I ALWAYS WEAR HEADPHONES SO MY HAIR'S PRESSED DOWN IN THE MIDDLE, WHICH MAKES IT LOOK EVEN WORSE.

MY CHILD BROKE MY GLASSES, SO I'M WEARING CONTACTS NOW.

村田雄介

Yusuke Murata

Whenever I finish a busy spell at work, I've always got horrendous bedhead. When I get my hair cut, I get it shaved, but I can't go to the barber very often, so it always ends up like this. Ugh...

In this volume we finally make it to the Christmas Bowl!! Whew! It took a while! When we started, the stadium was still called Tokyo Stadium. Along the way, Tokyo sold the naming rights, and the name changed... I can really feel the passage of time. But if the name of the site for the championship game kept changing, it would be strange, so we're sticking with Tokyo Stadium! (Anyway, it seems like that's still the official name...)

稲垣理一郎

Riichiro Inagaki

Eyeshield 21 is the most exciting football manga to hit the scene. A collaborative effort between writer Riichiro Inagaki and artist Yusuke Murata, *Eyeshield 21* was originally serialized in Japan's *Weekly Shonen Jump*. An OAV created for Shueisha's Anime Tour is available in Japan, and the *Eyeshield 21* hit animated TV series debuted in spring 2005!

EYESHIELD 21
Vol. 32: Christmas Bowl
SHONEN JUMP ADVANCED Manga Edition

STORY BY RIICHIRO INAGAKI
ART BY YUSUKE MURATA

English Adaptation & Translation/John Werry, HC Language Solutions, Inc.
Touch-up Art & Lettering/James Gaubatz
Cover & Graphic Design/Sean Lee
Editor/Kit Fox

VP, Production/Alvin Lu
VP, Sales & Product Marketing/Gonzalo Ferreyra
VP, Creative/Linda Espinosa
Publisher/Hyoe Narita

Printed in Canada

Published by VIZ Media, LLC
P.O. Box 77010
San Francisco, CA 94107

10 9 8 7 6 5 4 3 2 1
First printing, July 2010

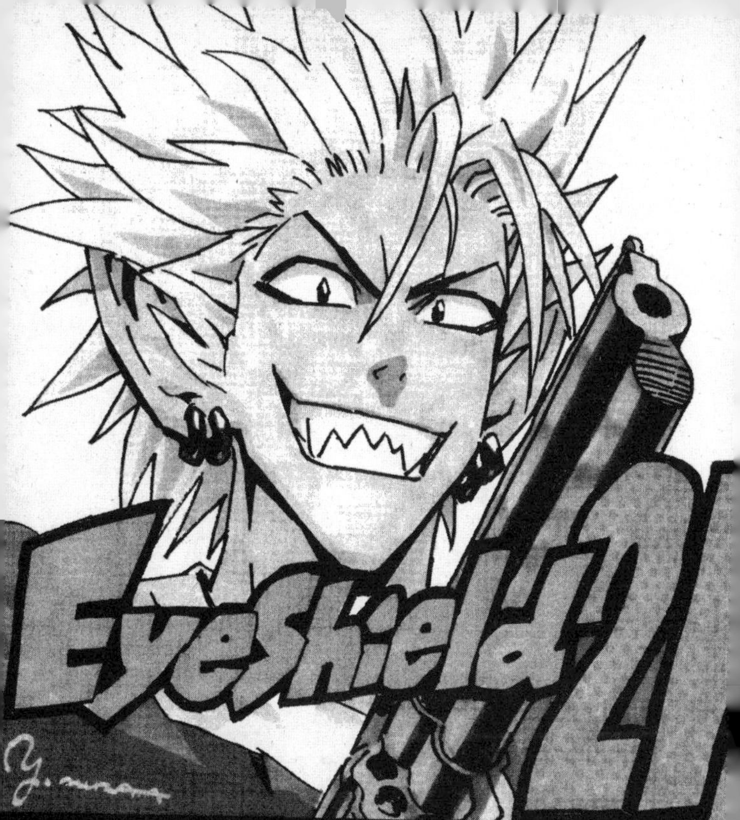
EyeShield 21

Vol. 32:
Christmas Bowl

STORY BY RIICHIRO INAGAKI ART BY YUSUKE MURATA

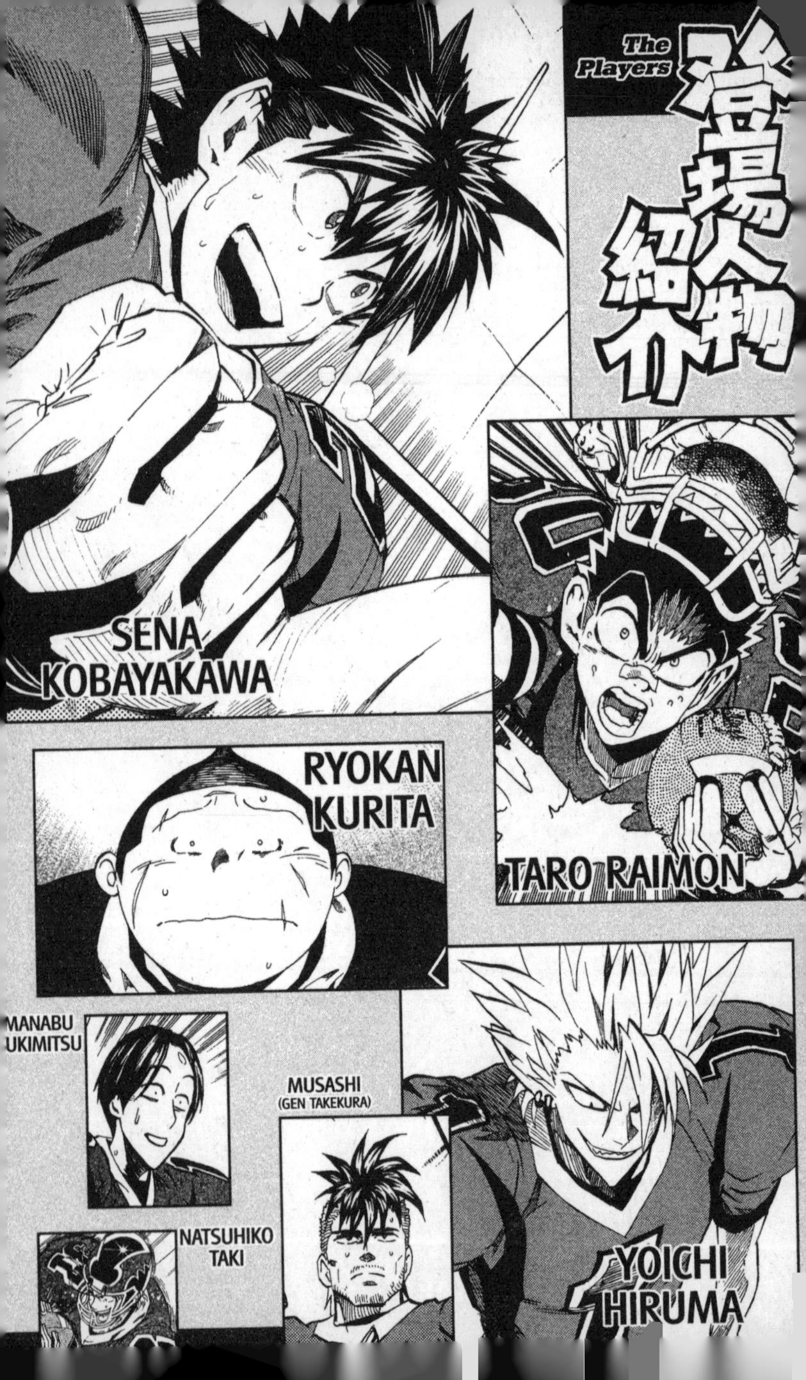
The Players
登場人物紹介
SENA KOBAYAKAWA
TARO RAIMON
RYOKAN KURITA
YOICHI HIRUMA
MUSASHI (GEN TAKEKURA)
MANABU YUKIMITSU
NATSUHIKO TAKI

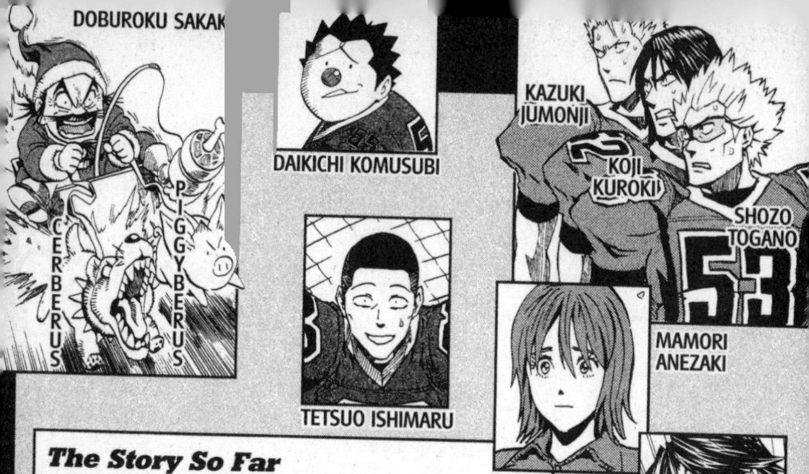
KAZUKI JUMONJI
KOJI KUROKI
SHOZO TOGANO
DAIKICHI KOMUSUBI
DOBUROKU SAKAK
PIGGYBERUS
CERBERUS
MAMORI ANEZAKI
TETSUO ISHIMARU

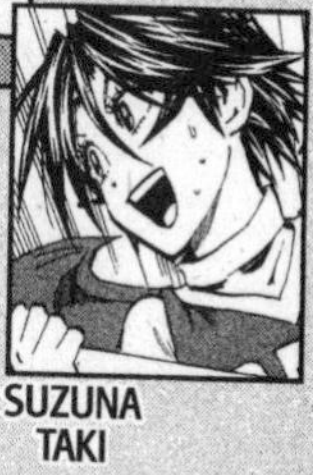
SUZUNA TAKI

The Story So Far

Shy Sena Kobayakawa joins the Deimon High School football team to reinvent himself. Sena's exceptional running ability comes to light and he competes under a secret identity, Eyeshield 21.

Deimon advances to the finals, where they must battle the frightfully powerful Hakushu Dinosaurs. Hiruma's right arm is broken, but the game is a close one until the Devil Bats pull a stunning upset and advance to the Christmas Bowl!!

Their opponents will be Teikoku High School—said to be undefeatable. In preparation for the big game, Deimon gathers together its former rivals and begins special training!!

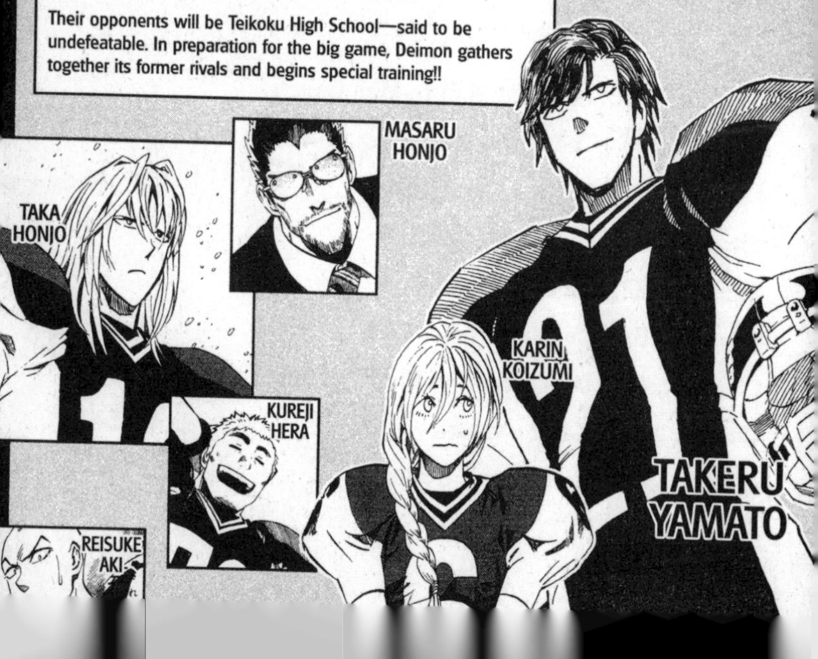
TAKERU YAMATO
MASARU HONJO
TAKA HONJO
KARIN KOIZUMI
KUREJI HERA
REISUKE AKI

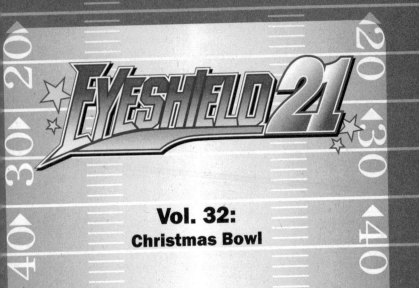

Vol. 32:
Christmas Bowl

CONTENTS

Chapter 278	The Best Man-to-Man Coach	7
Chapter 279	The World's Greatest Glove	27
Chapter 280	Natural Born Talent	47
Chapter 281	Christmas Bowl	67
Chapter 282	All-Star Spirits	87
Chapter 283	Certain Prediction	107
Chapter 284	Descendant of the Sky People	127
Chapter 285	Karin Koizumi	147
Chapter 286	Running vs. Running	167

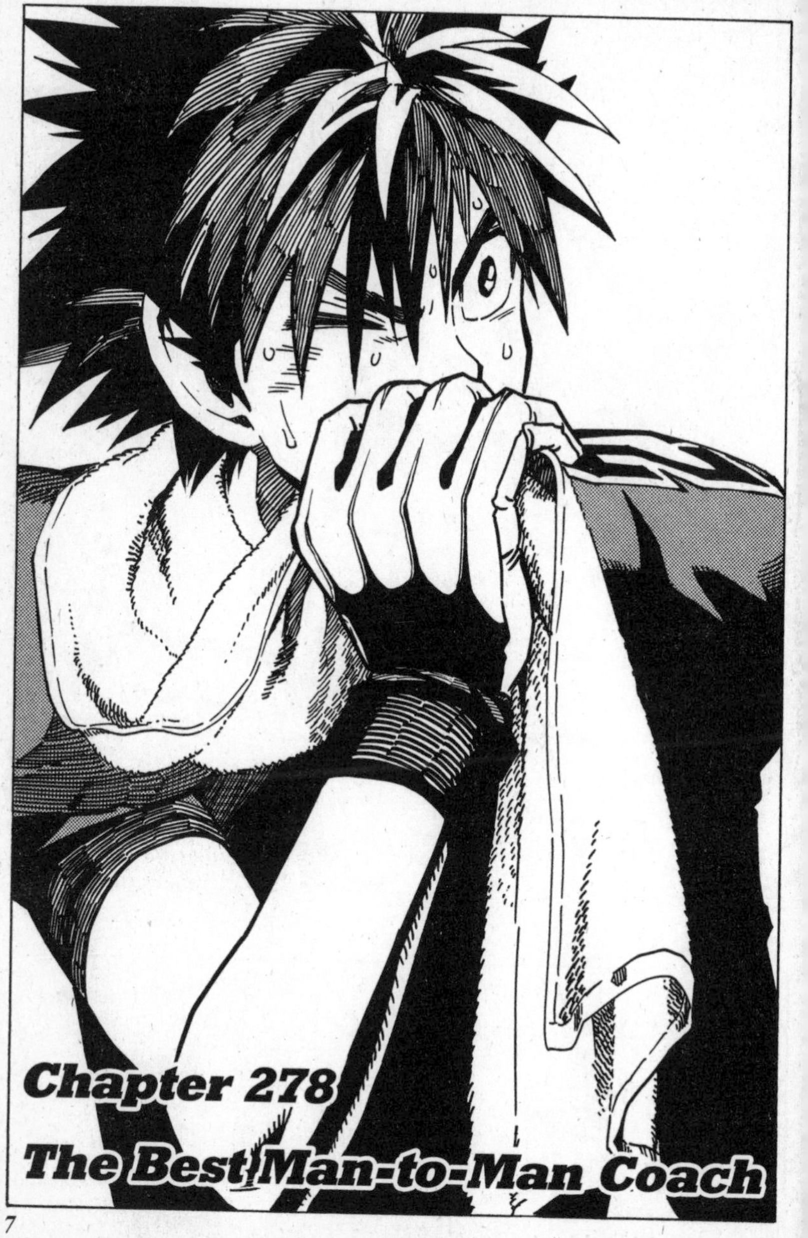
Chapter 278
The Best Man-to-Man Coach

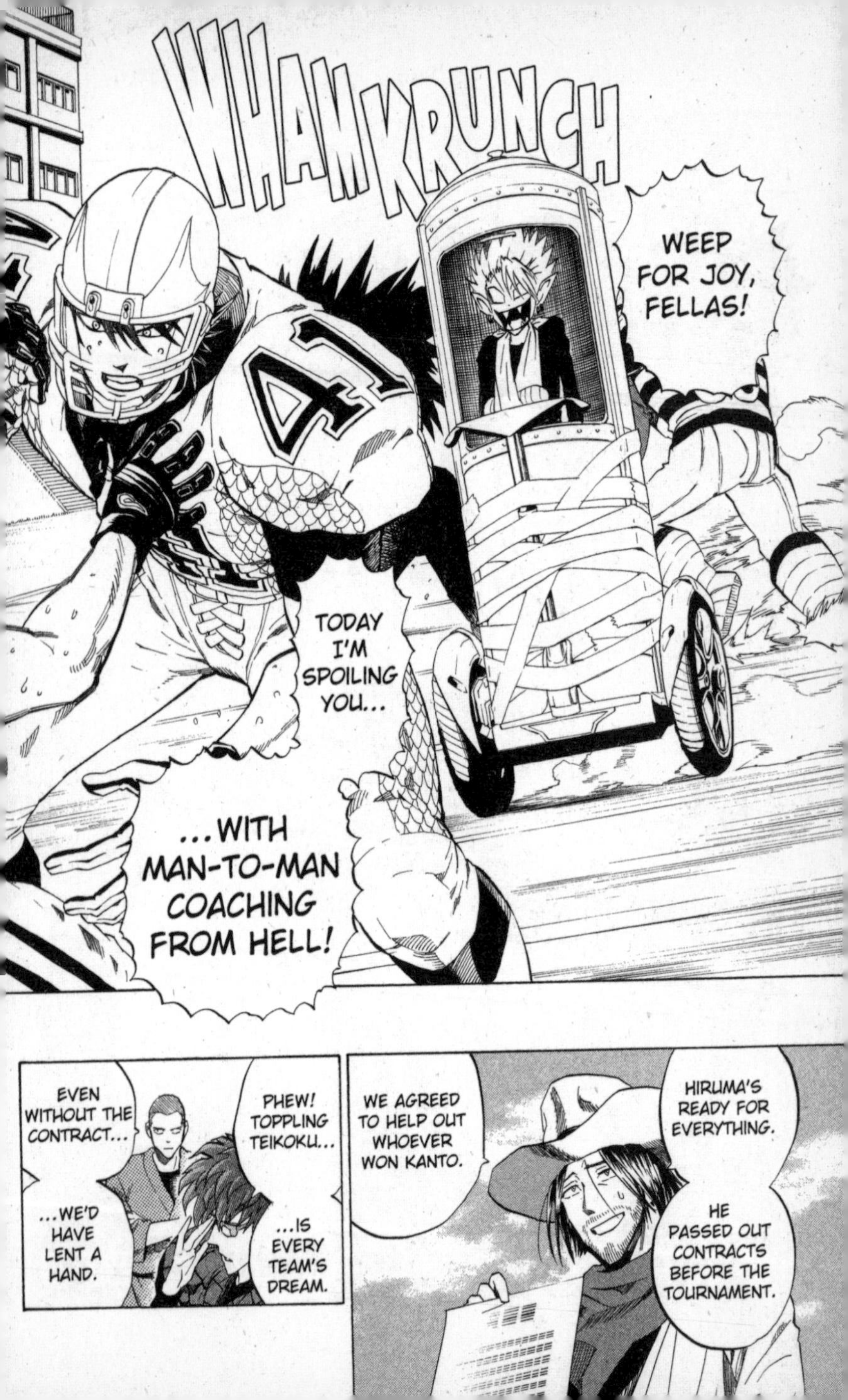
WHAMKRUNCH
WEEP FOR JOY, FELLAS!
TODAY I'M SPOILING YOU...
...WITH MAN-TO-MAN COACHING FROM HELL!
HIRUMA'S READY FOR EVERYTHING.
WE AGREED TO HELP OUT WHOEVER WON KANTO.
HE PASSED OUT CONTRACTS BEFORE THE TOURNAMENT.
PHEW! TOPPLING TEIKOKU...
...IS EVERY TEAM'S DREAM.
EVEN WITHOUT THE CONTRACT...
...WE'D HAVE LENT A HAND.

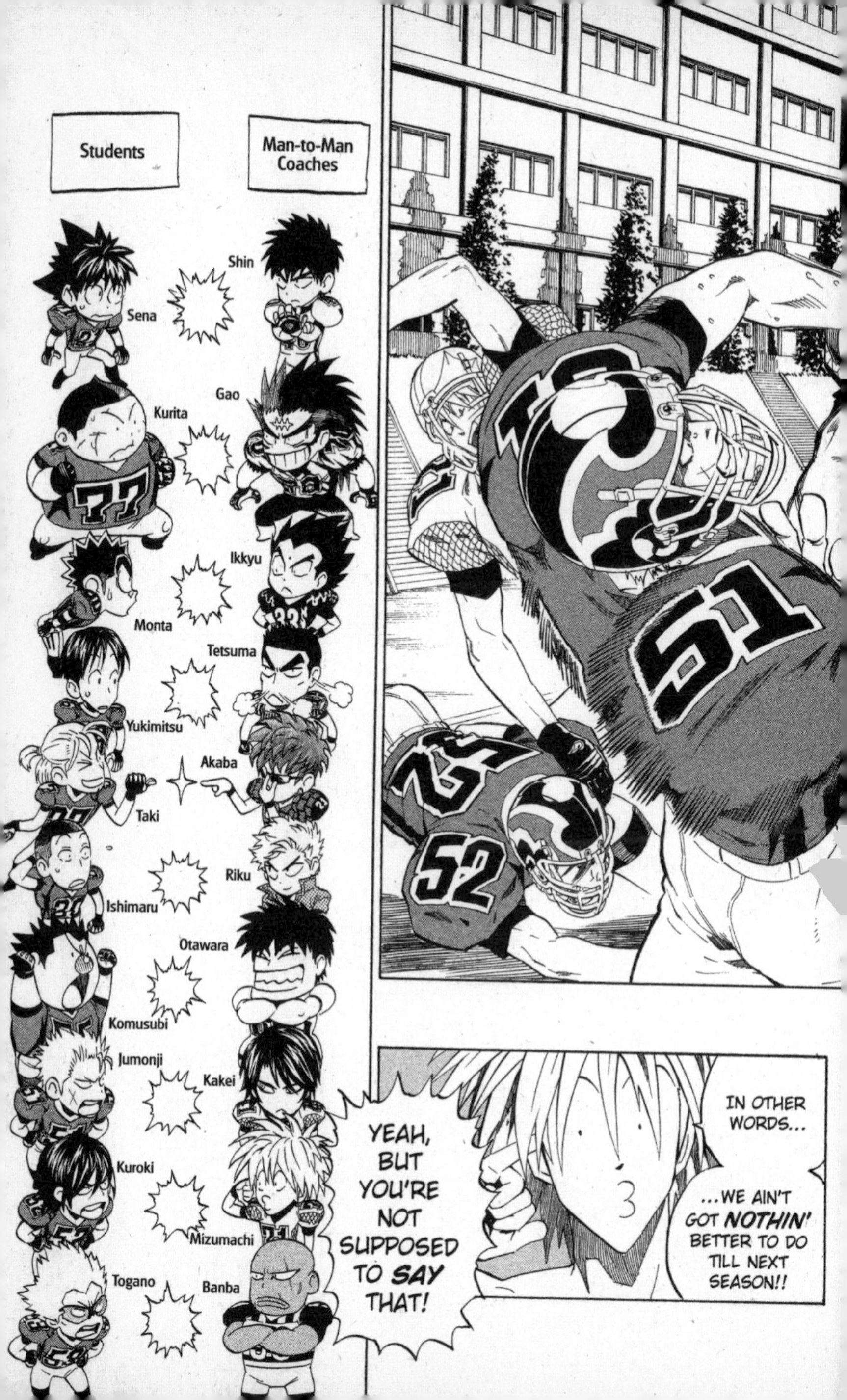
IN OTHER WORDS...
...WE AIN'T GOT NOTHIN' BETTER TO DO TILL NEXT SEASON!!
YEAH, BUT YOU'RE NOT SUPPOSED TO SAY THAT!
Man-to-Man Coaches
Students
Shin
Sena
Gao
Kurita
Ikkyu
Monta
Tetsuma
Yukimitsu
Akaba
Taki
Riku
Ishimaru
Otawara
Komusubi
Kakei
Jumonji
Mizumachi
Kuroki
Banba
Togano

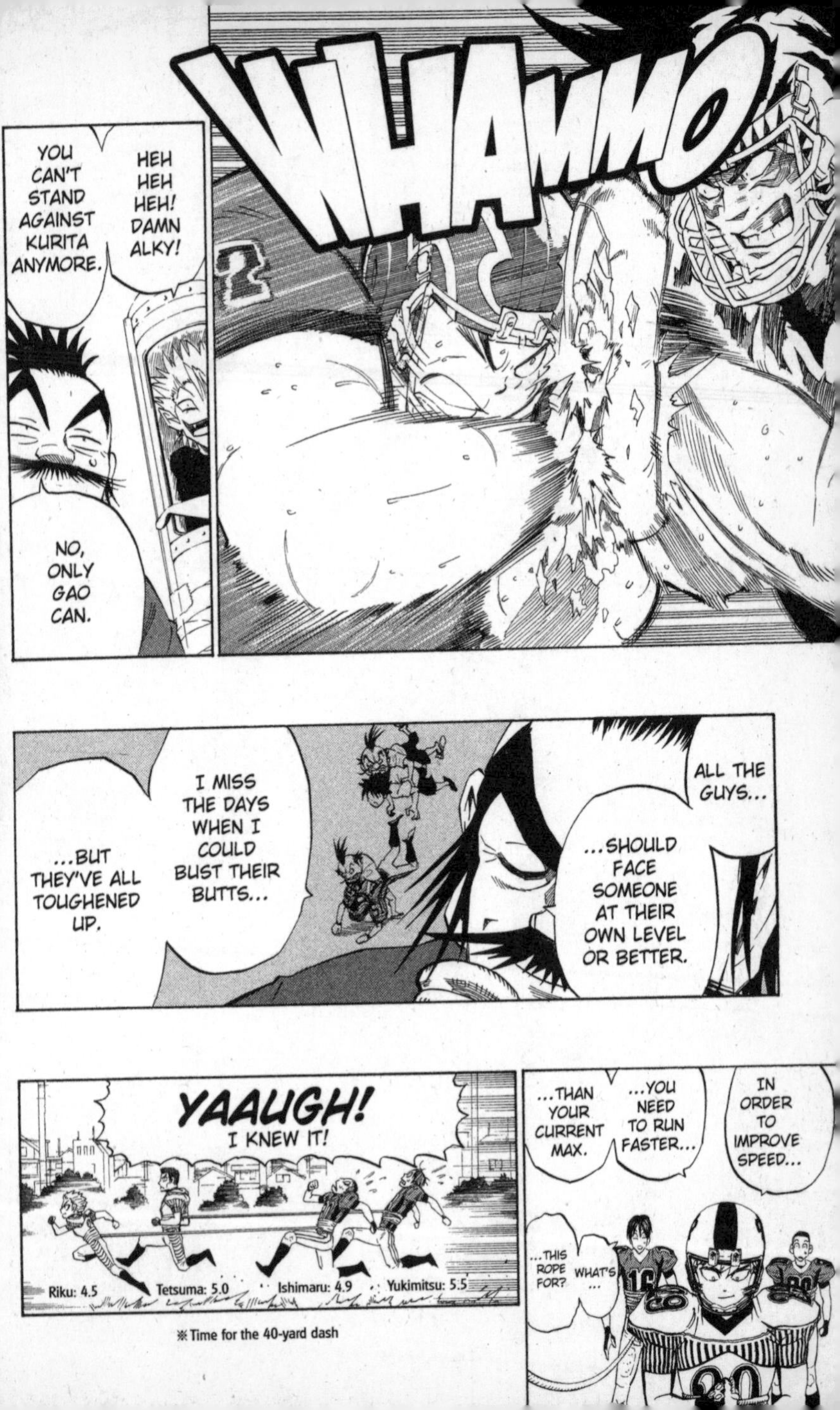
WHAMMO
HEH HEH HEH! DAMN ALKY!
YOU CAN'T STAND AGAINST KURITA ANYMORE.
NO, ONLY GAO CAN.
ALL THE GUYS...
...SHOULD FACE SOMEONE AT THEIR OWN LEVEL OR BETTER.
I MISS THE DAYS WHEN I COULD BUST THEIR BUTTS...
...BUT THEY'VE ALL TOUGHENED UP.
IN ORDER TO IMPROVE SPEED...
...YOU NEED TO RUN FASTER...
...THAN YOUR CURRENT MAX.
WHAT'S ...
...THIS ROPE FOR?
YAAUGH! I KNEW IT!
Riku: 4.5
Tetsuma: 5.0
Ishimaru: 4.9
Yukimitsu: 5.5
※Time for the 40-yard dash

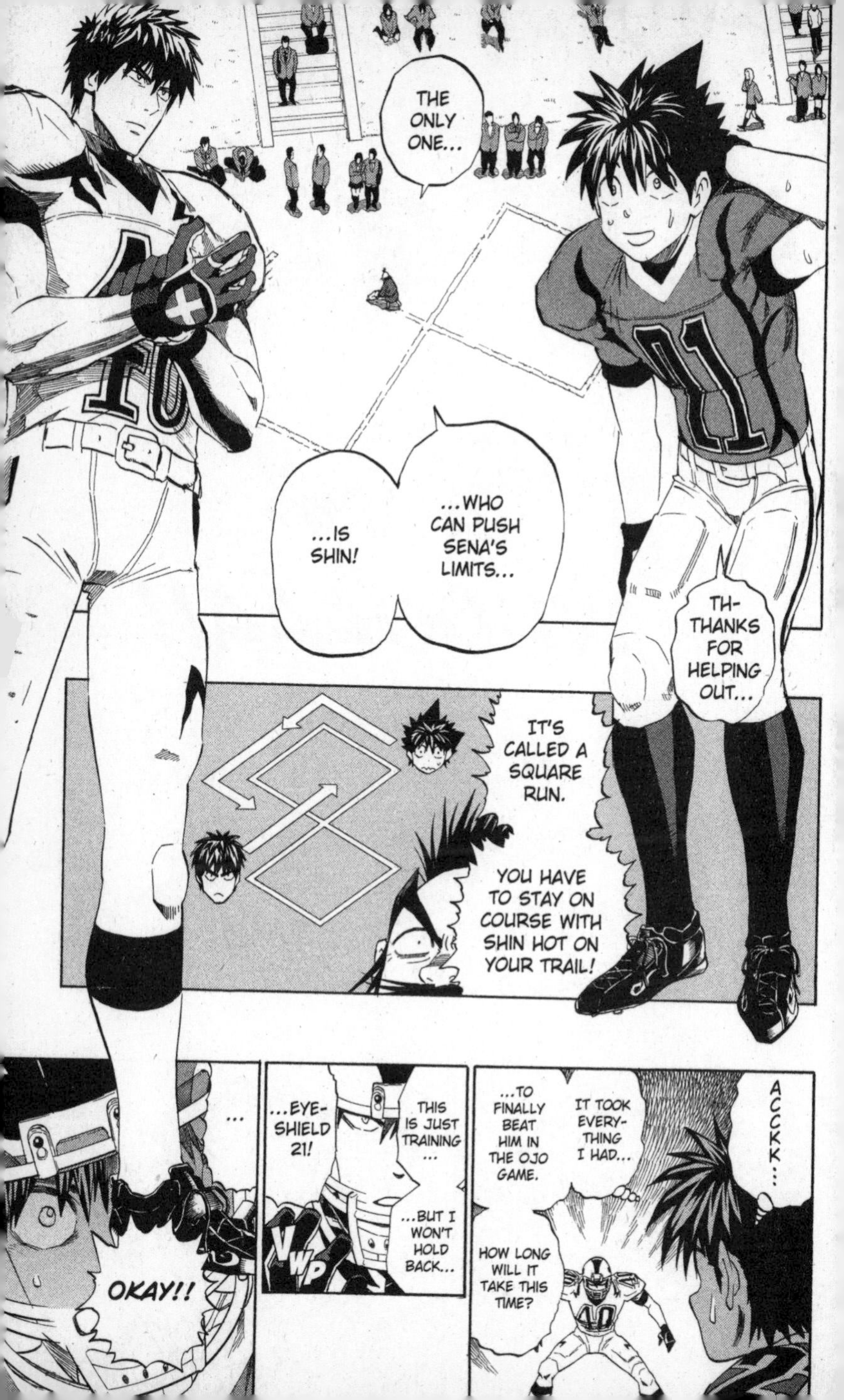
THE ONLY ONE...
...WHO CAN PUSH SENA'S LIMITS...
...IS SHIN!
TH-THANKS FOR HELPING OUT...
IT'S CALLED A SQUARE RUN.
YOU HAVE TO STAY ON COURSE WITH SHIN HOT ON YOUR TRAIL!
ACCKK...
IT TOOK EVERY-THING I HAD...
...TO FINALLY BEAT HIM IN THE OJO GAME.
HOW LONG WILL IT TAKE THIS TIME?
THIS IS JUST TRAINING...
...EYE-SHIELD 21!
...BUT I WON'T HOLD BACK...
VWP
...
OKAY!!

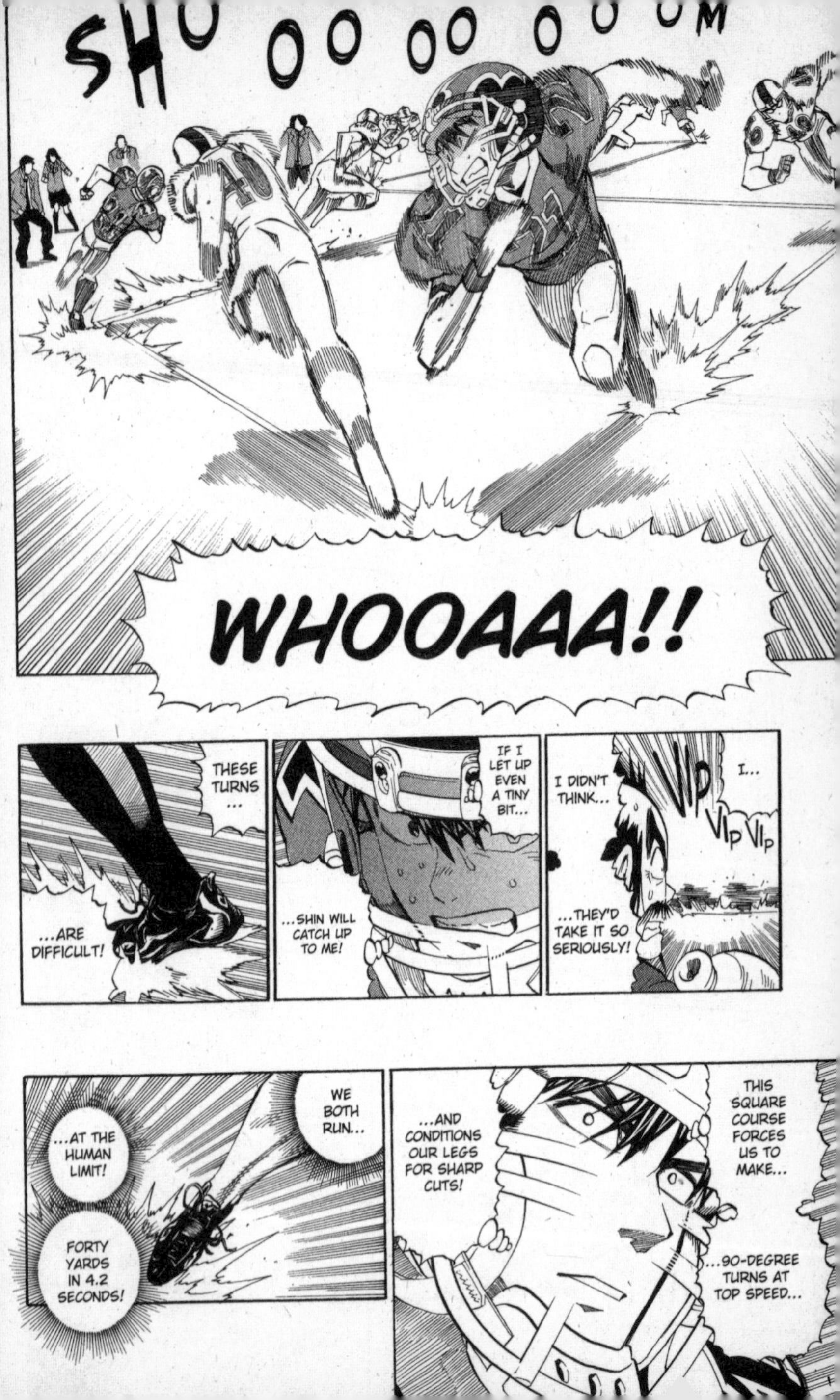

SHU OO OO O O OM
WHOOAAA!!
I...
VIP VIP VIP
I DIDN'T THINK...
...THEY'D TAKE IT SO SERIOUSLY!
IF I LET UP EVEN A TINY BIT...
...SHIN WILL CATCH UP TO ME!
THESE TURNS...
...ARE DIFFICULT!
THIS SQUARE COURSE FORCES US TO MAKE...
...90-DEGREE TURNS AT TOP SPEED...
...AND CONDITIONS OUR LEGS FOR SHARP CUTS!
WE BOTH RUN...
...AT THE HUMAN LIMIT!
FORTY YARDS IN 4.2 SECONDS!

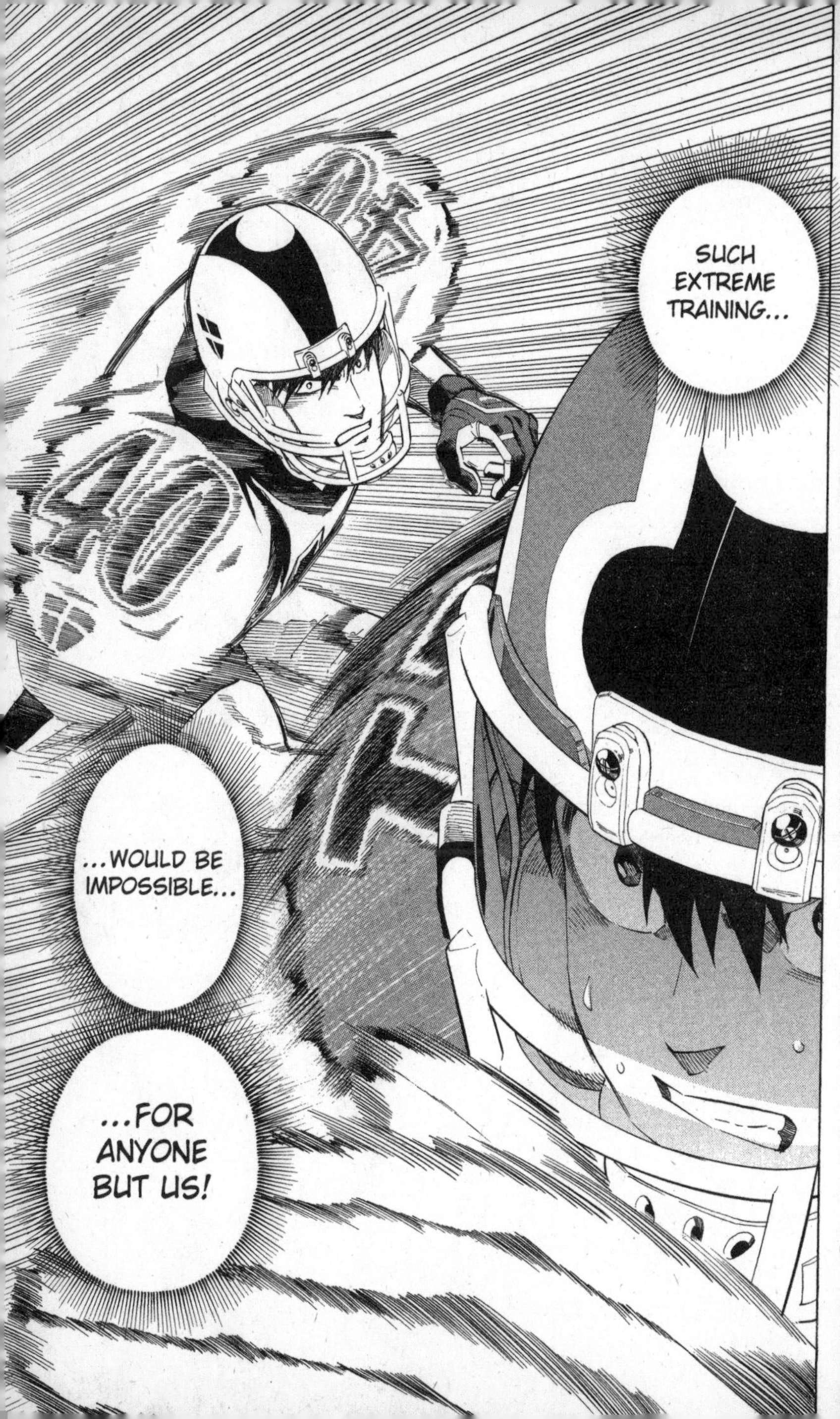
SUCH EXTREME TRAINING...
...WOULD BE IMPOSSIBLE...
...FOR ANYONE BUT US!

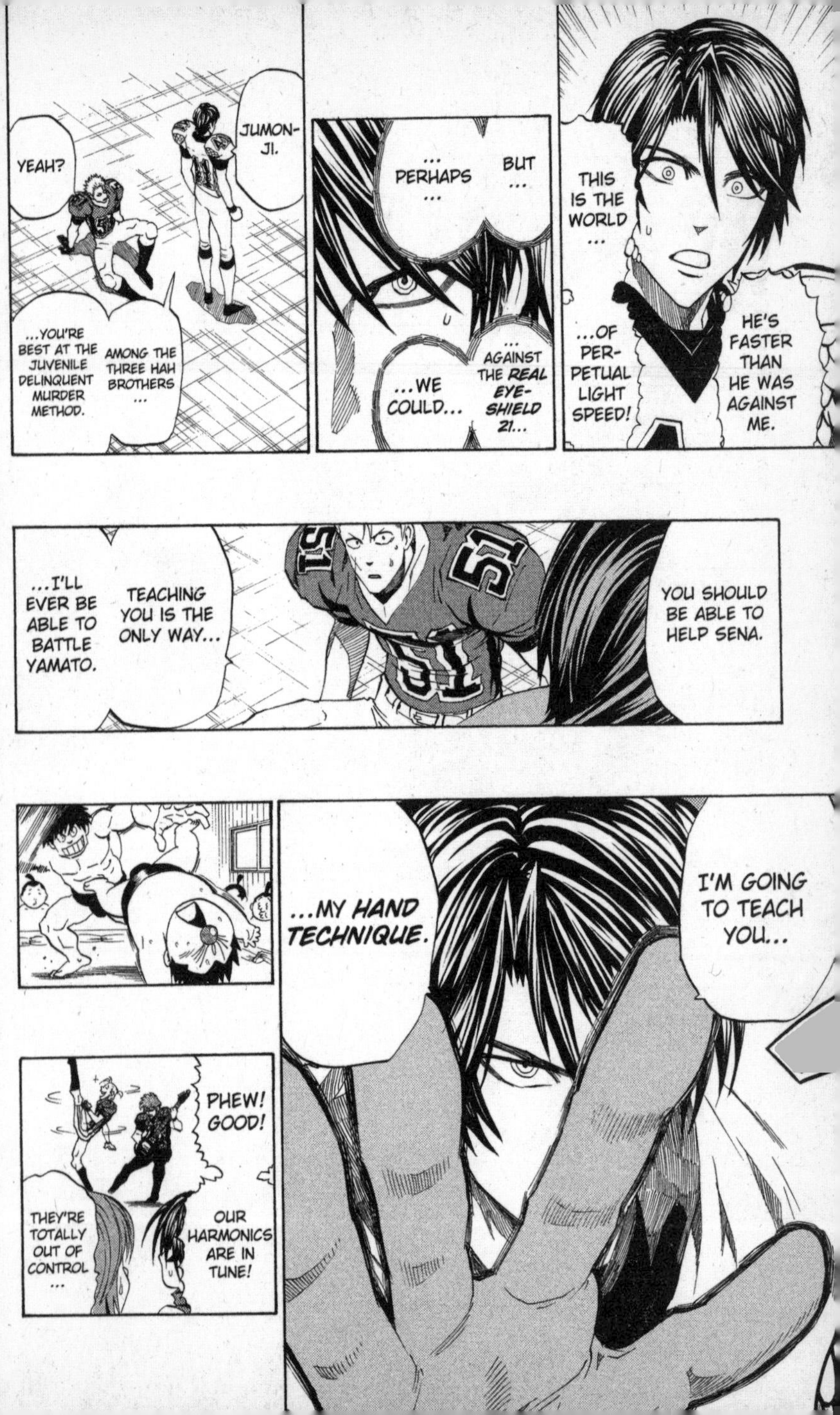
THIS IS THE WORLD...
...OF PER-PETUAL LIGHT SPEED!
HE'S FASTER THAN HE WAS AGAINST ME.
BUT...
...PERHAPS...
...AGAINST THE *REAL EYE-SHIELD 21*...
...WE COULD...
JUMON-JI.
YEAH?
AMONG THE THREE HAH BROTHERS...
...YOU'RE BEST AT THE JUVENILE DELINQUENT MURDER METHOD.
YOU SHOULD BE ABLE TO HELP SENA.
TEACHING YOU IS THE ONLY WAY...
...I'LL EVER BE ABLE TO BATTLE YAMATO.
I'M GOING TO TEACH YOU...
...MY *HAND TECHNIQUE*.
PHEW! GOOD!
OUR HARMONICS ARE IN TUNE!
THEY'RE TOTALLY OUT OF CONTROL...

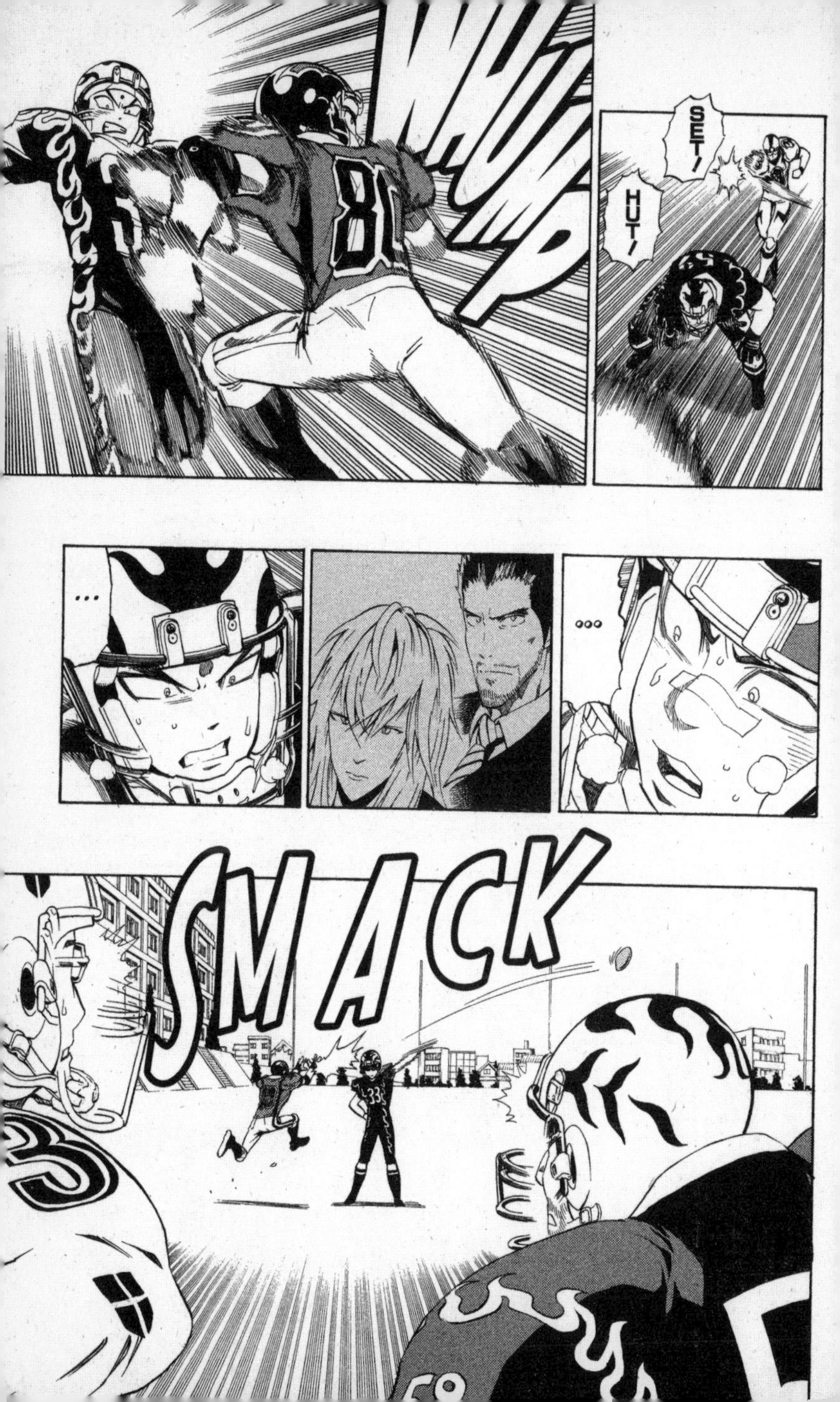
SET!
HUT!
WHUMP
...
...
SMACK

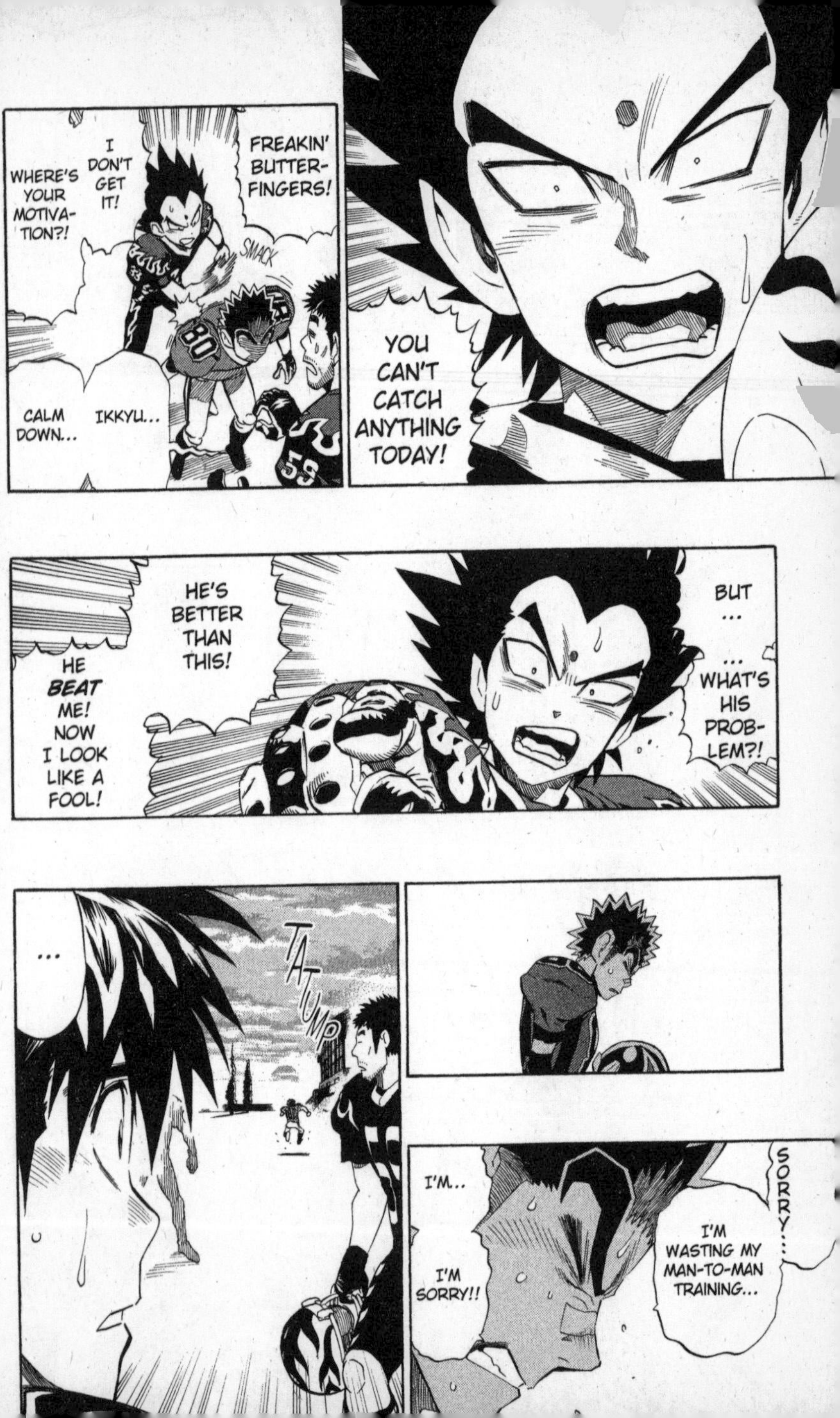
YOU CAN'T CATCH ANYTHING TODAY!
FREAKIN' BUTTER-FINGERS!
I DON'T GET IT!
WHERE'S YOUR MOTIVATION?!
SMACK
IKKYU...
CALM DOWN...
BUT ...
... WHAT'S HIS PROBLEM?!
HE'S BETTER THAN THIS!
HE *BEAT* ME! NOW I LOOK LIKE A FOOL!
SORRY...
I'M WASTING MY MAN-TO-MAN TRAINING...
I'M..
I'M SORRY!!
TATUMP
...

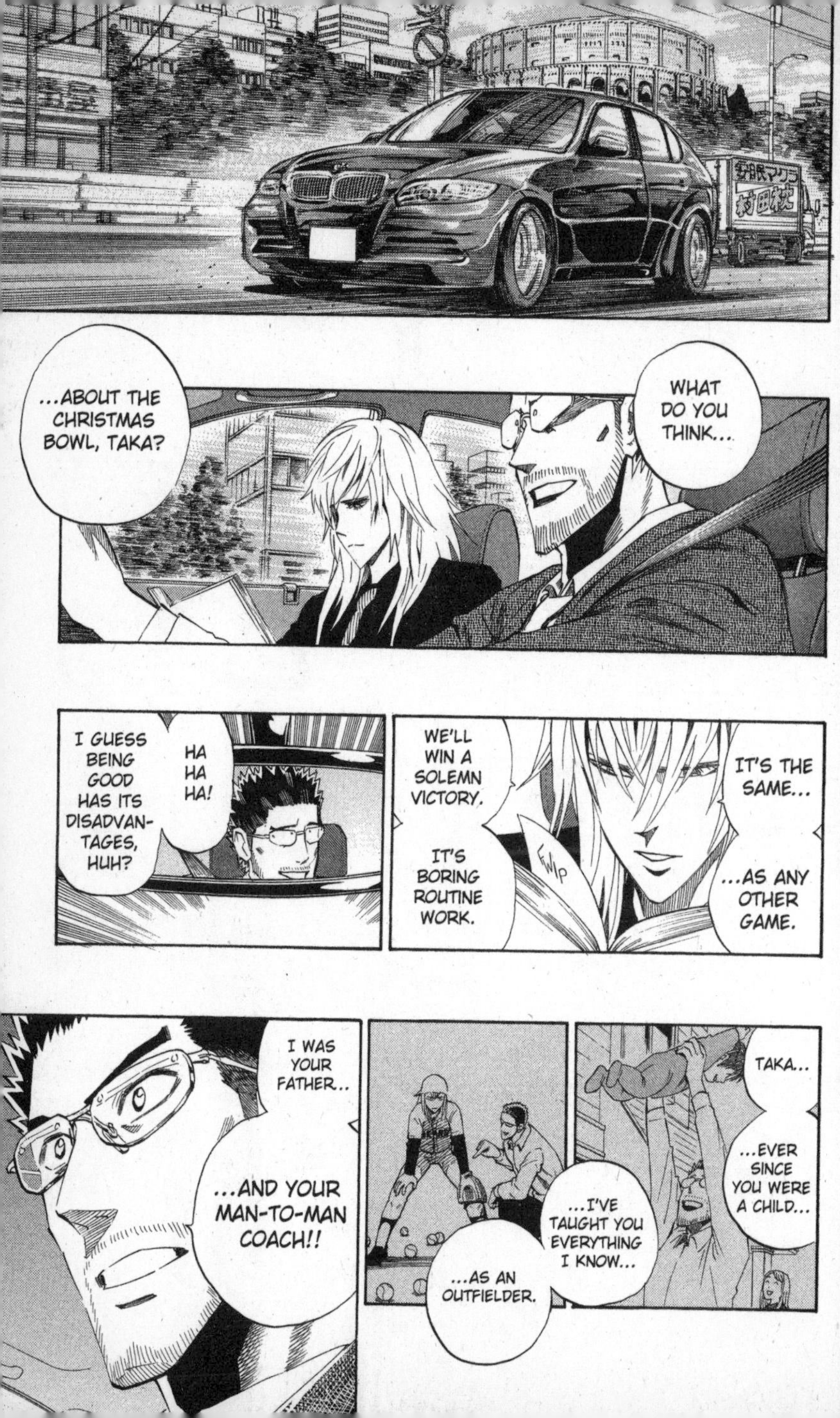
WHAT DO YOU THINK...
...ABOUT THE CHRISTMAS BOWL, TAKA?
IT'S THE SAME...
...AS ANY OTHER GAME.
WE'LL WIN A SOLEMN VICTORY.
IT'S BORING ROUTINE WORK.
FWIP
HA HA HA!
I GUESS BEING GOOD HAS ITS DISADVANTAGES, HUH?
TAKA...
...EVER SINCE YOU WERE A CHILD...
...I'VE TAUGHT YOU EVERYTHING I KNOW...
...AS AN OUTFIELDER.
I WAS YOUR FATHER...
...AND YOUR MAN-TO-MAN COACH!!

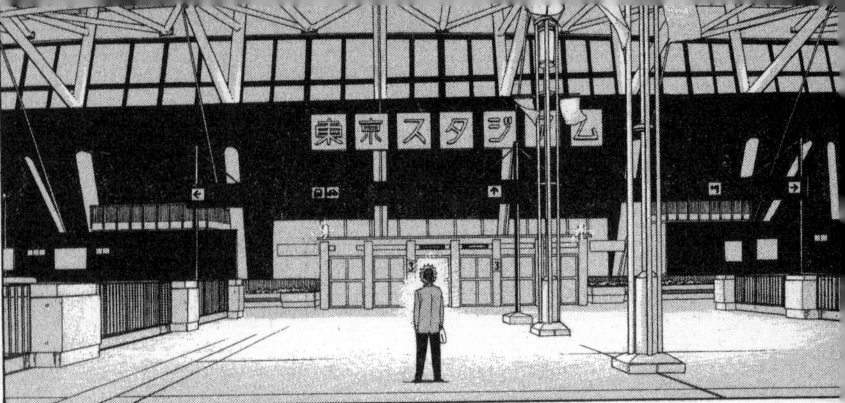

SIGN: TOKYO STADIUM

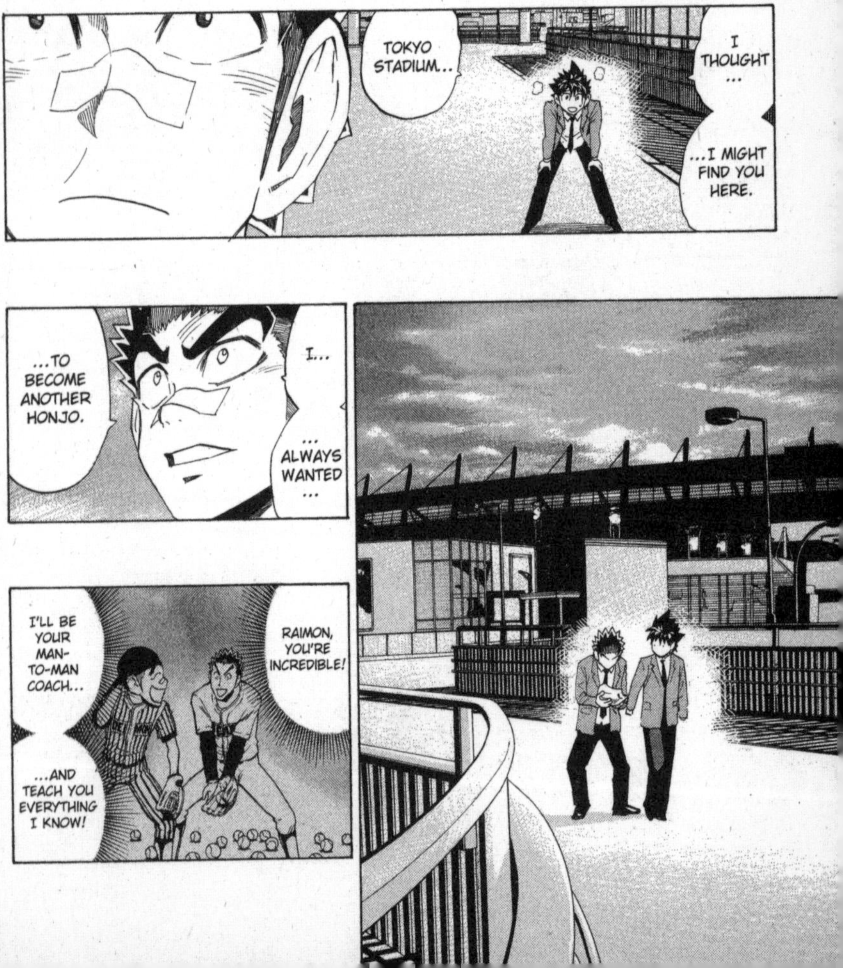
I THOUGHT ...
...I MIGHT FIND YOU HERE.
TOKYO STADIUM...
I...
...ALWAYS WANTED ...
...TO BECOME ANOTHER HONJO.
RAIMON, YOU'RE INCREDIBLE!
I'LL BE YOUR MAN-TO-MAN COACH...
...AND TEACH YOU EVERYTHING I KNOW!

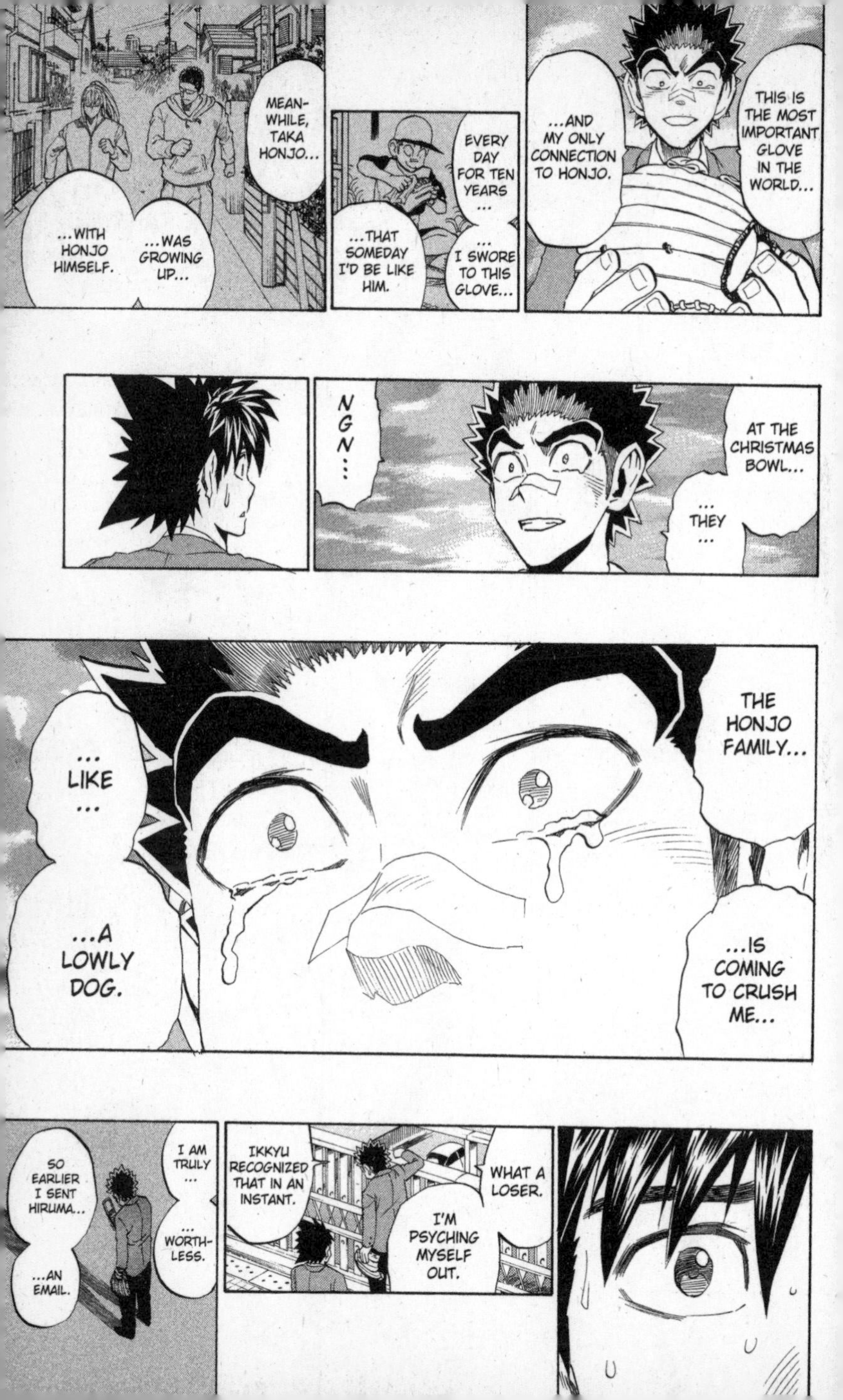
THIS IS THE MOST IMPORTANT GLOVE IN THE WORLD...
...AND MY ONLY CONNECTION TO HONJO.
EVERY DAY FOR TEN YEARS...
...I SWORE TO THIS GLOVE...
...THAT SOMEDAY I'D BE LIKE HIM.
MEAN-WHILE, TAKA HONJO...
...WAS GROWING UP...
...WITH HONJO HIMSELF.
AT THE CHRISTMAS BOWL...
...THEY...
NGN...
THE HONJO FAMILY...
...IS COMING TO CRUSH ME...
...LIKE...
...A LOWLY DOG.
WHAT A LOSER.
I'M PSYCHING MYSELF OUT.
IKKYU RECOGNIZED THAT IN AN INSTANT.
I AM TRULY...
...WORTHLESS.
SO EARLIER I SENT HIRUMA...
...AN EMAIL.

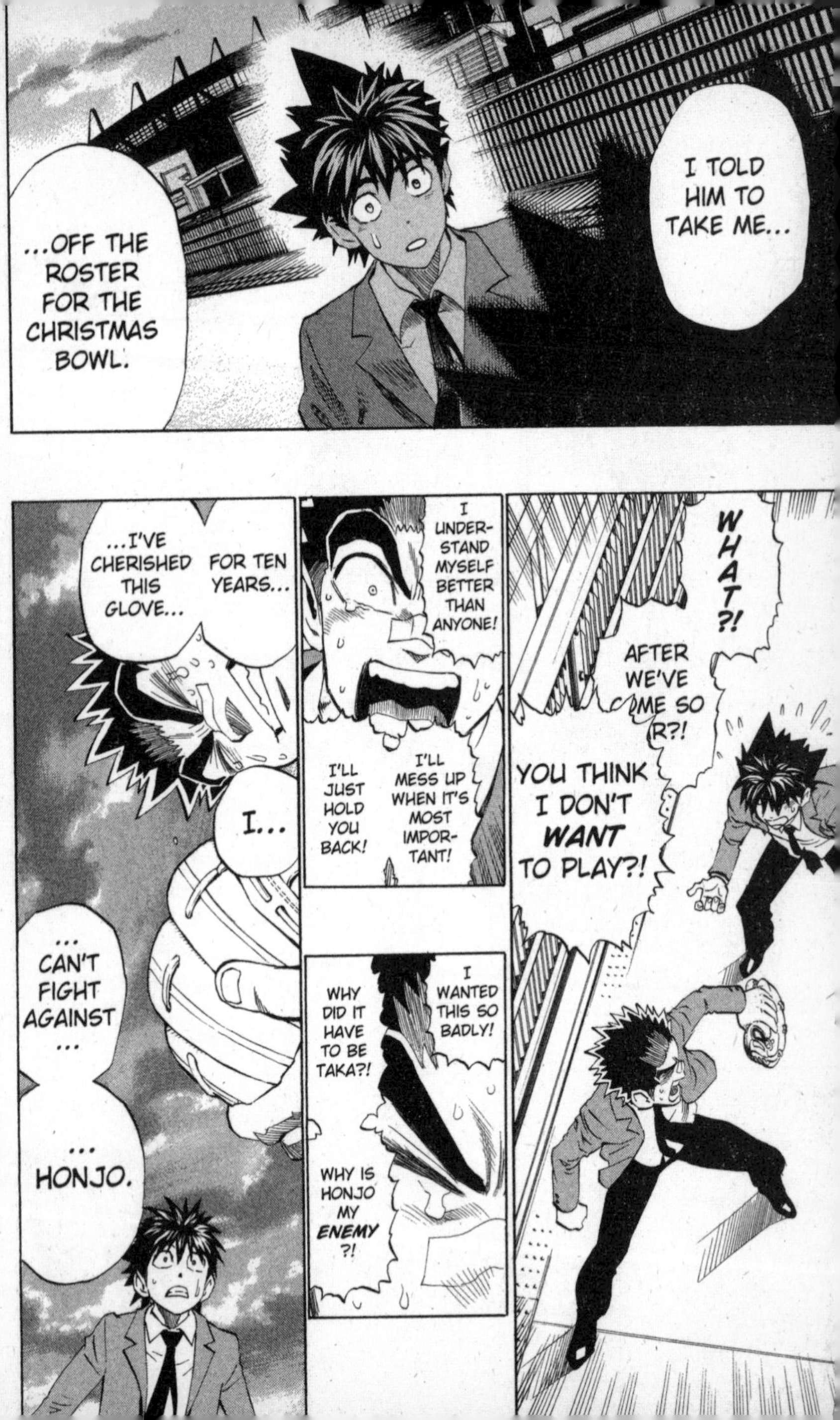
I TOLD HIM TO TAKE ME...
...OFF THE ROSTER FOR THE CHRISTMAS BOWL.
WHAT?!
AFTER WE'VE ME SO R?!
YOU THINK I DON'T *WANT* TO PLAY?!
I UNDER-STAND MYSELF BETTER THAN ANYONE!
I'LL MESS UP WHEN IT'S MOST IMPOR-TANT!
I'LL JUST HOLD YOU BACK!
I WANTED THIS SO BADLY!
WHY DID IT HAVE TO BE TAKA?!
WHY IS HONJO MY *ENEMY* ?!
FOR TEN YEARS...
...I'VE CHERISHED THIS GLOVE...
I...
...CAN'T FIGHT AGAINST...
...HONJO.

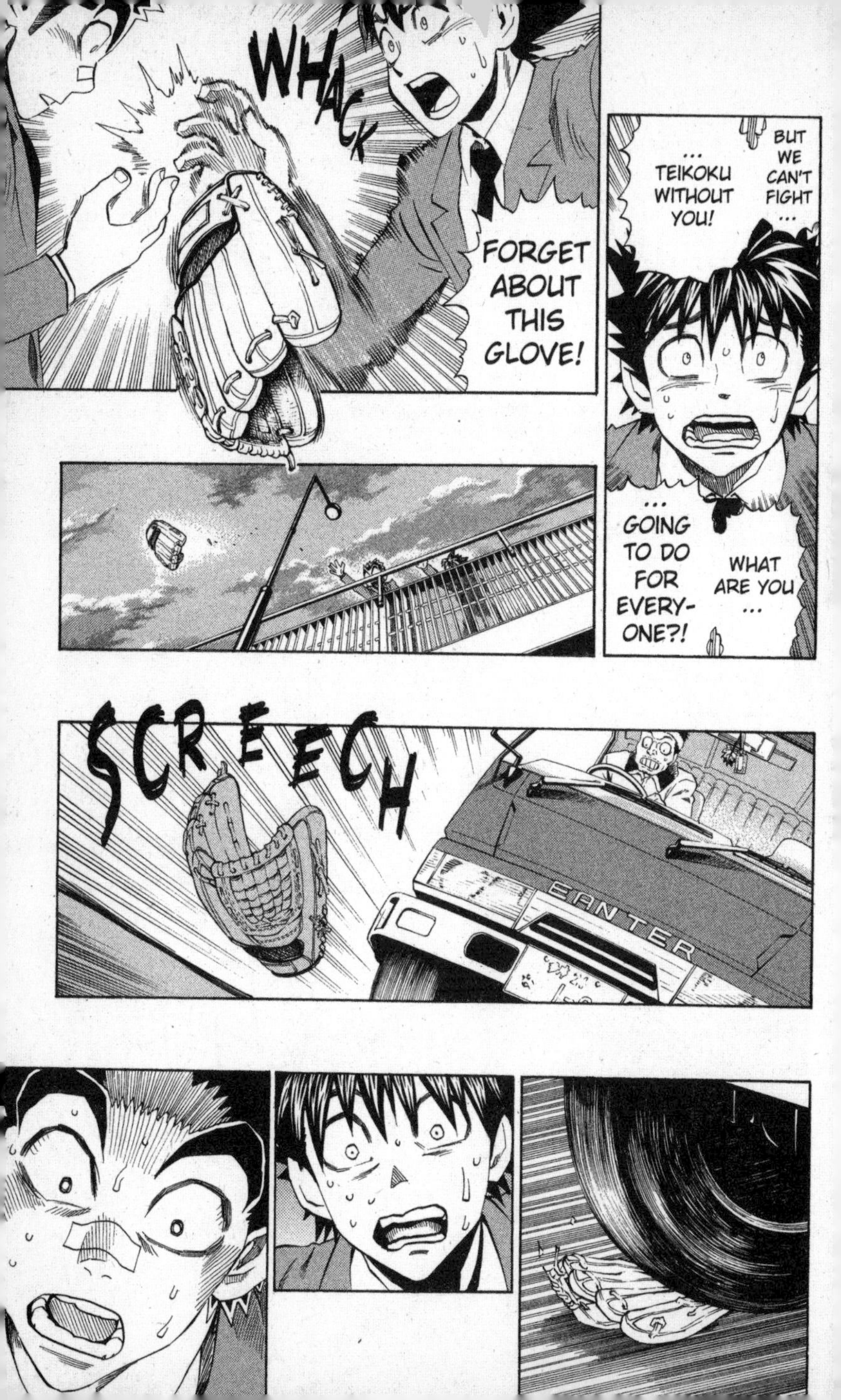
WHACK
FORGET ABOUT THIS GLOVE!
BUT WE CAN'T FIGHT ...
... TEIKOKU WITHOUT YOU!
WHAT ARE YOU ...
... GOING TO DO FOR EVERY-ONE?!
SCREECH
CANTER

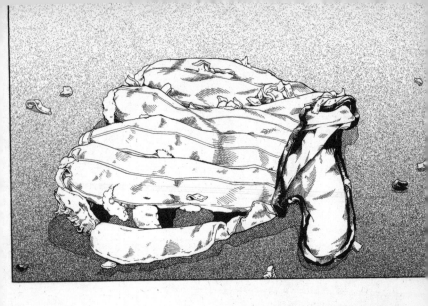

CAREFUL, MONTA!

WATCH OUT FOR THE CARS!

MY...

...GLOVE!

HONJO'S...

...GLOVE...

HONK

HONK

THNK

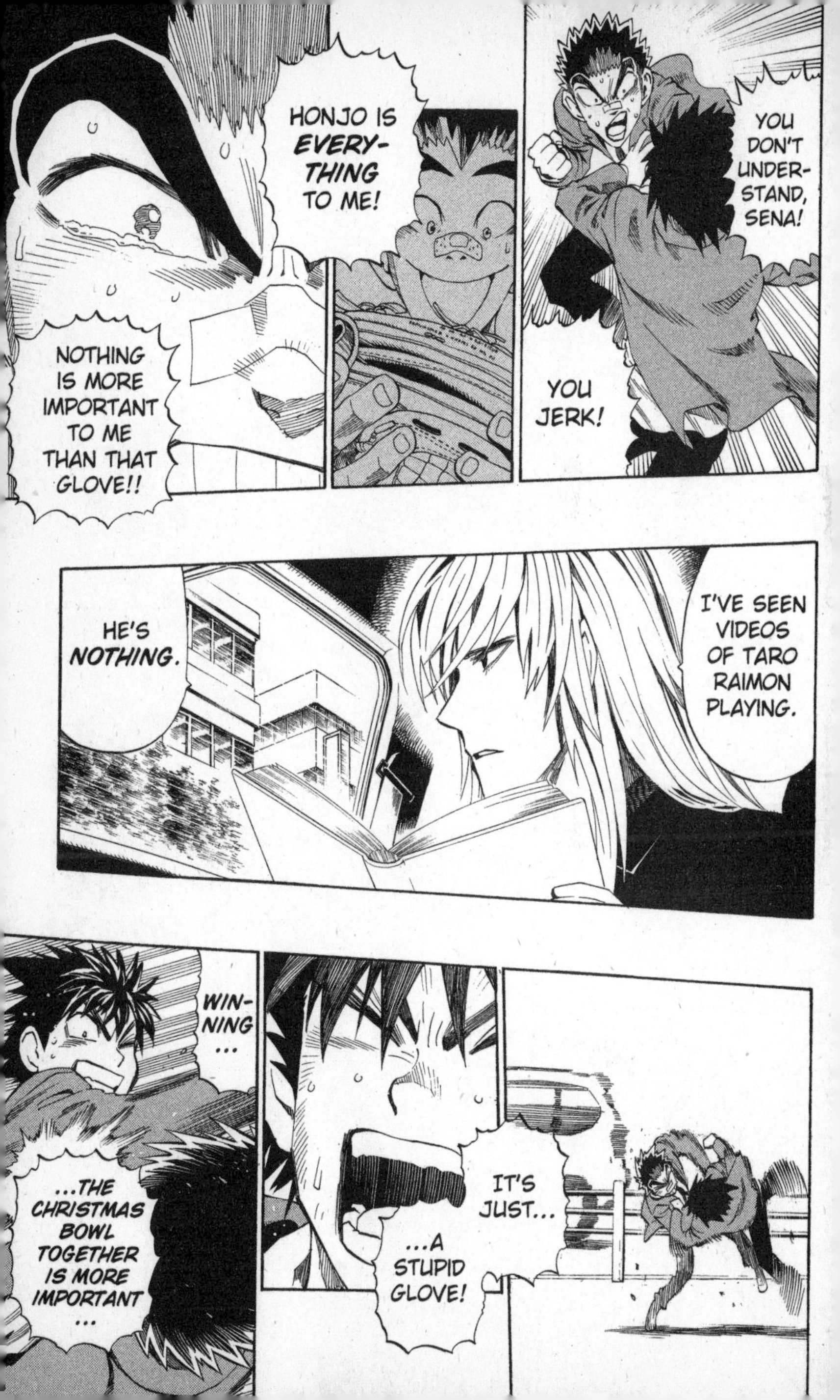
YOU DON'T UNDERSTAND, SENA!
YOU JERK!
HONJO IS *EVERYTHING* TO ME!
NOTHING IS MORE IMPORTANT TO ME THAN THAT GLOVE!!
I'VE SEEN VIDEOS OF TARO RAIMON PLAYING.
HE'S *NOTHING*.
IT'S JUST...
...A STUPID GLOVE!
WINNING...
...THE CHRISTMAS BOWL TOGETHER IS MORE IMPORTANT...

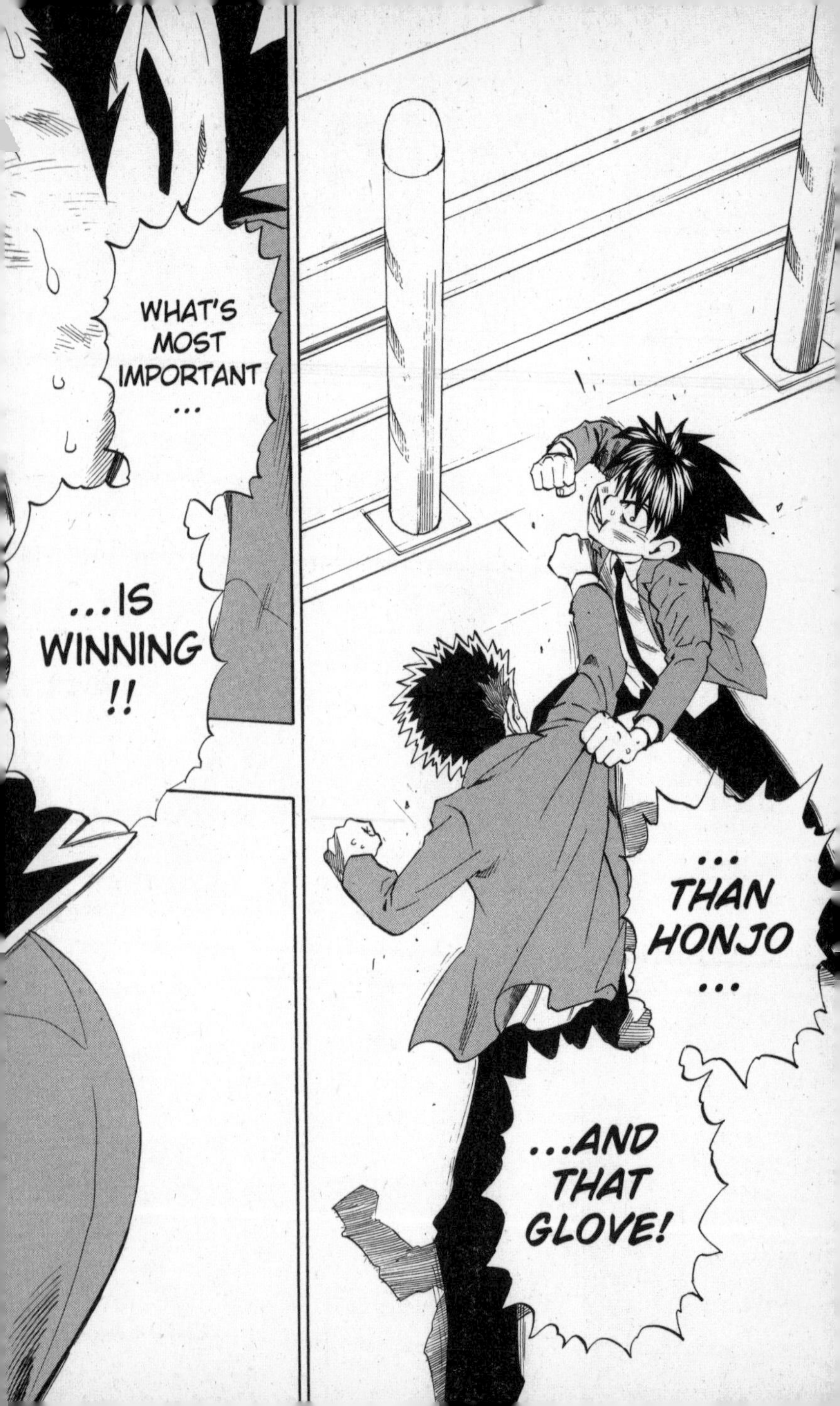
... THAN HONJO ...
...AND THAT GLOVE!
WHAT'S MOST IMPORTANT ...
...IS WINNING !!

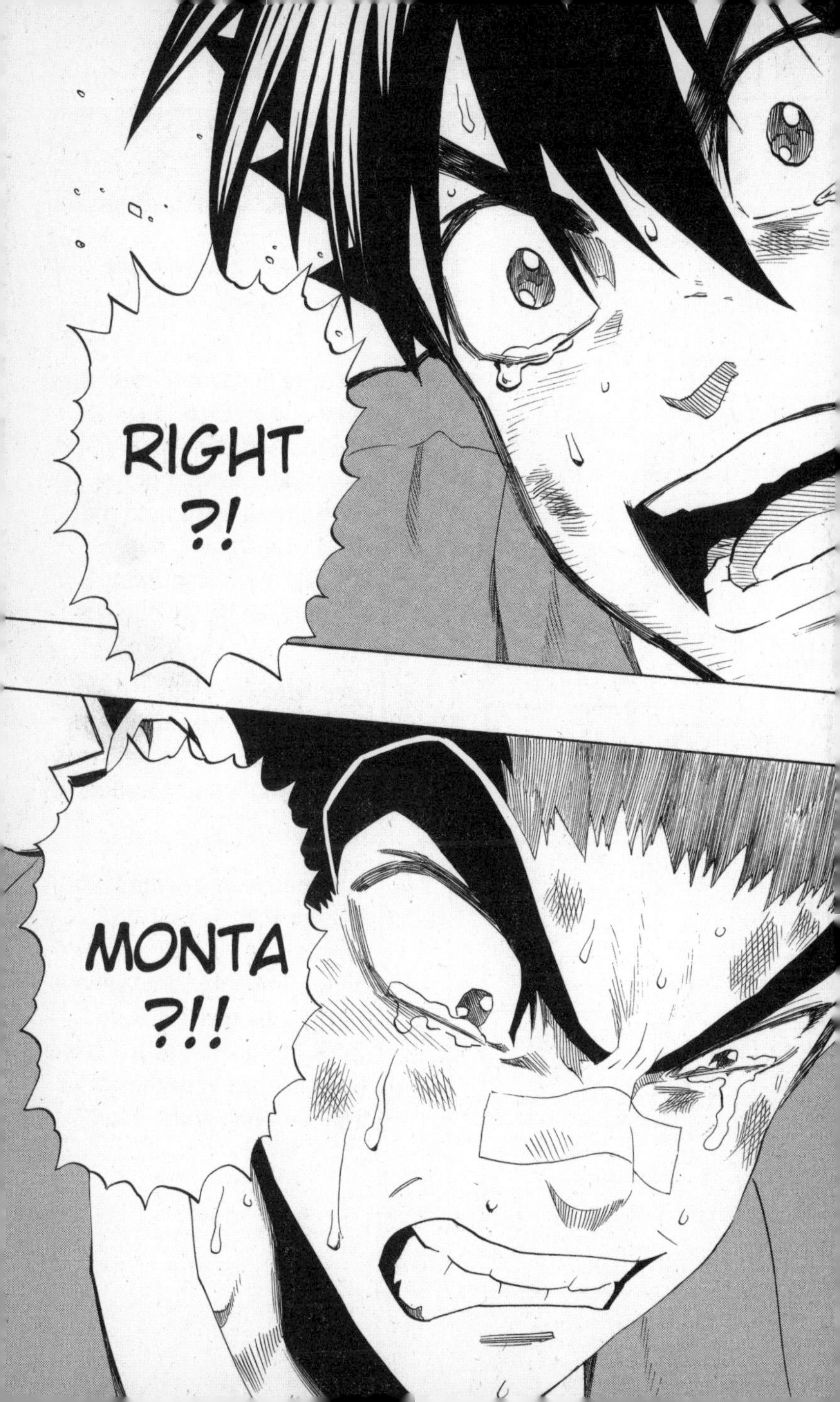
RIGHT ?!
MONTA ?!!

●TEIKOKU PERSONAL HISTORIES

◂Taka Honjo▸

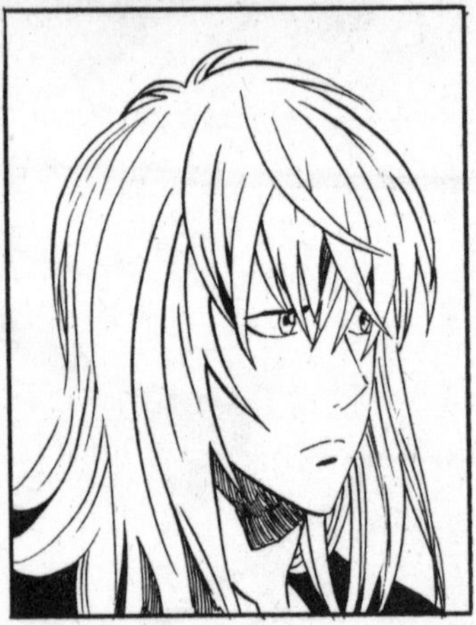

CURRENT AGE: 16

Height	178 cm
Weight	67 kg
Blood type	A
Birthday	June 26
Siblings	One elder sister
Talents/Hobbies	Reading books
Favorite type of girl	
Quiet girls	

0 YEARS OLD

Born in Kyoto to catching master Masaru Honjo.

It is said he learned to ***jump*** before he learned to crawl, and that when riding in trains he would jump out of his baby stroller, grab onto the hand straps and swing around... but these ***baby legends*** are highly dubious...

12 YEARS OLD

Graduates from Little League. On defense they call him the ***Flying Grab*** and he becomes No. 1 in both name and deed.

14 YEARS OLD

In response to a scout from Teikoku High School, he switches to football in hopes of encountering some serious catching battles. He soon gains recognition as a receiver and once again becomes No. 1 in both name and deed.

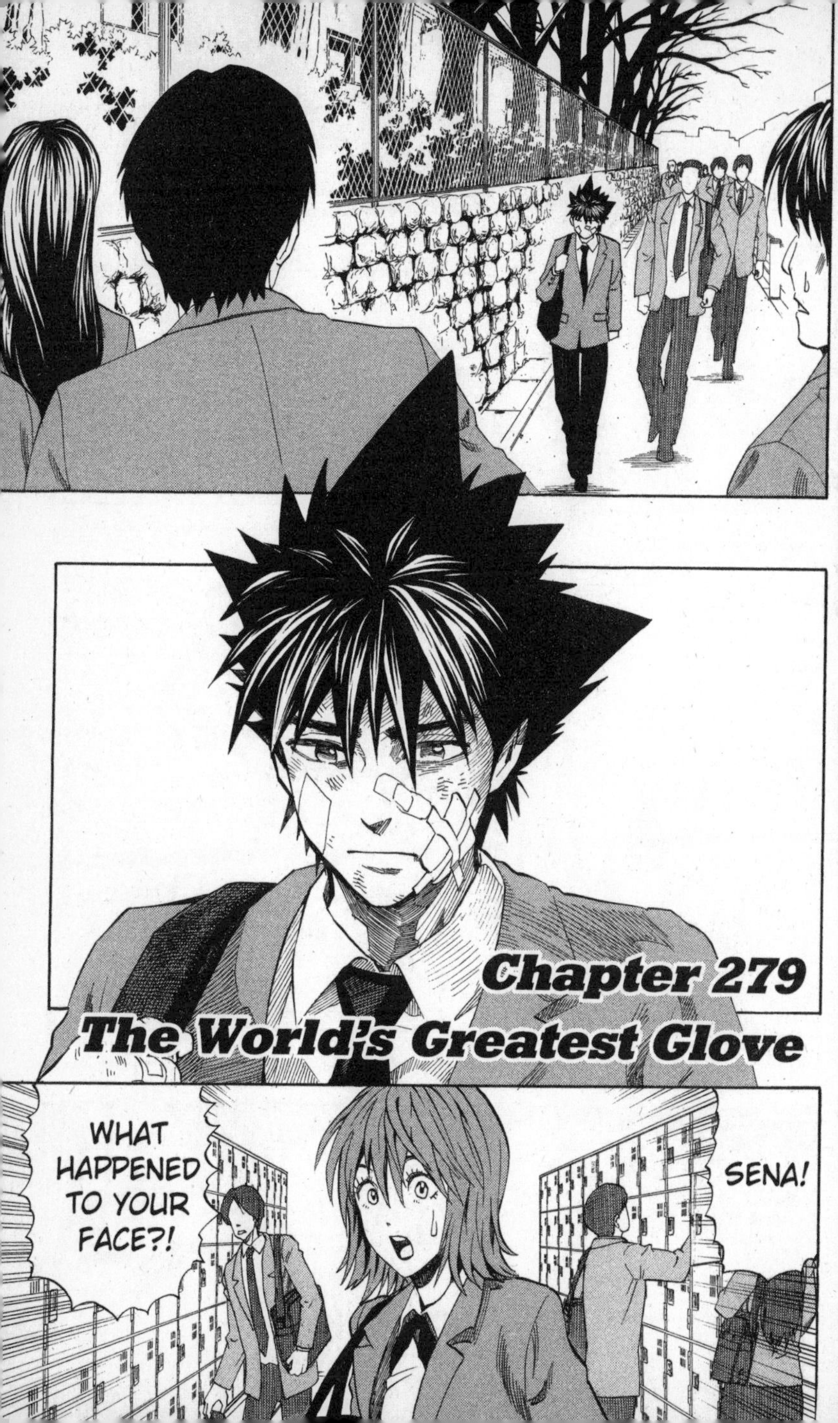
Chapter 279
The World's Greatest Glove
SENA!
WHAT HAPPENED TO YOUR FACE?!

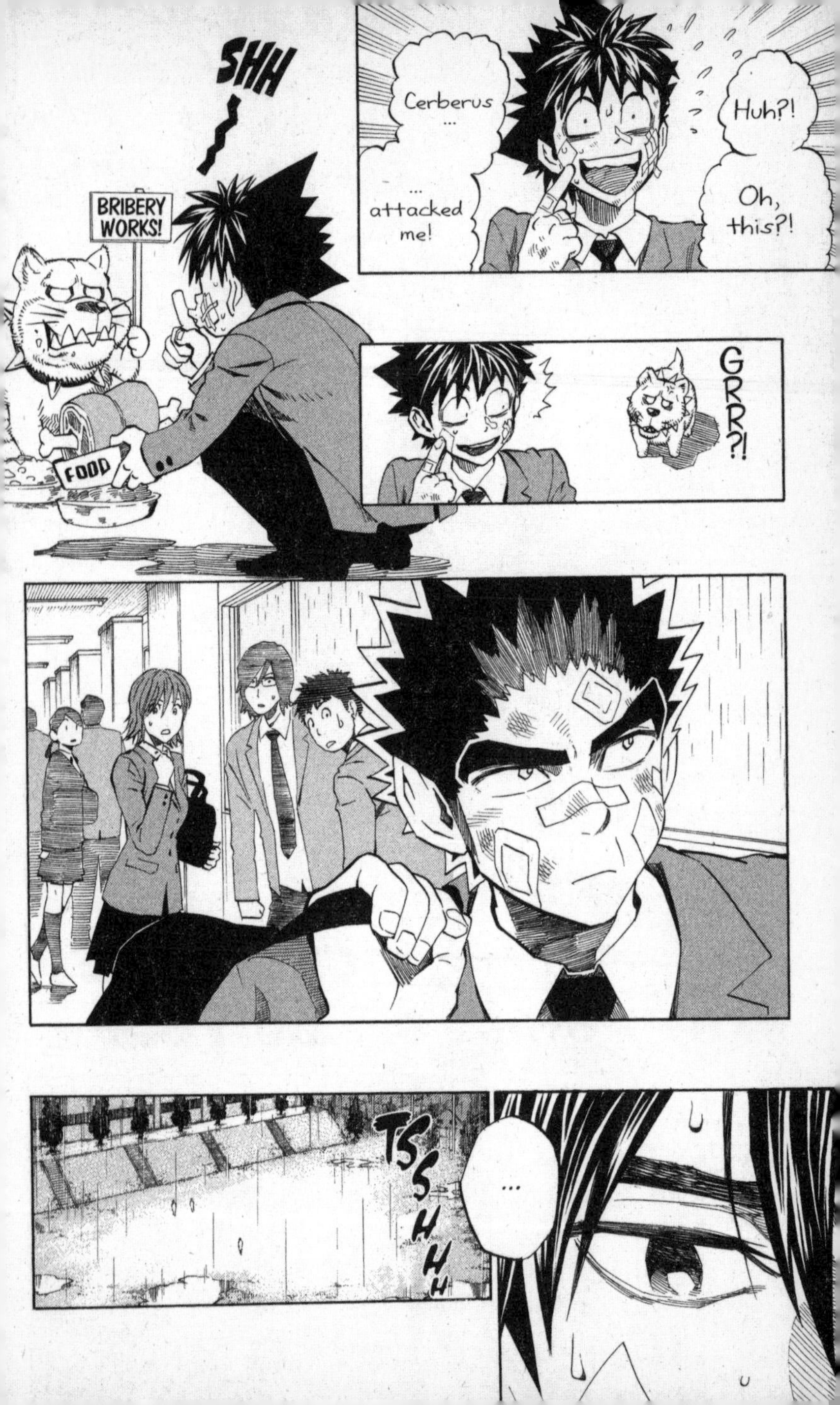
Huh?!
Oh, this?!
Cerberus...
...attacked me!
GRR?!
SHH
BRIBERY WORKS!
FOOD
...
TSSHHH

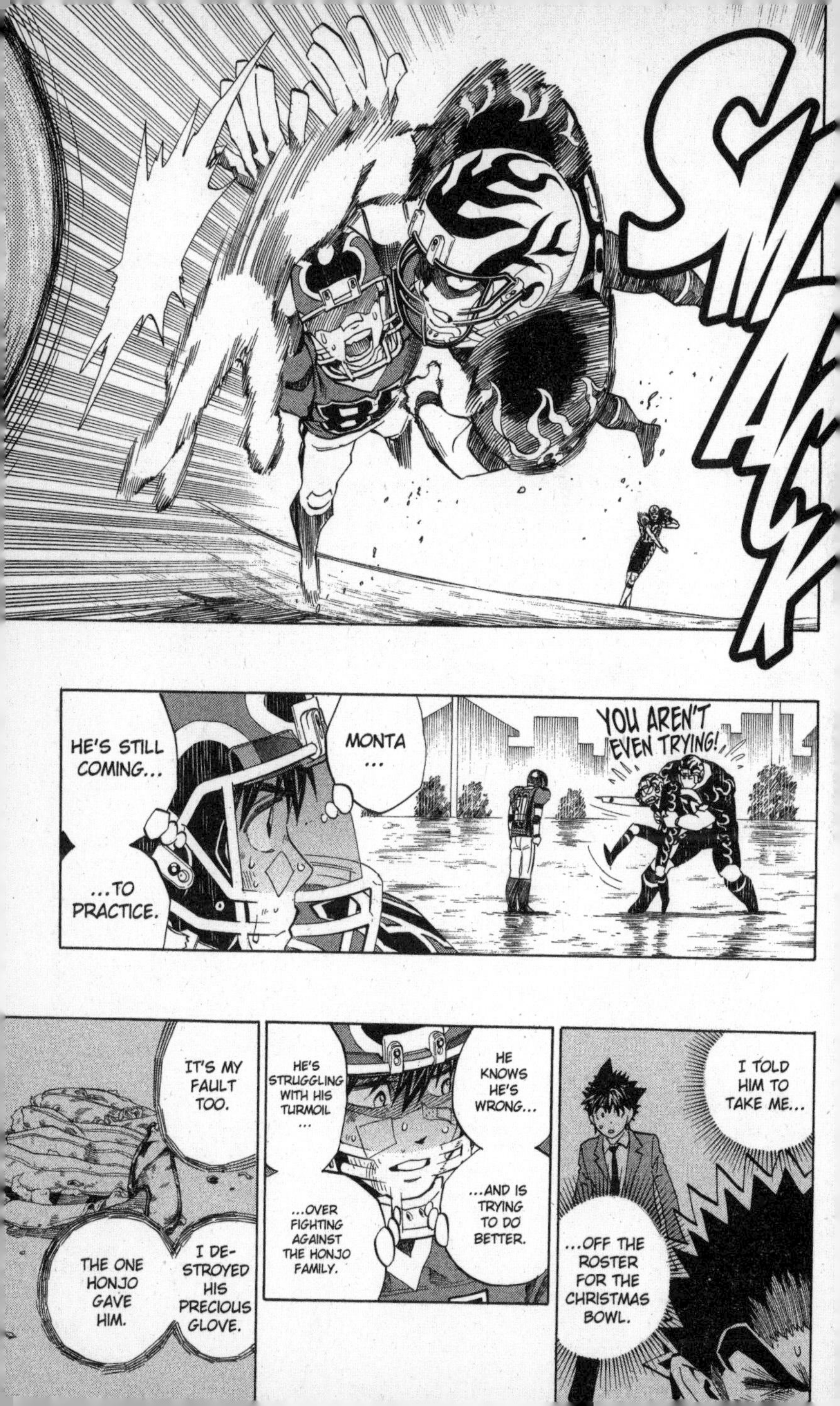
SMACK
YOU AREN'T EVEN TRYING!
MONTA...
HE'S STILL COMING...
...TO PRACTICE.
I TOLD HIM TO TAKE ME...
...OFF THE ROSTER FOR THE CHRISTMAS BOWL.
HE KNOWS HE'S WRONG...
...AND IS TRYING TO DO BETTER.
HE'S STRUGGLING WITH HIS TURMOIL...
...OVER FIGHTING AGAINST THE HONJO FAMILY.
IT'S MY FAULT TOO.
I DE-STROYED HIS PRECIOUS GLOVE.
THE ONE HONJO GAVE HIM.

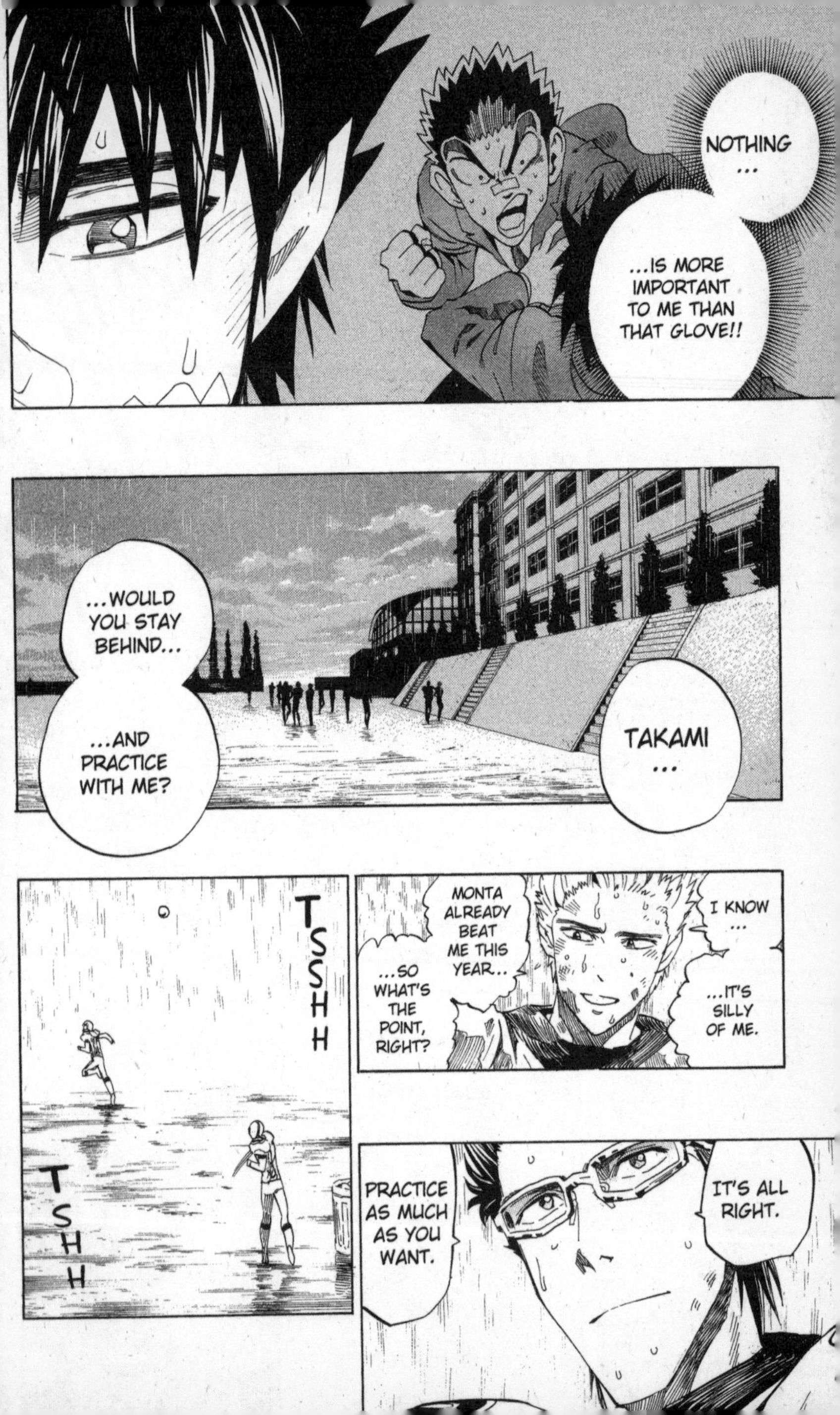
NOTHING ...
...IS MORE IMPORTANT TO ME THAN THAT GLOVE!!
TAKAMI ...
...WOULD YOU STAY BEHIND...
...AND PRACTICE WITH ME?
I KNOW ...
...IT'S SILLY OF ME.
MONTA ALREADY BEAT ME THIS YEAR...
...SO WHAT'S THE POINT, RIGHT?
IT'S ALL RIGHT.
PRACTICE AS MUCH AS YOU WANT.
TSSHH
TSHH

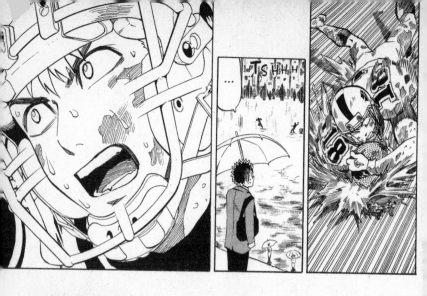

...

TSHHH

UM...

...SAKU-RABA?

SPLOSH

SPLISH

SPLISH

WHAT...

...IS MY PROB-LEM?!

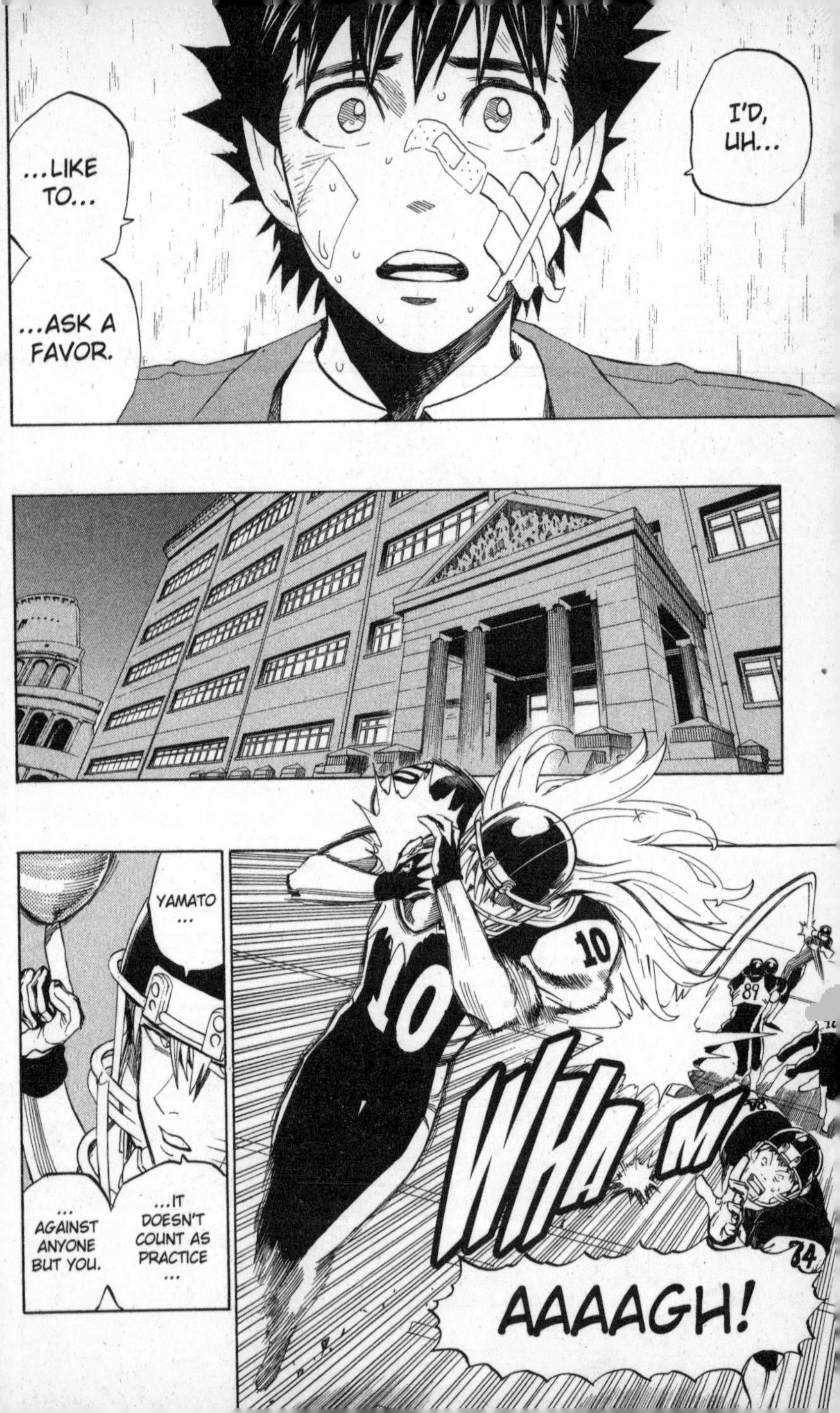
I'D, UH...
...LIKE TO...
...ASK A FAVOR.
WHAM
AAAAGH!
YAMATO...
...IT DOESN'T COUNT AS PRACTICE...
...AGAINST ANYONE BUT YOU.

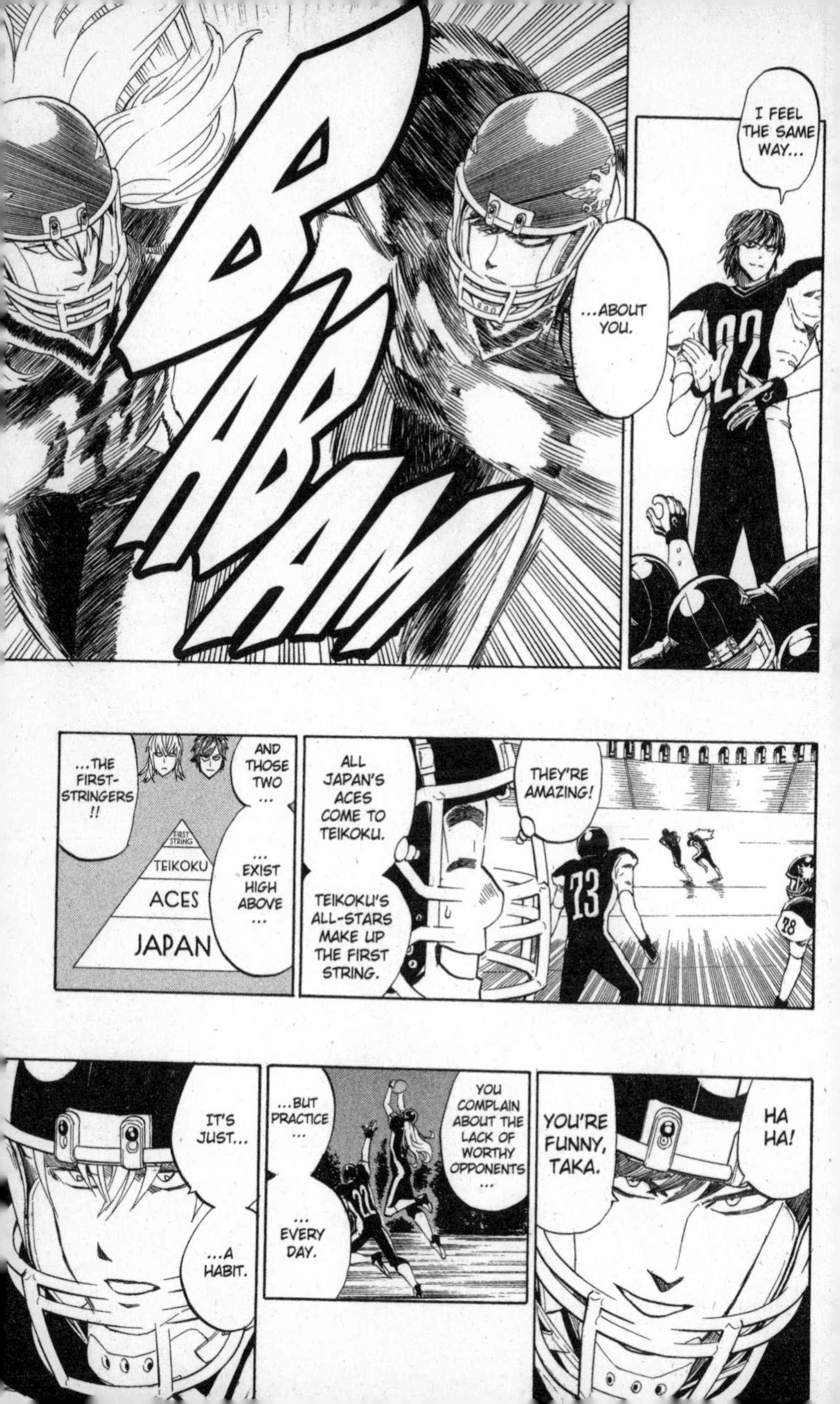
I FEEL THE SAME WAY...
...ABOUT YOU.
BABAM
THEY'RE AMAZING!
ALL JAPAN'S ACES COME TO TEIKOKU.
TEIKOKU'S ALL-STARS MAKE UP THE FIRST STRING.
AND THOSE TWO...
...EXIST HIGH ABOVE...
...THE FIRST-STRINGERS!!
FIRST STRING
TEIKOKU
ACES
JAPAN
HA HA!
YOU'RE FUNNY, TAKA.
YOU COMPLAIN ABOUT THE LACK OF WORTHY OPPONENTS...
...BUT PRACTICE...
...EVERY DAY.
IT'S JUST...
...A HABIT.

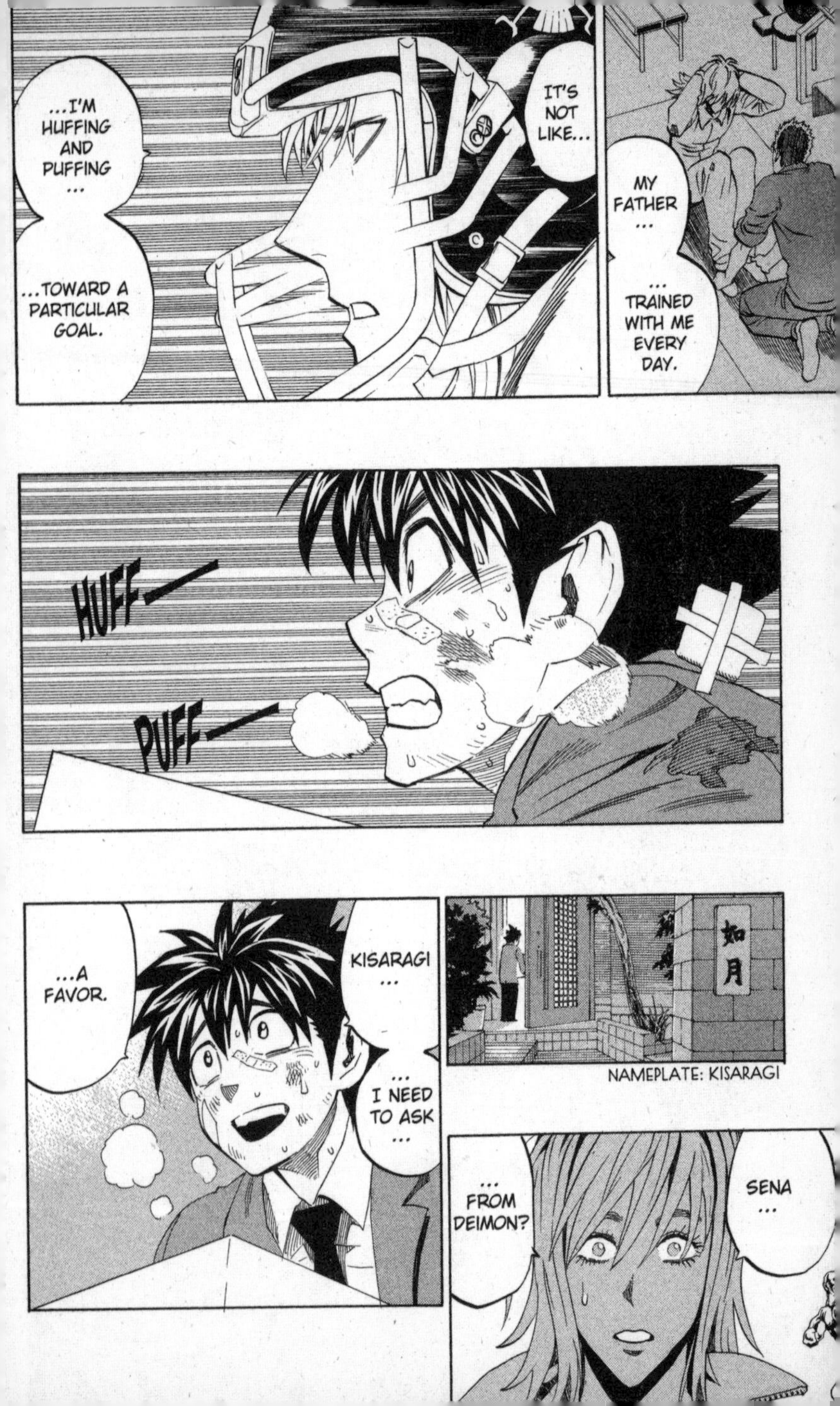
MY FATHER ...
... TRAINED WITH ME EVERY DAY.
IT'S NOT LIKE...
...I'M HUFFING AND PUFFING ...
...TOWARD A PARTICULAR GOAL.
HUFF——
PUFF——
如月
NAMEPLATE: KISARAGI
KISARAGI ...
... I NEED TO ASK ...
...A FAVOR.
SENA ...
... FROM DEIMON?

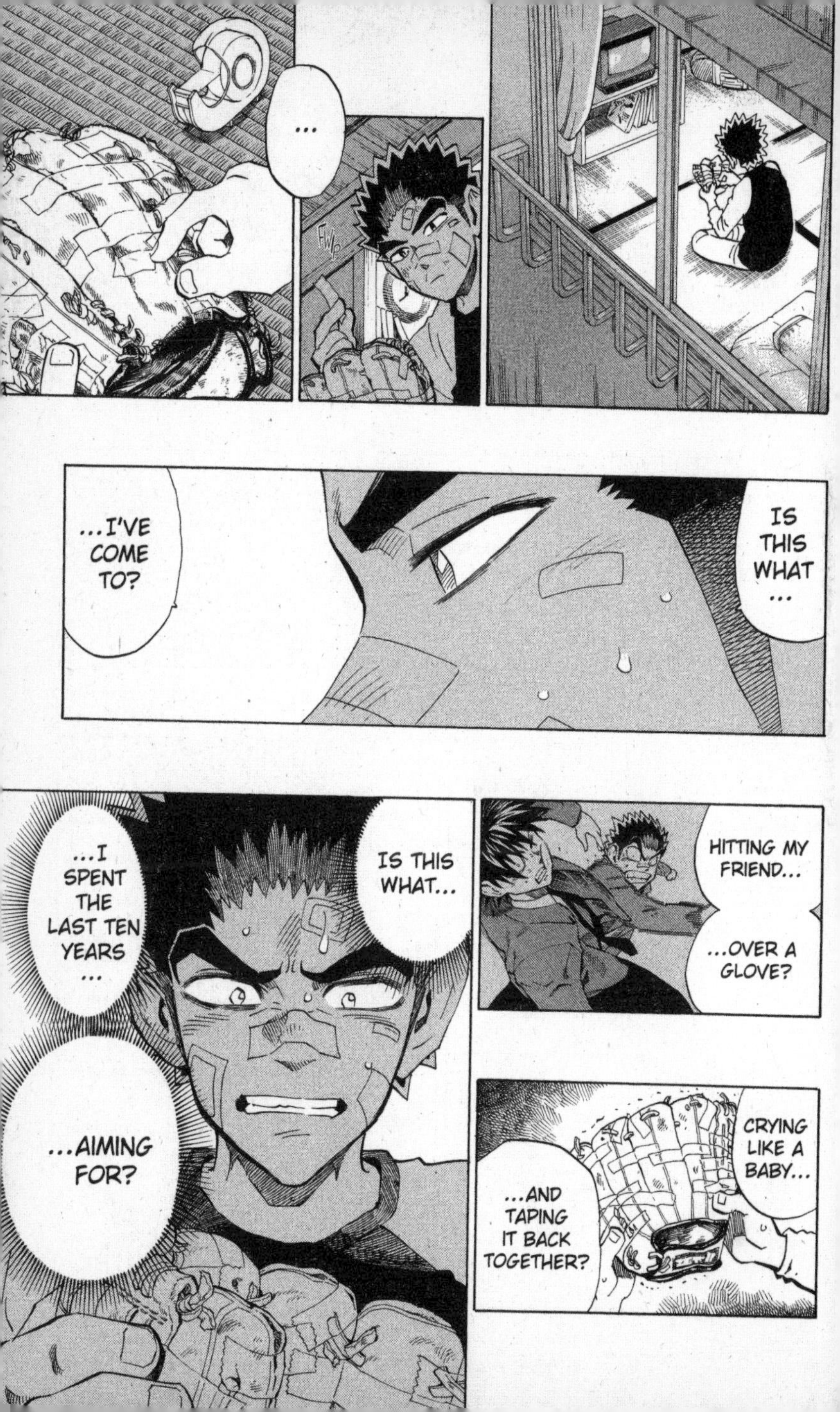
FWIP
...
IS THIS WHAT...
...I'VE COME TO?
HITTING MY FRIEND...
...OVER A GLOVE?
CRYING LIKE A BABY...
...AND TAPING IT BACK TOGETHER?
IS THIS WHAT...
...I SPENT THE LAST TEN YEARS...
...AIMING FOR?

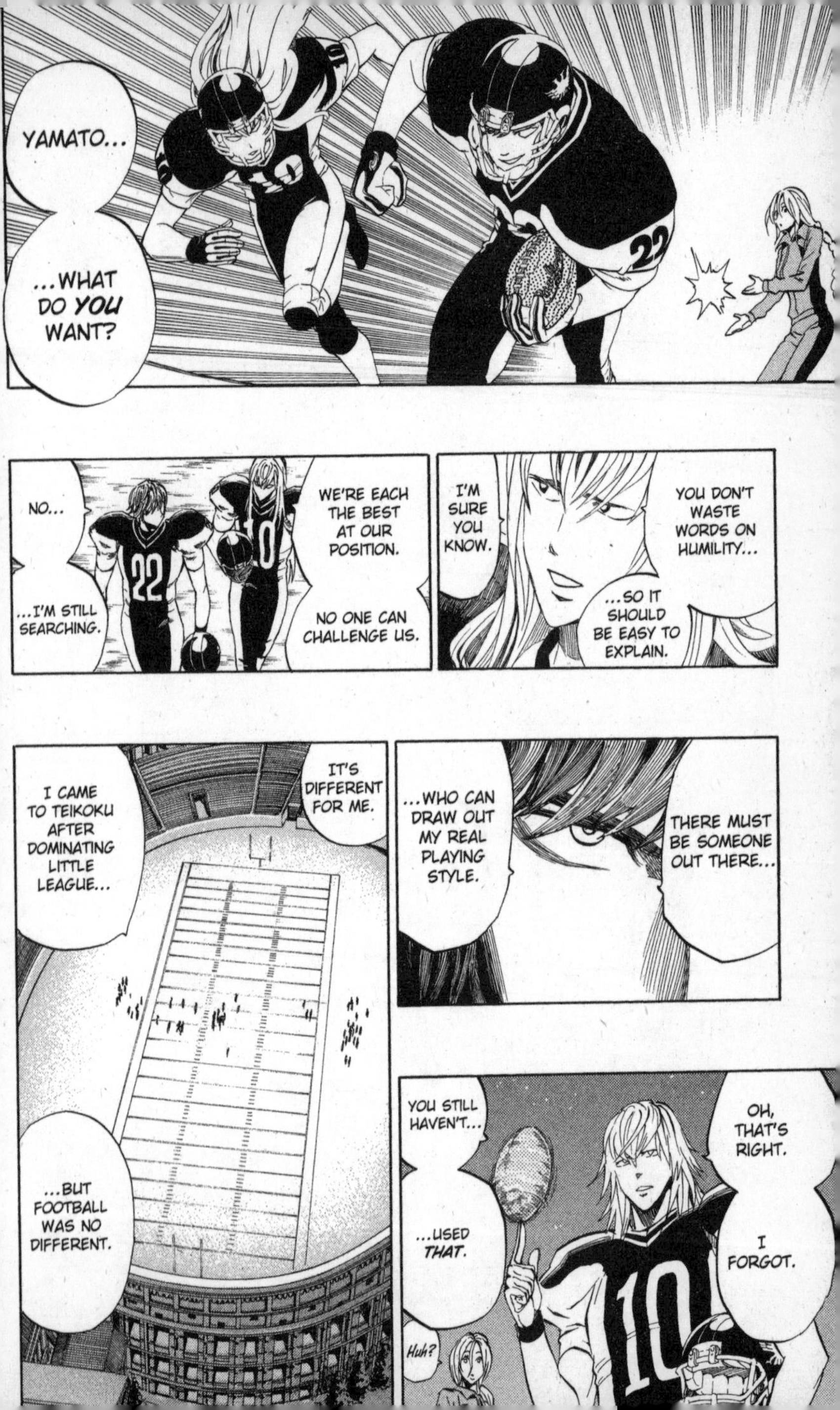
YAMATO...
...WHAT DO *YOU* WANT?
YOU DON'T WASTE WORDS ON HUMILITY...
I'M SURE YOU KNOW.
...SO IT SHOULD BE EASY TO EXPLAIN.
WE'RE EACH THE BEST AT OUR POSITION.
NO ONE CAN CHALLENGE US.
NO...
...I'M STILL SEARCHING.
THERE MUST BE SOMEONE OUT THERE...
...WHO CAN DRAW OUT MY REAL PLAYING STYLE.
OH, THAT'S RIGHT.
I FORGOT.
YOU STILL HAVEN'T...
...USED *THAT*.
Huh?
IT'S DIFFERENT FOR ME.
I CAME TO TEIKOKU AFTER DOMINATING LITTLE LEAGUE...
...BUT FOOTBALL WAS NO DIFFERENT.

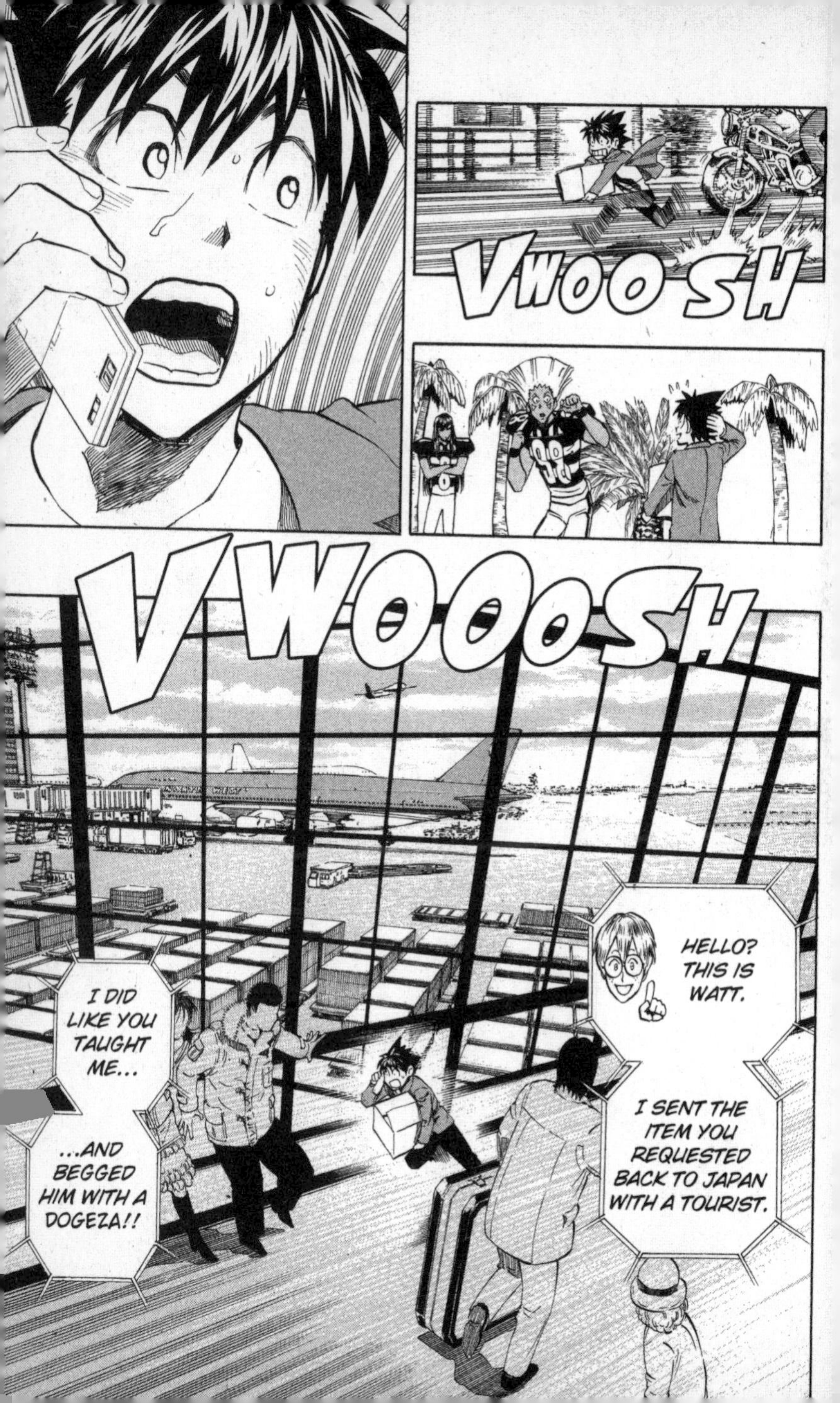
VWOO SH
VWOOOSH
HELLO? THIS IS WATT.
I SENT THE ITEM YOU REQUESTED BACK TO JAPAN WITH A TOURIST.
I DID LIKE YOU TAUGHT ME...
...AND BEGGED HIM WITH A DOGEZA!!

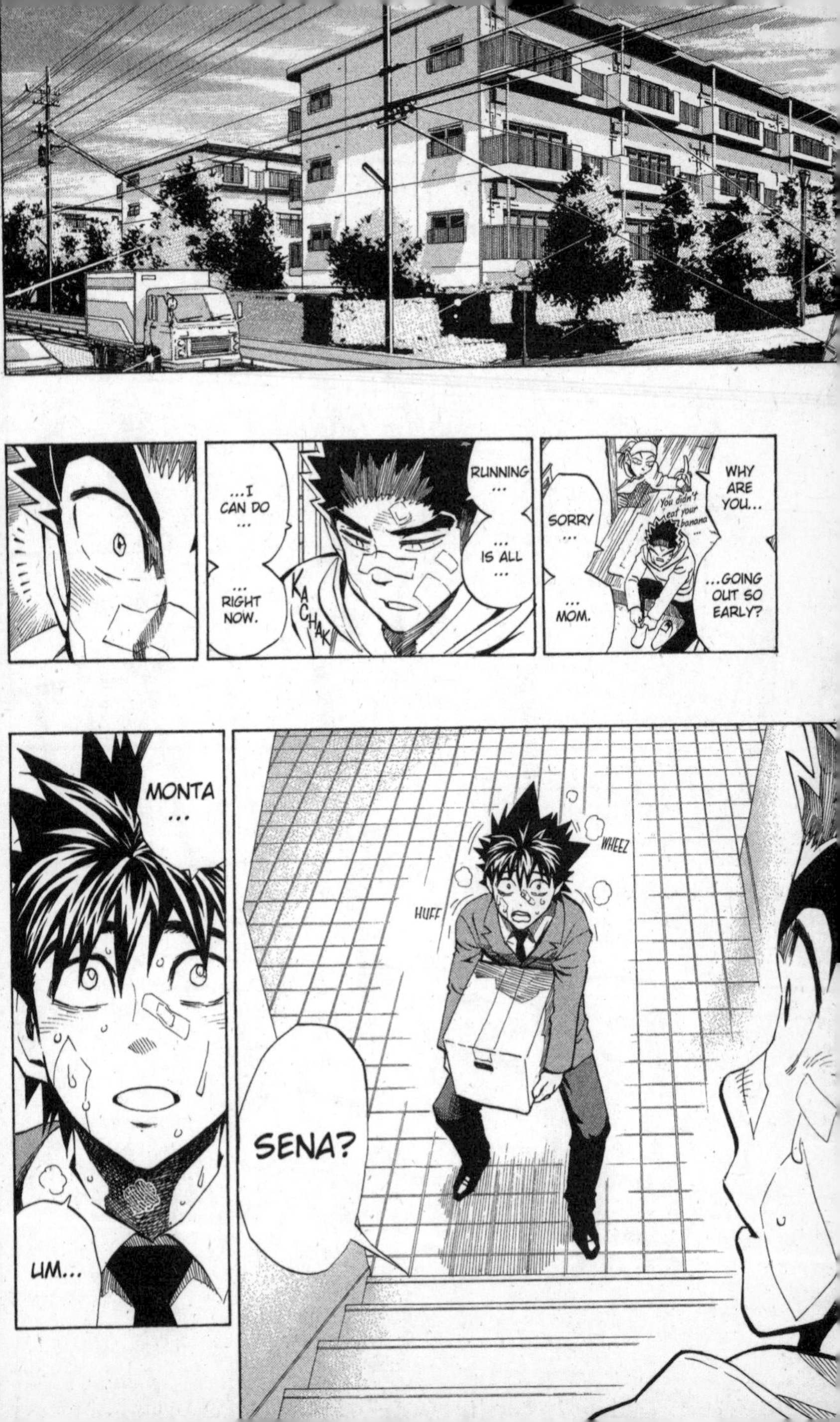
WHY ARE YOU...
You didn't eat your banana...
...GOING OUT SO EARLY?
SORRY...
...MOM.
RUNNING...
...IS ALL...
...I CAN DO...
...RIGHT NOW.
KACHAK
WHEEZ
HUFF
SENA?
MONTA...
UM...

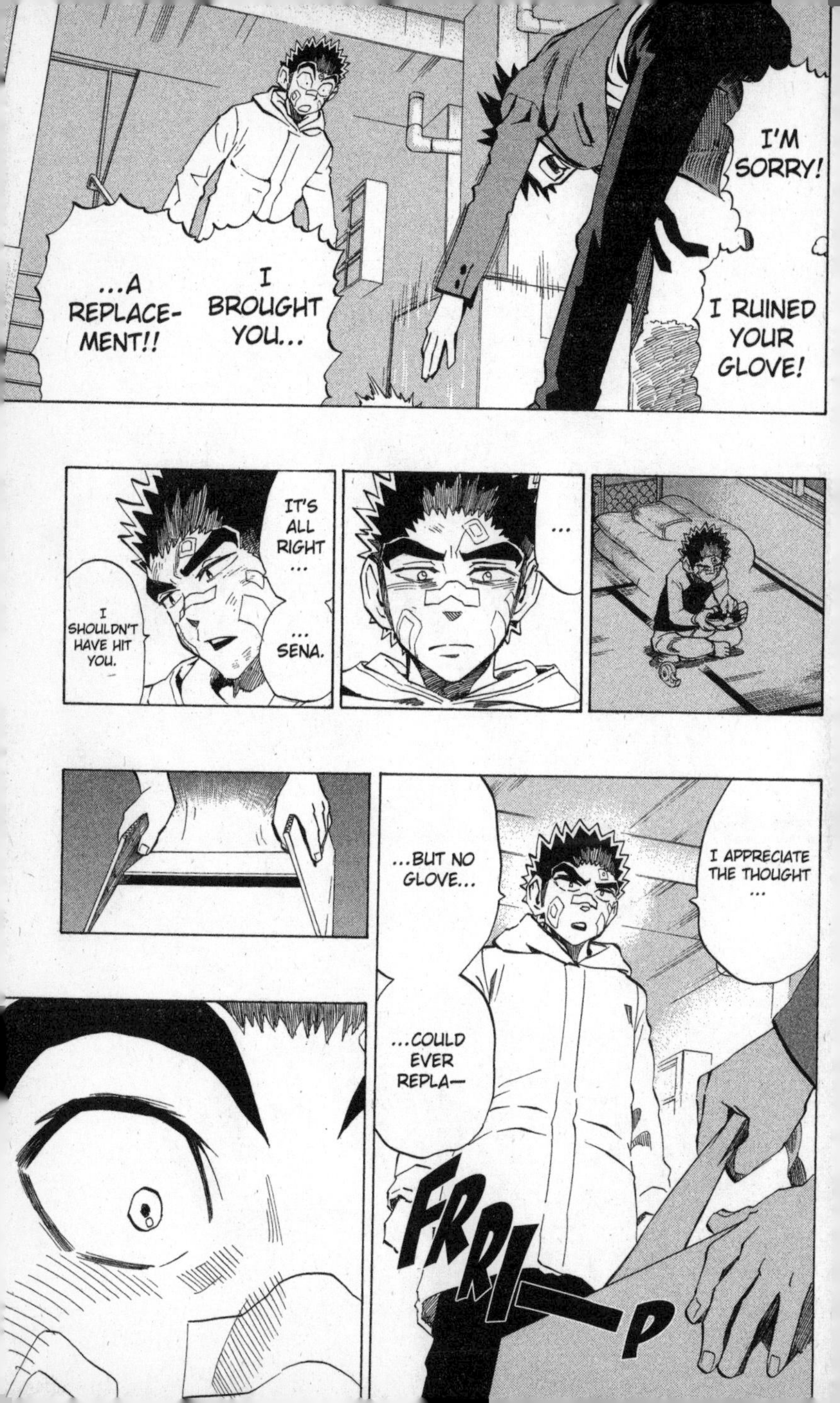
I'M SORRY!
I RUINED YOUR GLOVE!
I BROUGHT YOU...
...A REPLACE-MENT!!
...
IT'S ALL RIGHT...
...SENA.
I SHOULDN'T HAVE HIT YOU.
I APPRECIATE THE THOUGHT...
...BUT NO GLOVE...
...COULD EVER REPLA—
FRRI—P

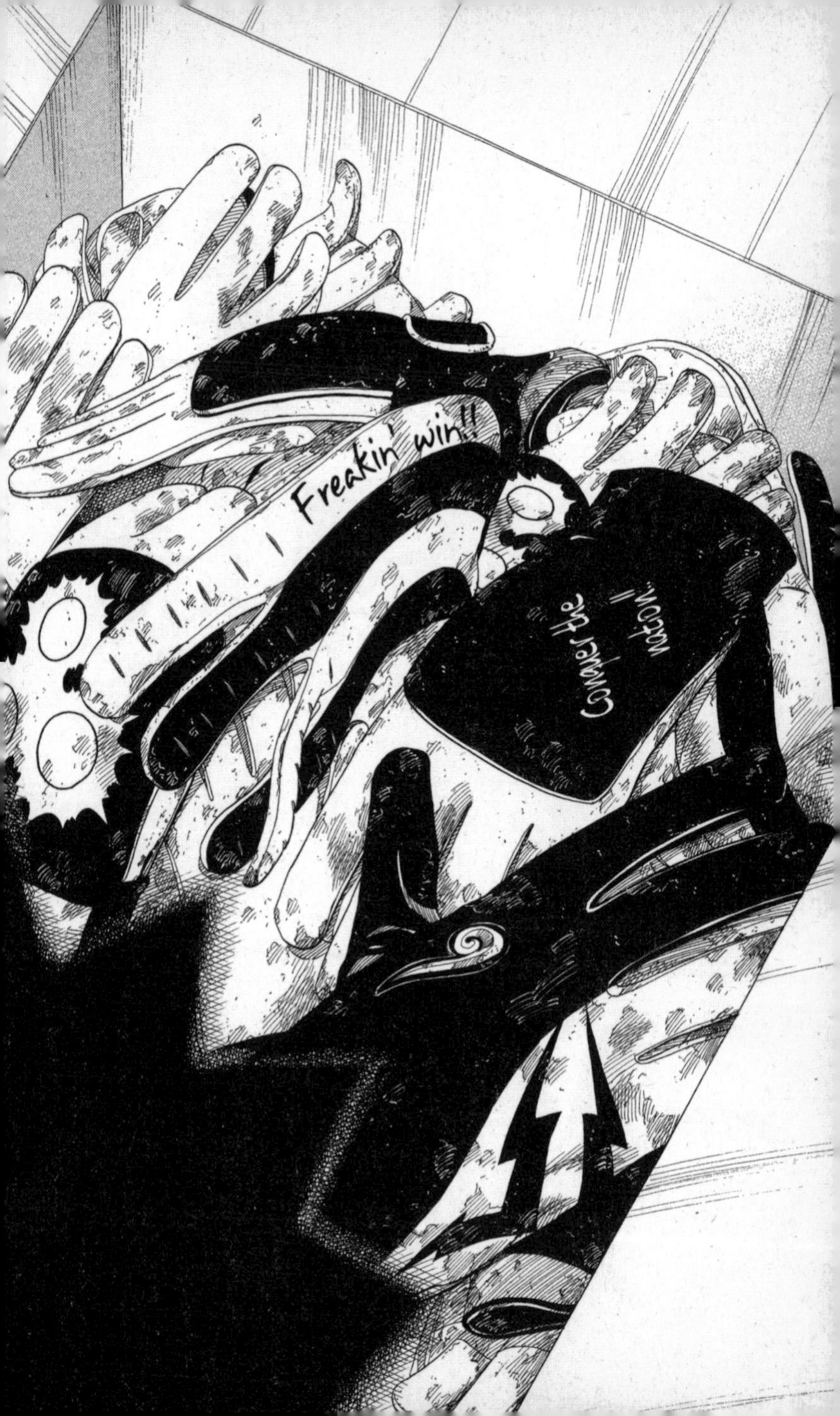
Freakin' win!!
Conquer the nation!!

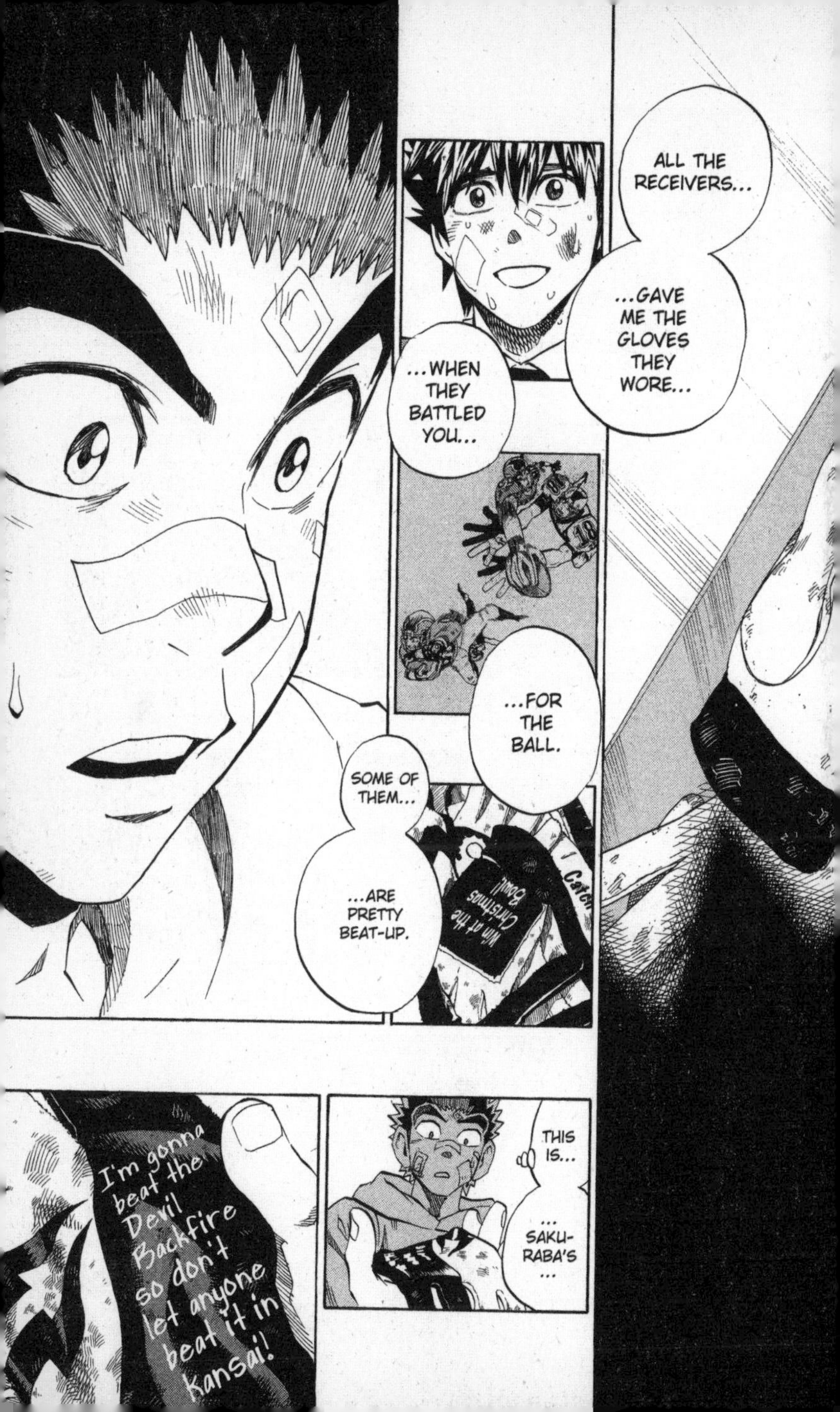

ALL THE RECEIVERS...
...GAVE ME THE GLOVES THEY WORE...
...WHEN THEY BATTLED YOU...
...FOR THE BALL.
SOME OF THEM...
...ARE PRETTY BEAT-UP.
Win at the Christmas Bowl!
Catch
THIS IS...
...SAKU-RABA'S...
I'm gonna beat the Devil Backfire so don't let anyone beat it in Kansai!

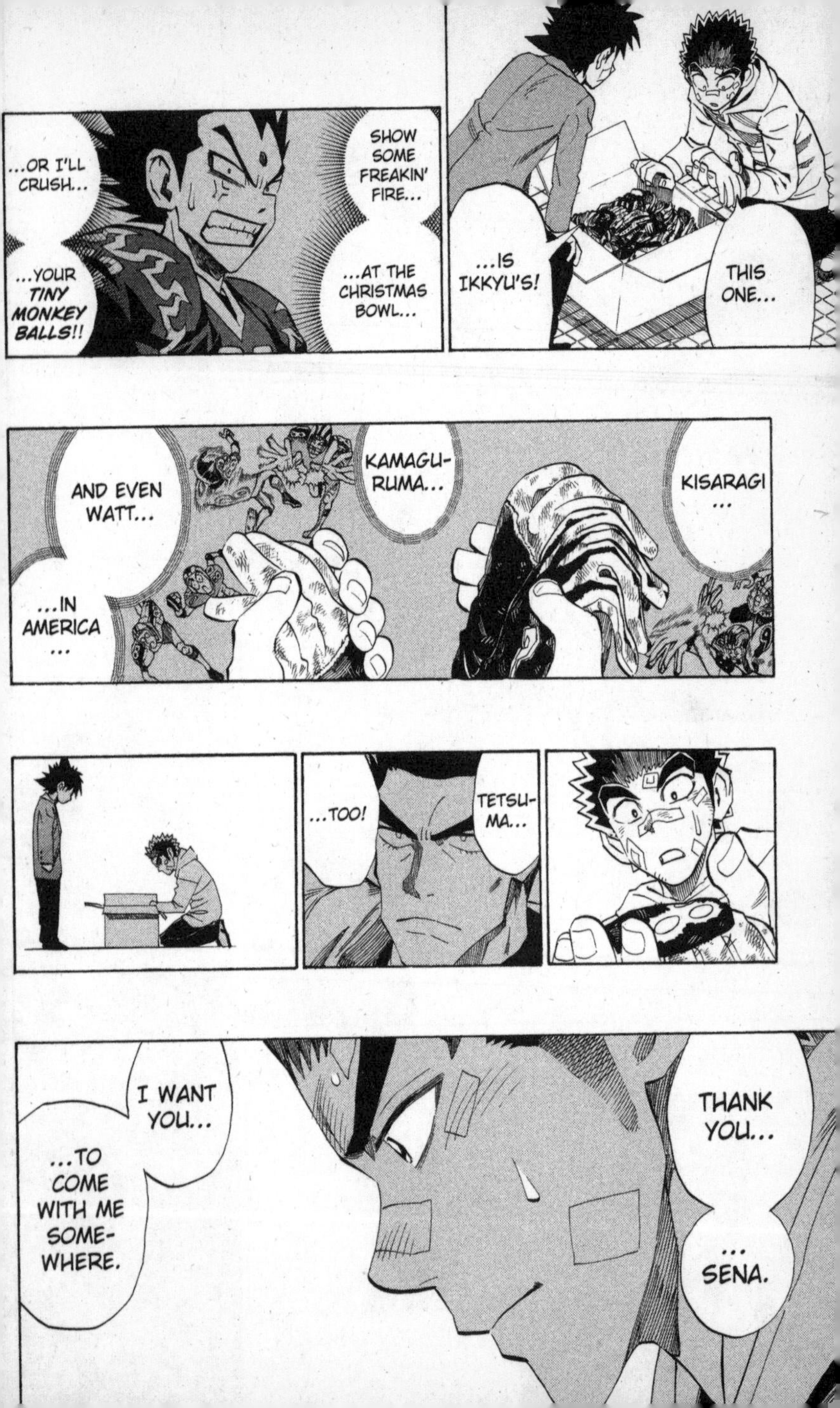
THIS ONE...
...IS IKKYU'S!
SHOW SOME FREAKIN' FIRE...
...AT THE CHRISTMAS BOWL...
...OR I'LL CRUSH...
...YOUR *TINY MONKEY BALLS!!*
KISARAGI ...
KAMAGU-RUMA...
AND EVEN WATT...
...IN AMERICA ...
TETSU-MA...
...TOO!
THANK YOU...
... SENA.
I WANT YOU...
...TO COME WITH ME SOME-WHERE.

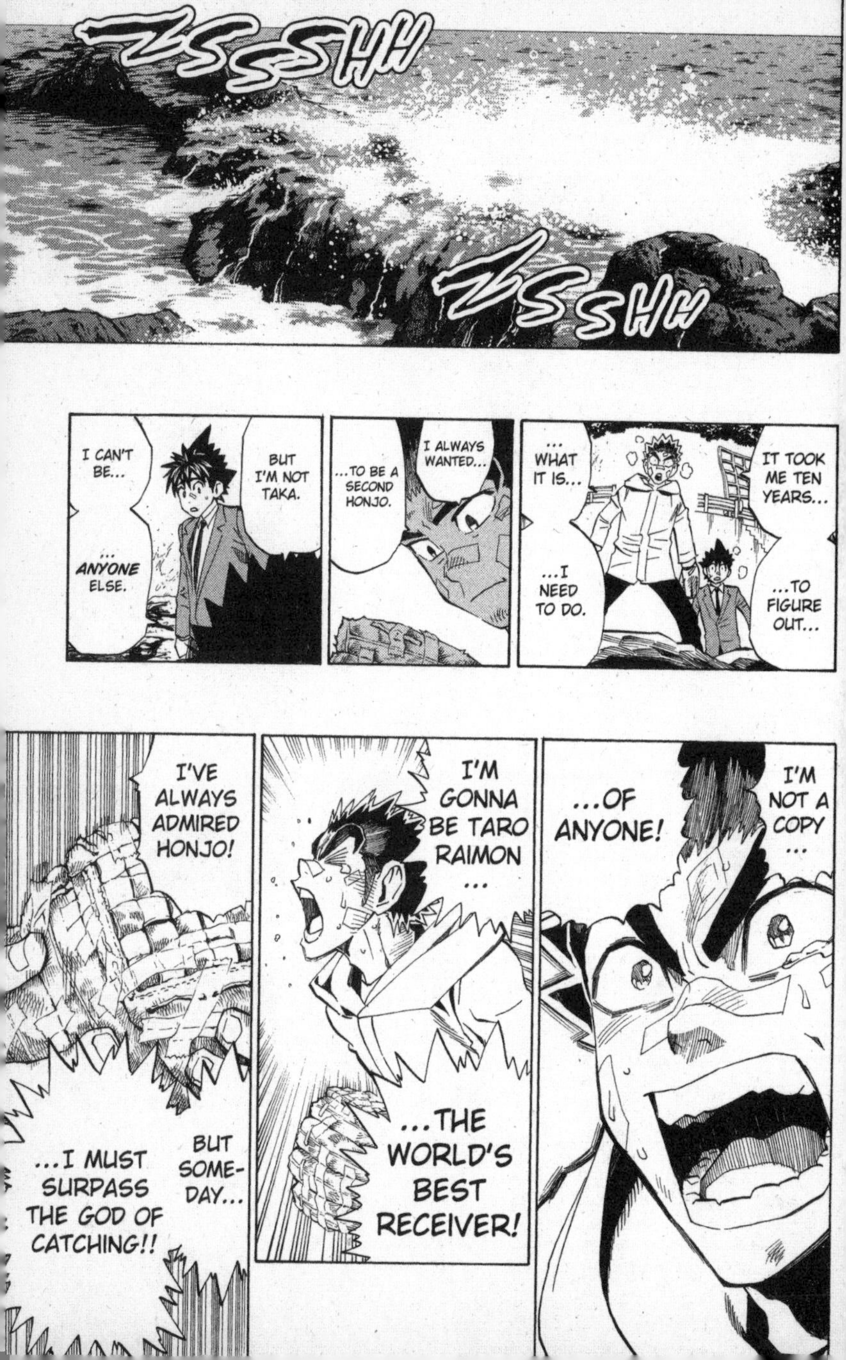
ZSSSHH
ZSSHH
IT TOOK ME TEN YEARS...
...TO FIGURE OUT...
... WHAT IT IS...
...I NEED TO DO.
I ALWAYS WANTED...
...TO BE A SECOND HONJO.
BUT I'M NOT TAKA.
I CAN'T BE...
... ANYONE ELSE.
I'M NOT A COPY ...
...OF ANYONE!
I'M GONNA BE TARO RAIMON ...
...THE WORLD'S BEST RECEIVER!
I'VE ALWAYS ADMIRED HONJO!
BUT SOME-DAY...
...I MUST SURPASS THE GOD OF CATCHING!!

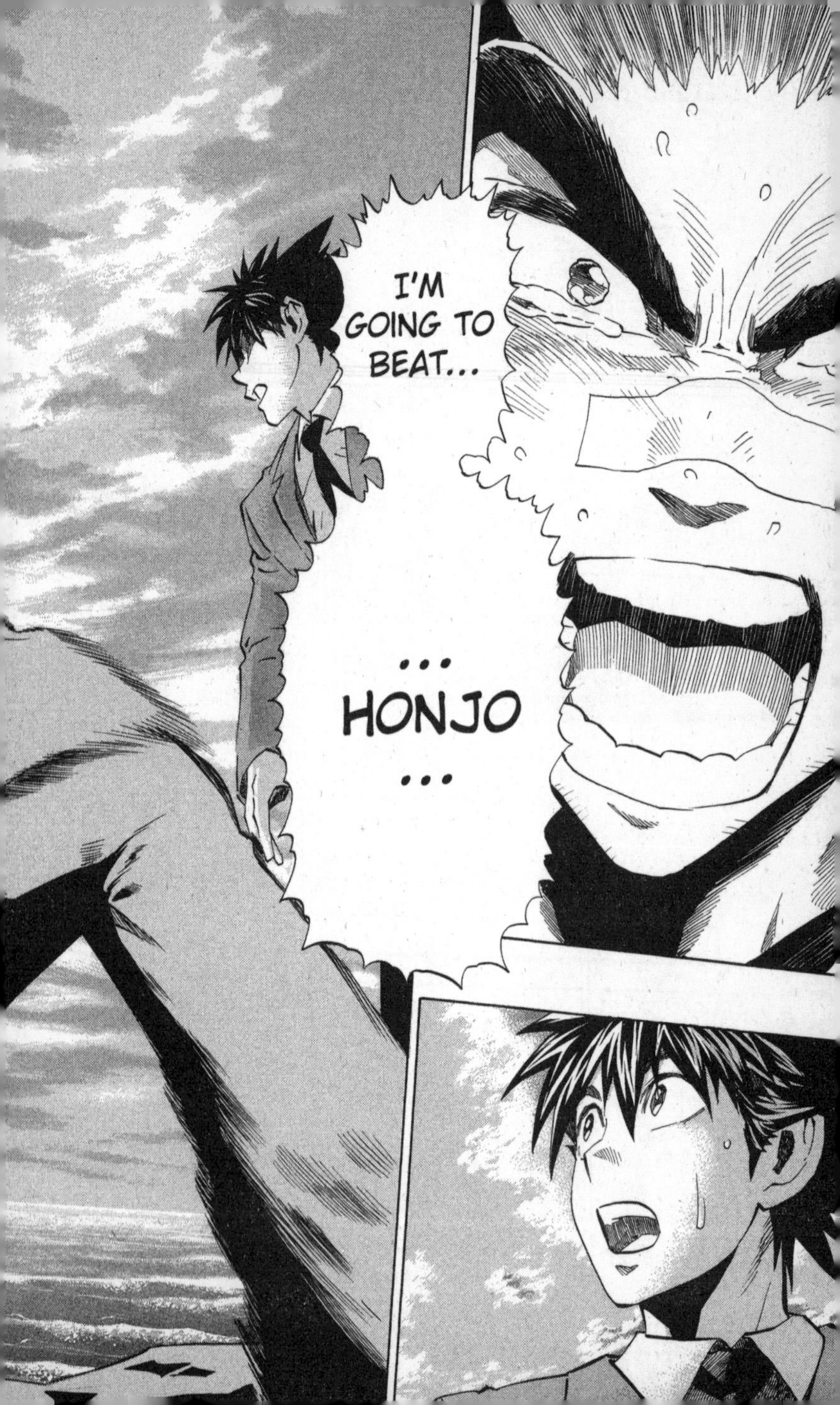
I'M GOING TO BEAT...
... HONJO ...

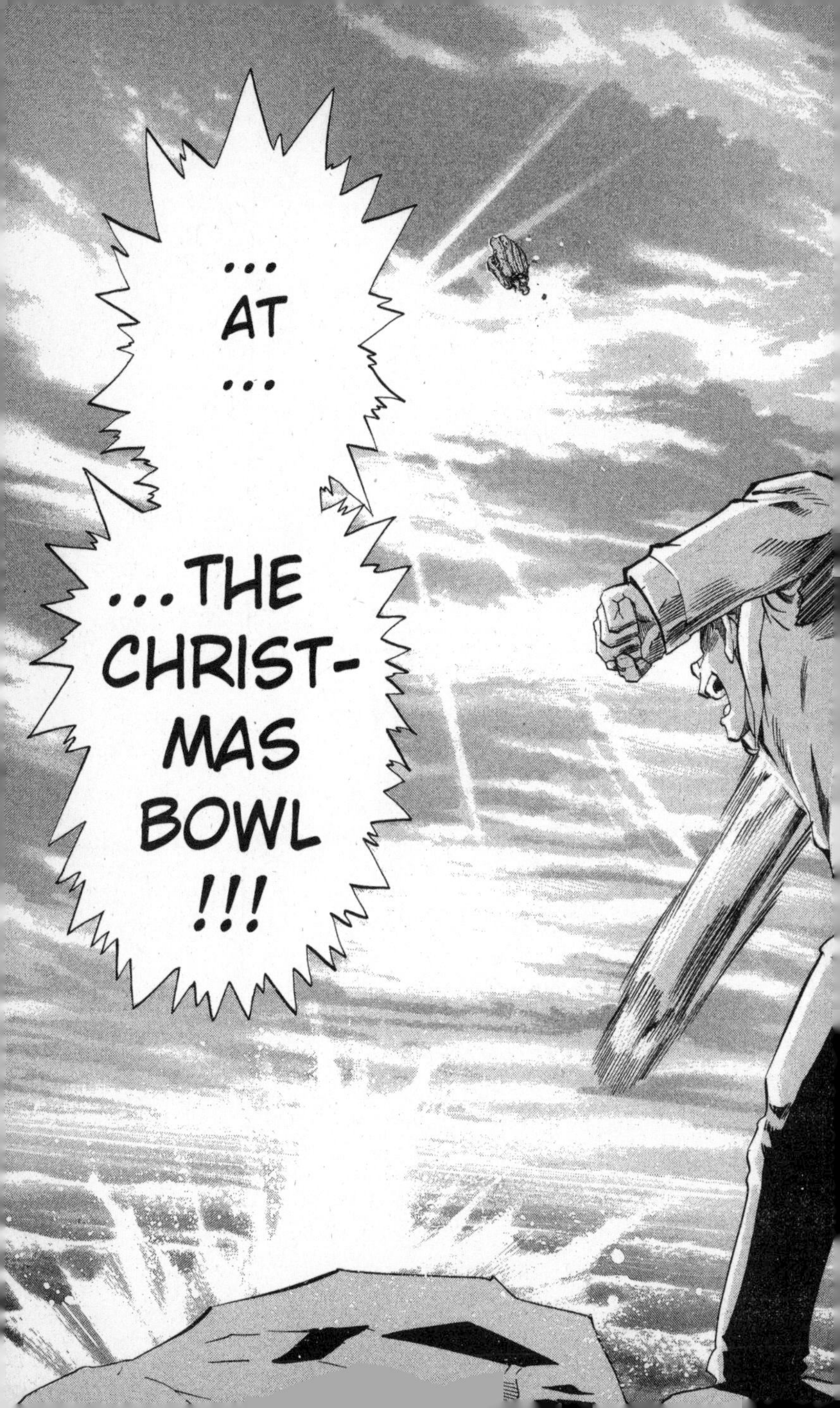
...AT...
...THE CHRIST-MAS BOWL!!!

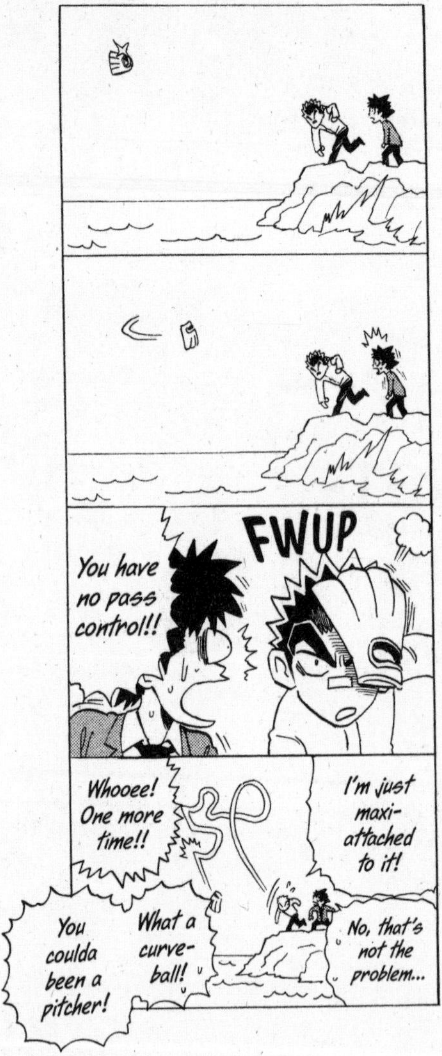
FWUP
You have no pass control!!
I'm just maxi-attached to it!
Whooee! One more time!!
No, that's not the problem...
What a curveball!
You coulda been a pitcher!

Chapter 280 Natural Born Talent

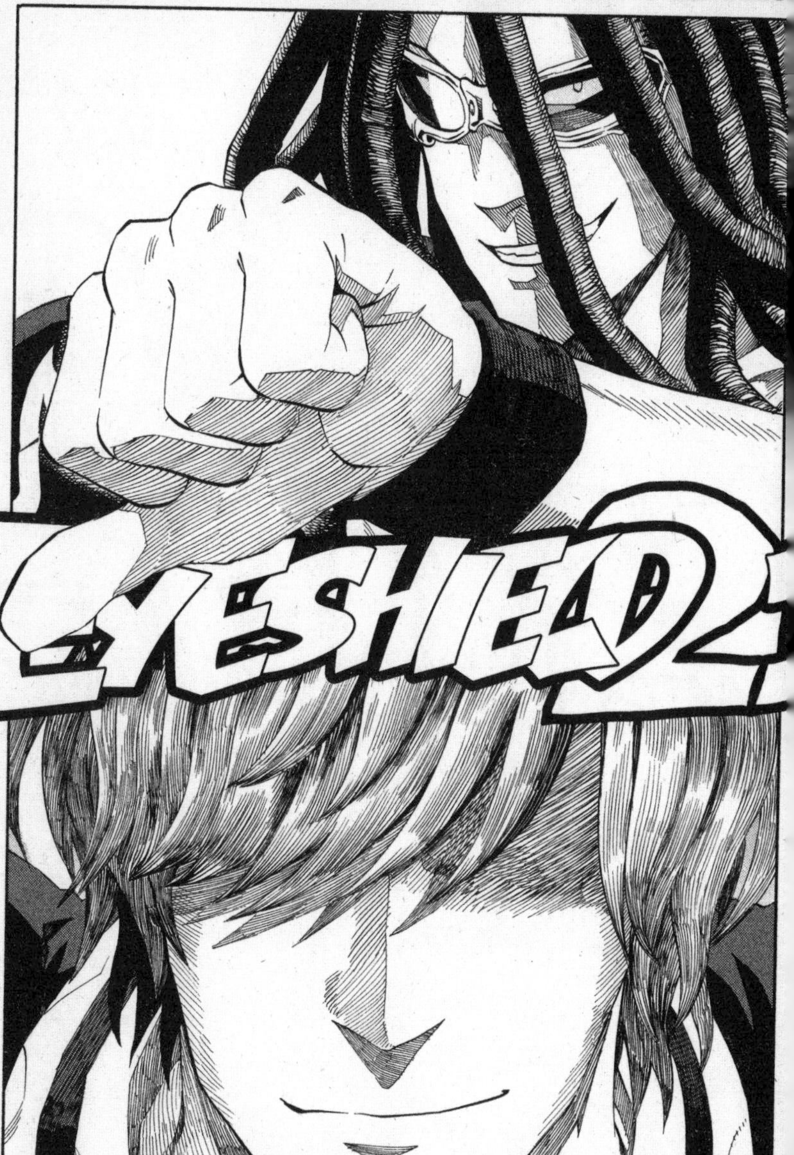
EYESHIELD 21

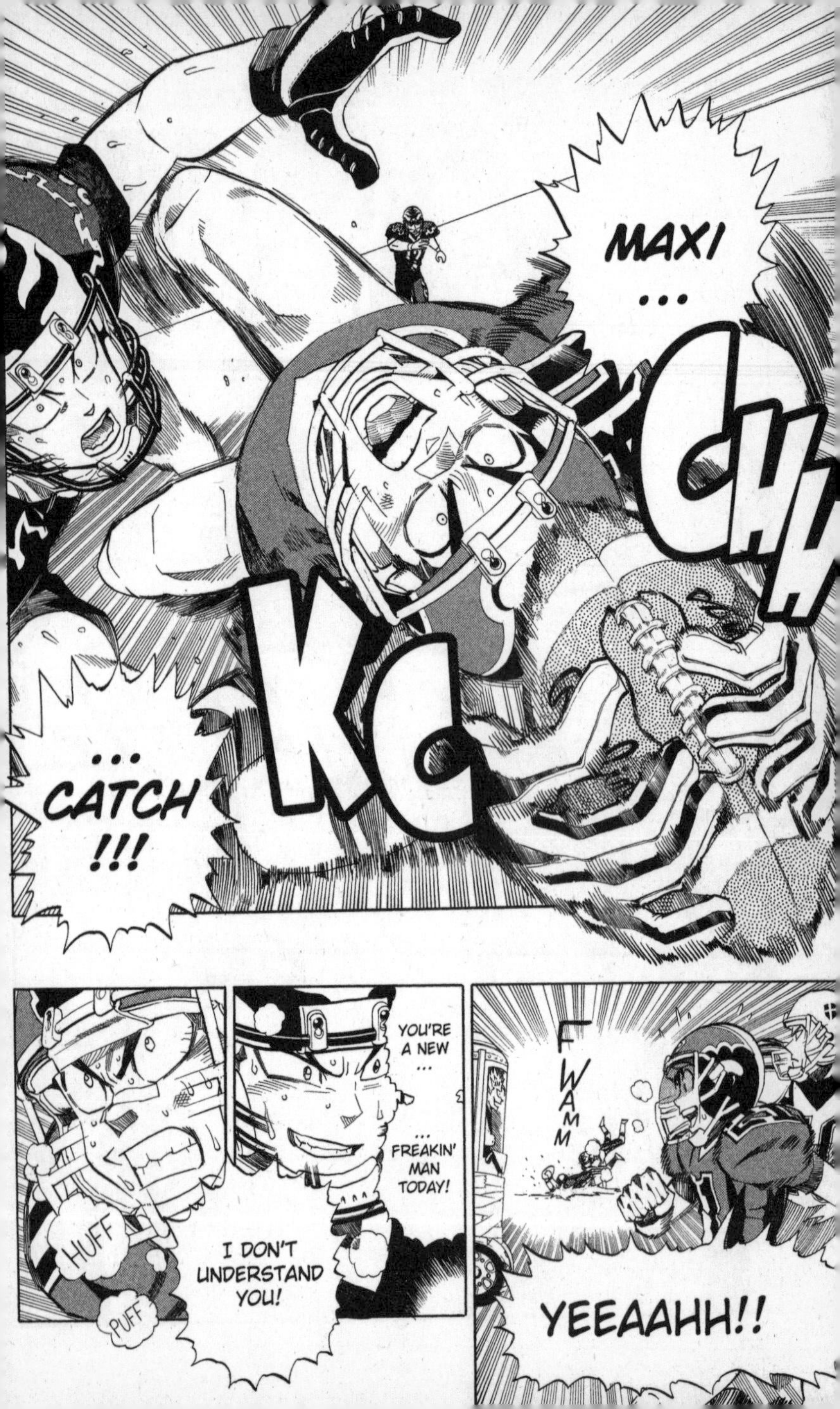

MAXI ...
CH
KC
... CATCH !!!
FWAMM
YEEAAHH!!
YOU'RE A NEW ...
... FREAKIN' MAN TODAY!
HUFF
PUFF
I DON'T UNDERSTAND YOU!

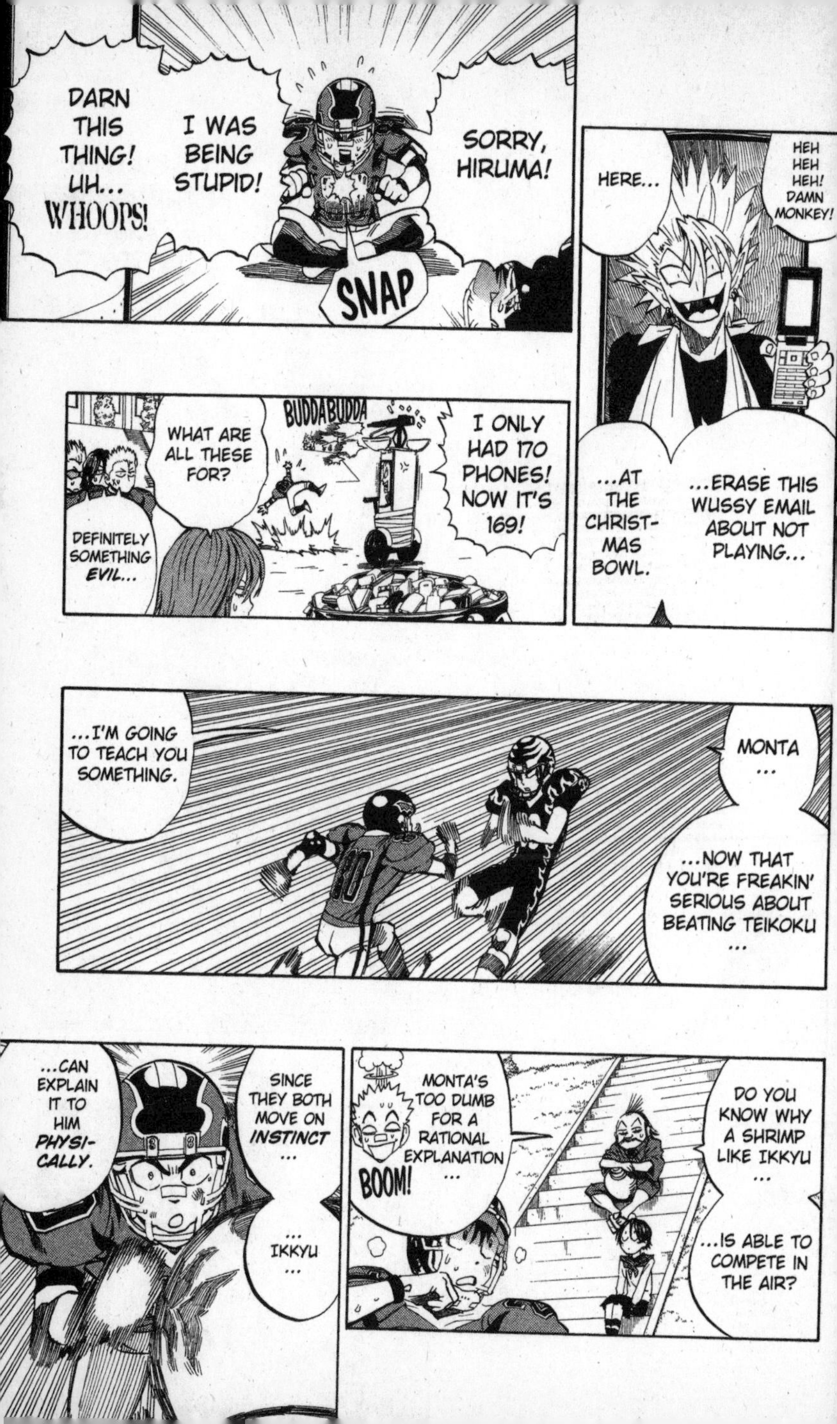

HEH HEH HEH! DAMN MONKEY!
HERE...
...ERASE THIS WUSSY EMAIL ABOUT NOT PLAYING...
...AT THE CHRISTMAS BOWL.
SORRY, HIRUMA!
I WAS BEING STUPID!
DARN THIS THING! UH... WHOOPS!
SNAP
I ONLY HAD 170 PHONES! NOW IT'S 169!
BUDDABUDDA
WHAT ARE ALL THESE FOR?
DEFINITELY SOMETHING *EVIL*...
MONTA ...
...NOW THAT YOU'RE FREAKIN' SERIOUS ABOUT BEATING TEIKOKU ...
...I'M GOING TO TEACH YOU SOMETHING.
DO YOU KNOW WHY A SHRIMP LIKE IKKYU ...
...IS ABLE TO COMPETE IN THE AIR?
MONTA'S TOO DUMB FOR A RATIONAL EXPLANATION ...
BOOM!
SINCE THEY BOTH MOVE ON *INSTINCT* ...
... IKKYU ...
...CAN EXPLAIN IT TO HIM *PHYSICALLY*.

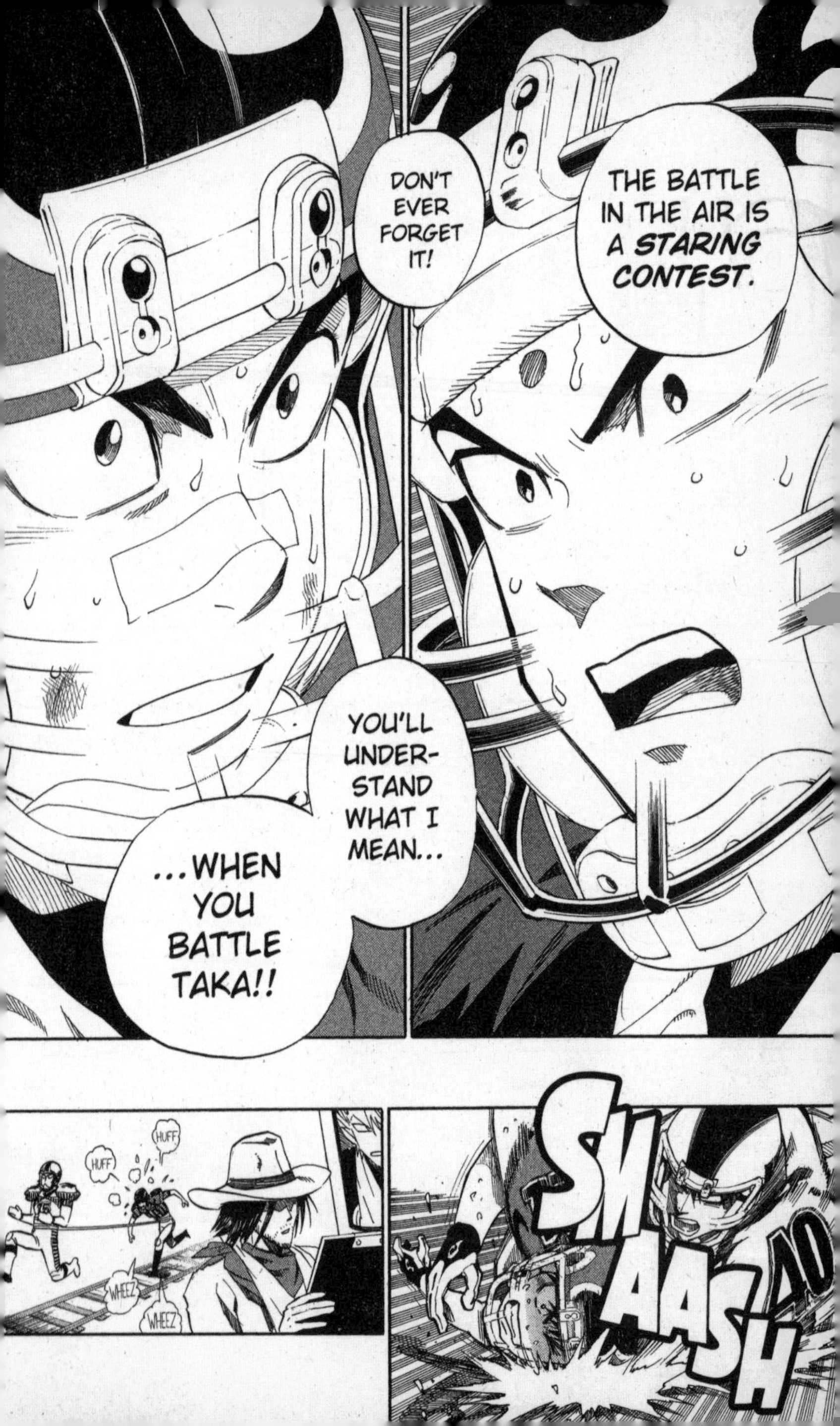
THE BATTLE IN THE AIR IS A STARING CONTEST.
DON'T EVER FORGET IT!
YOU'LL UNDER-STAND WHAT I MEAN...
...WHEN YOU BATTLE TAKA!!
HUFF
HUFF
WHEEZ
WHEEZ
SHAASH

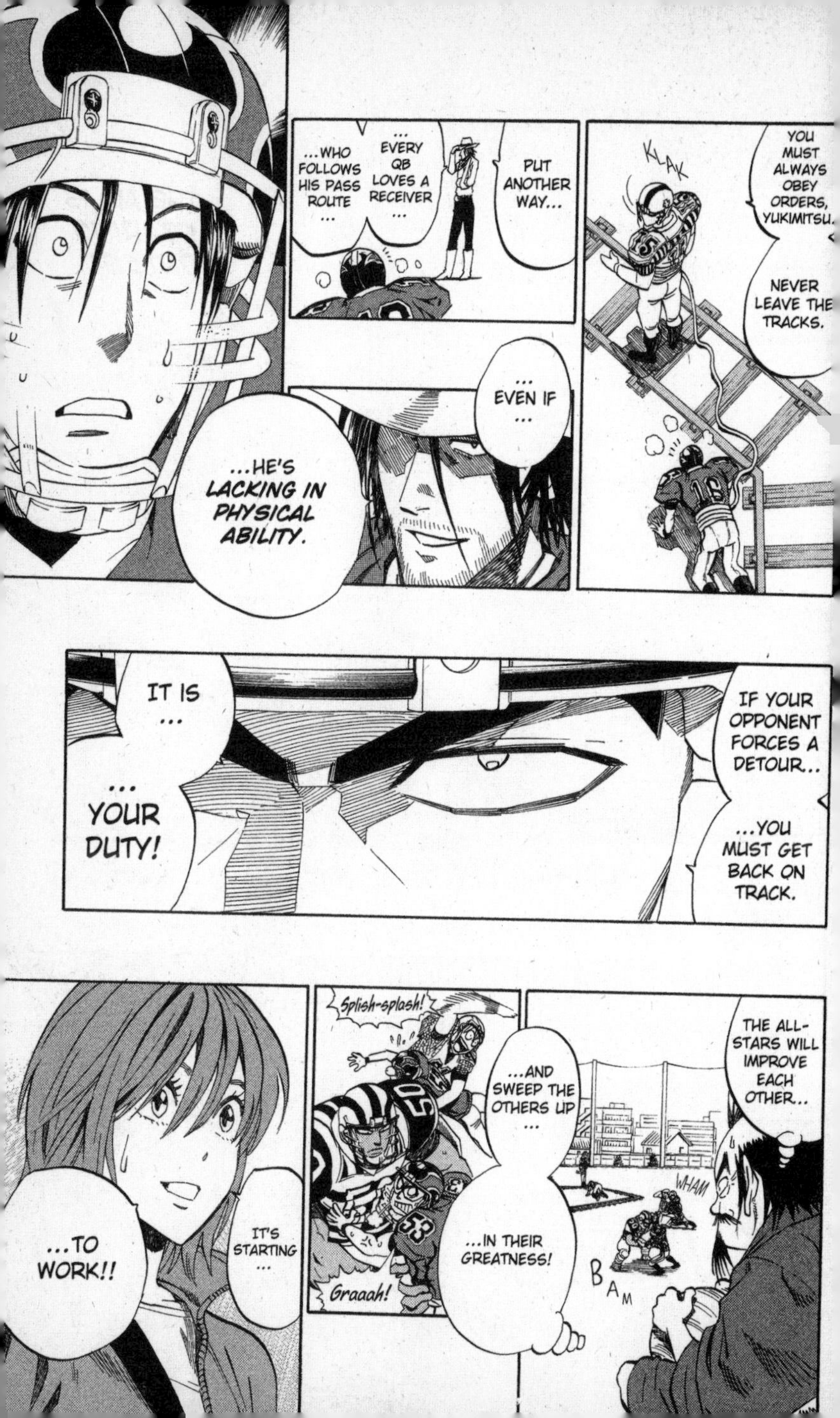
KLAK
YOU MUST ALWAYS OBEY ORDERS, YUKIMITSU.
NEVER LEAVE THE TRACKS.
PUT ANOTHER WAY...
...EVERY QB LOVES A RECEIVER...
...WHO FOLLOWS HIS PASS ROUTE...
...EVEN IF...
...HE'S LACKING IN PHYSICAL ABILITY.
IF YOUR OPPONENT FORCES A DETOUR...
...YOU MUST GET BACK ON TRACK.
IT IS...
...YOUR DUTY!
THE ALL-STARS WILL IMPROVE EACH OTHER...
WHAM
BAM
Splish-splash!
...AND SWEEP THE OTHERS UP...
...IN THEIR GREATNESS!
Graaah!
IT'S STARTING...
...TO WORK!!

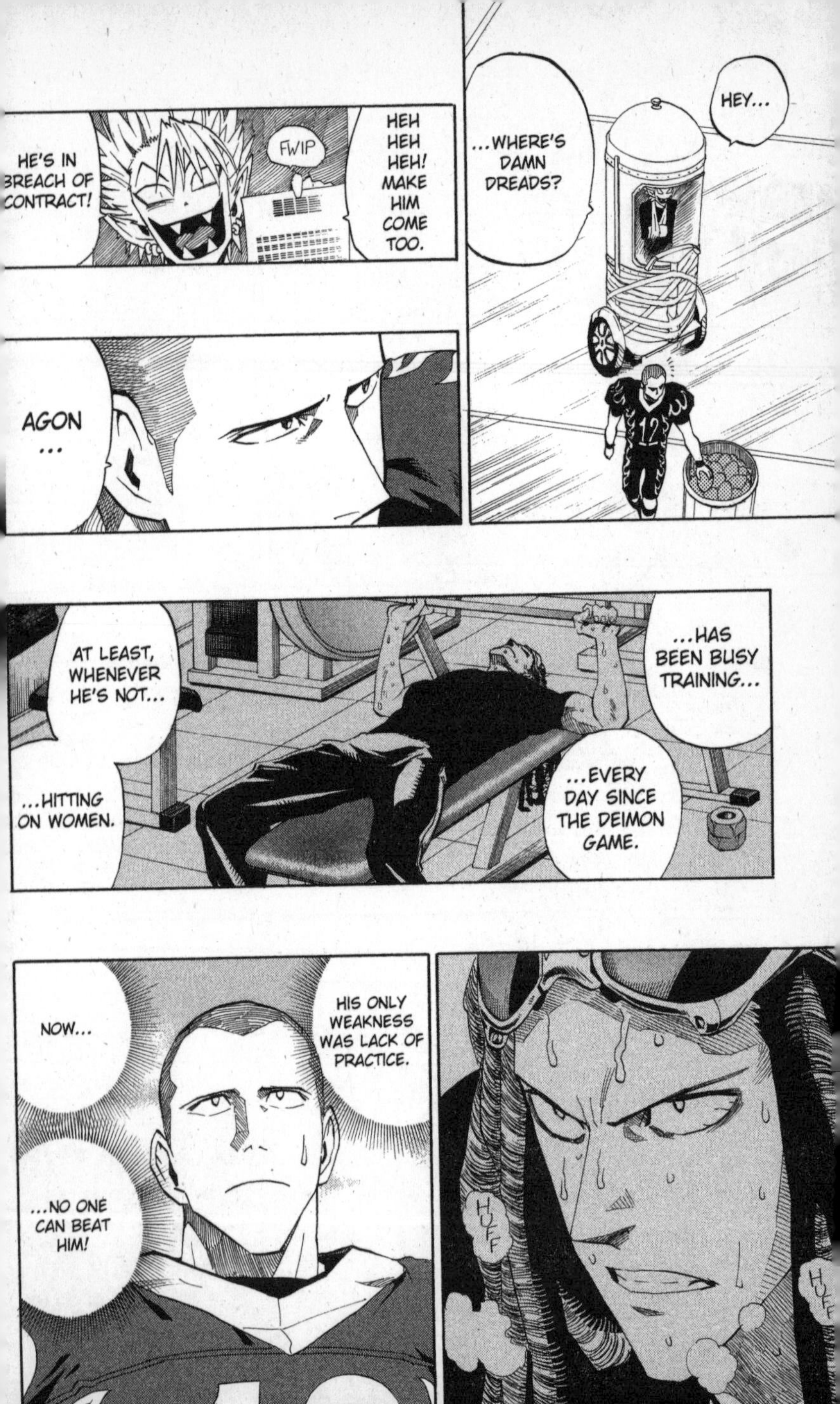
HEY...
...WHERE'S DAMN DREADS?
HEH HEH HEH! MAKE HIM COME TOO.
FWIP
HE'S IN BREACH OF CONTRACT!
AGON ...
...HAS BEEN BUSY TRAINING...
...EVERY DAY SINCE THE DEIMON GAME.
AT LEAST, WHENEVER HE'S NOT...
...HITTING ON WOMEN.
HUFF
HUFF
HIS ONLY WEAKNESS WAS LACK OF PRACTICE.
NOW...
...NO ONE CAN BEAT HIM!

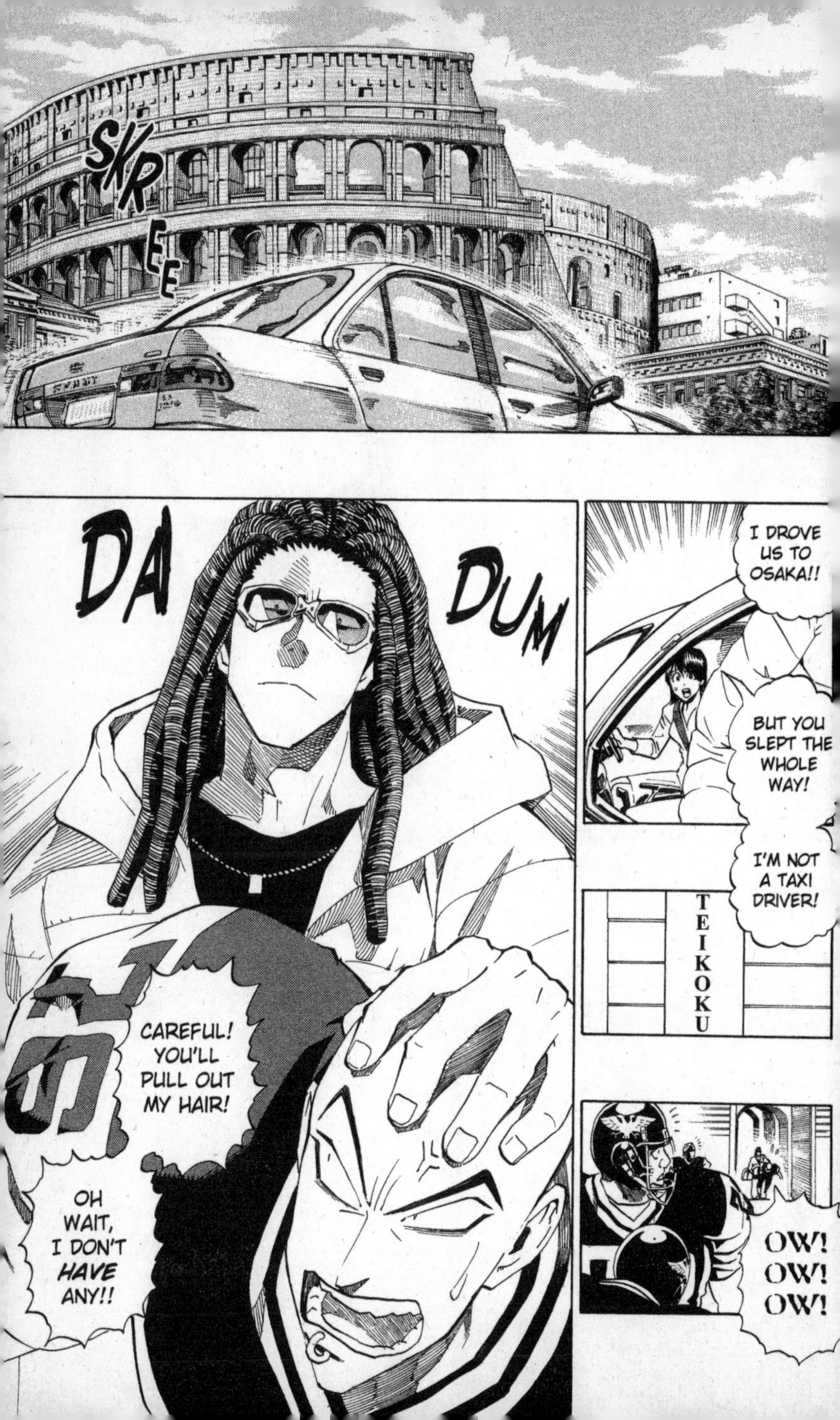
SKREEE
I DROVE US TO OSAKA!!
BUT YOU SLEPT THE WHOLE WAY!
I'M NOT A TAXI DRIVER!
TEIKOKU
OW! OW! OW!
DA DUM
CAREFUL! YOU'LL PULL OUT MY HAIR!
OH WAIT, I DON'T *HAVE* ANY!!

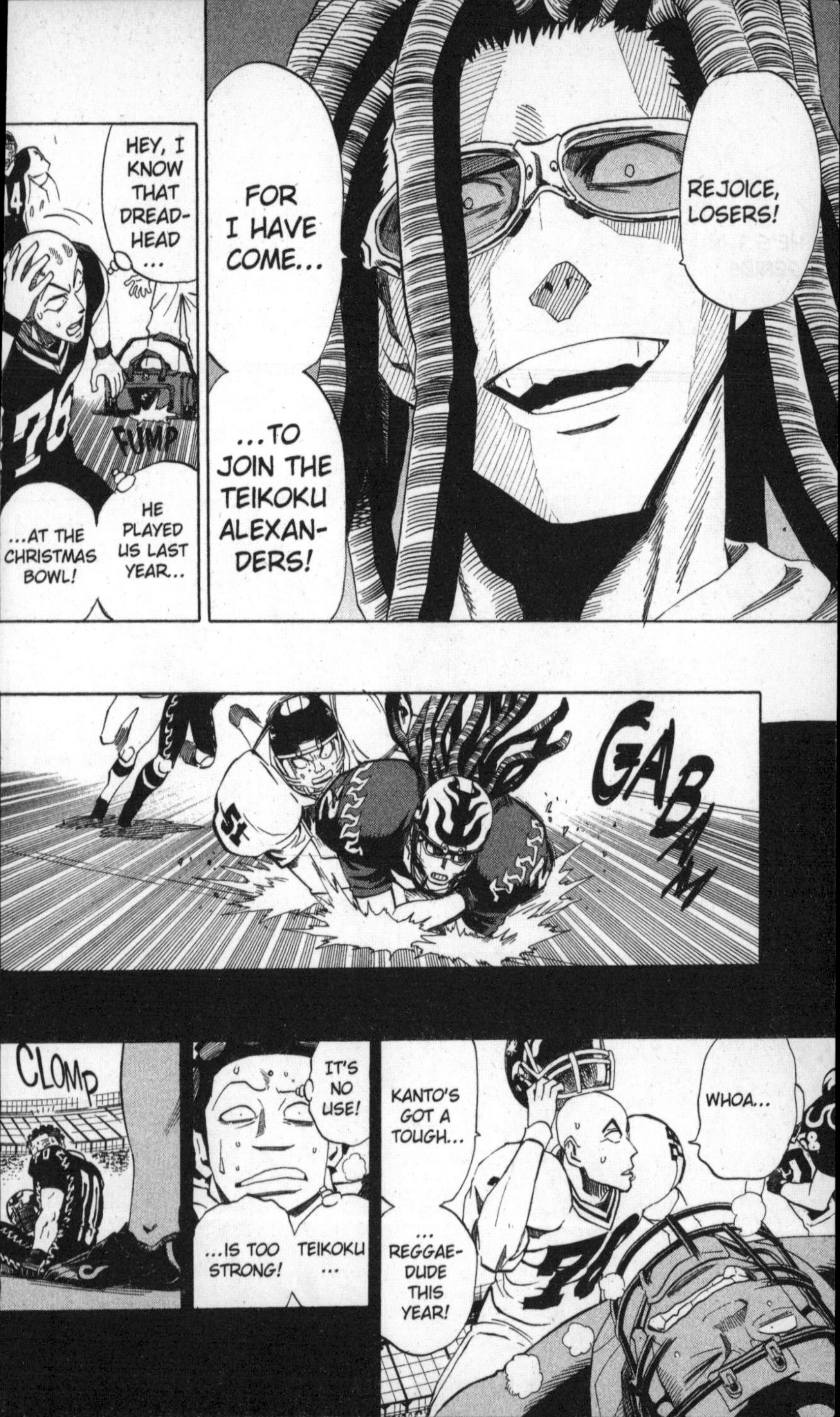
REJOICE, LOSERS!
FOR I HAVE COME...
...TO JOIN THE TEIKOKU ALEXANDERS!
HEY, I KNOW THAT DREAD-HEAD...
FUMP
HE PLAYED US LAST YEAR...
...AT THE CHRISTMAS BOWL!
GABAM
WHOA...
KANTO'S GOT A TOUGH...
...REGGAE-DUDE THIS YEAR!
IT'S NO USE!
TEIKOKU...
...IS TOO STRONG!
CLOMP

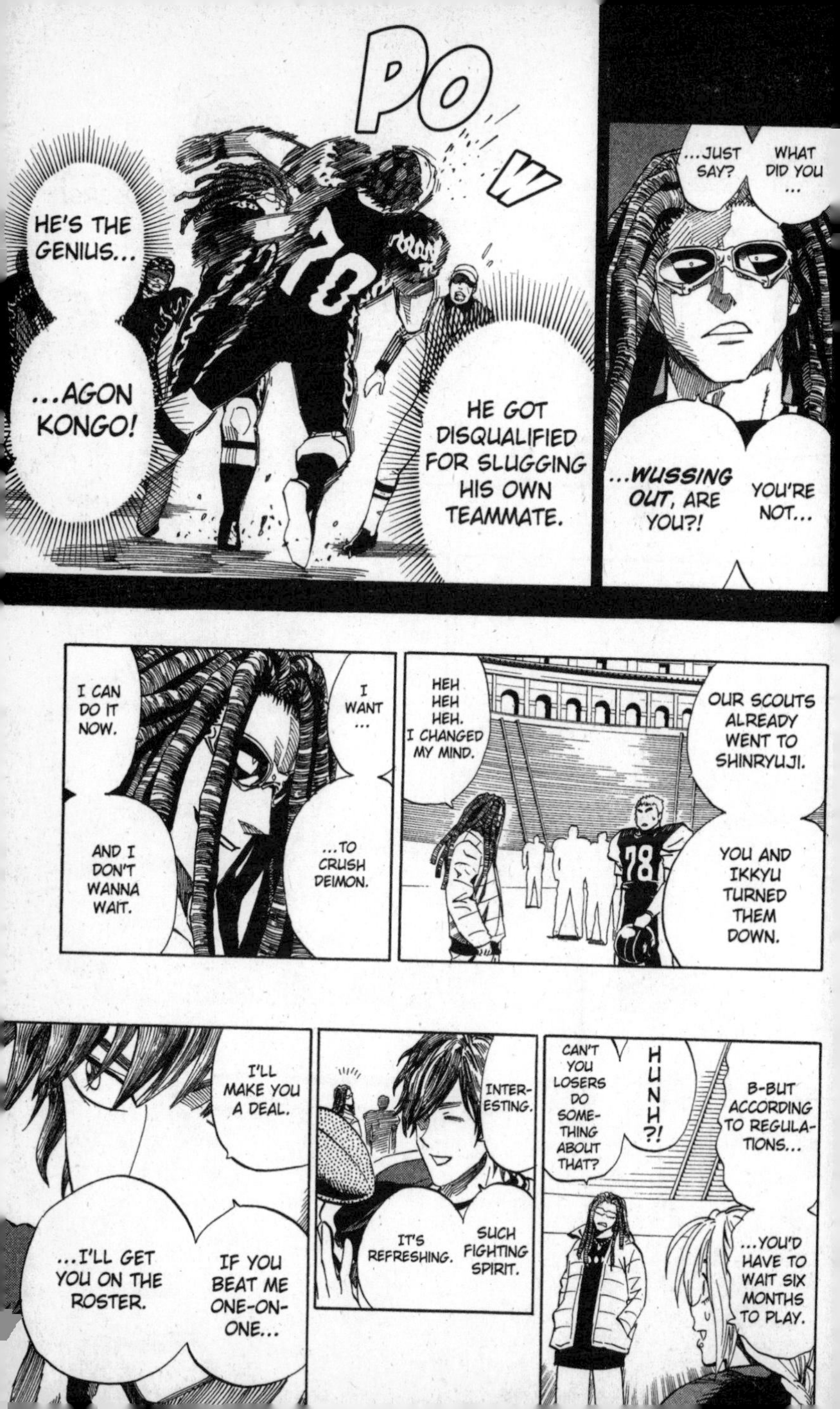
WHAT DID YOU ...
...JUST SAY?
YOU'RE NOT...
...WUSSING OUT, ARE YOU?!
POW
HE GOT DISQUALIFIED FOR SLUGGING HIS OWN TEAMMATE.
HE'S THE GENIUS...
...AGON KONGO!
OUR SCOUTS ALREADY WENT TO SHINRYUJI.
YOU AND IKKYU TURNED THEM DOWN.
HEH HEH HEH. I CHANGED MY MIND.
I WANT ...
...TO CRUSH DEIMON.
I CAN DO IT NOW.
AND I DON'T WANNA WAIT.
B-BUT ACCORDING TO REGULATIONS...
...YOU'D HAVE TO WAIT SIX MONTHS TO PLAY.
HUNH?!
CAN'T YOU LOSERS DO SOMETHING ABOUT THAT?
INTERESTING.
SUCH FIGHTING SPIRIT.
IT'S REFRESHING.
I'LL MAKE YOU A DEAL.
IF YOU BEAT ME ONE-ON-ONE...
...I'LL GET YOU ON THE ROSTER.

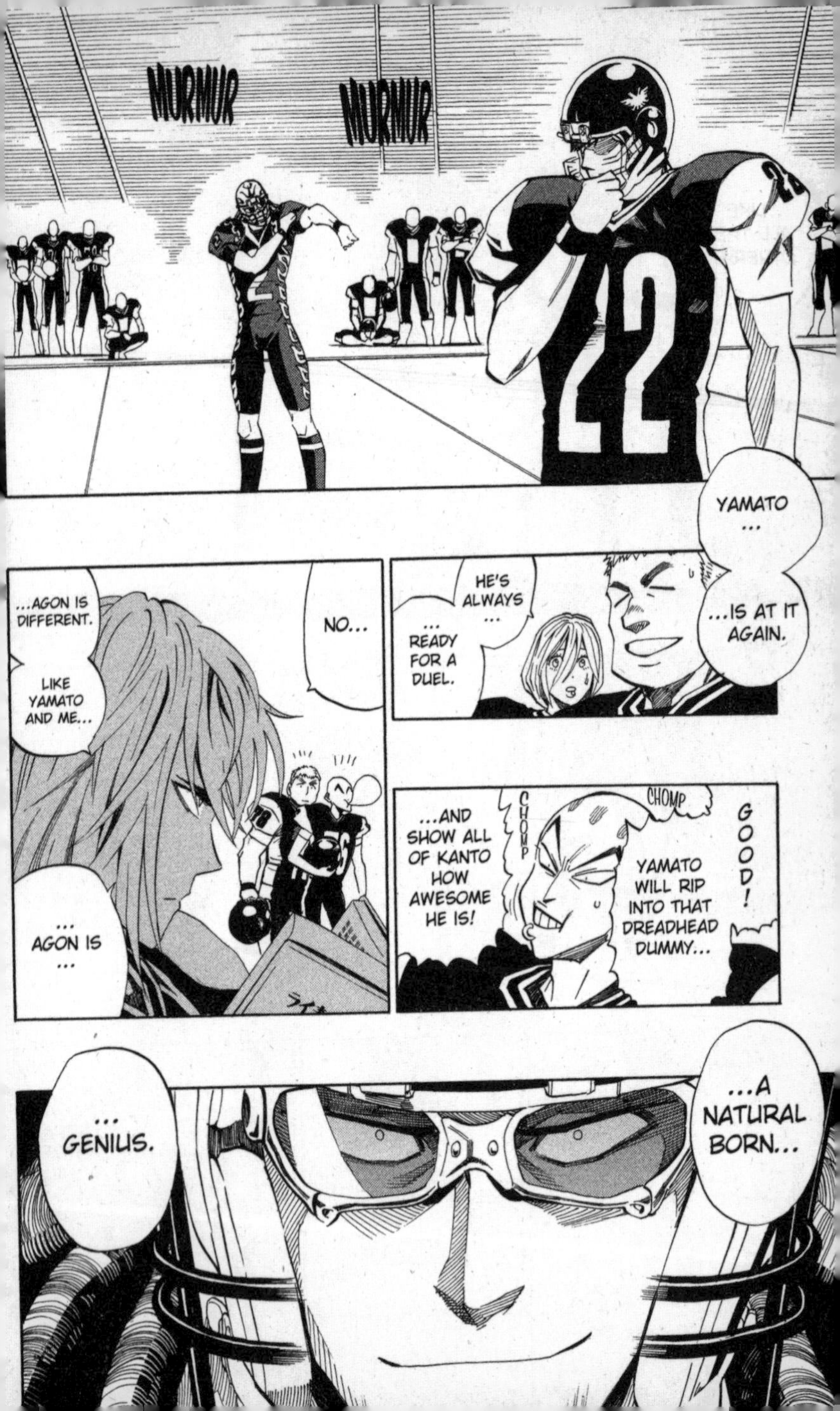
MURMUR
MURMUR
YAMATO ...
...IS AT IT AGAIN.
HE'S ALWAYS ...
... READY FOR A DUEL.
GOOD!
CHOMP
CHOMP
YAMATO WILL RIP INTO THAT DREADHEAD DUMMY...
...AND SHOW ALL OF KANTO HOW AWESOME HE IS!
NO...
...AGON IS DIFFERENT.
LIKE YAMATO AND ME...
... AGON IS ...
...A NATURAL BORN...
... GENIUS.

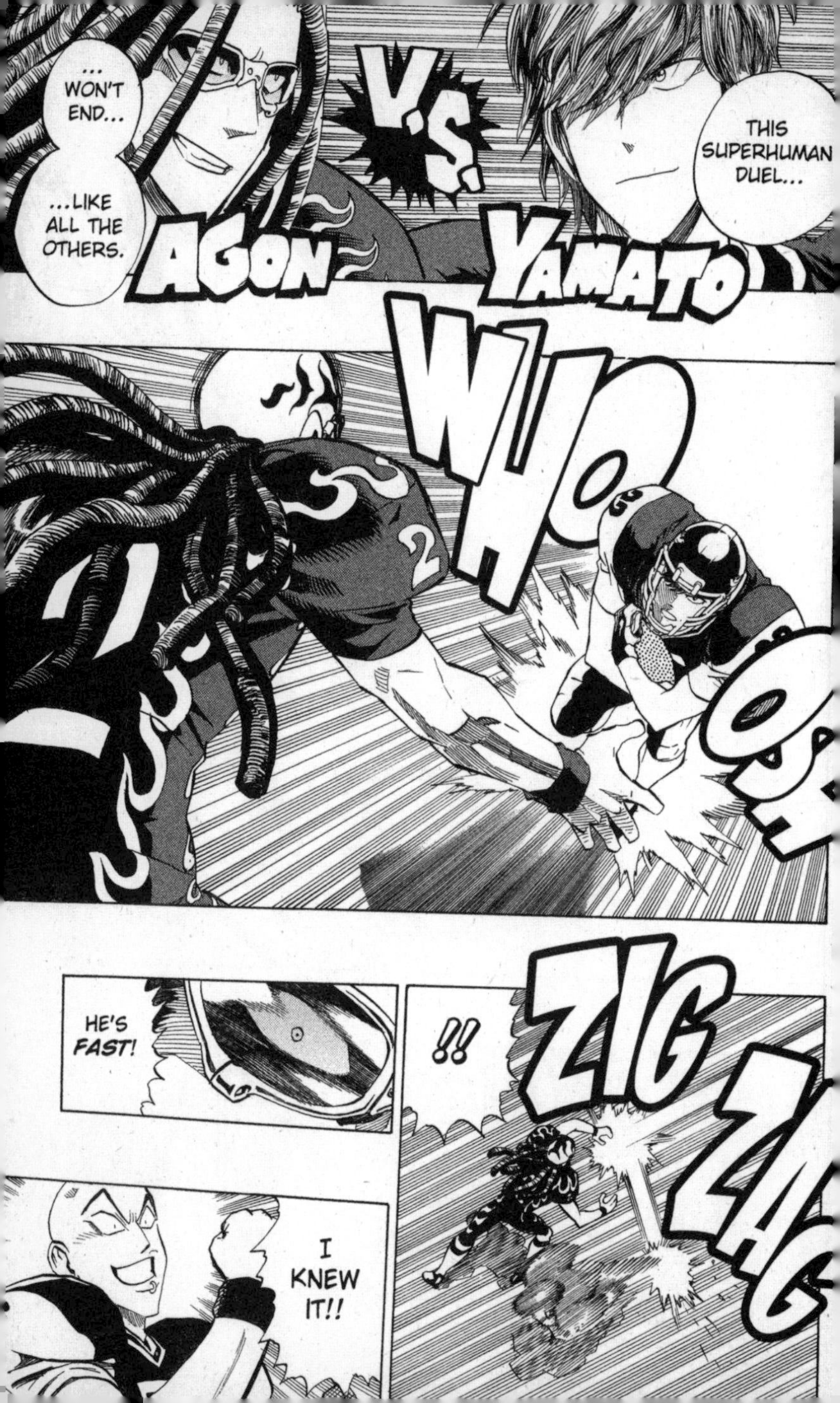
THIS SUPERHUMAN DUEL...
... WON'T END...
...LIKE ALL THE OTHERS.
AGON V.S. YAMATO
WHOOSH
ZIG ZAG
!!
HE'S FAST!
I KNEW IT!!

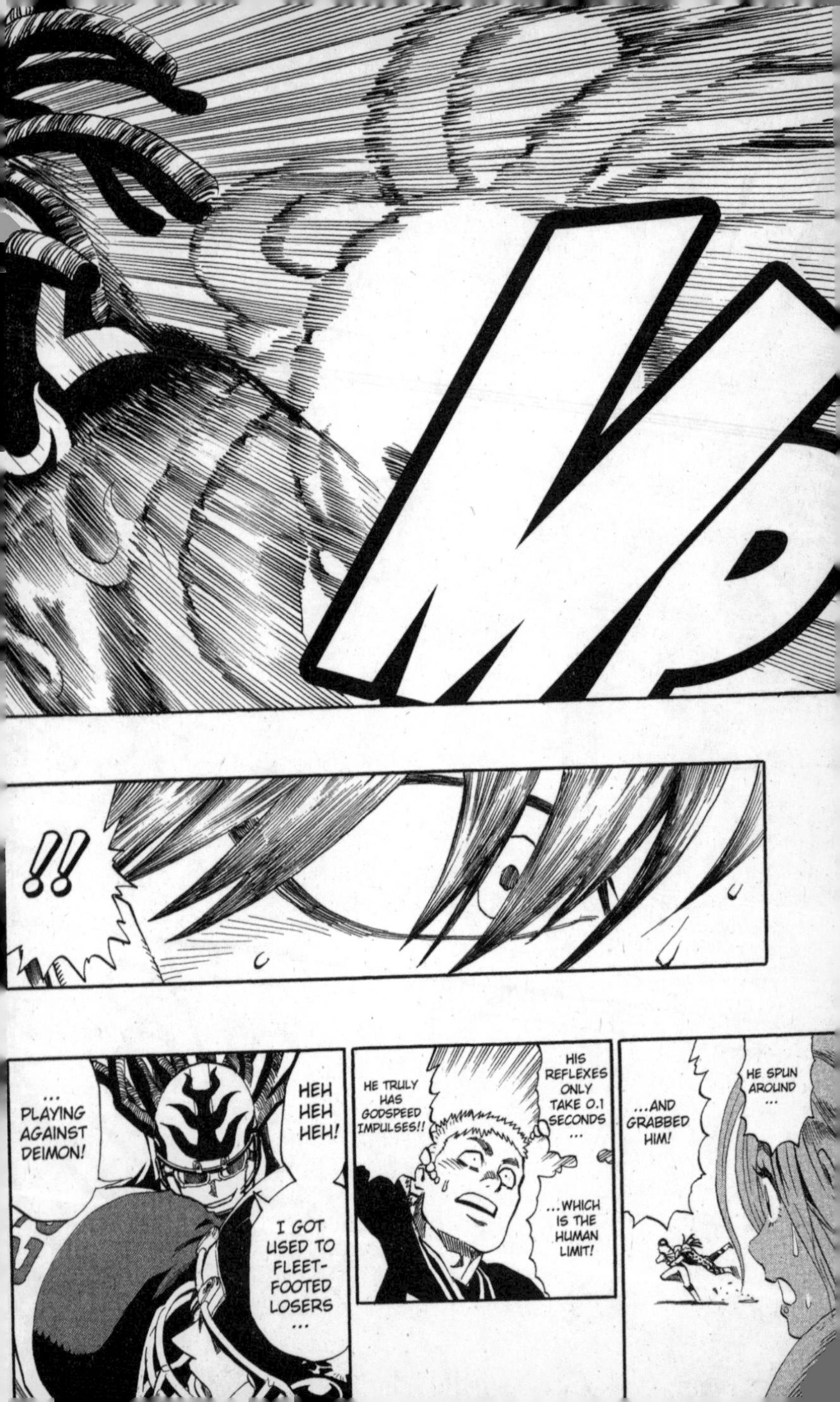
!!
HE SPUN AROUND ...
...AND GRABBED HIM!
HIS REFLEXES ONLY TAKE 0.1 SECONDS ...
...WHICH IS THE HUMAN LIMIT!
HE TRULY HAS GODSPEED IMPULSES!!
HEH HEH HEH!
I GOT USED TO FLEET-FOOTED LOSERS ...
... PLAYING AGAINST DEIMON!

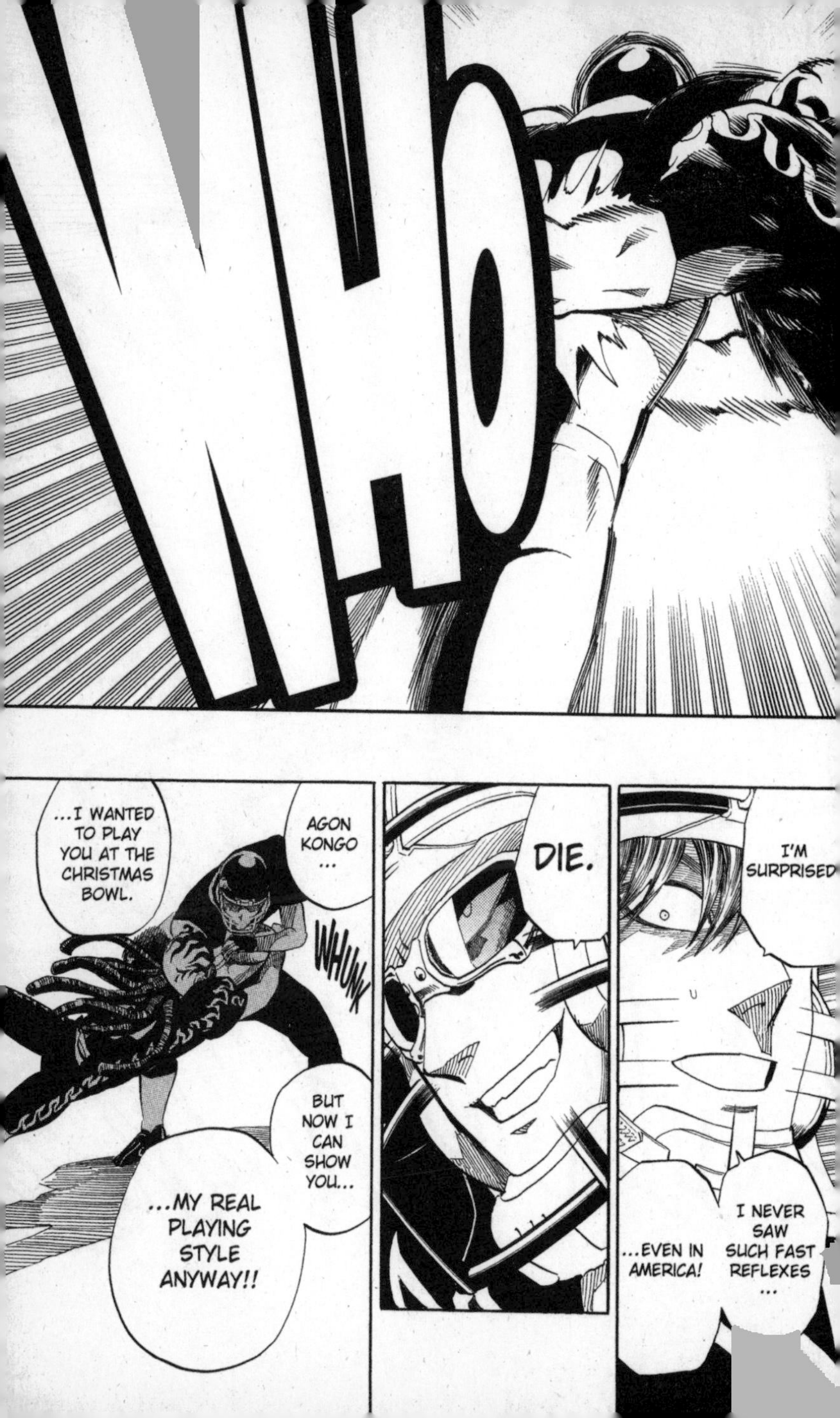
WHO
I'M SURPRISED
I NEVER SAW SUCH FAST REFLEXES ...
...EVEN IN AMERICA!
DIE.
AGON KONGO ...
...I WANTED TO PLAY YOU AT THE CHRISTMAS BOWL.
WHUNK
BUT NOW I CAN SHOW YOU...
...MY REAL PLAYING STYLE ANYWAY!!

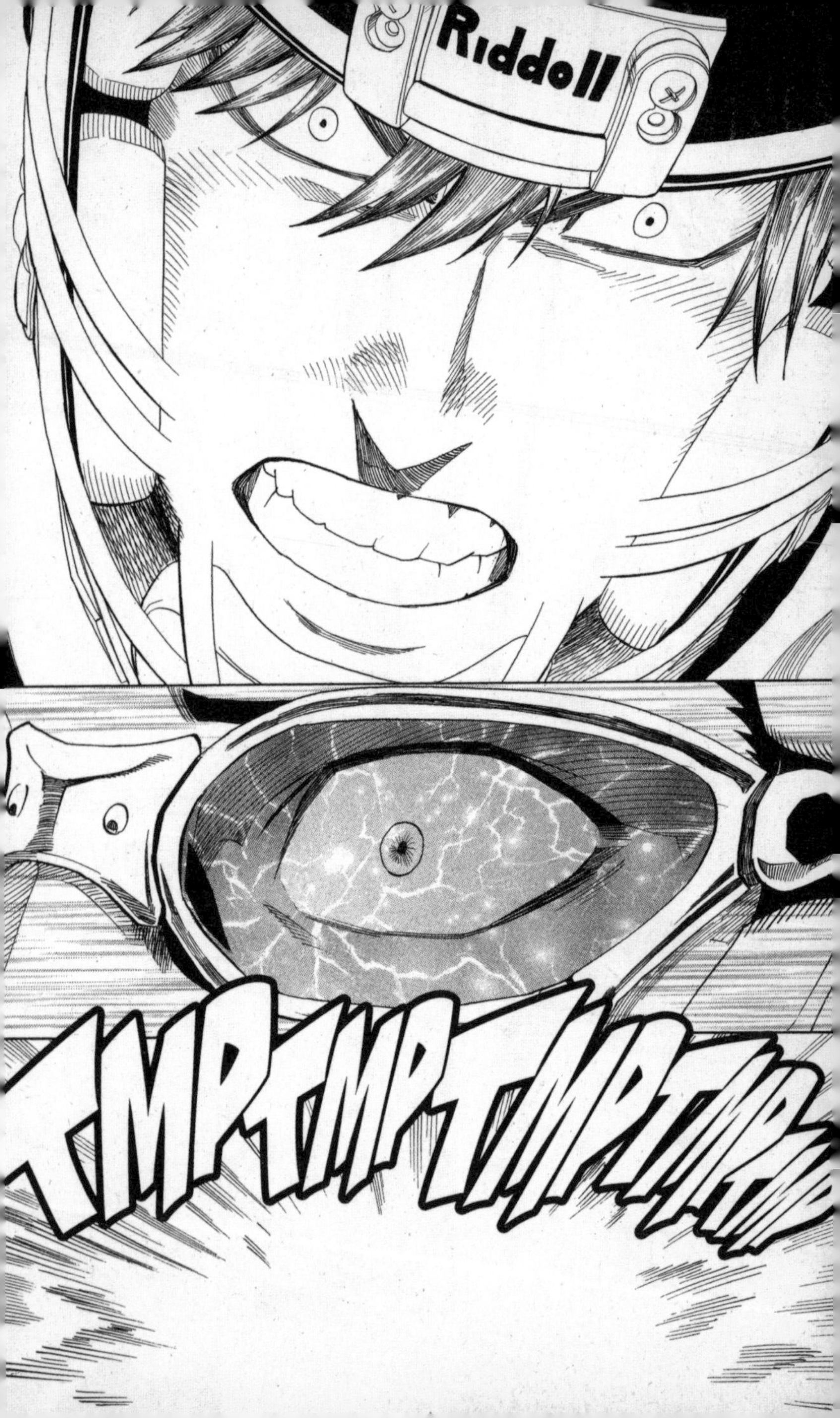
Riddoll
TMP TMP TMP TMP

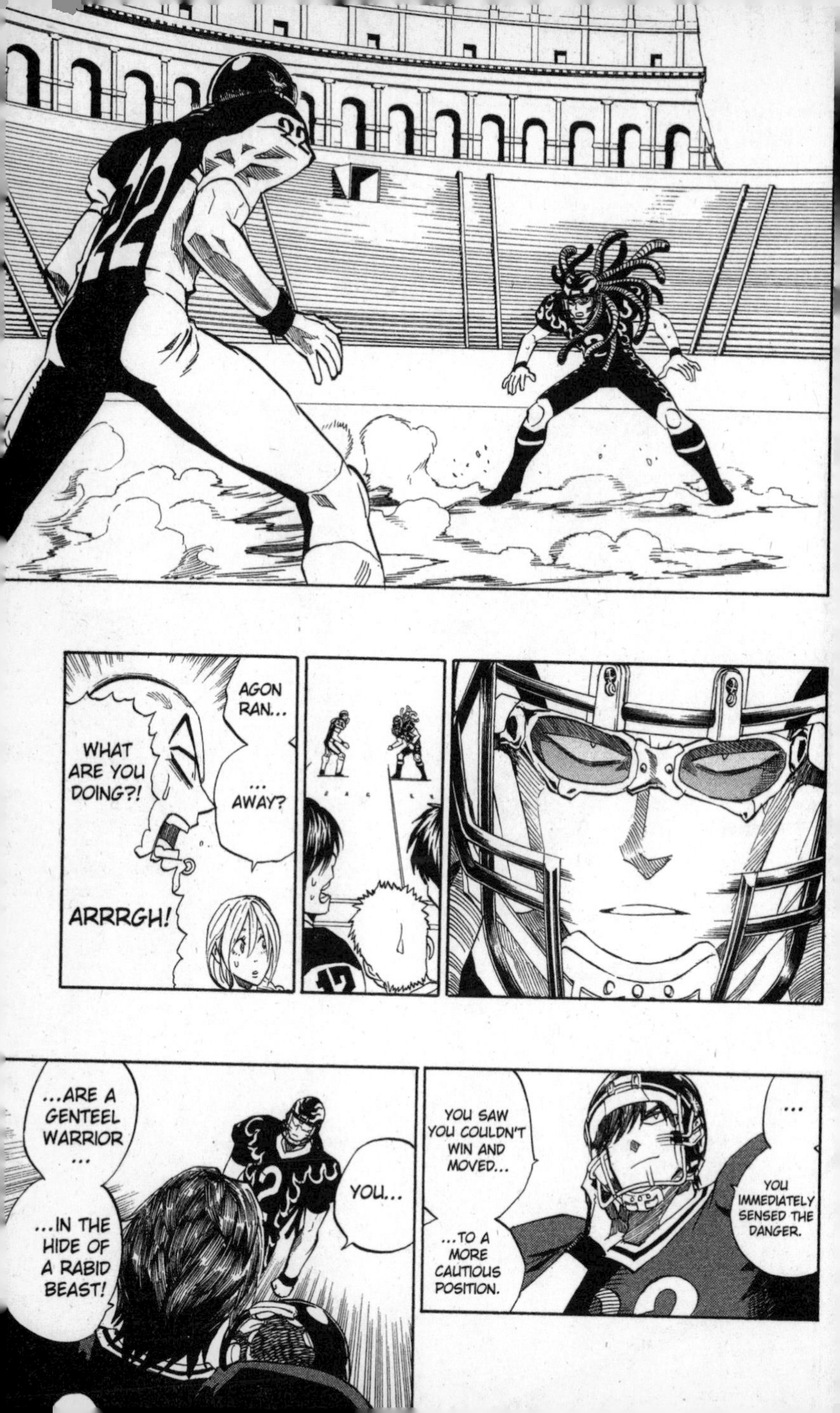

AGON RAN...
... AWAY?
WHAT ARE YOU DOING?!
ARRRGH!
...
YOU IMMEDIATELY SENSED THE DANGER.
YOU SAW YOU COULDN'T WIN AND MOVED...
...TO A MORE CAUTIOUS POSITION.
YOU...
...ARE A GENTEEL WARRIOR ...
...IN THE HIDE OF A RABID BEAST!

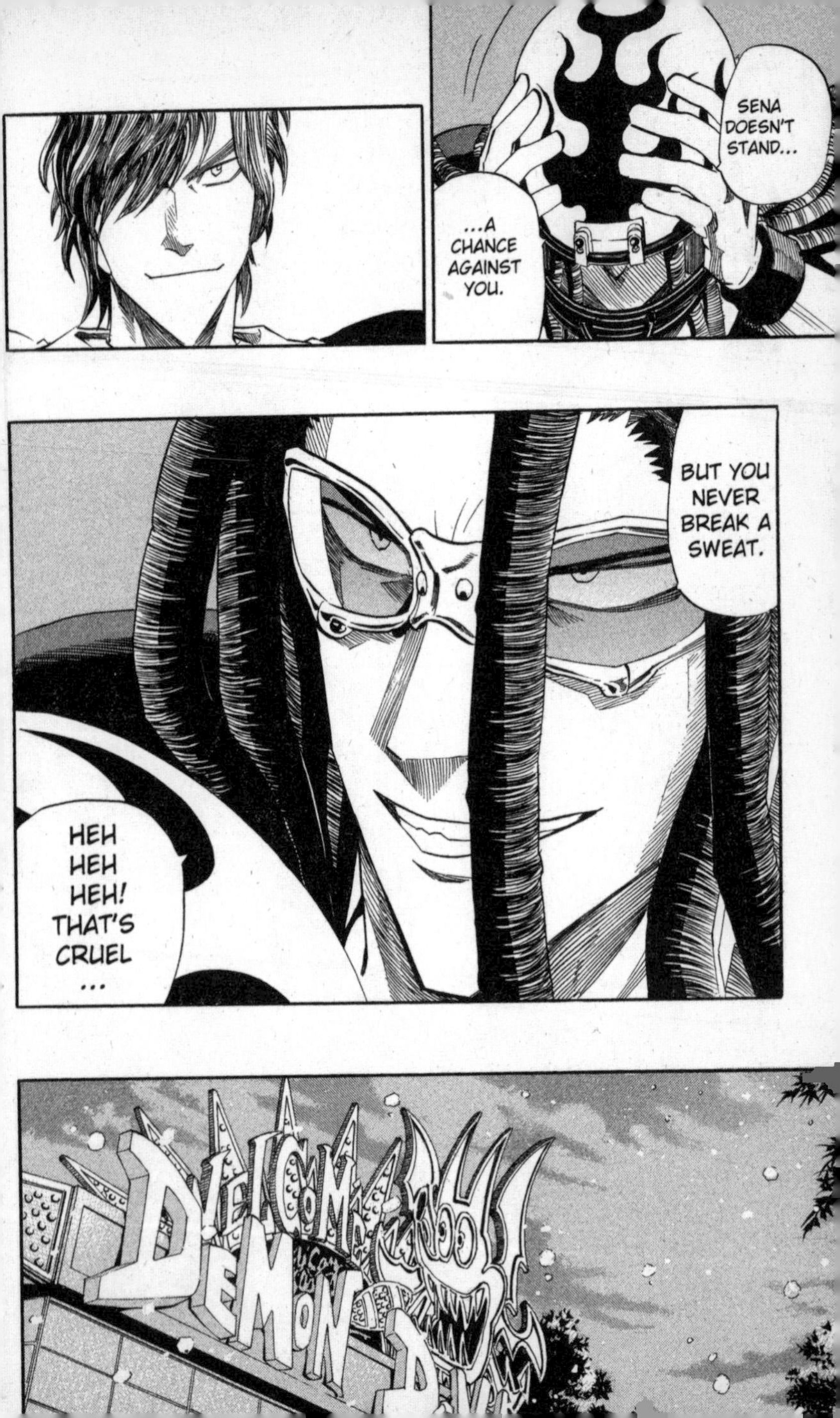
SENA DOESN'T STAND...
...A CHANCE AGAINST YOU.
BUT YOU NEVER BREAK A SWEAT.
HEH HEH HEH! THAT'S CRUEL ...

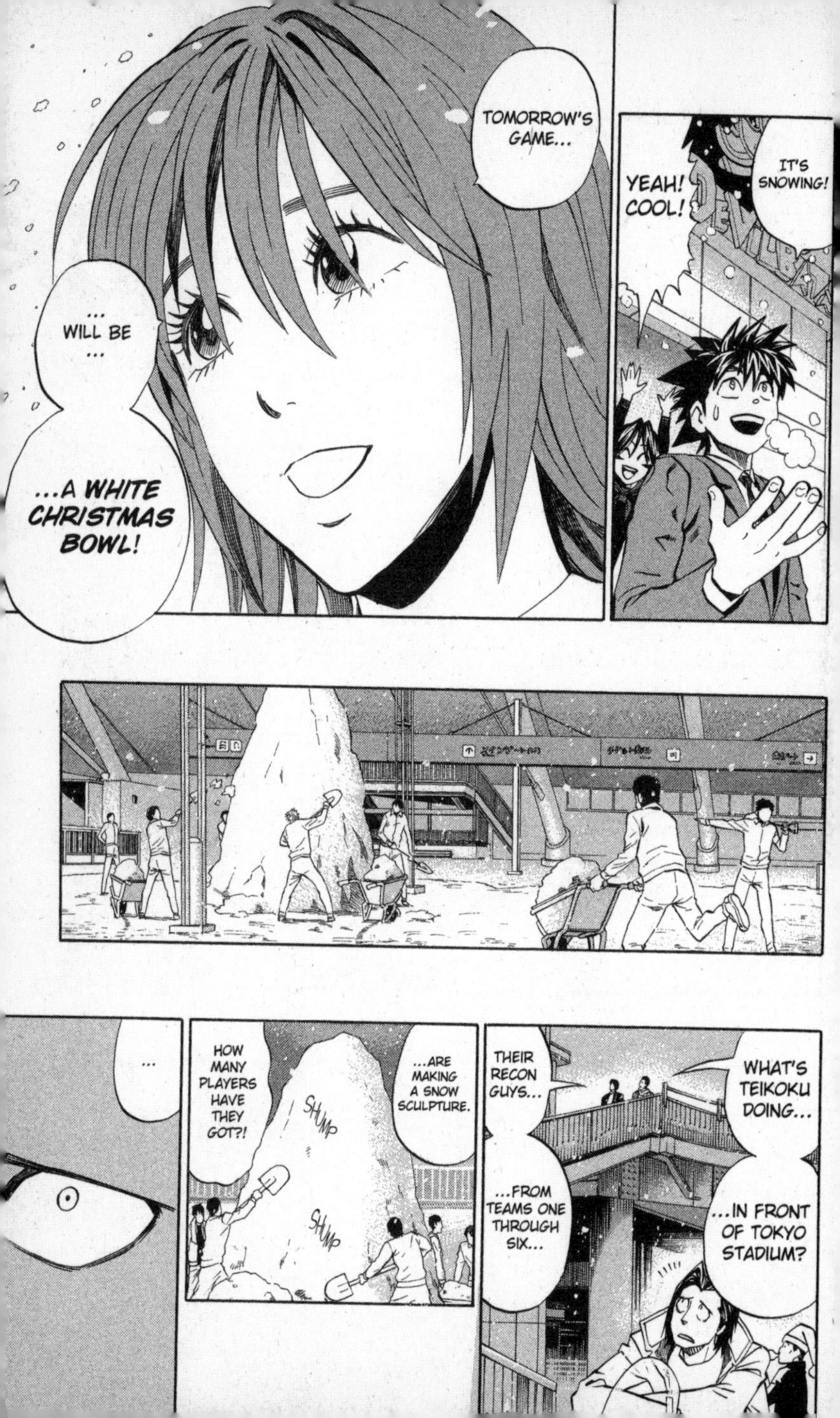
IT'S SNOWING!
YEAH! COOL!
TOMORROW'S GAME...
... WILL BE ...
...A *WHITE* CHRISTMAS BOWL!
WHAT'S TEIKOKU DOING...
...IN FRONT OF TOKYO STADIUM?
THEIR RECON GUYS...
...FROM TEAMS ONE THROUGH SIX...
...ARE MAKING A SNOW SCULPTURE.
HOW MANY PLAYERS HAVE THEY GOT?!
SHUMP
SHUMP
...

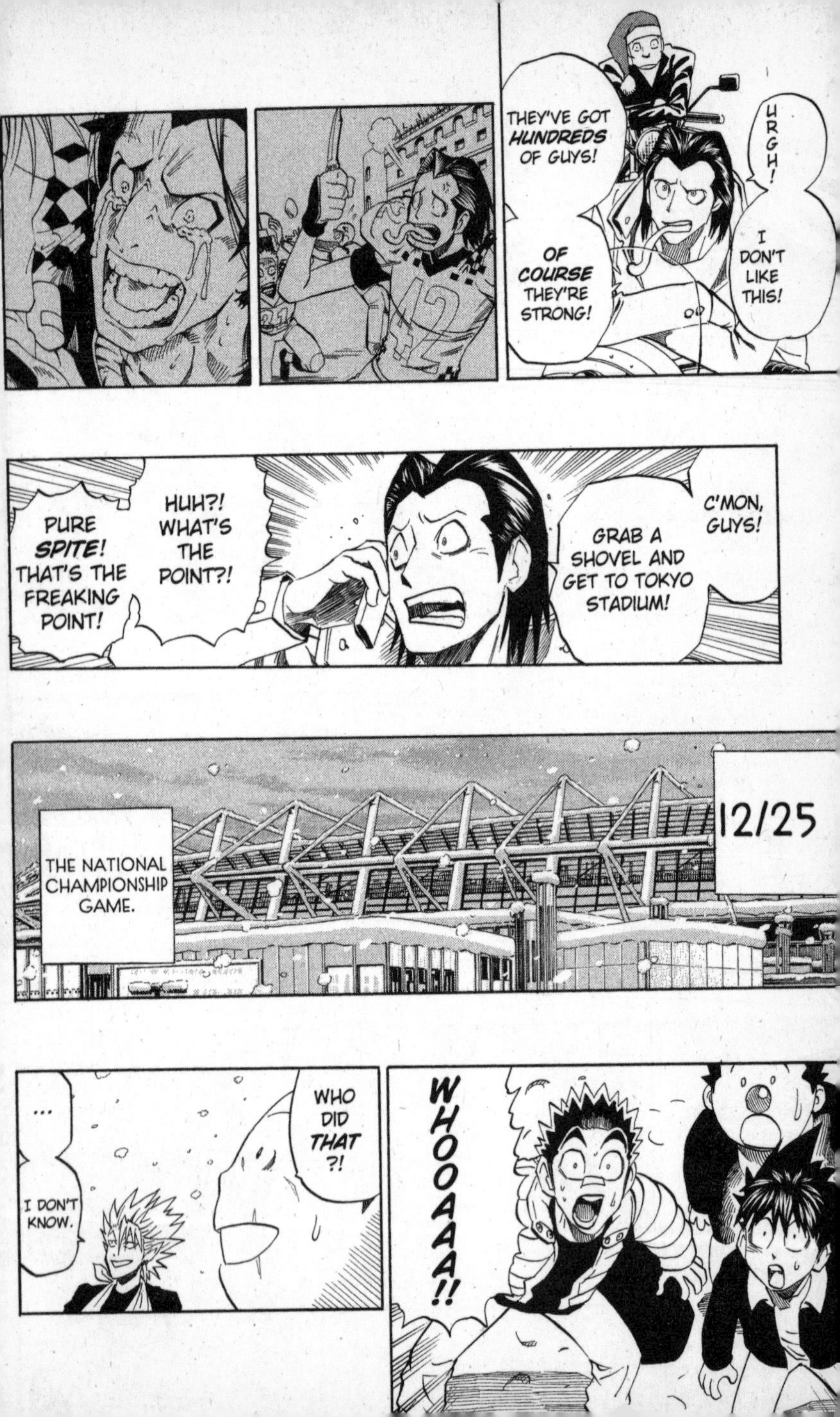
URGH!
I DON'T LIKE THIS!
THEY'VE GOT HUNDREDS OF GUYS!
OF COURSE THEY'RE STRONG!
C'MON, GUYS!
GRAB A SHOVEL AND GET TO TOKYO STADIUM!
HUH?! WHAT'S THE POINT?!
PURE SPITE! THAT'S THE FREAKING POINT!
12/25
THE NATIONAL CHAMPIONSHIP GAME.
WHOOAAAA!!
WHO DID THAT?!
...
I DON'T KNOW.

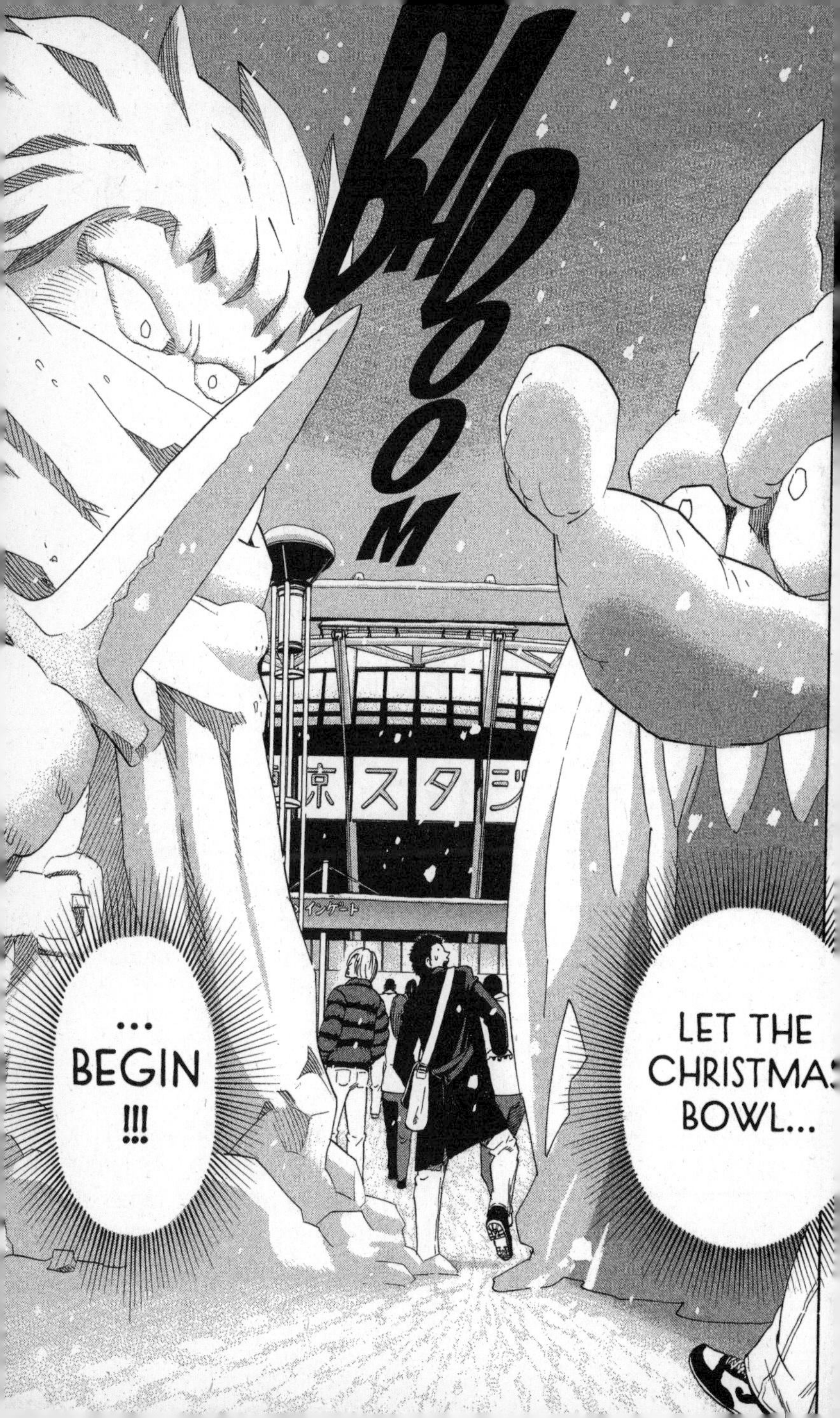
BADOOOM
LET THE CHRISTMAS BOWL...
...BEGIN!!!

TEIKOKU PERSONAL HISTORIES

◀Takeru Yamato▶

CURRENT AGE: 16

Height	190 cm
Weight	79 kg
Blood type	A
Birthday	October 10
Siblings	One younger brother
Talents/Hobbies	Camping
Favorite type of girl	
A decent, strong-willed girl	

0 YEARS OLD

Born in Kagoshima Prefecture. He drinks milk all the time and grows at an *alarming speed*.

He always stares at his mother *with great confidence*, almost as if to say, "Drink my milk? I'll drink it dry!"

6 YEARS OLD

Joins the *Boy Scouts*. With great confidence and conviction, he pulls everyone along.

11 YEARS OLD

Studies abroad in America at the junior high school affiliated with Notre Dame University. He creates an uproar as "*Eyeshield 21*."

13 YEARS OLD

Scouts entice him to join Teikoku High School's junior high. He returns to Japan and becomes an unbeatable ace.

Chapter 281
Christmas Bowl

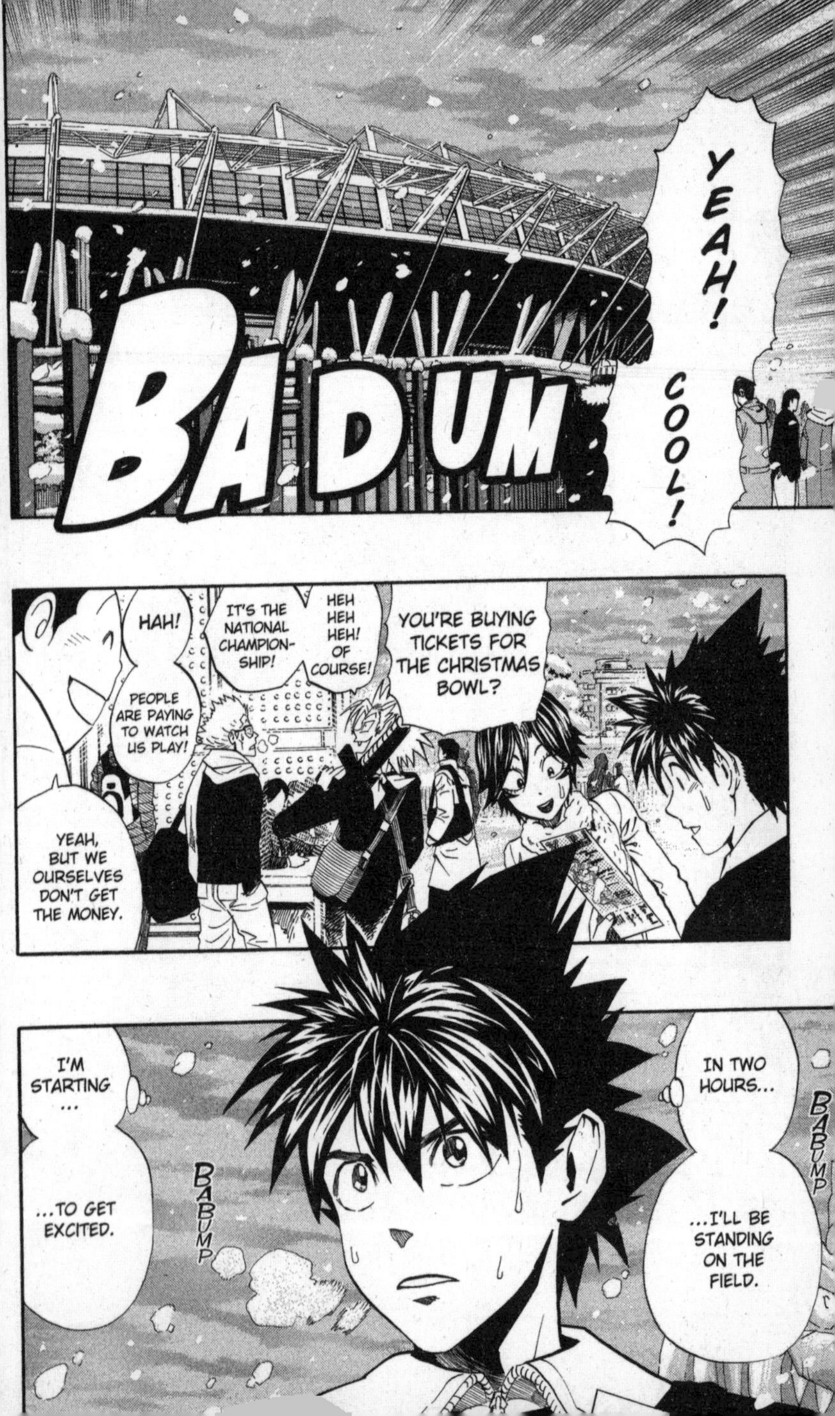
YEAH!
COOL!
BADUM
YOU'RE BUYING TICKETS FOR THE CHRISTMAS BOWL?
HEH HEH HEH! OF COURSE!
IT'S THE NATIONAL CHAMPIONSHIP!
HAH!
PEOPLE ARE PAYING TO WATCH US PLAY!
YEAH, BUT WE OURSELVES DON'T GET THE MONEY.
IN TWO HOURS...
BABUMP
...I'LL BE STANDING ON THE FIELD.
BABUMP
I'M STARTING...
...TO GET EXCITED.

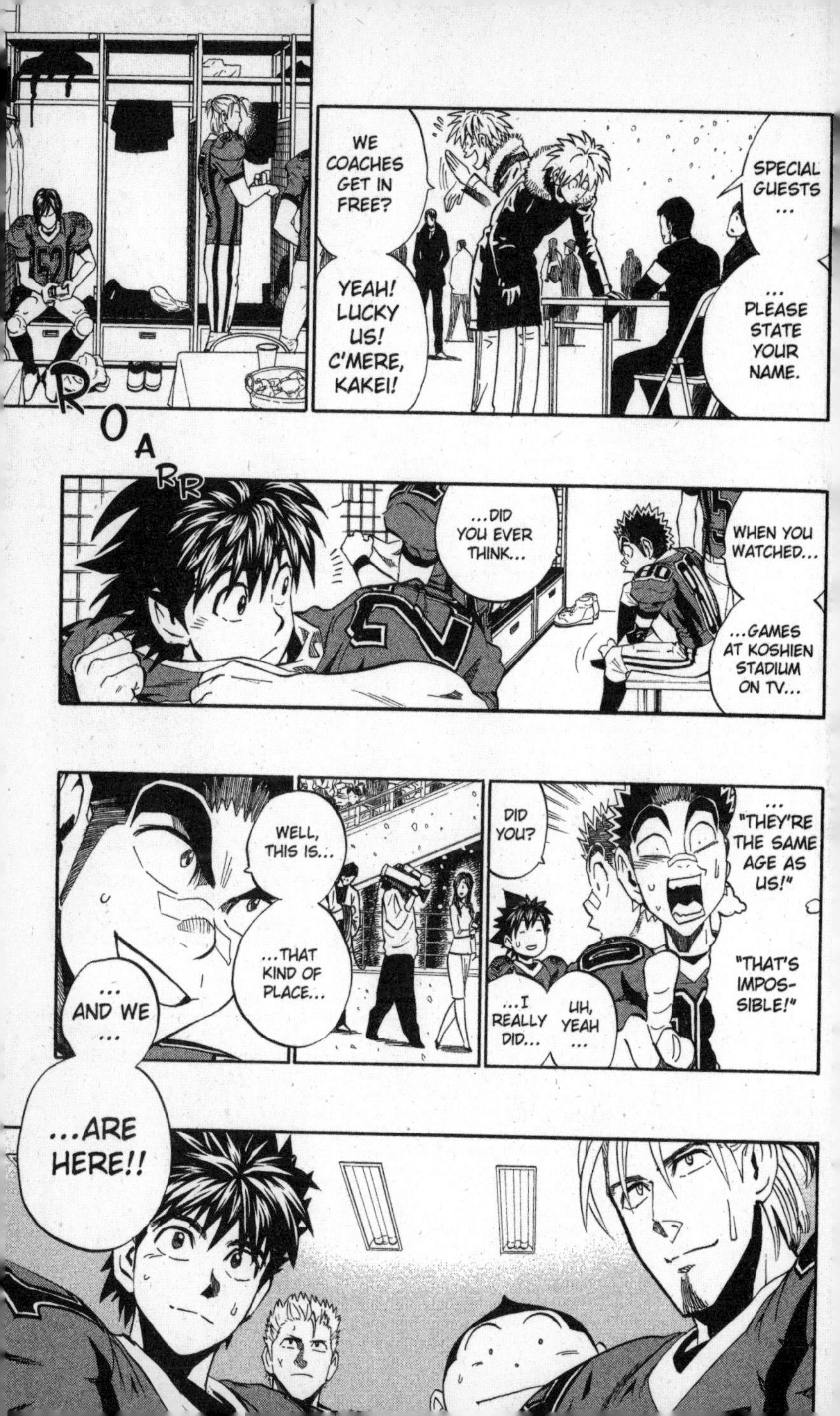
SPECIAL GUESTS ...
... PLEASE STATE YOUR NAME.
WE COACHES GET IN FREE?
YEAH! LUCKY US! C'MERE, KAKEI!
ROARR
WHEN YOU WATCHED...
...GAMES AT KOSHIEN STADIUM ON TV...
...DID YOU EVER THINK...
... "THEY'RE THE SAME AGE AS US!"
"THAT'S IMPOS-SIBLE!"
DID YOU?
UH, YEAH ...
...I REALLY DID...
WELL, THIS IS...
...THAT KIND OF PLACE...
... AND WE ...
...ARE HERE!!

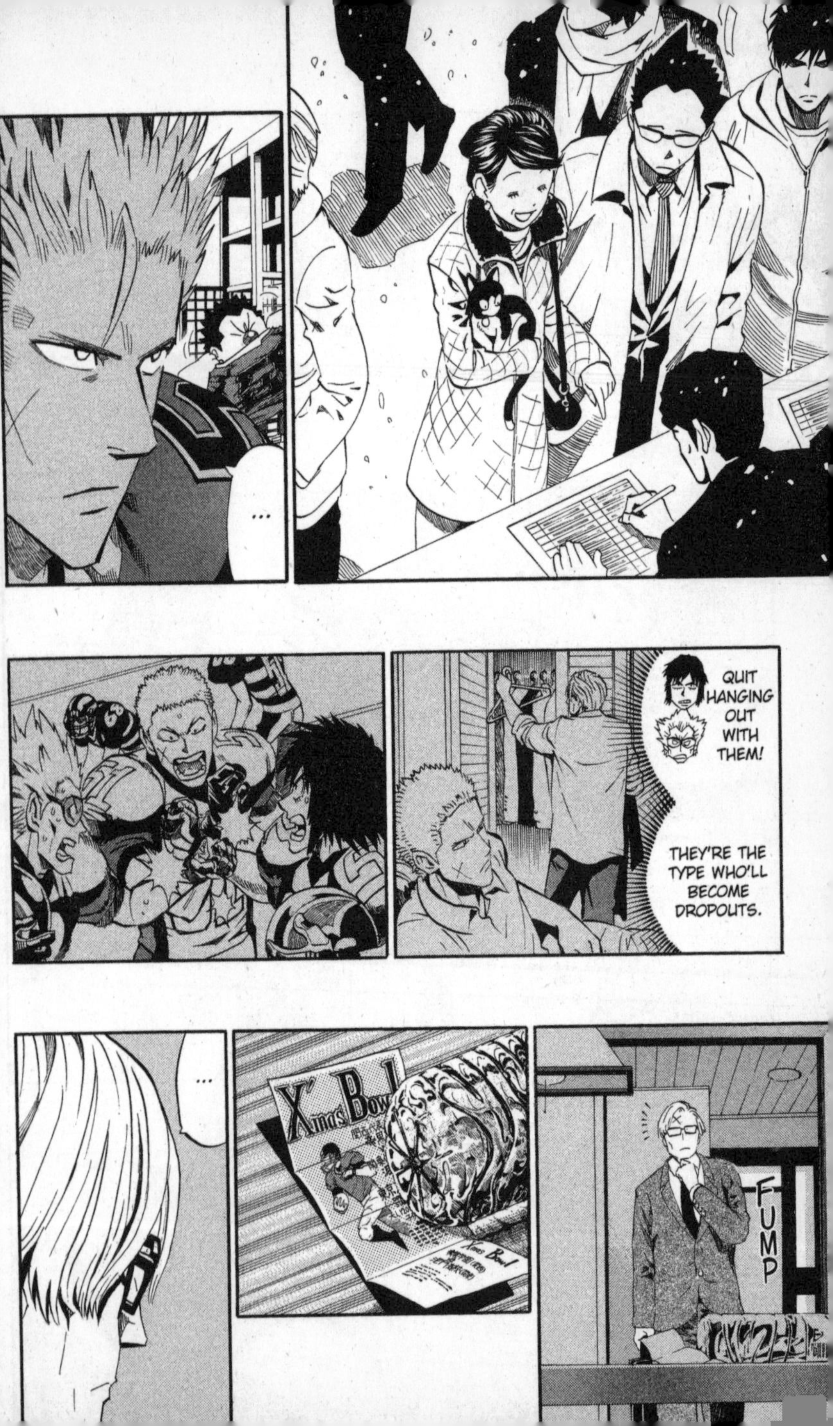
...
QUIT HANGING OUT WITH THEM!
THEY'RE THE TYPE WHO'LL BECOME DROPOUTS.
FUMP
...

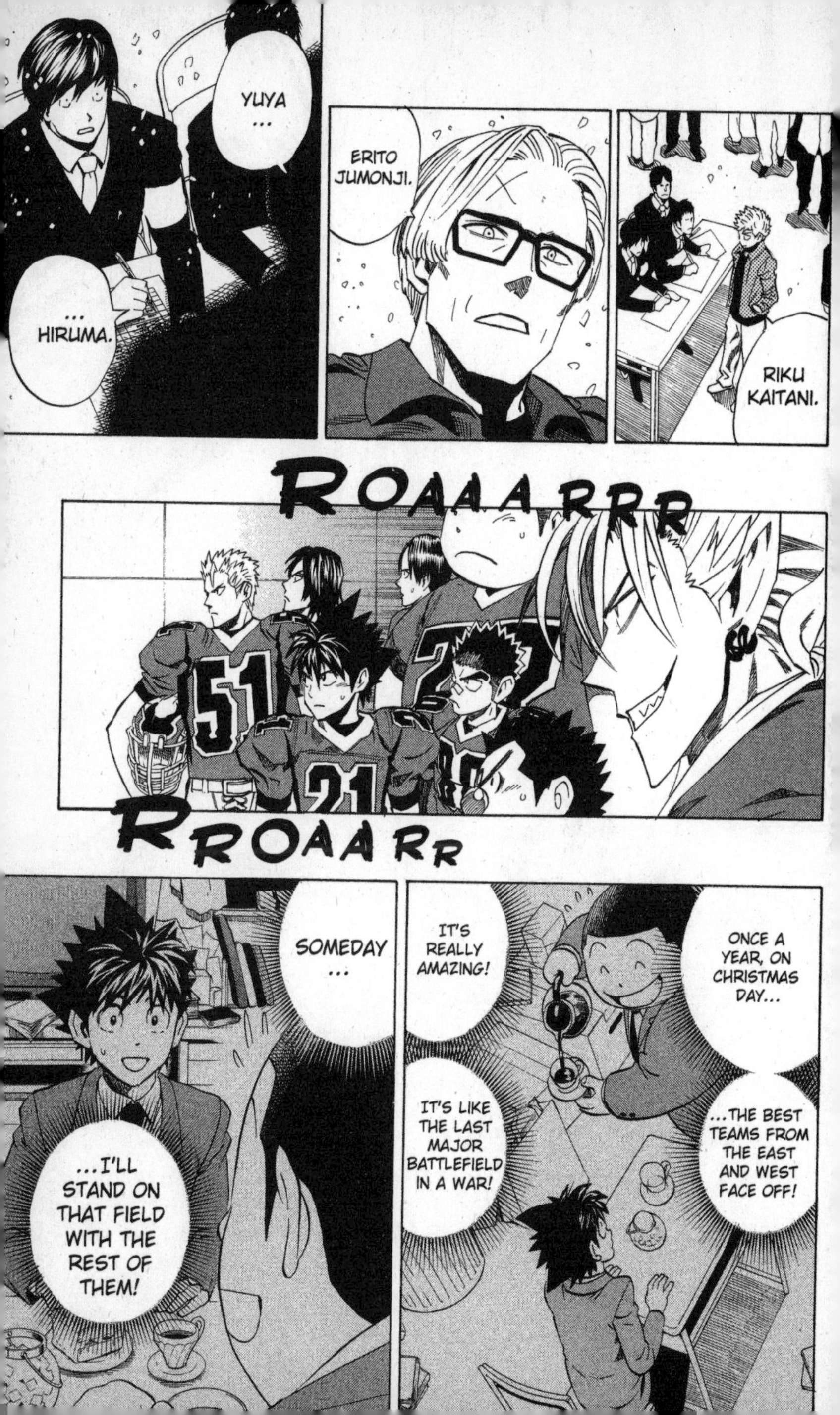
RIKU KAITANI.
ERITO JUMONJI.
YUYA ...
... HIRUMA.
ROAAARRR
RROAARR
ONCE A YEAR, ON CHRISTMAS DAY...
...THE BEST TEAMS FROM THE EAST AND WEST FACE OFF!
IT'S REALLY AMAZING!
IT'S LIKE THE LAST MAJOR BATTLEFIELD IN A WAR!
SOMEDAY ...
...I'LL STAND ON THAT FIELD WITH THE REST OF THEM!

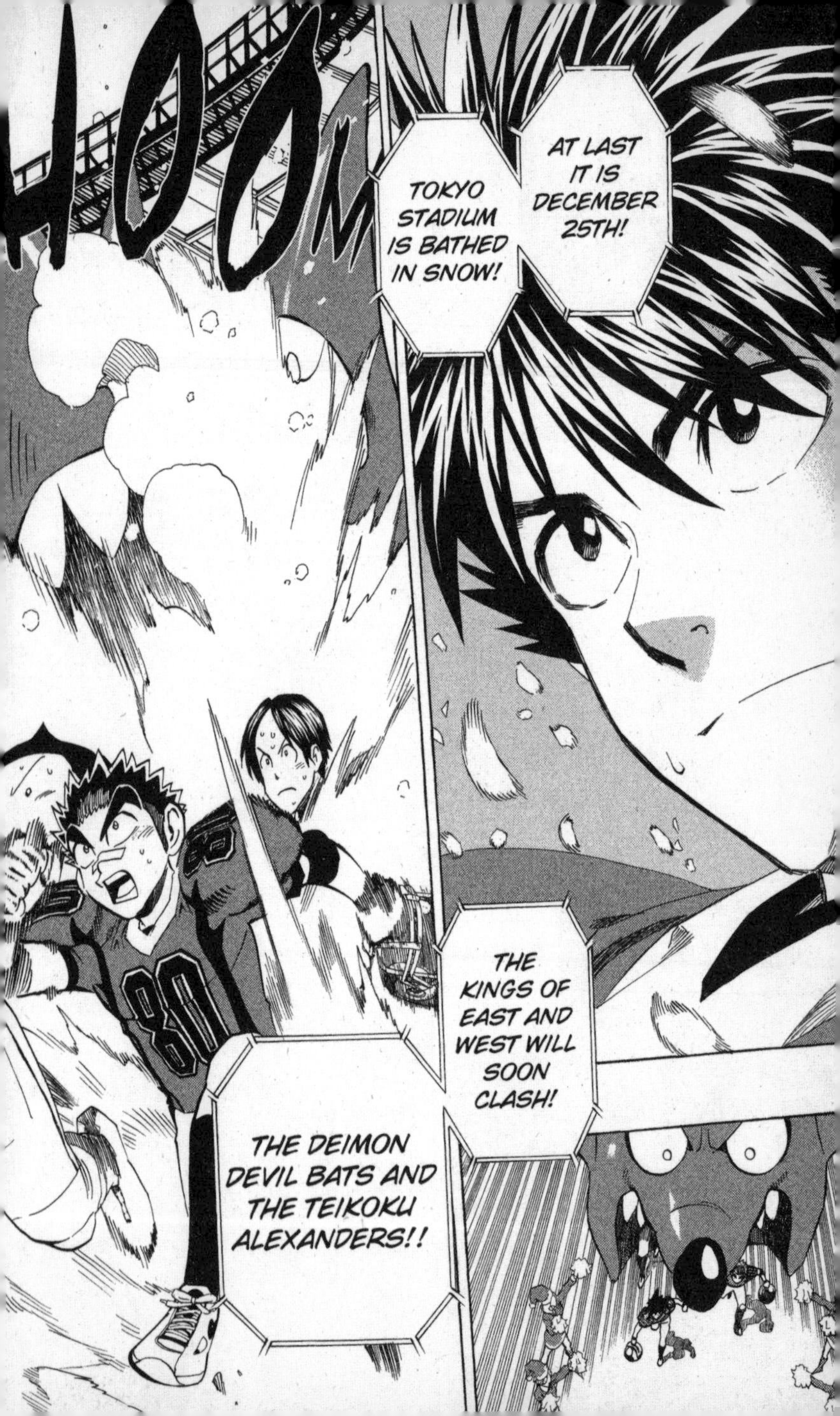
AT LAST IT IS DECEMBER 25TH!
TOKYO STADIUM IS BATHED IN SNOW!
HOOM
THE KINGS OF EAST AND WEST WILL SOON CLASH!
THE DEIMON DEVIL BATS AND THE TEIKOKU ALEXANDERS!!

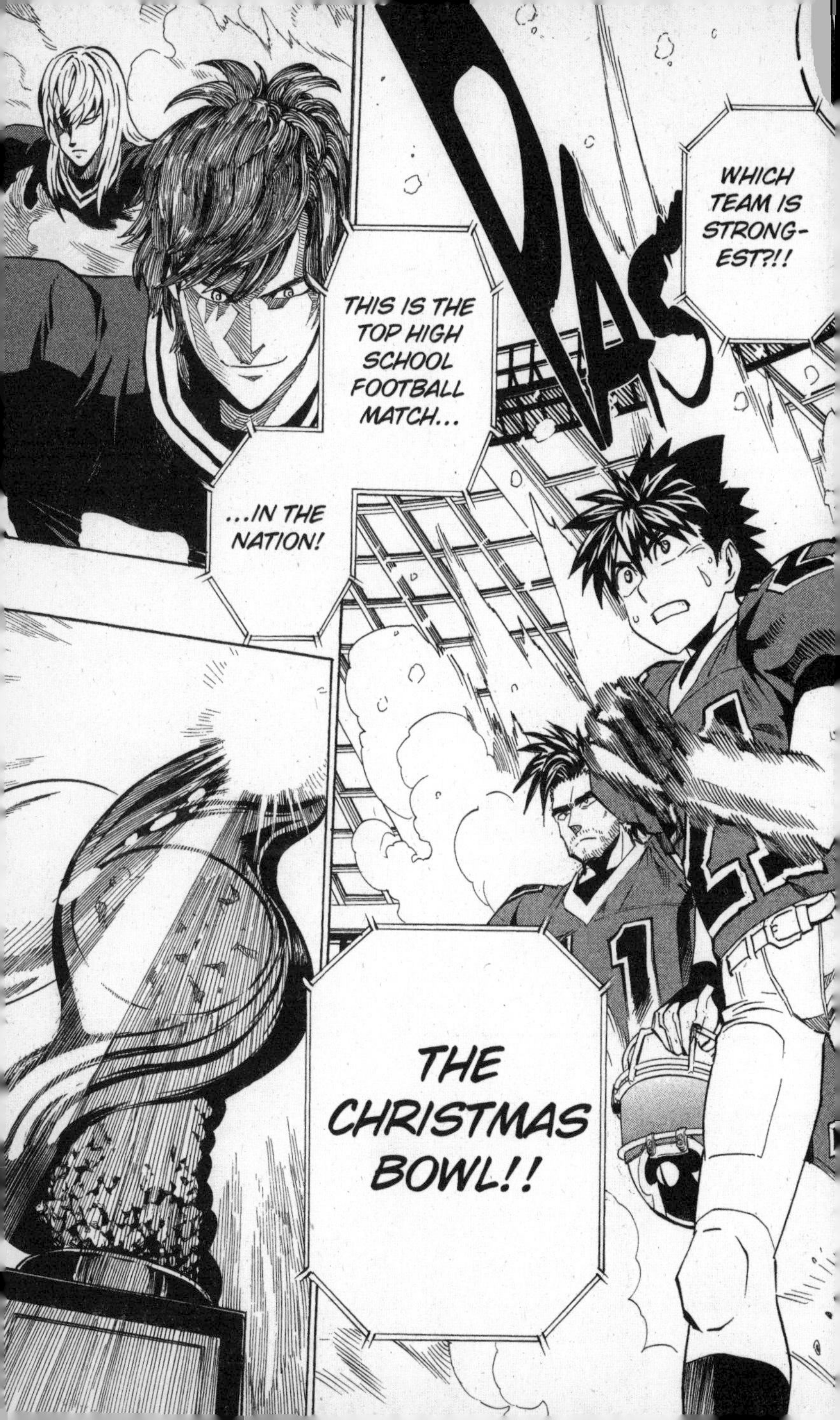
WHICH TEAM IS STRONG-EST?!!
THIS IS THE TOP HIGH SCHOOL FOOTBALL MATCH...
...IN THE NATION!
THE CHRISTMAS BOWL!!

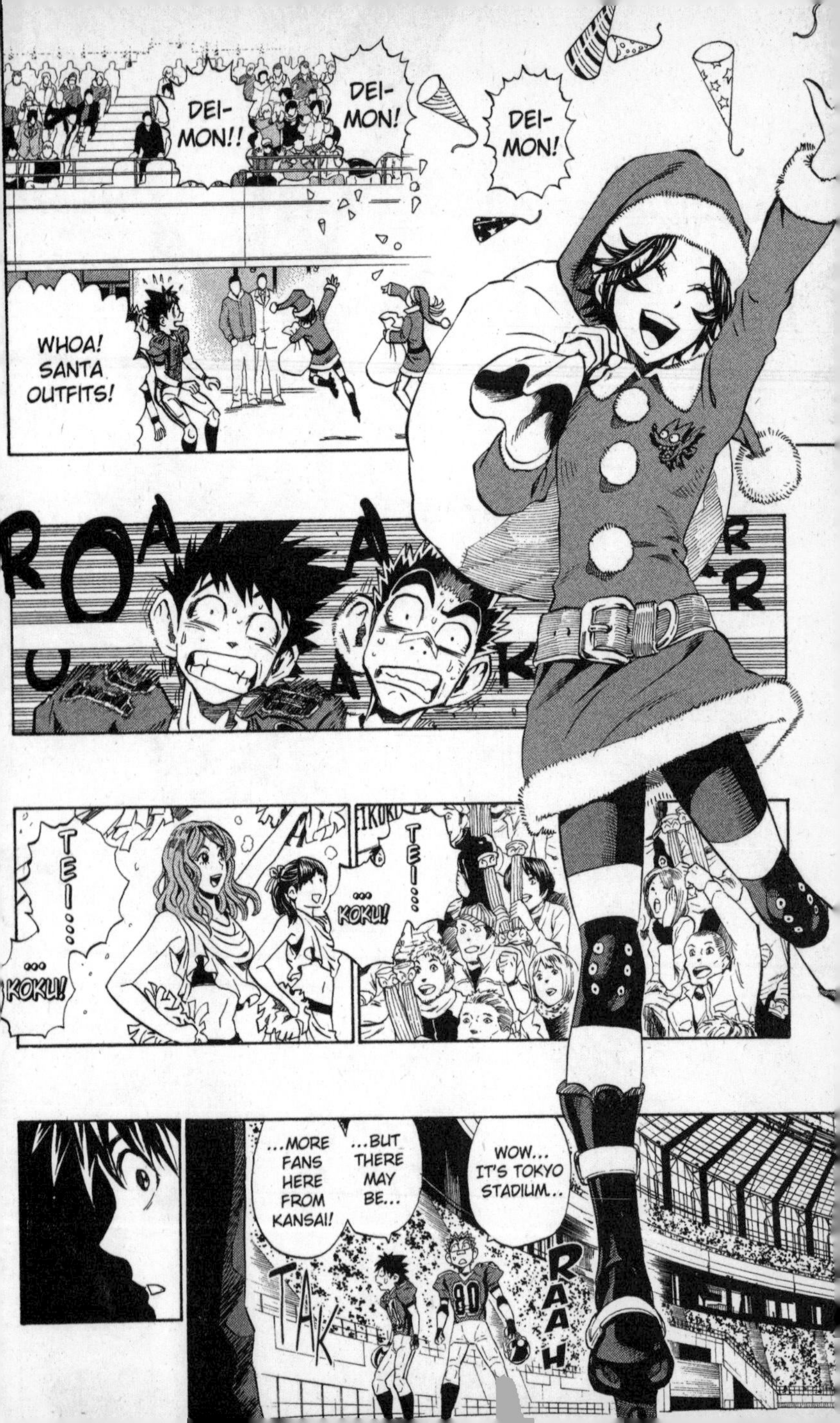

DEI-MON!
DEI-MON!
DEI-MON!!
WHOA! SANTA OUTFITS!
TEI...
...KOKU!
TEI...
...KOKU!
WOW... IT'S TOKYO STADIUM..
...BUT THERE MAY BE...
...MORE FANS HERE FROM KANSAI!
RAAH
TAK

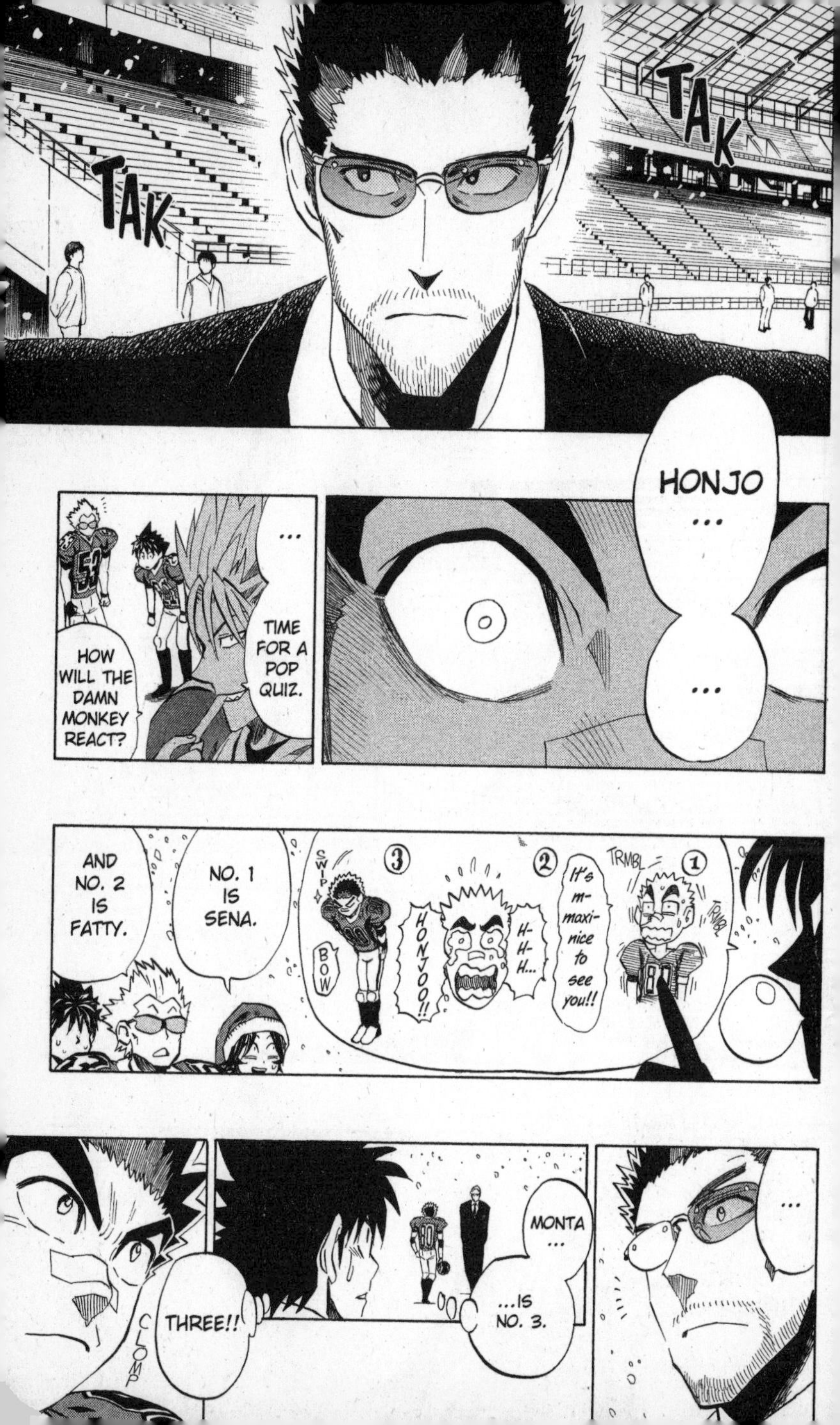
TAK
TAK
HONJO ... ...
...
TIME FOR A POP QUIZ.
HOW WILL THE DAMN MONKEY REACT?
① TRMBL TRMBL
It's m-maxi-nice to see you!!
② H-H-H...
HONJOO!!
③ SWIP
BOW
NO. 1 IS SENA.
AND NO. 2 IS FATTY.
...
MONTA ...
...IS NO. 3.
THREE!!
CLOMP

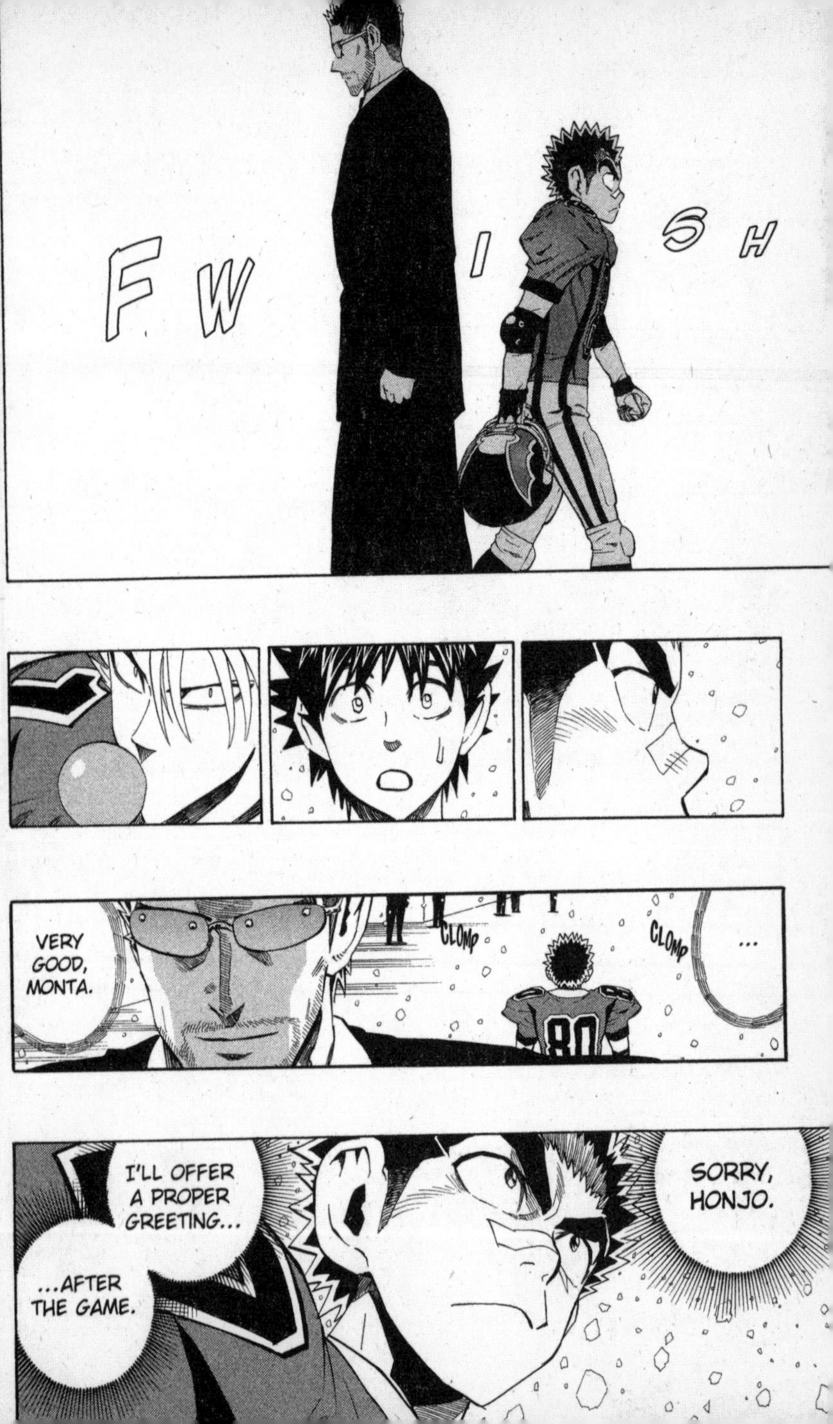
FWISH
...
CLOMP
CLOMP
VERY GOOD, MONTA.
SORRY, HONJO.
I'LL OFFER A PROPER GREETING...
...AFTER THE GAME.

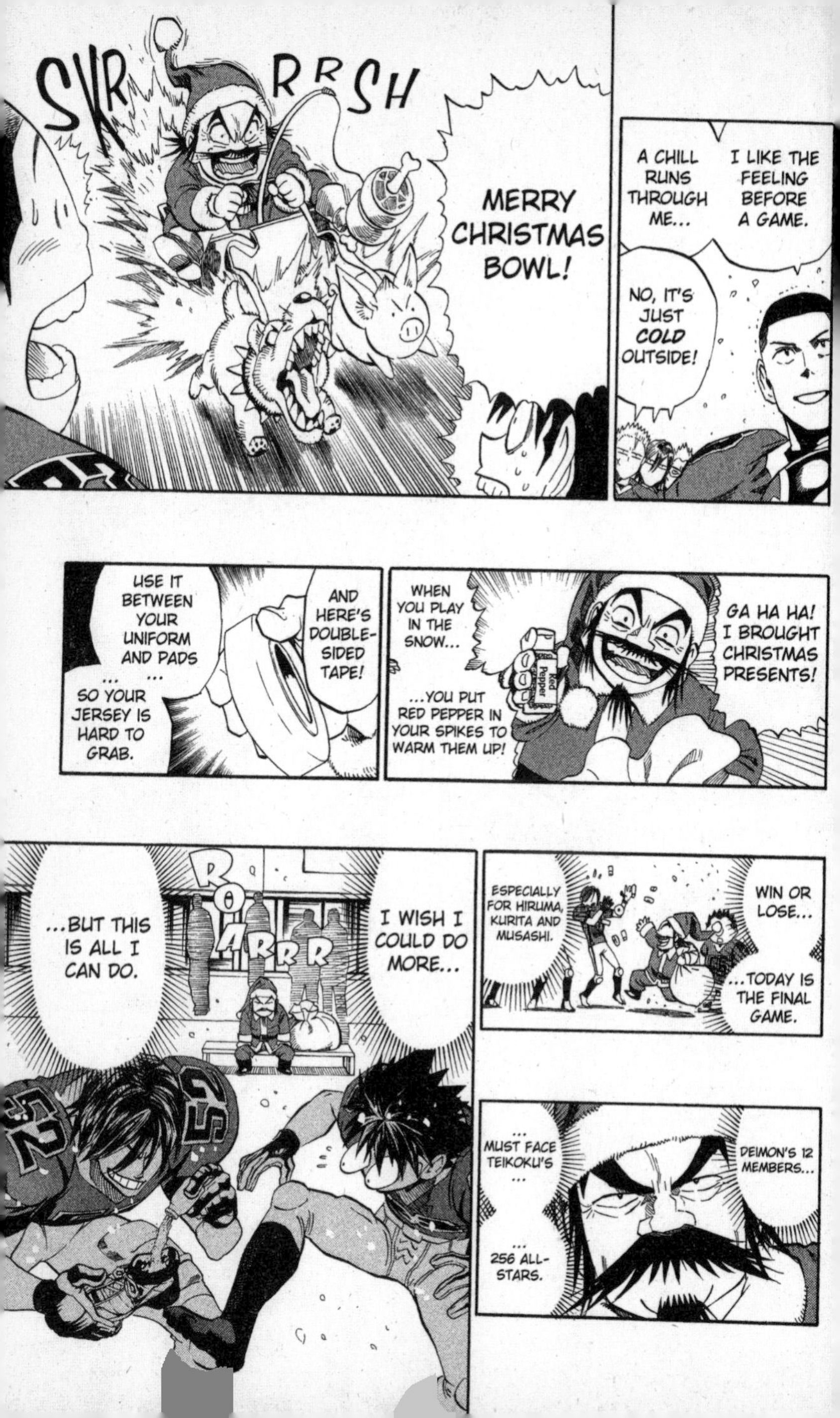
I LIKE THE FEELING BEFORE A GAME.
A CHILL RUNS THROUGH ME...
NO, IT'S JUST **COLD** OUTSIDE!
SKRRRSH
MERRY CHRISTMAS BOWL!
GA HA HA! I BROUGHT CHRISTMAS PRESENTS!
Red Pepper
WHEN YOU PLAY IN THE SNOW...
...YOU PUT RED PEPPER IN YOUR SPIKES TO WARM THEM UP!
AND HERE'S DOUBLE-SIDED TAPE!
USE IT BETWEEN YOUR UNIFORM AND PADS... ...SO YOUR JERSEY IS HARD TO GRAB.
WIN OR LOSE...
...TODAY IS THE FINAL GAME.
ESPECIALLY FOR HIRUMA, KURITA AND MUSASHI.
DEIMON'S 12 MEMBERS...
...MUST FACE TEIKOKU'S...
...256 ALL-STARS.
I WISH I COULD DO MORE...
ROARRR
...BUT THIS IS ALL I CAN DO.

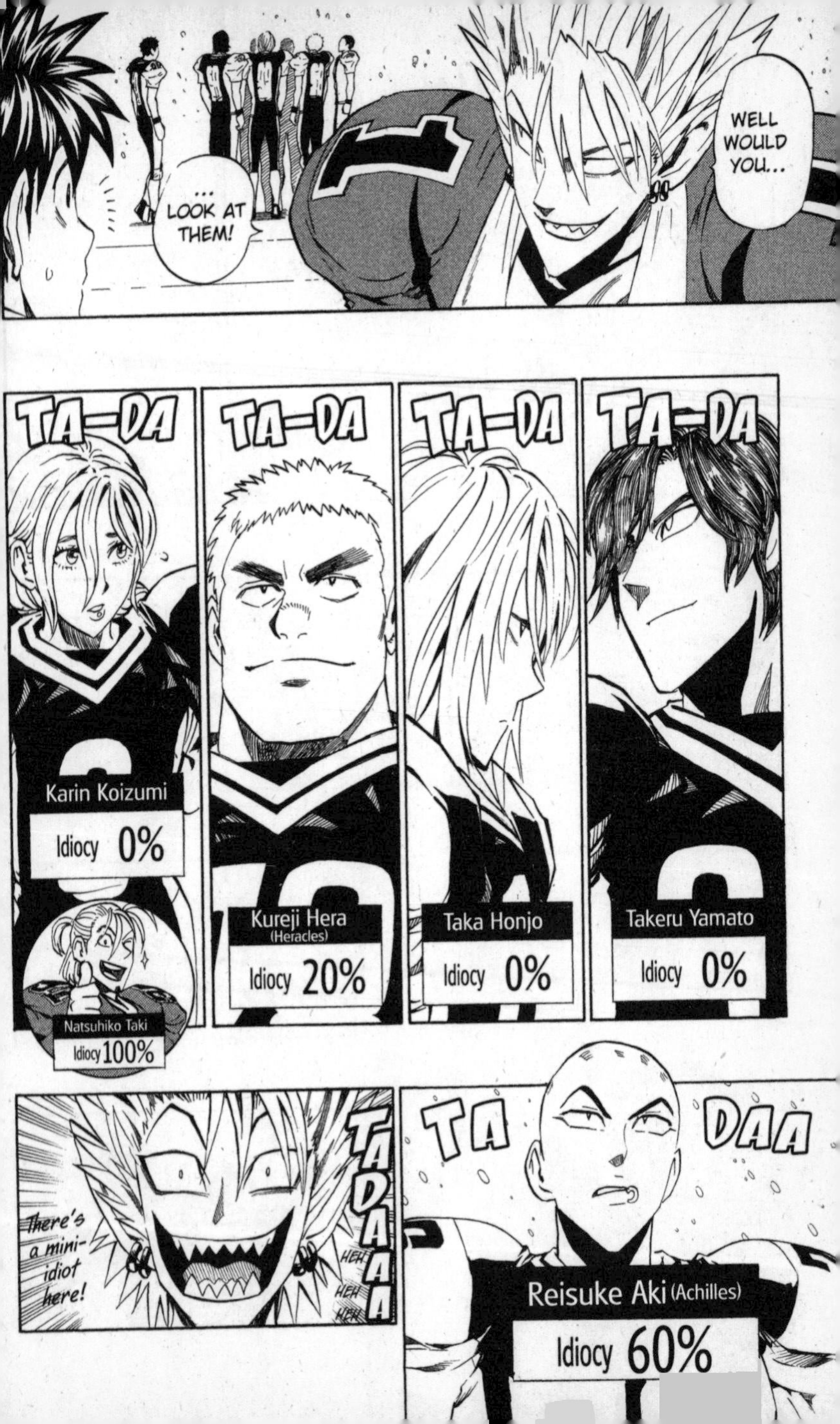
WELL WOULD YOU...
...LOOK AT THEM!
TA-DA
Takeru Yamato
Idiocy 0%
TA-DA
Taka Honjo
Idiocy 0%
TA-DA
Kureji Hera (Heracles)
Idiocy 20%
TA-DA
Karin Koizumi
Idiocy 0%
Natsuhiko Taki
Idiocy 100%
TA DAA
Reisuke Aki (Achilles)
Idiocy 60%
TADAAAA
HEH HEH HEH
There's a mini-idiot here!

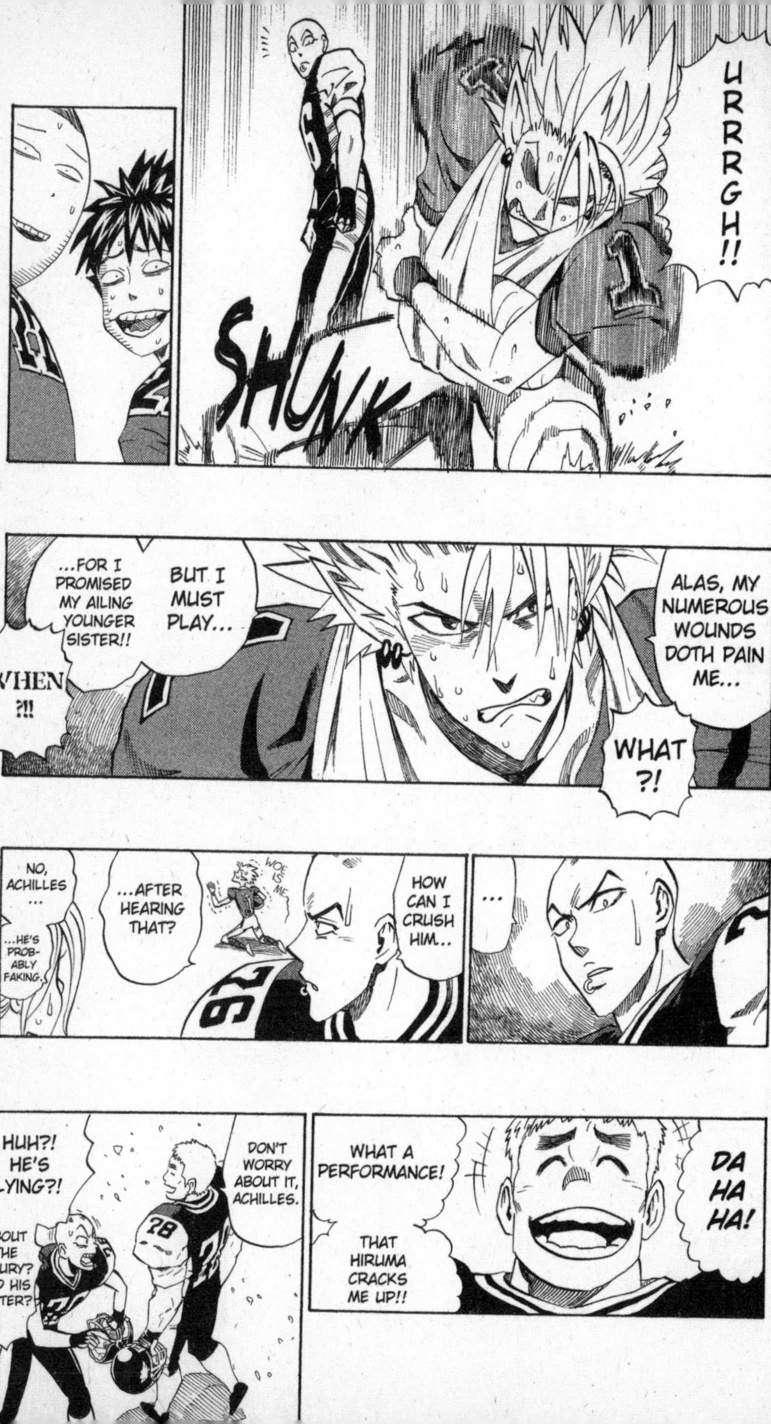
URRRGH!!
SHUNK
ALAS, MY NUMEROUS WOUNDS DOTH PAIN ME...
WHAT ?!
BUT I MUST PLAY...
...FOR I PROMISED MY AILING YOUNGER SISTER!!
WHEN ?!!
...
HOW CAN I CRUSH HIM..
...AFTER HEARING THAT?
WOE IS ME
NO, ACHILLES ...
...HE'S PROBABLY FAKING.
DA HA HA!
WHAT A PERFORMANCE!
THAT HIRUMA CRACKS ME UP!!
DON'T WORRY ABOUT IT, ACHILLES.
HUH?! HE'S LYING?!
ABOUT THE INJURY? AND HIS SISTER?

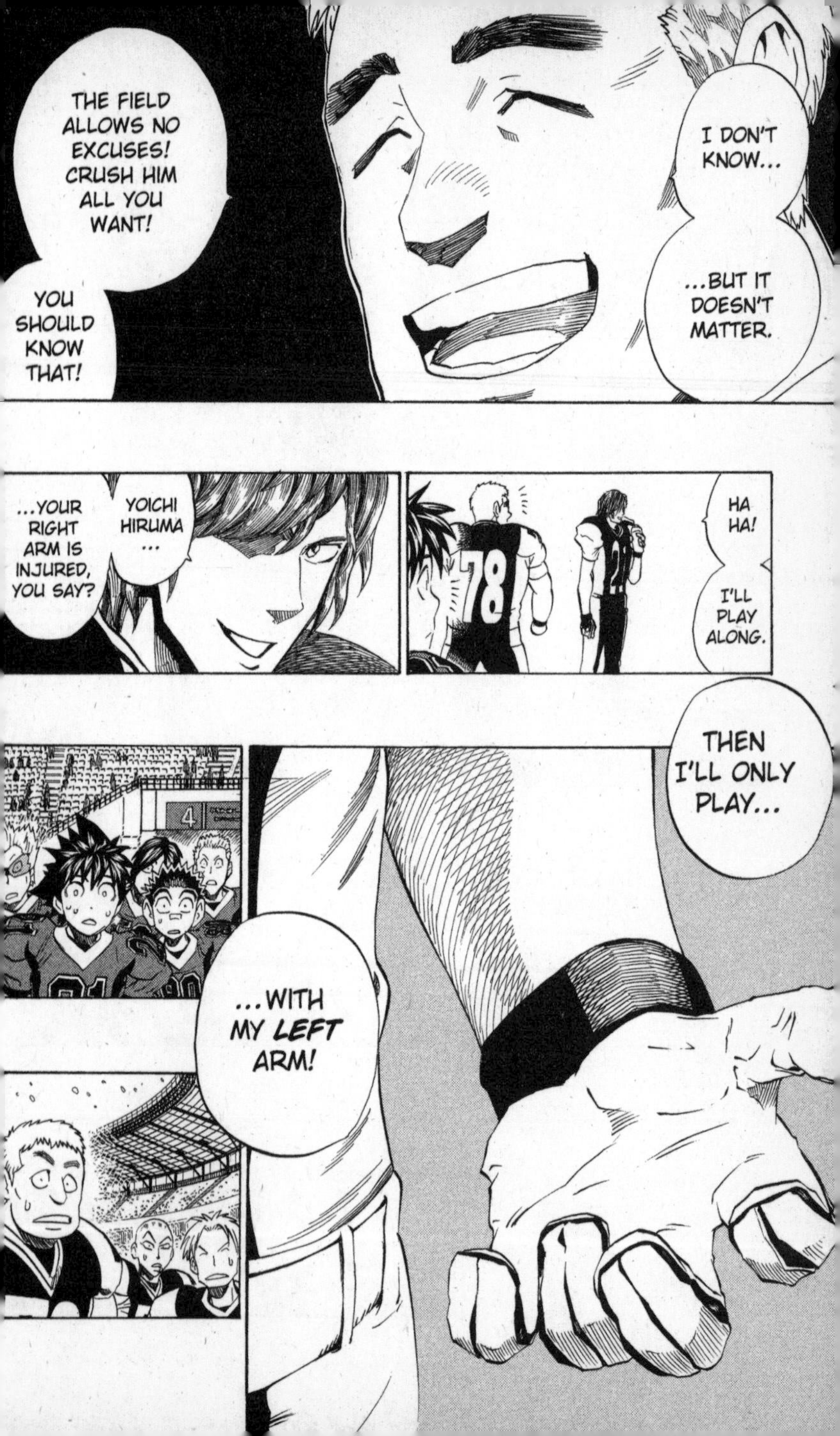
I DON'T KNOW...
...BUT IT DOESN'T MATTER.
THE FIELD ALLOWS NO EXCUSES! CRUSH HIM ALL YOU WANT!
YOU SHOULD KNOW THAT!
HA HA!
I'LL PLAY ALONG.
YOICHI HIRUMA...
...YOUR RIGHT ARM IS INJURED, YOU SAY?
THEN I'LL ONLY PLAY...
...WITH MY *LEFT* ARM!

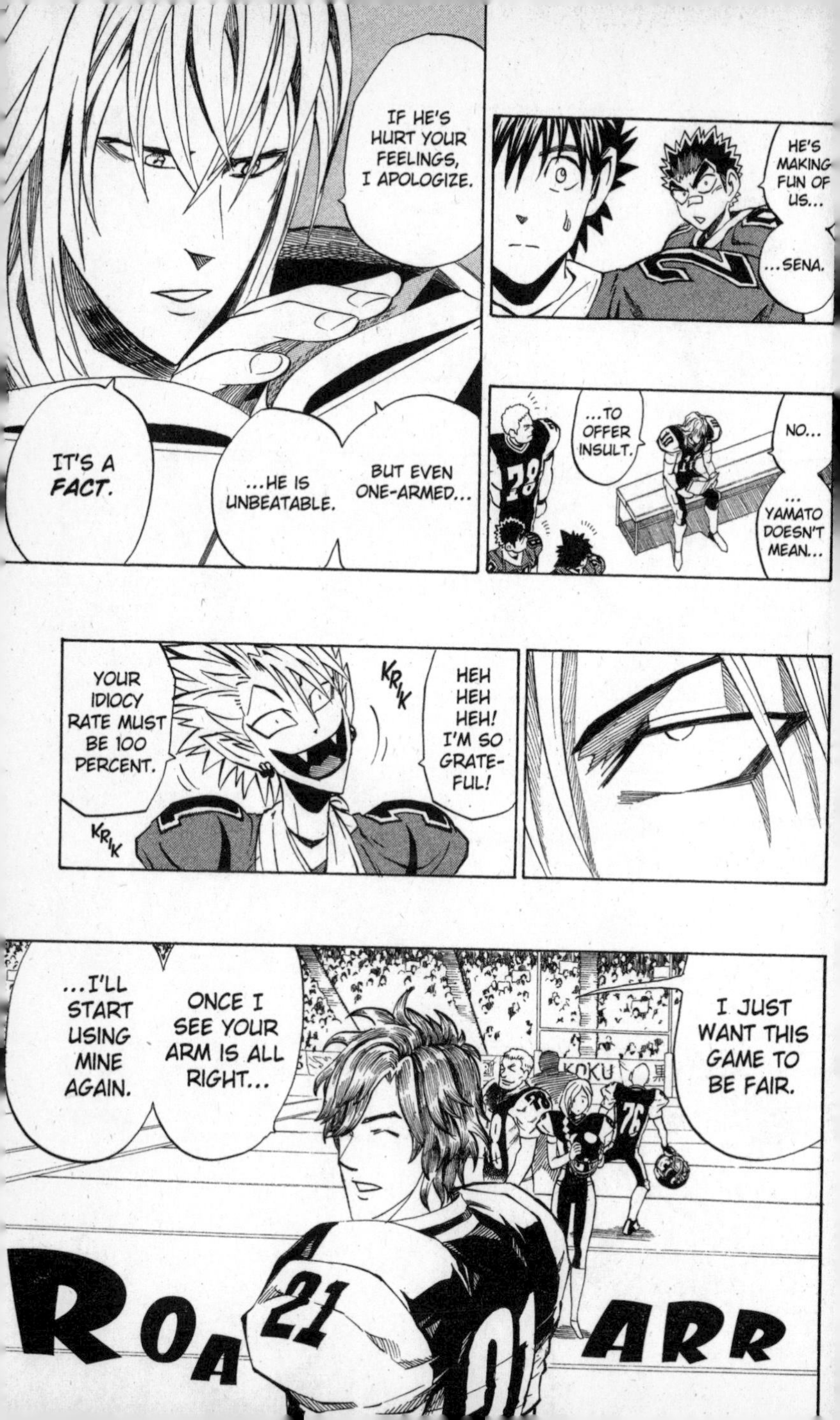
HE'S MAKING FUN OF US...
...SENA.
NO...
...YAMATO DOESN'T MEAN...
...TO OFFER INSULT.
IF HE'S HURT YOUR FEELINGS, I APOLOGIZE.
BUT EVEN ONE-ARMED...
...HE IS UNBEATABLE.
IT'S A *FACT*.
HEH HEH HEH! I'M SO GRATEFUL!
KRIK
YOUR IDIOCY RATE MUST BE 100 PERCENT.
KRIK
I JUST WANT THIS GAME TO BE FAIR.
ONCE I SEE YOUR ARM IS ALL RIGHT...
...I'LL START USING MINE AGAIN.
ROAARR

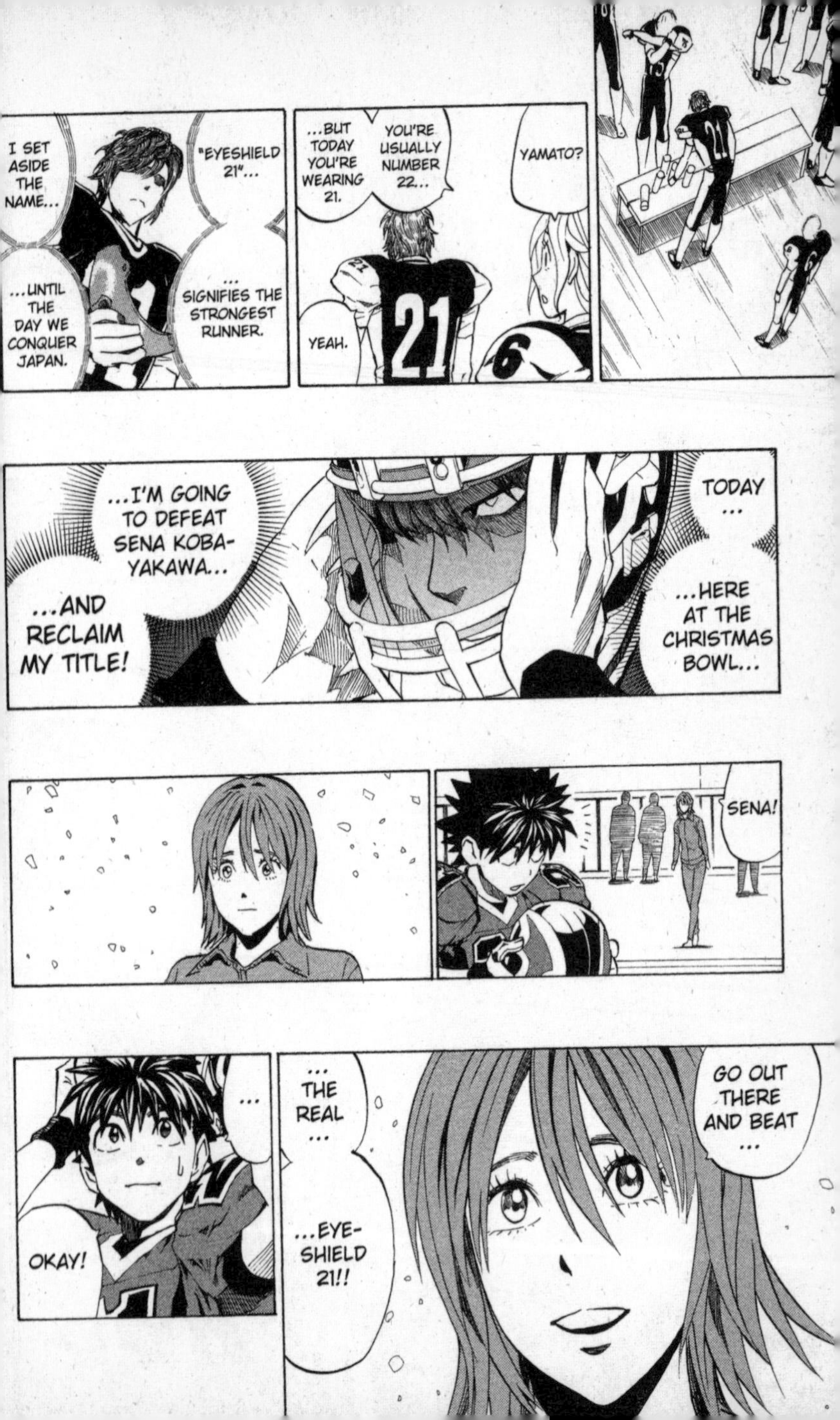
YAMATO?
YOU'RE USUALLY NUMBER 22...
...BUT TODAY YOU'RE WEARING 21.
YEAH.
"EYESHIELD 21"...
...SIGNIFIES THE STRONGEST RUNNER.
I SET ASIDE THE NAME...
...UNTIL THE DAY WE CONQUER JAPAN.
TODAY...
...HERE AT THE CHRISTMAS BOWL...
...I'M GOING TO DEFEAT SENA KOBA-YAKAWA...
...AND RECLAIM MY TITLE!
SENA!
GO OUT THERE AND BEAT...
...THE REAL...
...EYE-SHIELD 21!!
...
OKAY!

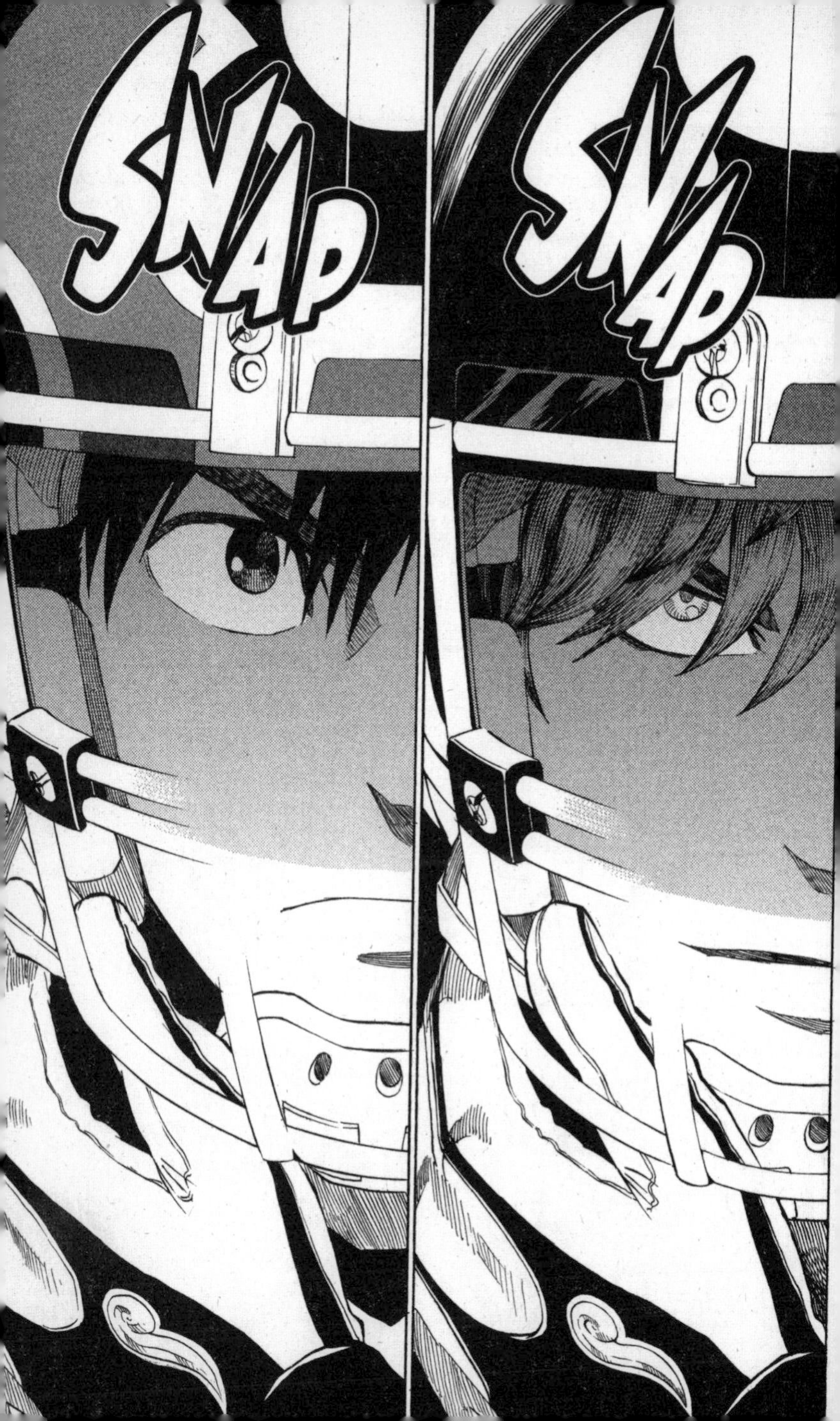
SNAP
SNAP

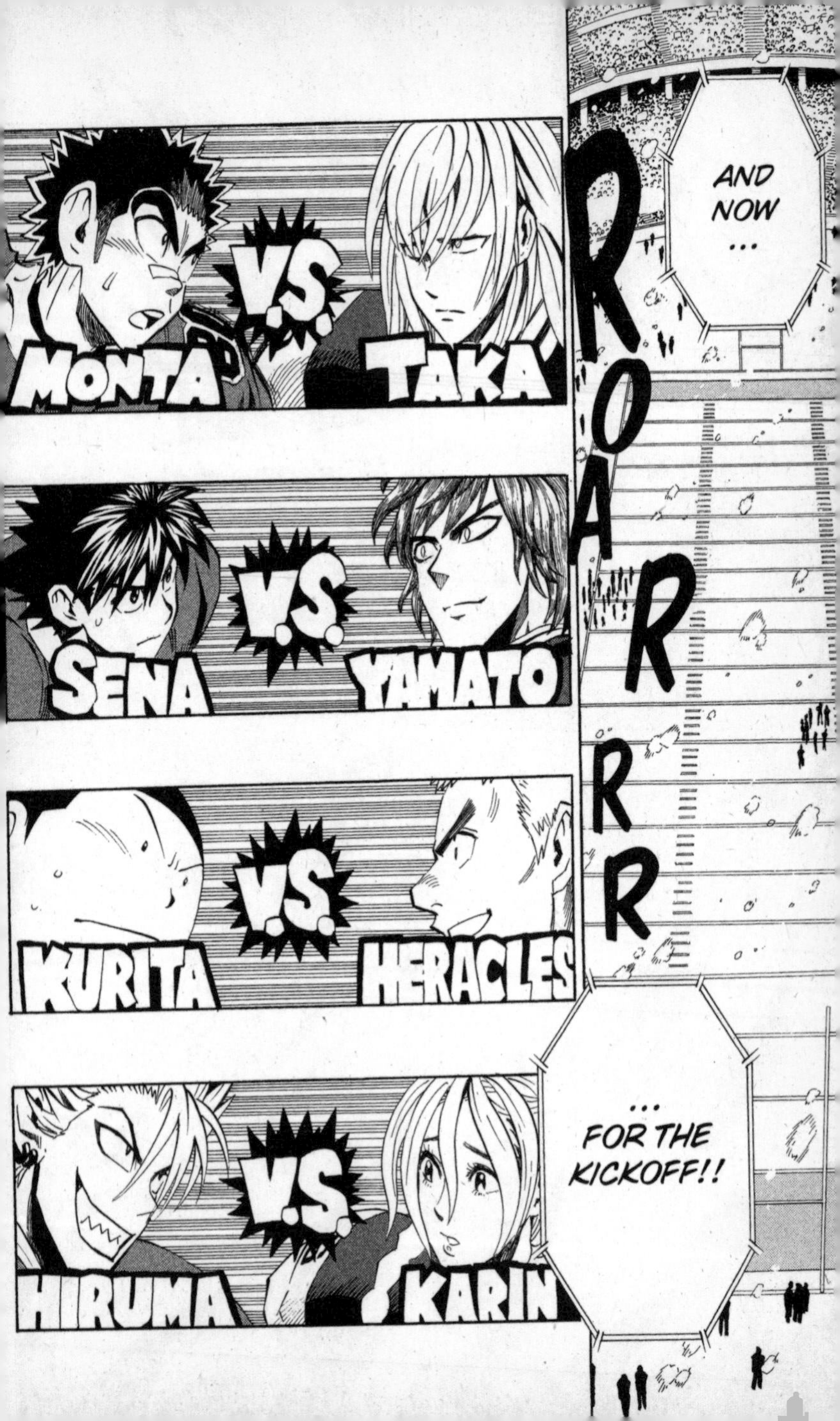
AND NOW ...
ROARRRR
... FOR THE KICKOFF!!
MONTA V.S. TAKA
SENA V.S. YAMATO
KURITA V.S. HERACLES
HIRUMA V.S. KARIN

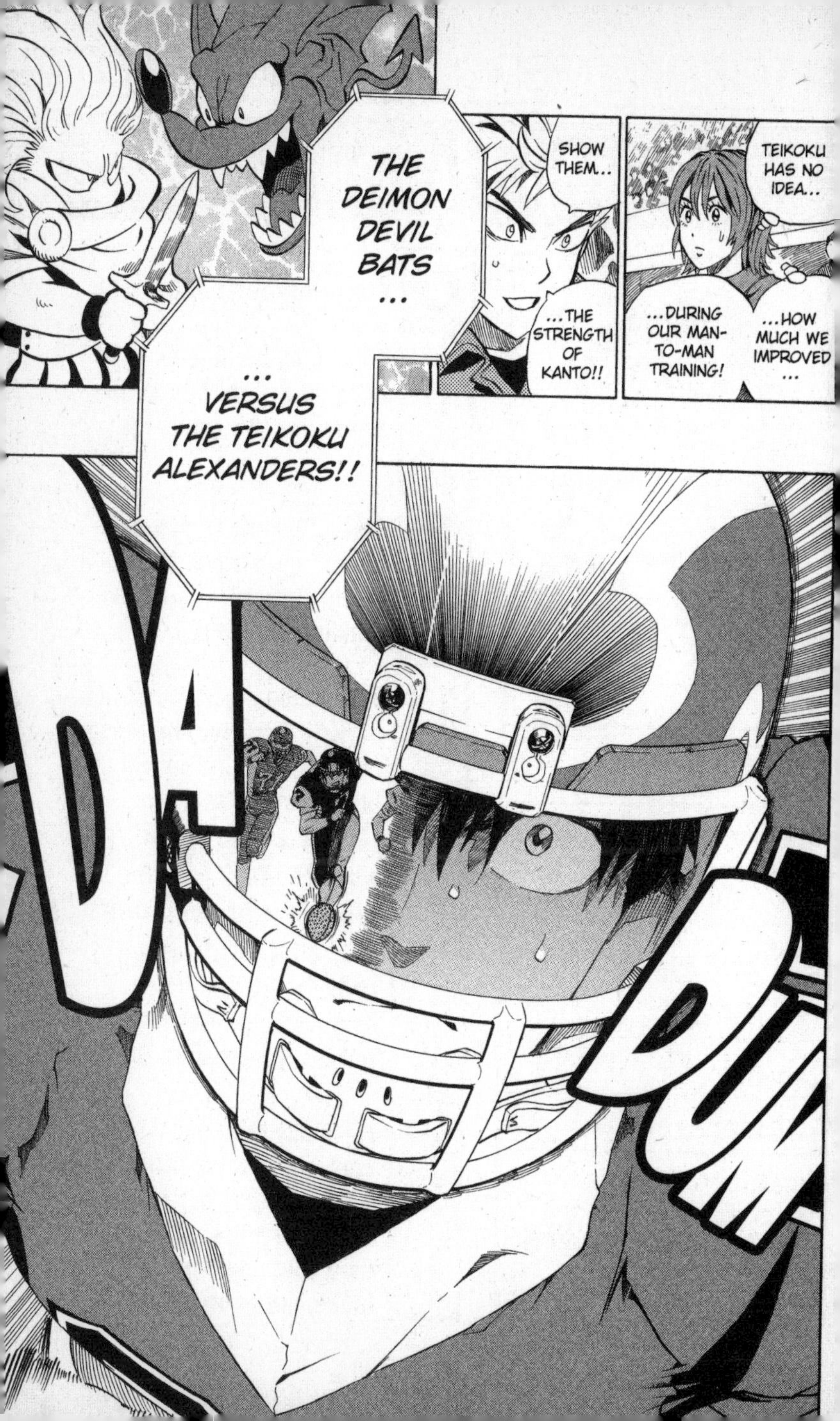
TEIKOKU HAS NO IDEA...
...HOW MUCH WE IMPROVED...
...DURING OUR MAN-TO-MAN TRAINING!
SHOW THEM...
...THE STRENGTH OF KANTO!!
THE DEIMON DEVIL BATS...
...VERSUS THE TEIKOKU ALEXANDERS!!
DUM
DA

TEIKOKU PERSONAL HISTORIES

◂Kureji Hera (Heracles)▸

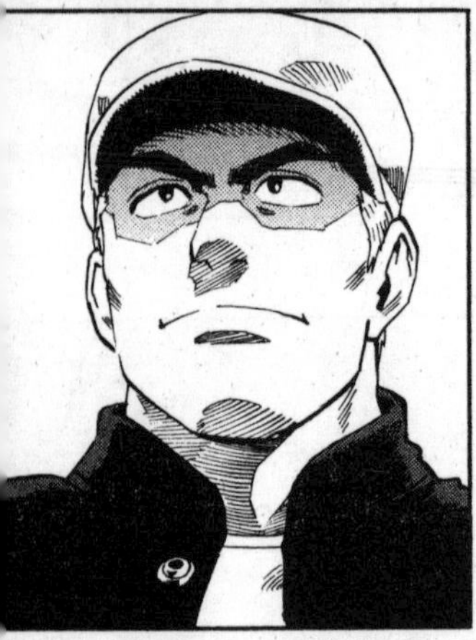

CURRENT AGE: 18

Height	177 cm
Weight	100 kg
Blood type	O
Birthday	May 14
Siblings	One younger sister
Talents/Hobbies	Comedy, Karaoke
Favorite type of girl	
Easygoing girls	

0 YEARS OLD

Born and raised in Osaka.

As a child, he dreams of becoming a ***chubby comedian*** when he grows up.

12 YEARS OLD

Enters Teikoku High School's junior high school. Moves on to high school without ever making first string.

16 YEARS OLD

When drinking at a football party is disclosed, he bursts out laughing and covers the other players, saying,

"What are you talking about? Sure, I drank alcohol, but everyone else just drank mapo tofu."

As a result, he has to reclimb Teikoku's football ranks.

18 YEARS OLD

He finally blossoms in his final year of high school. ***His personality is a riot***, but everyone respects him, so they vote unanimously to make him team captain.

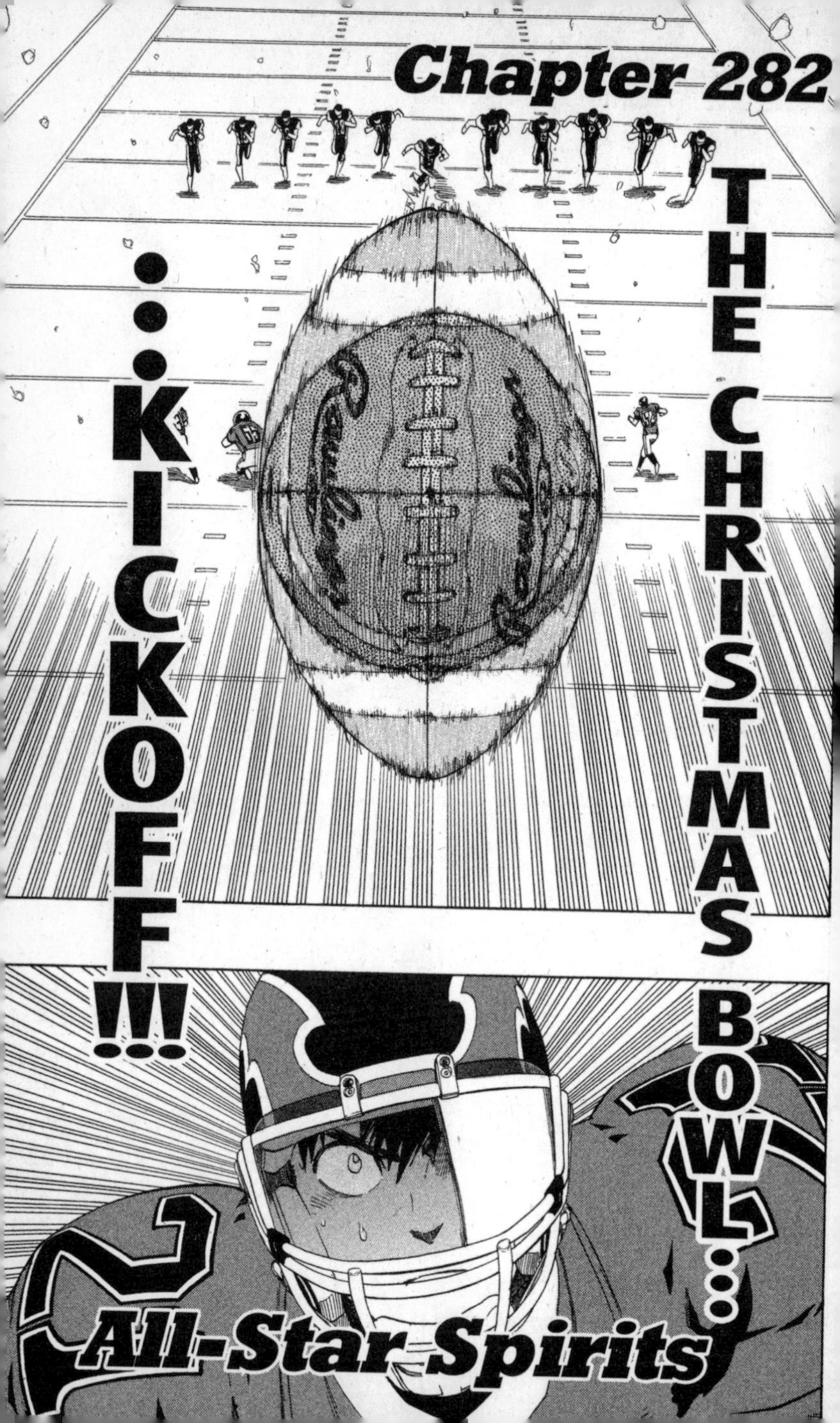
Chapter 282
THE CHRISTMAS BOWL...
...KICKOFF!!!
All-Star Spirits

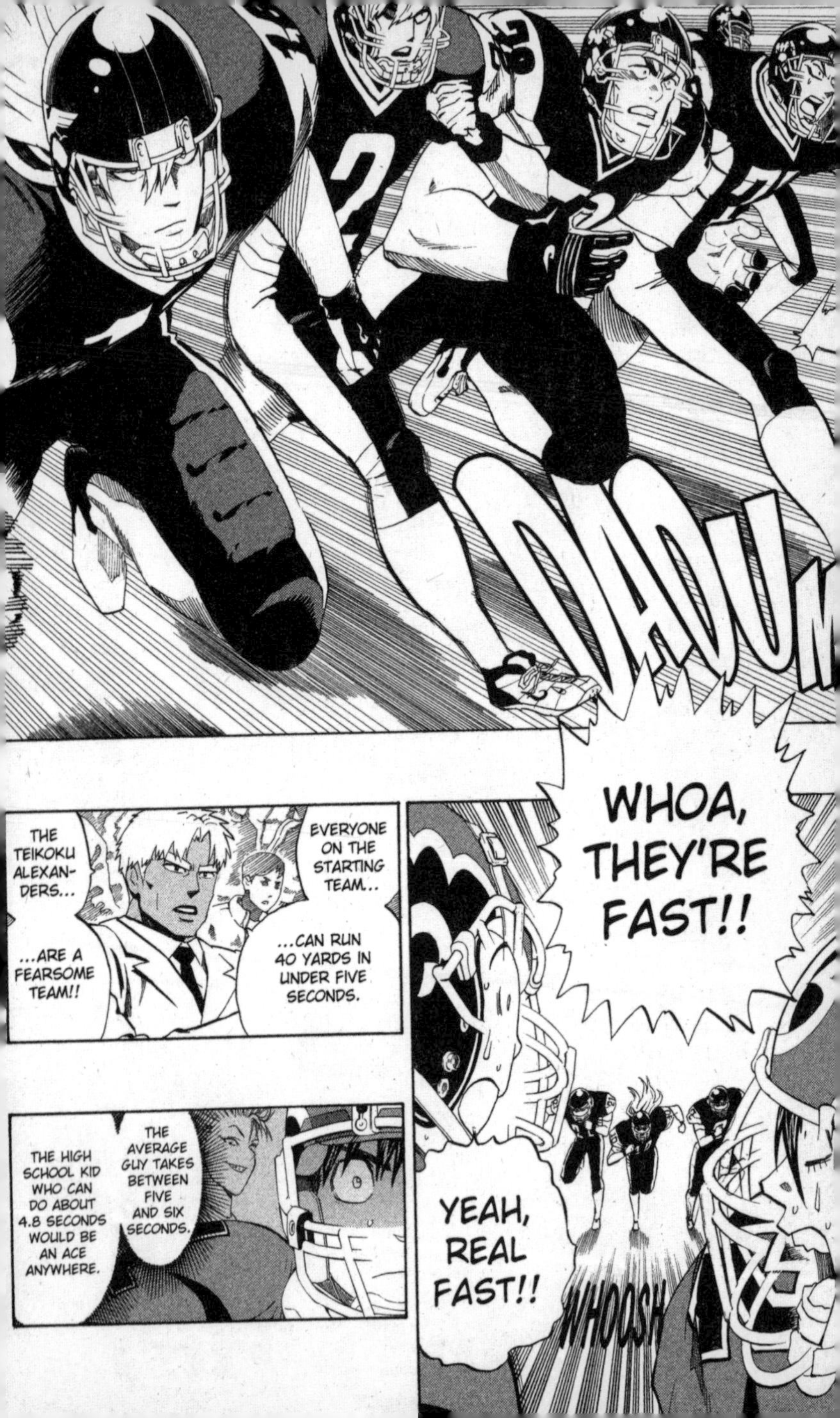
DADUM
WHOA, THEY'RE FAST!!
YEAH, REAL FAST!!
WHOOSH
EVERYONE ON THE STARTING TEAM...
...CAN RUN 40 YARDS IN UNDER FIVE SECONDS.
THE TEIKOKU ALEXANDERS...
...ARE A FEARSOME TEAM!!
THE AVERAGE GUY TAKES BETWEEN FIVE AND SIX SECONDS.
THE HIGH SCHOOL KID WHO CAN DO ABOUT 4.8 SECONDS WOULD BE AN ACE ANYWHERE.

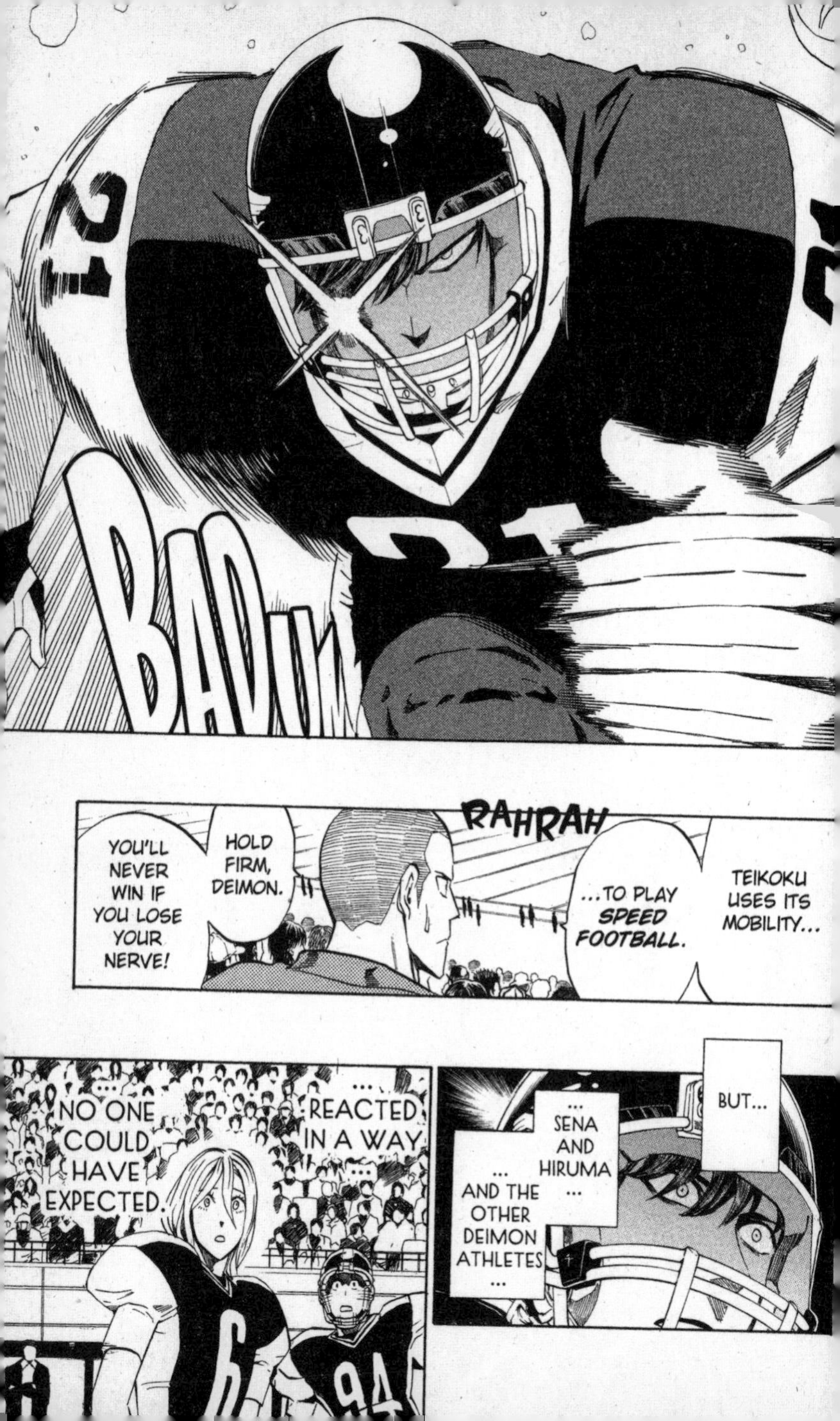
BADUM
TEIKOKU USES ITS MOBILITY...
...TO PLAY SPEED FOOTBALL.
RAHRAH
HOLD FIRM, DEIMON.
YOU'LL NEVER WIN IF YOU LOSE YOUR NERVE!
BUT...
... SENA AND HIRUMA ...
... AND THE OTHER DEIMON ATHLETES ...
... REACTED IN A WAY
... NO ONE COULD HAVE EXPECTED.

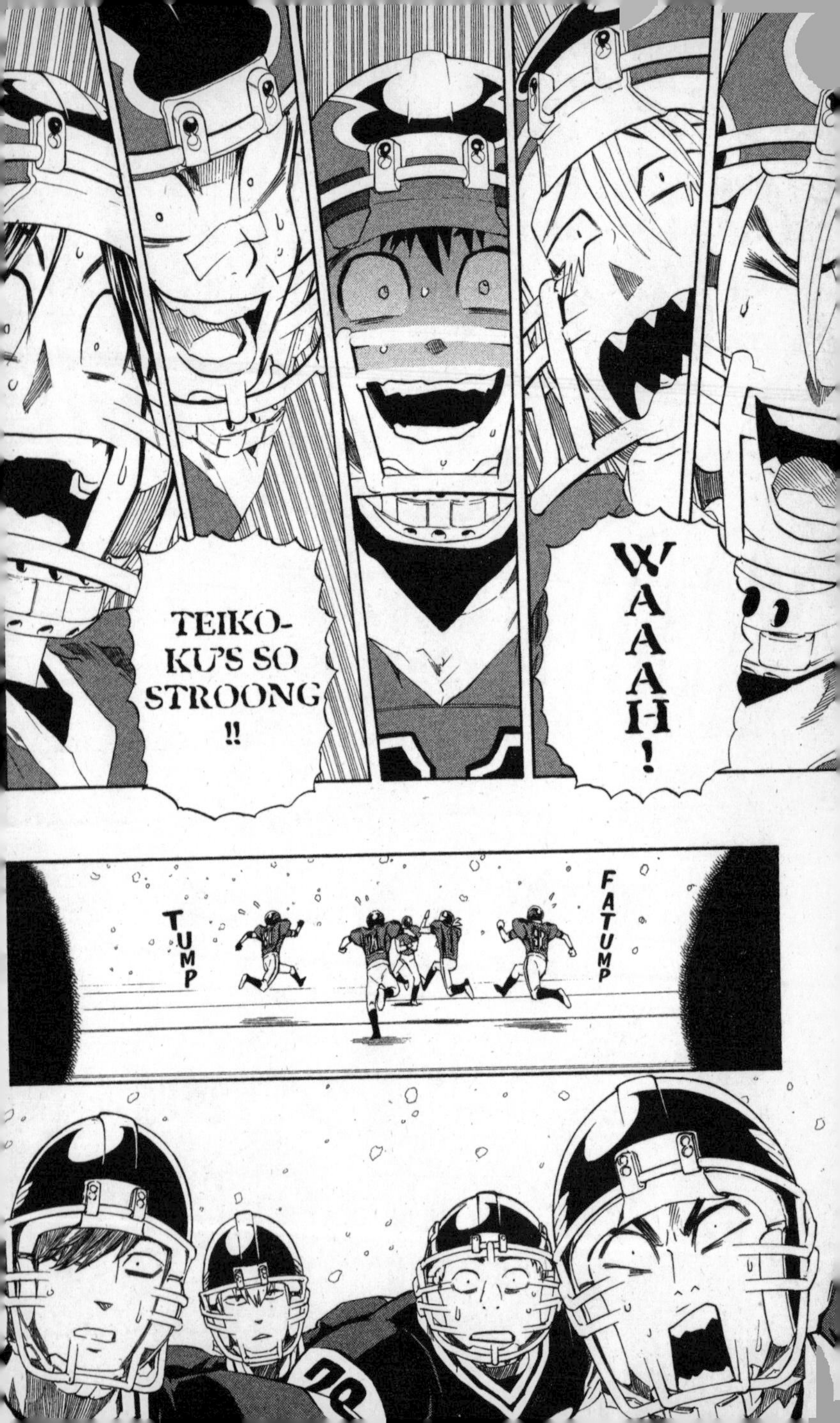
WAAAH!
TEIKO-KU'S SO STROONG!!
FATUMP
TUMP

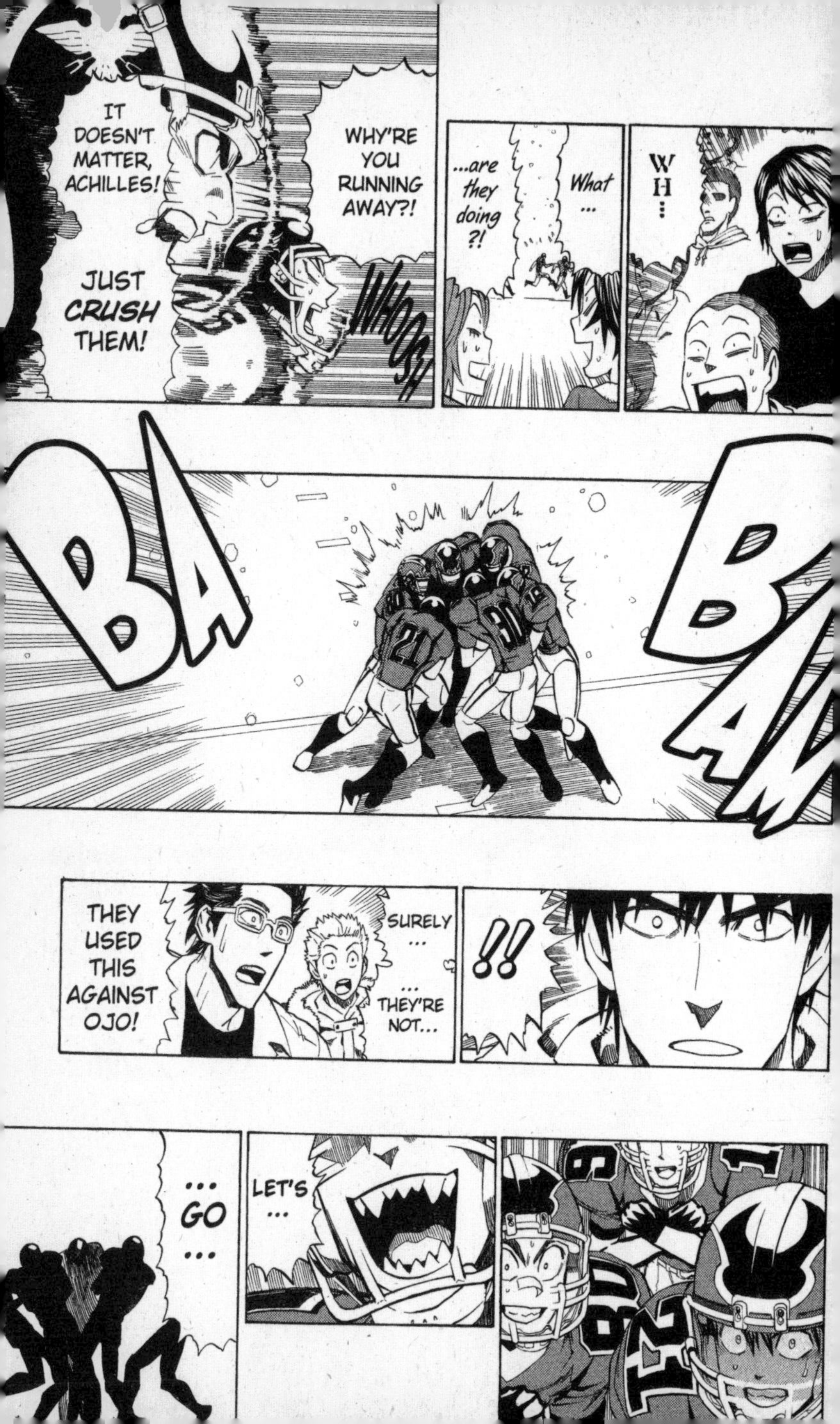
WH...
What ...
...are they doing ?!
WHY'RE YOU RUNNING AWAY?!
IT DOESN'T MATTER, ACHILLES!
JUST CRUSH THEM!
WHOOSH
BA
BAM
!!
SURELY ...
... THEY'RE NOT...
THEY USED THIS AGAINST OJO!
LET'S ...
... GO ...

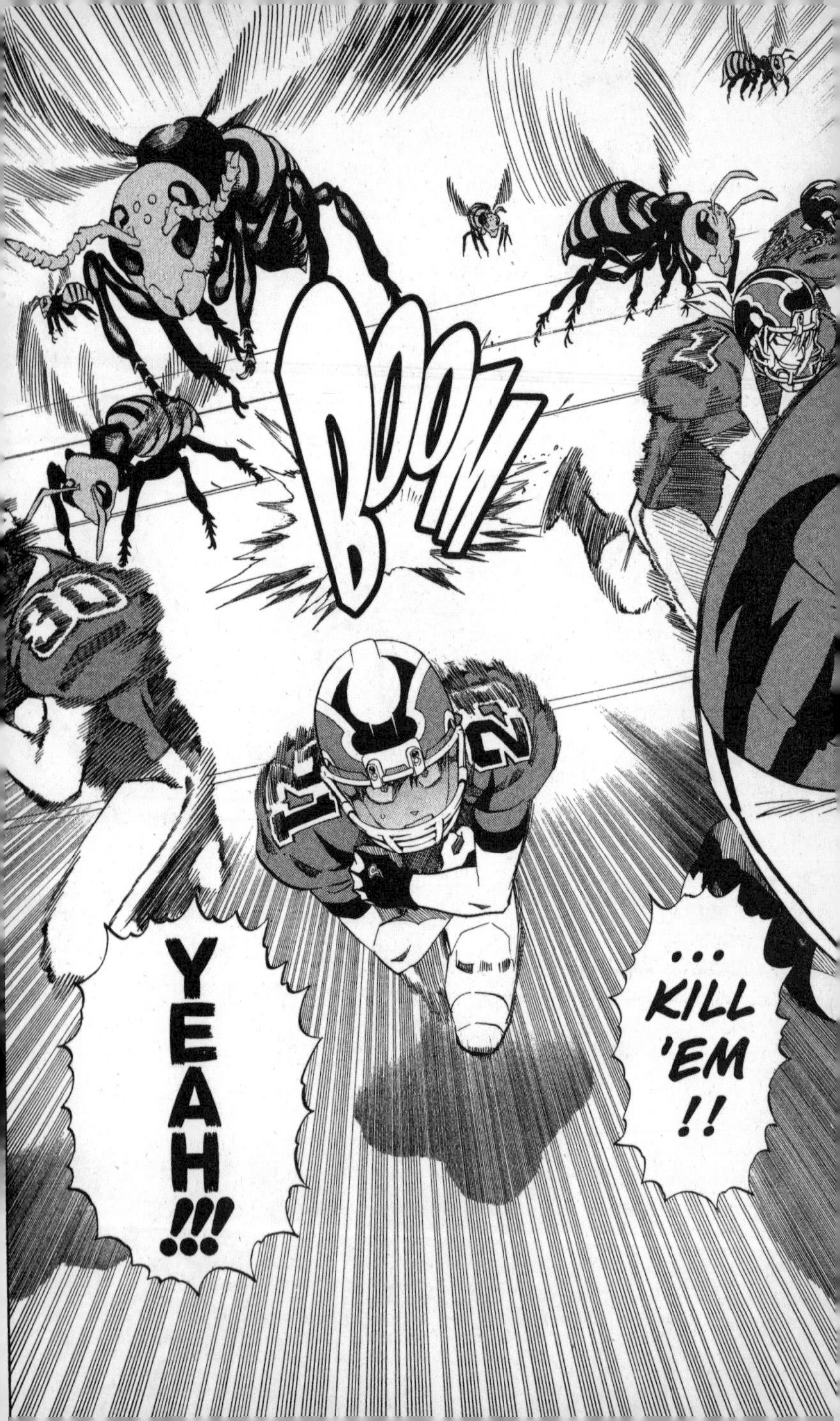
BOOM
... KILL 'EM !!
YEAH!!!

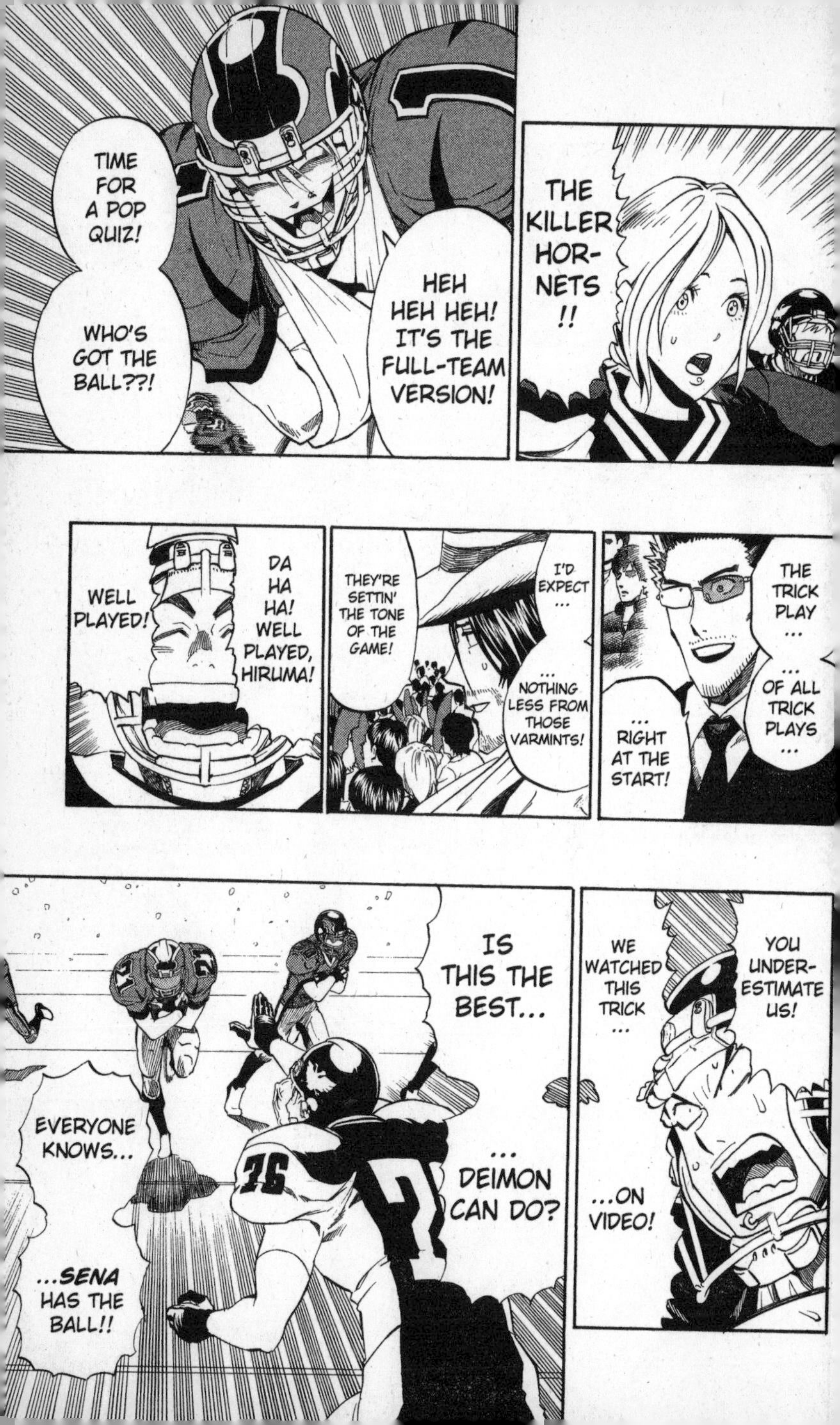
THE KILLER HOR-NETS!!
TIME FOR A POP QUIZ!
WHO'S GOT THE BALL??!
HEH HEH HEH! IT'S THE FULL-TEAM VERSION!
THE TRICK PLAY...
...OF ALL TRICK PLAYS...
...RIGHT AT THE START!
I'D EXPECT...
...NOTHING LESS FROM THOSE VARMINTS!
THEY'RE SETTIN' THE TONE OF THE GAME!
DA HA HA! WELL PLAYED, HIRUMA!
WELL PLAYED!
YOU UNDER-ESTIMATE US!
WE WATCHED THIS TRICK...
...ON VIDEO!
IS THIS THE BEST...
...DEIMON CAN DO?
EVERYONE KNOWS...
...*SENA* HAS THE BALL!!

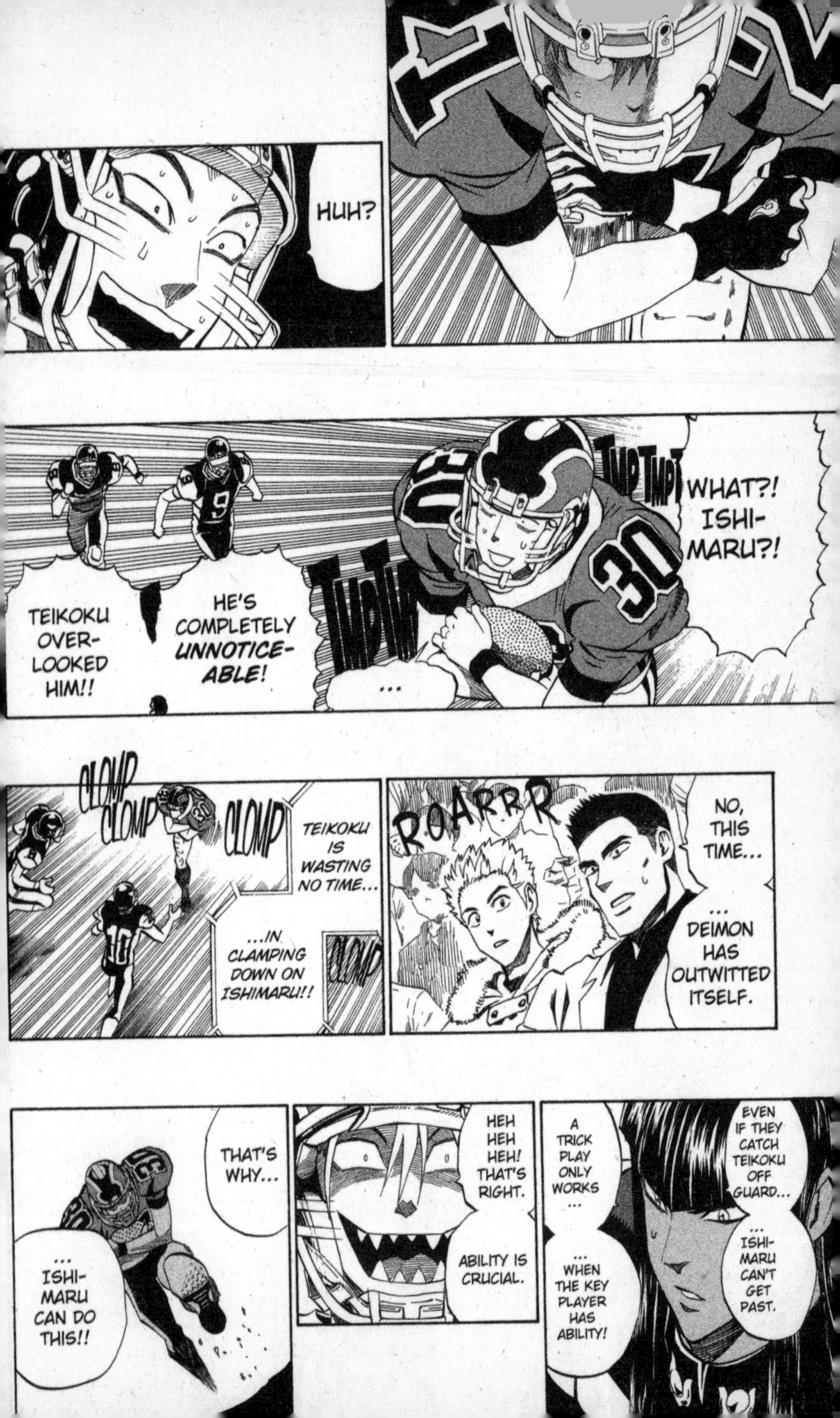
HUH?
TMPTMPT
WHAT?! ISHI-MARU?!
...
HE'S COMPLETELY UNNOTICE-ABLE!
TEIKOKU OVER-LOOKED HIM!!
TMPTMP
ROARRR
NO, THIS TIME...
... DEIMON HAS OUTWITTED ITSELF.
CLOMP CLOMP CLOMP
TEIKOKU IS WASTING NO TIME...
...IN CLAMPING DOWN ON ISHIMARU!!
CLOMP
EVEN IF THEY CATCH TEIKOKU OFF GUARD...
... ISHI-MARU CAN'T GET PAST.
A TRICK PLAY ONLY WORKS...
... WHEN THE KEY PLAYER HAS ABILITY!
HEH HEH HEH! THAT'S RIGHT.
ABILITY IS CRUCIAL.
THAT'S WHY...
... ISHI-MARU CAN DO THIS!!

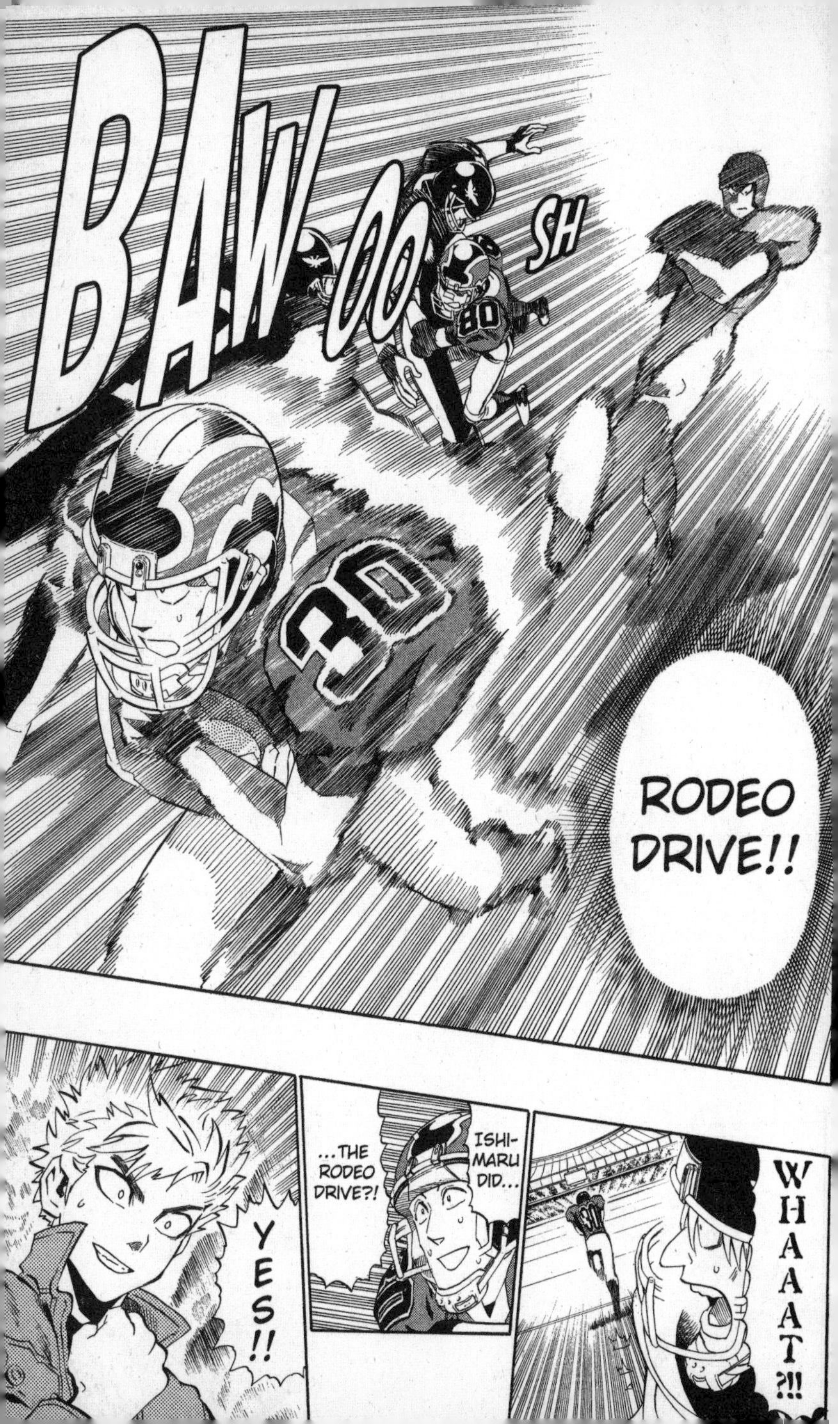
BAWOOSH
RODEO DRIVE!!
WHAAAT?!!
ISHI-MARU DID...
...THE RODEO DRIVE?!
YES!!

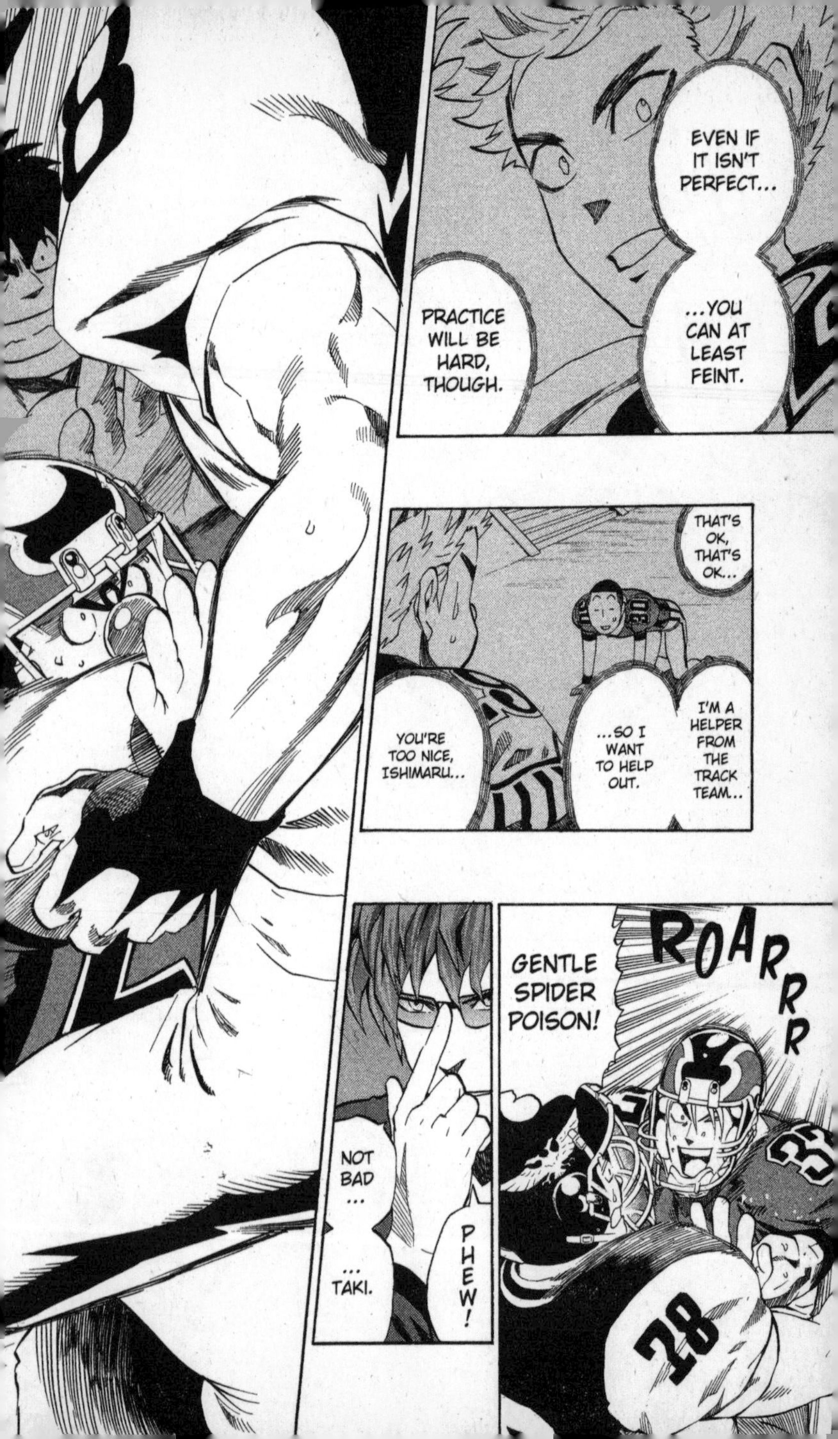
EVEN IF IT ISN'T PERFECT...
...YOU CAN AT LEAST FEINT.
PRACTICE WILL BE HARD, THOUGH.
THAT'S OK, THAT'S OK...
I'M A HELPER FROM THE TRACK TEAM...
...SO I WANT TO HELP OUT.
YOU'RE TOO NICE, ISHIMARU...
ROARRR
GENTLE SPIDER POISON!
PHEW!
NOT BAD...
...TAKI.

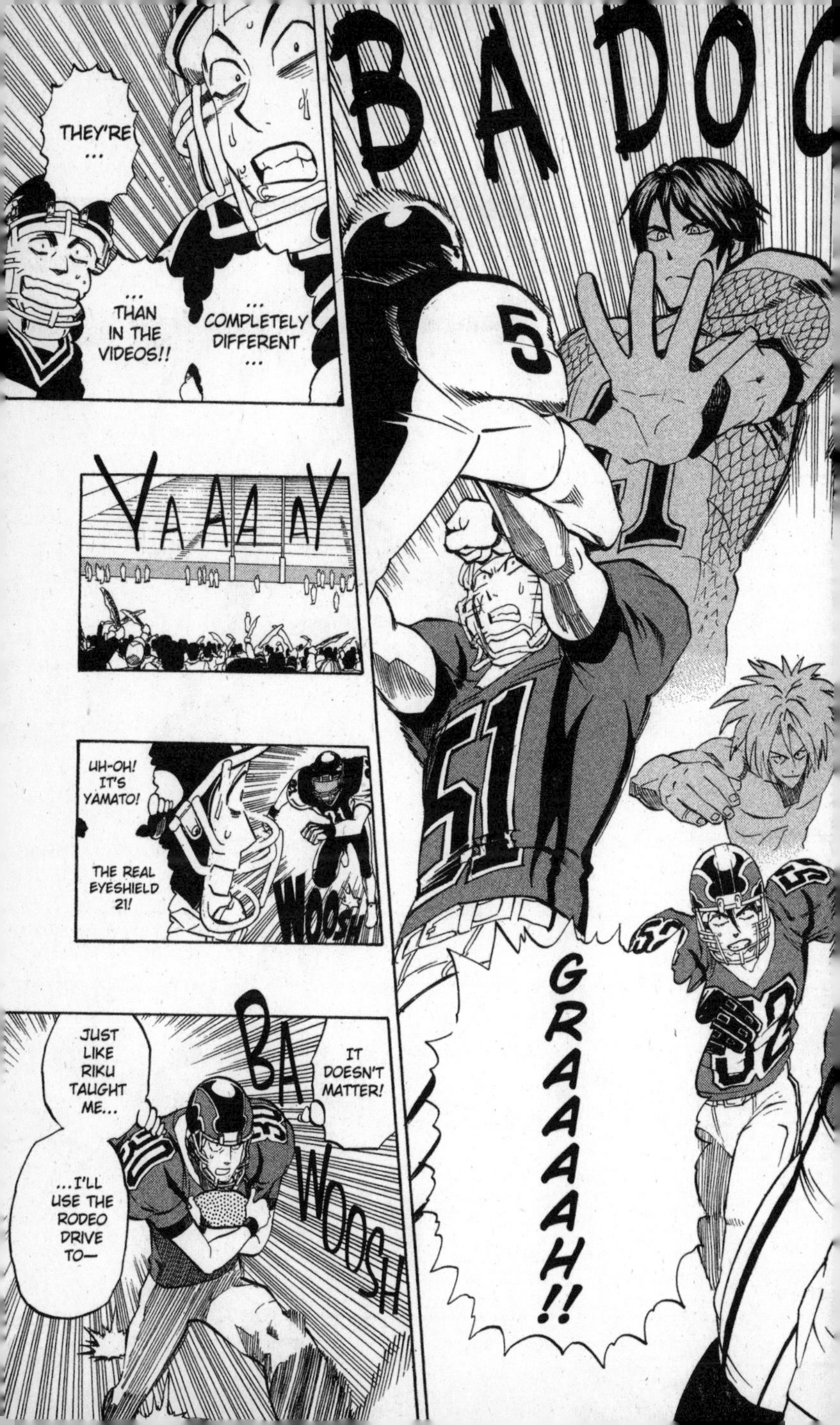
BADOO
GRAAAAAH!!
THEY'RE ...
... COMPLETELY DIFFERENT ...
... THAN IN THE VIDEOS!!
VAAAAY
UH-OH! IT'S YAMATO!
THE REAL EYESHIELD 21!
WOOSH
BA
IT DOESN'T MATTER!
JUST LIKE RIKU TAUGHT ME...
...I'LL USE THE RODEO DRIVE TO—
WOOSH

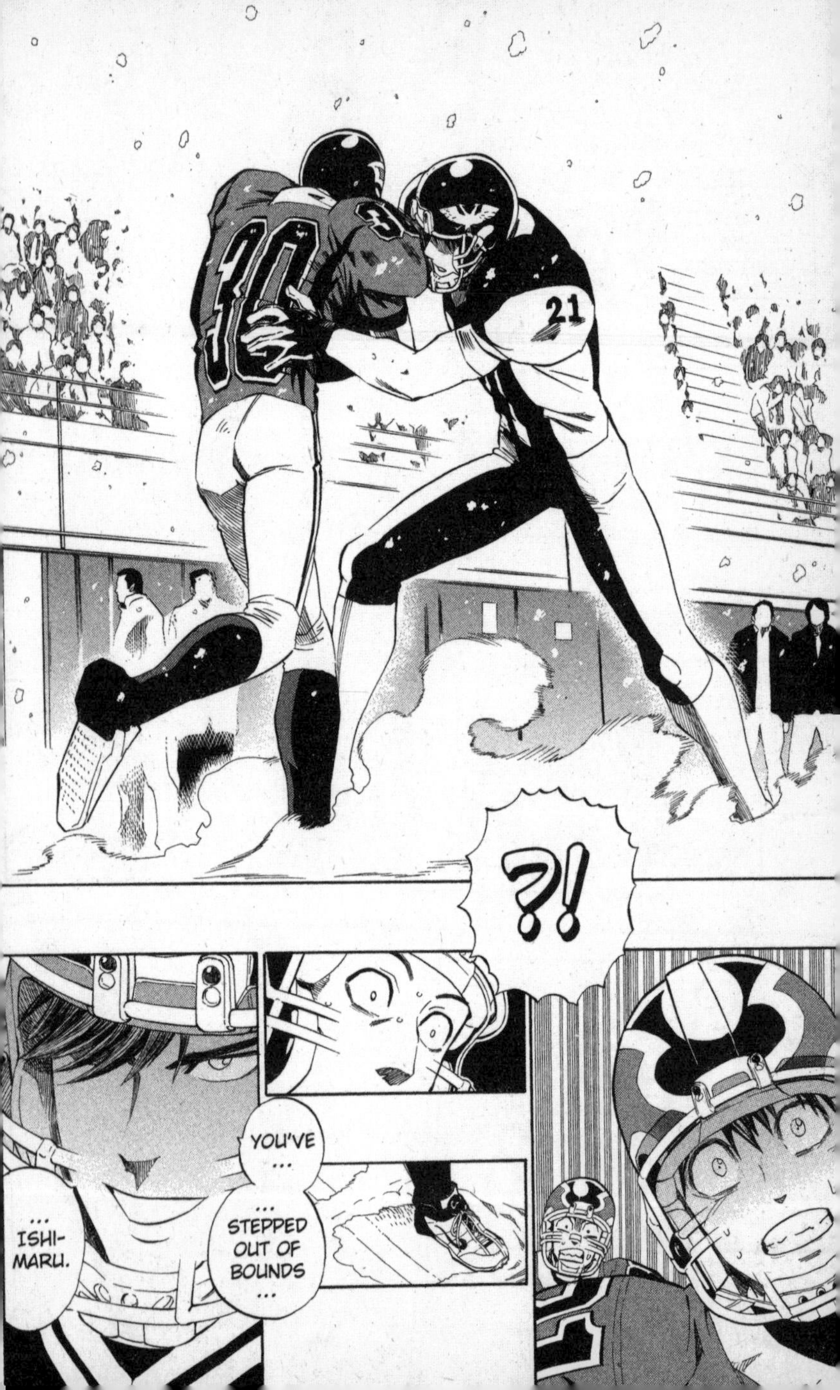
?!
YOU'VE ...
... STEPPED OUT OF BOUNDS ...
... ISHI-MARU.

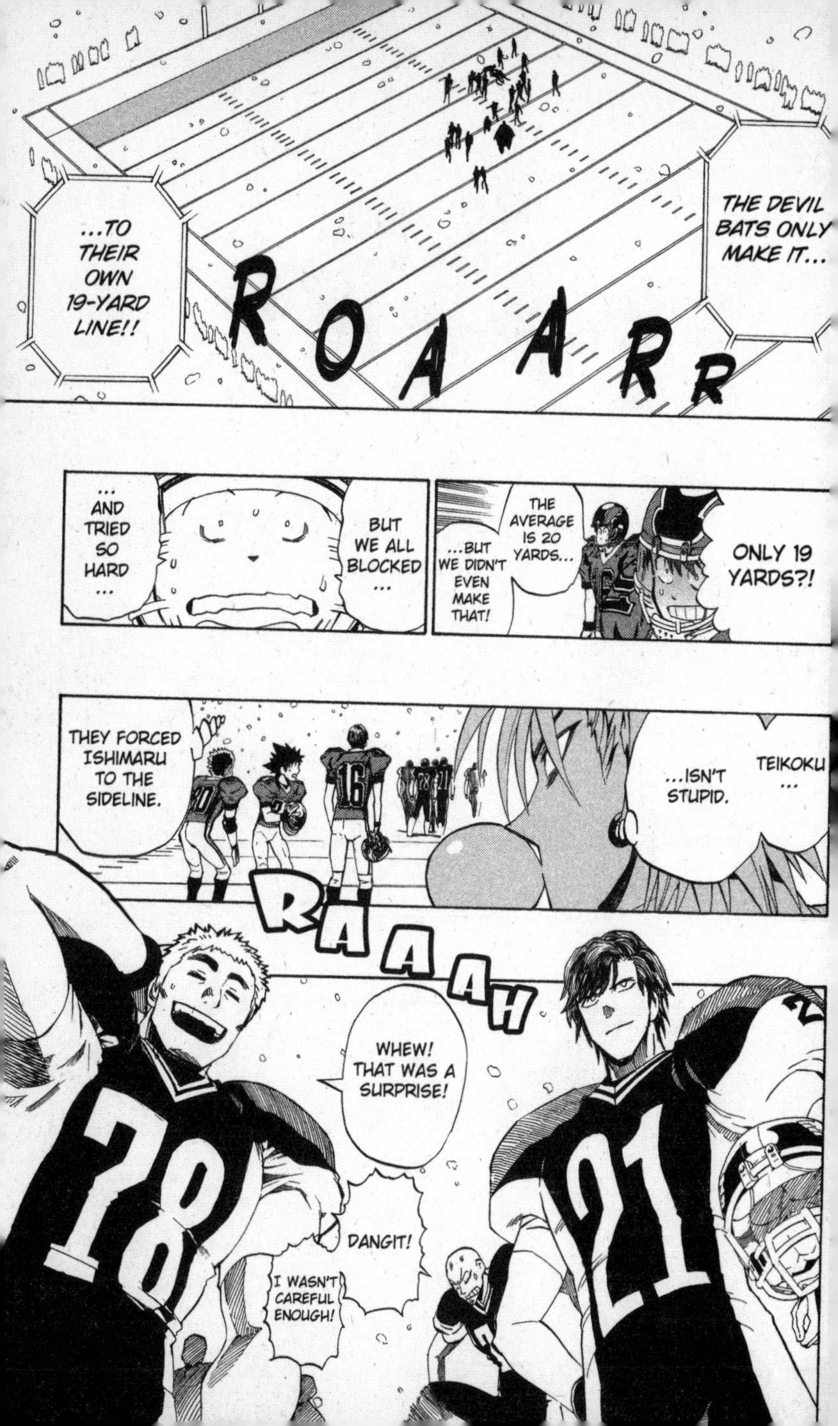
THE DEVIL BATS ONLY MAKE IT...
...TO THEIR OWN 19-YARD LINE!!
ROAARR
ONLY 19 YARDS?!
THE AVERAGE IS 20 YARDS...
...BUT WE DIDN'T EVEN MAKE THAT!
BUT WE ALL BLOCKED...
...AND TRIED SO HARD...
TEIKOKU...
...ISN'T STUPID.
THEY FORCED ISHIMARU TO THE SIDELINE.
RAAAH
WHEW! THAT WAS A SURPRISE!
DANGIT!
I WASN'T CAREFUL ENOUGH!

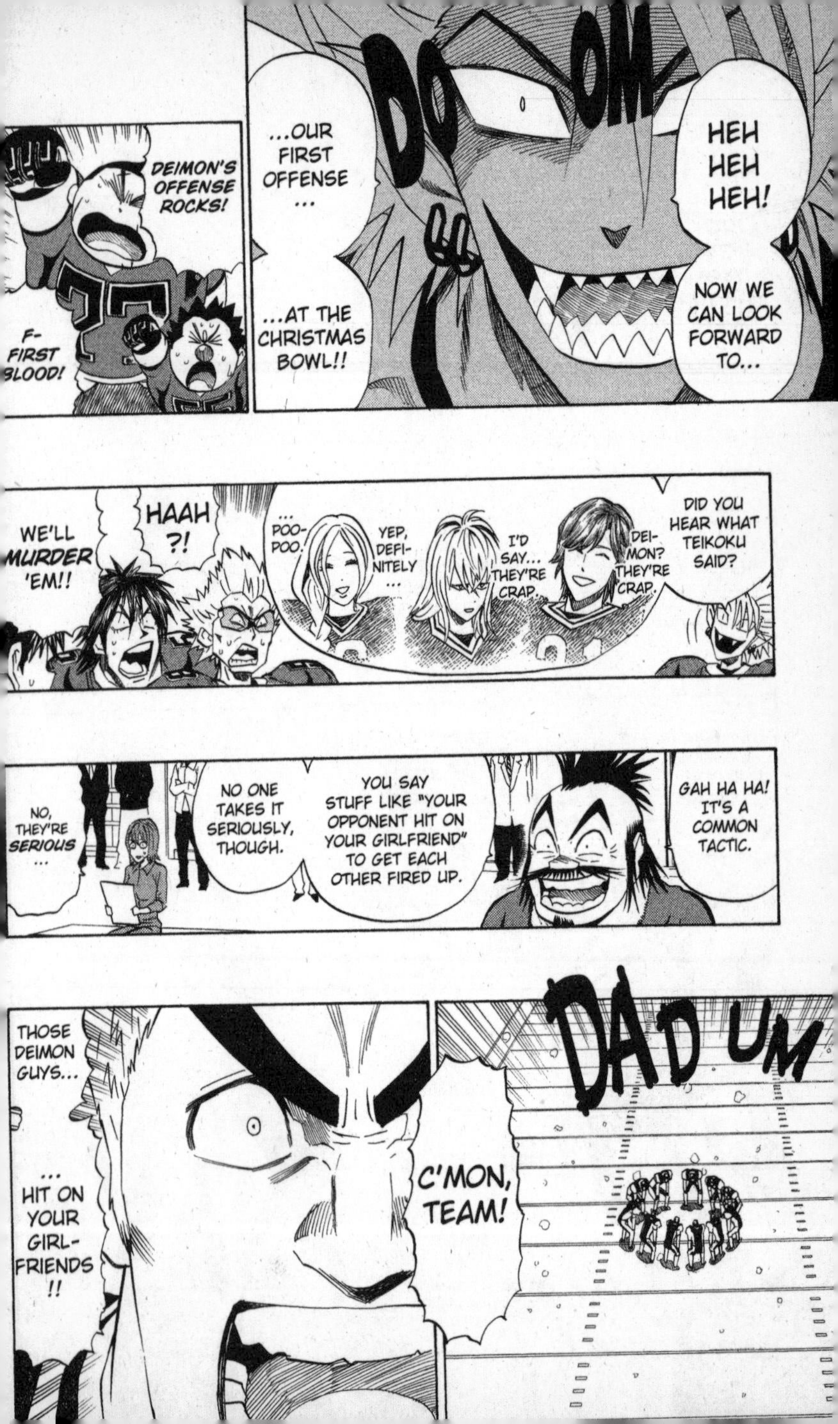
DOOM
HEH HEH HEH!
NOW WE CAN LOOK FORWARD TO...
...OUR FIRST OFFENSE...
...AT THE CHRISTMAS BOWL!!
DEIMON'S OFFENSE ROCKS!
F-FIRST BLOOD!
DID YOU HEAR WHAT TEIKOKU SAID?
DEIMON? THEY'RE CRAP.
I'D SAY... THEY'RE CRAP.
YEP, DEFINITELY...
...POO-POO.
HAAH?!
WE'LL MURDER 'EM!!
GAH HA HA! IT'S A COMMON TACTIC.
YOU SAY STUFF LIKE "YOUR OPPONENT HIT ON YOUR GIRLFRIEND" TO GET EACH OTHER FIRED UP.
NO ONE TAKES IT SERIOUSLY, THOUGH.
NO, THEY'RE SERIOUS...
DADUM
C'MON, TEAM!
THOSE DEIMON GUYS...
...HIT ON YOUR GIRLFRIENDS!!

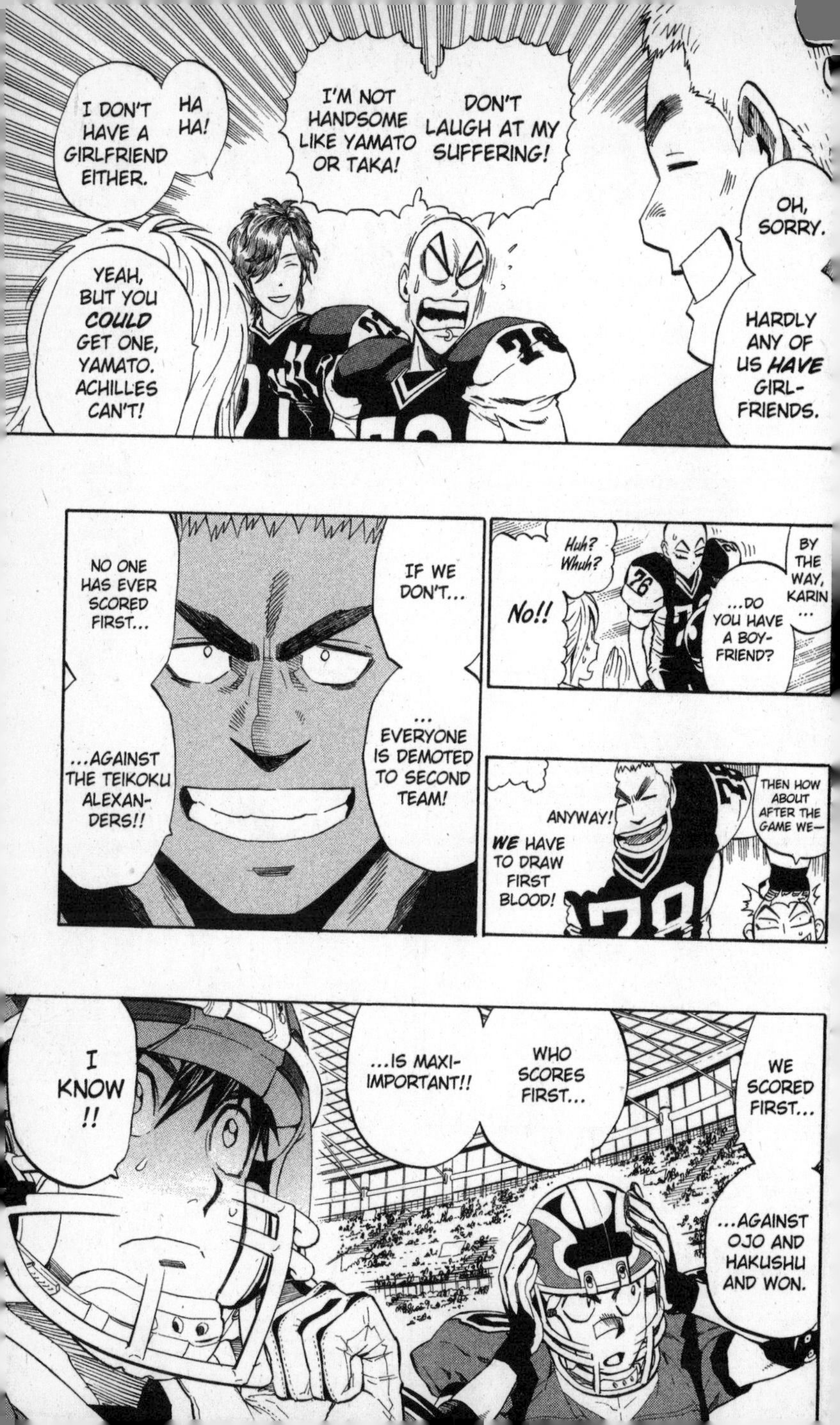
OH, SORRY.
HARDLY ANY OF US *HAVE* GIRL-FRIENDS.
DON'T LAUGH AT MY SUFFERING!
I'M NOT HANDSOME LIKE YAMATO OR TAKA!
HA HA!
I DON'T HAVE A GIRLFRIEND EITHER.
YEAH, BUT YOU *COULD* GET ONE, YAMATO. ACHILLES CAN'T!
BY THE WAY, KARIN...
...DO YOU HAVE A BOY-FRIEND?
Huh? Whuh?
No!!
THEN HOW ABOUT AFTER THE GAME WE—
ANYWAY!
WE HAVE TO DRAW FIRST BLOOD!
IF WE DON'T...
...EVERYONE IS DEMOTED TO SECOND TEAM!
NO ONE HAS EVER SCORED FIRST...
...AGAINST THE TEIKOKU ALEXANDERS!!
WE SCORED FIRST...
...AGAINST OJO AND HAKUSHU AND WON.
WHO SCORES FIRST...
...IS MAXI-IMPORTANT!!
I KNOW!!

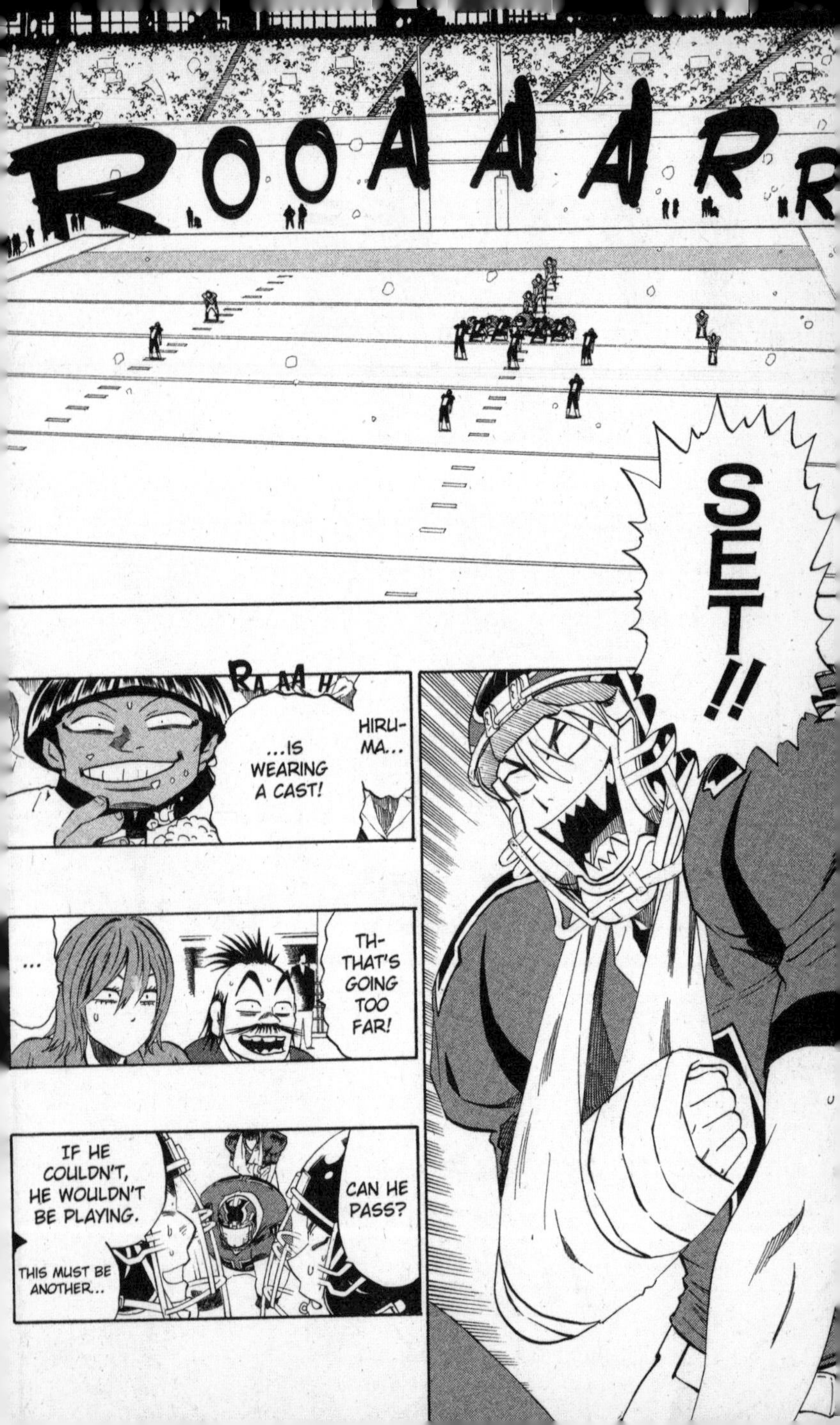
ROOAAARR
SET!!
RAAAH
HIRU-MA...
...IS WEARING A CAST!
TH-THAT'S GOING TOO FAR!
...
CAN HE PASS?
IF HE COULDN'T, HE WOULDN'T BE PLAYING.
THIS MUST BE ANOTHER...

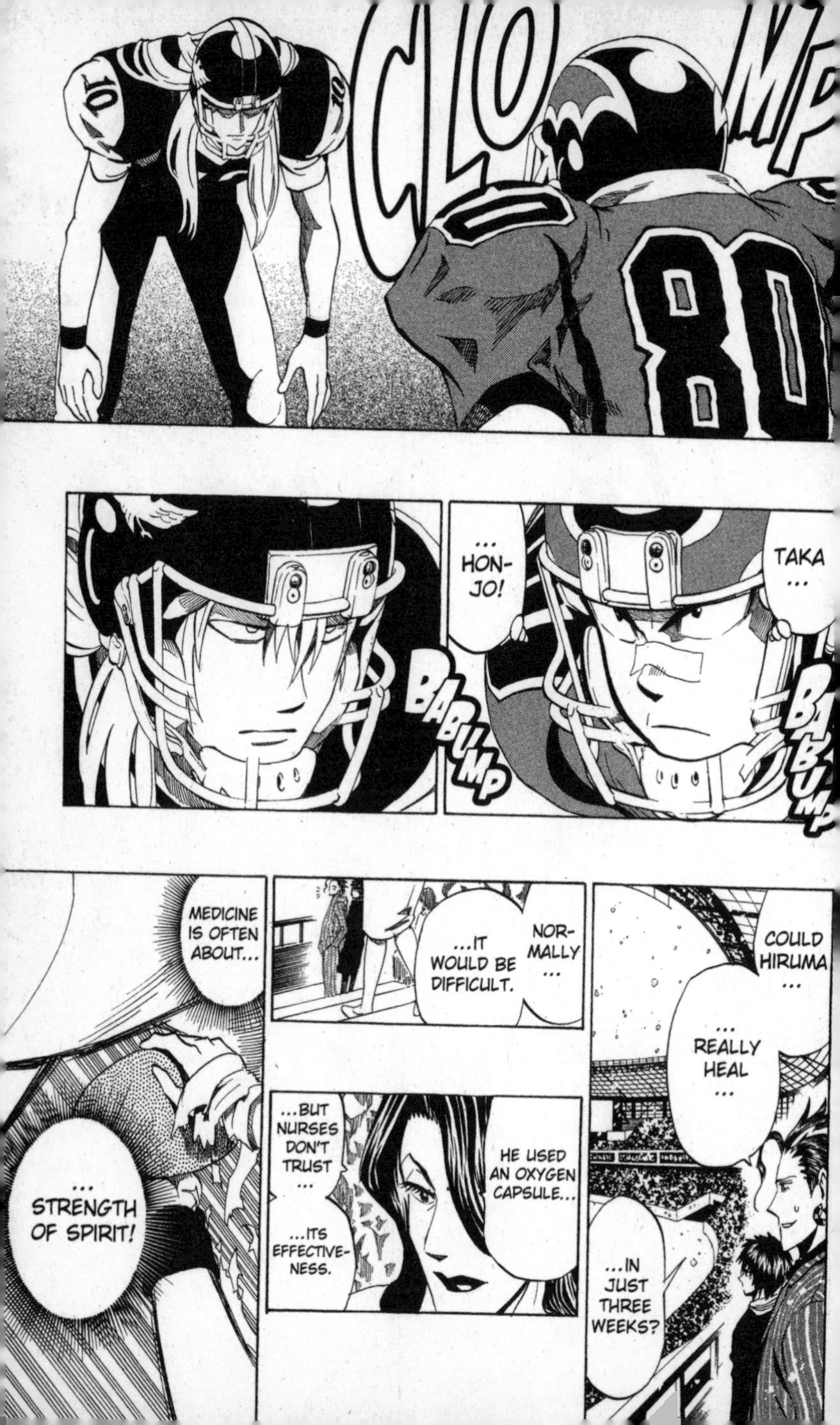
CLOMP
TAKA...
BABUMP
...HONJO!
BABUMP
COULD HIRUMA...
...REALLY HEAL...
...IN JUST THREE WEEKS?
NORMALLY...
...IT WOULD BE DIFFICULT.
HE USED AN OXYGEN CAPSULE...
...BUT NURSES DON'T TRUST...
...ITS EFFECTIVENESS.
MEDICINE IS OFTEN ABOUT...
...STRENGTH OF SPIRIT!

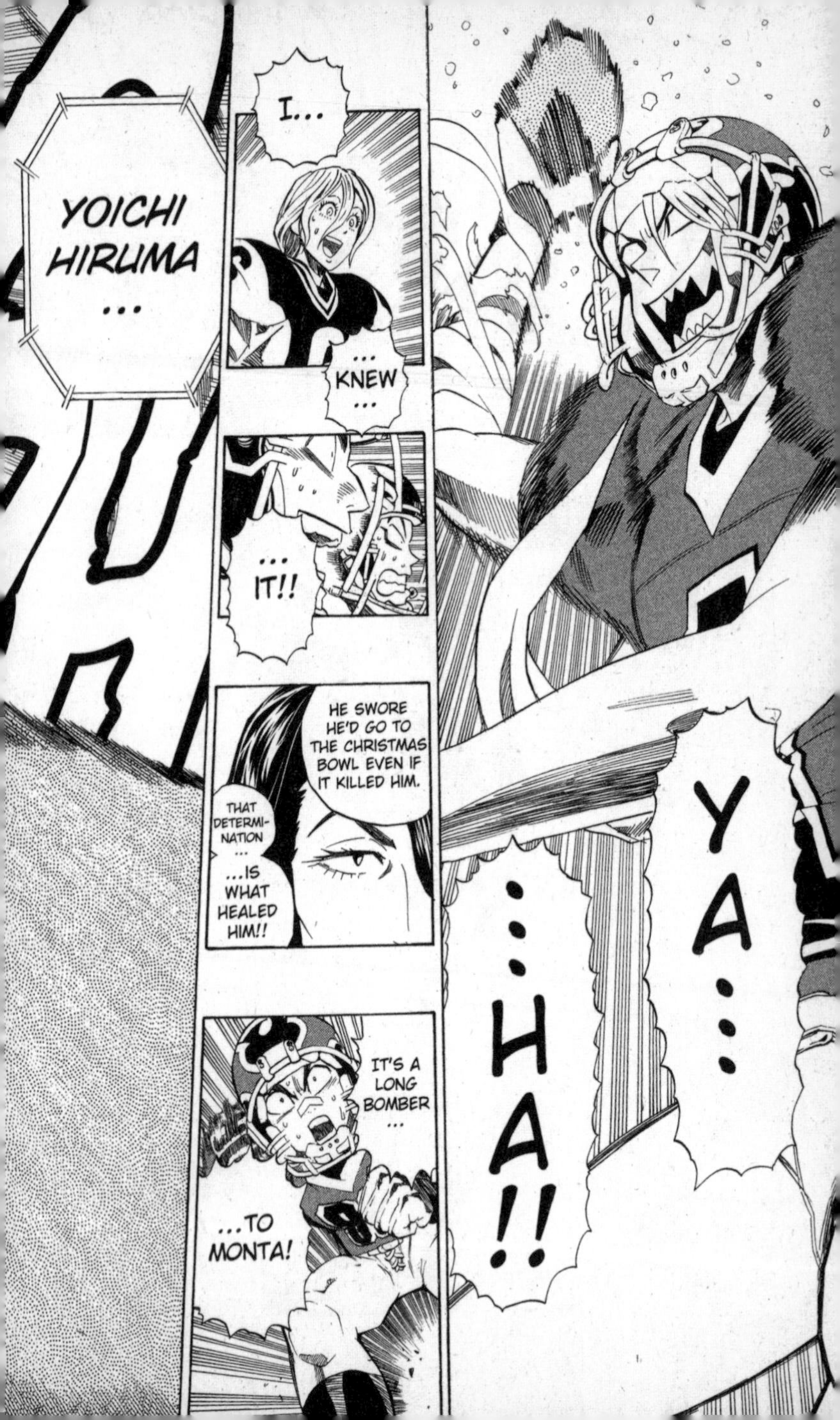
YA... ...HA!!
I...
...KNEW...
...IT!!
HE SWORE HE'D GO TO THE CHRISTMAS BOWL EVEN IF IT KILLED HIM.
THAT DETERMINATION...
...IS WHAT HEALED HIM!!
IT'S A LONG BOMBER...
...TO MONTA!
YOICHI HIRUMA ...

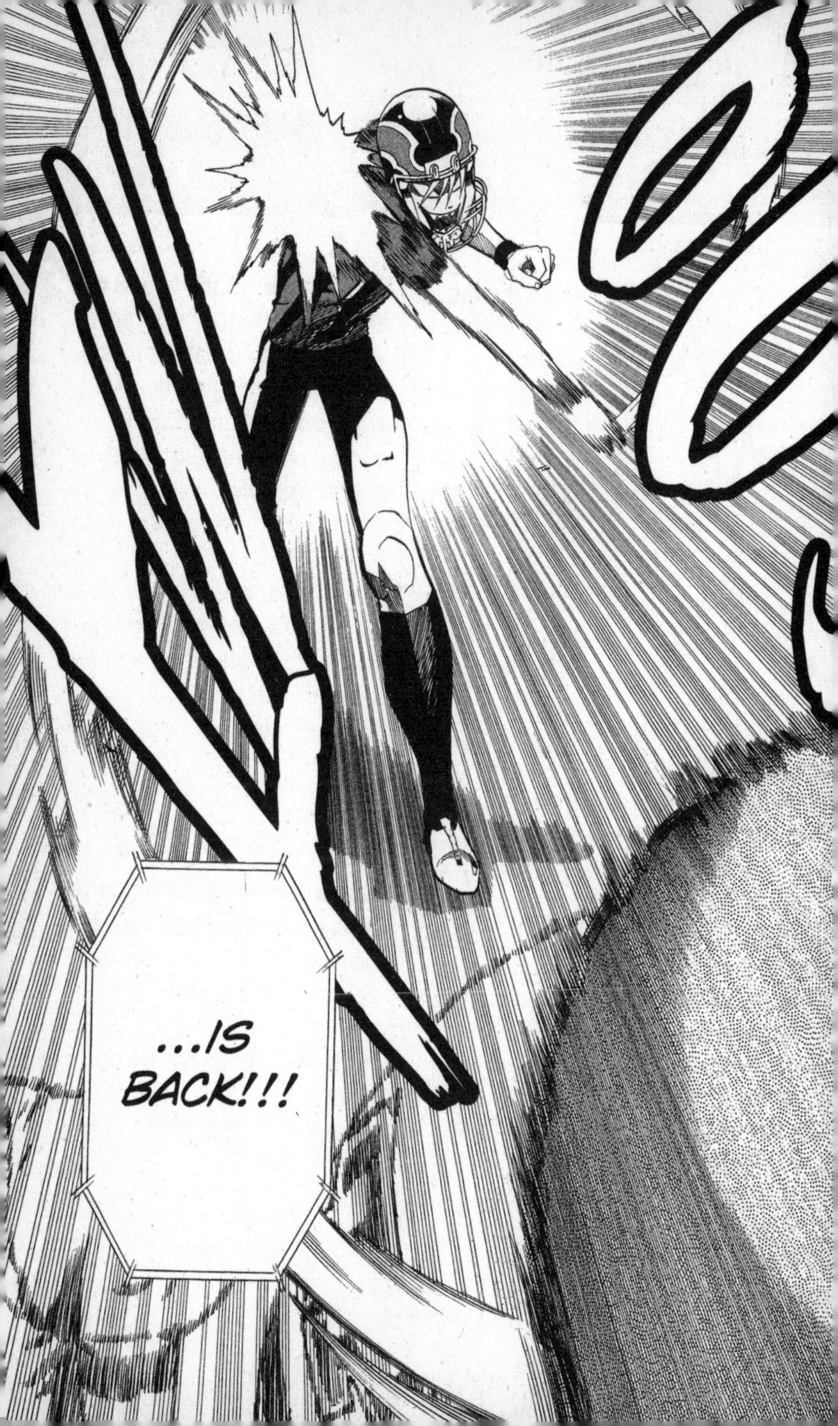
...IS BACK!!!

TEIKOKU PERSONAL HISTORIES

◀Reisuke Aki (Achilles)▶

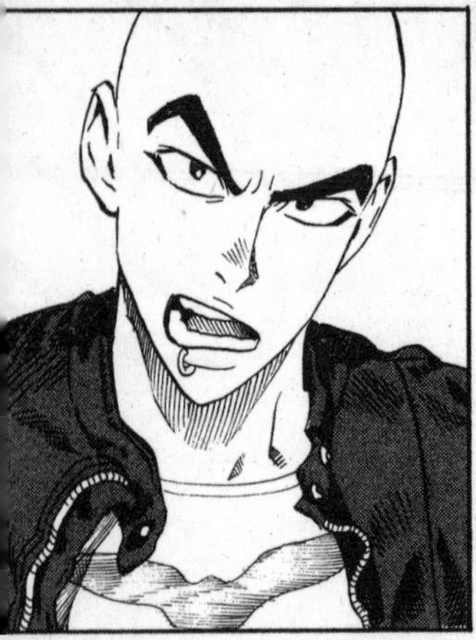

CURRENT AGE: 17

Height	173 cm
Weight	80 kg
Blood type	B
Birthday	August 28
Siblings	One elder brother
Talents/Hobbies	Listening to music
Favorite type of girl	
Karin	

0 YEARS OLD

Born in Kochi Prefecture. His father is a short-tempered, lecherous, softhearted man who is always getting dumped by women and ending up penniless. Reisuke is ***just like him***.

12 YEARS OLD

Enters Fukurahagi Junior High. He becomes an outstanding ace football player whose leg strength catches the eye of a Teikoku scout.

15 YEARS OLD

The scouts easily lure him to Teikoku High School with the ***obvious lie*** that he can date the beautiful cheerleaders.

He howls about not being able to get a girlfriend, but advances to first string in just one month.

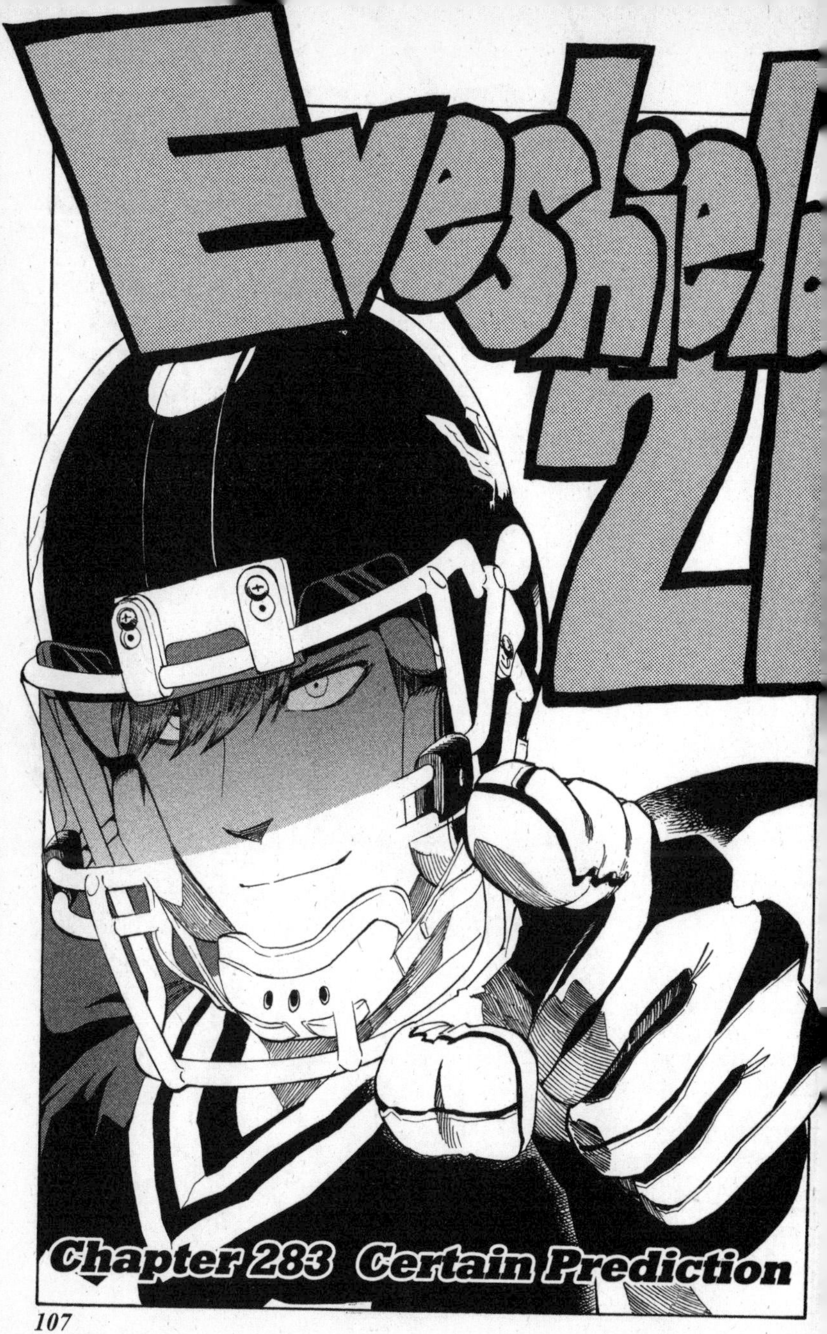
Chapter 283 Certain Prediction

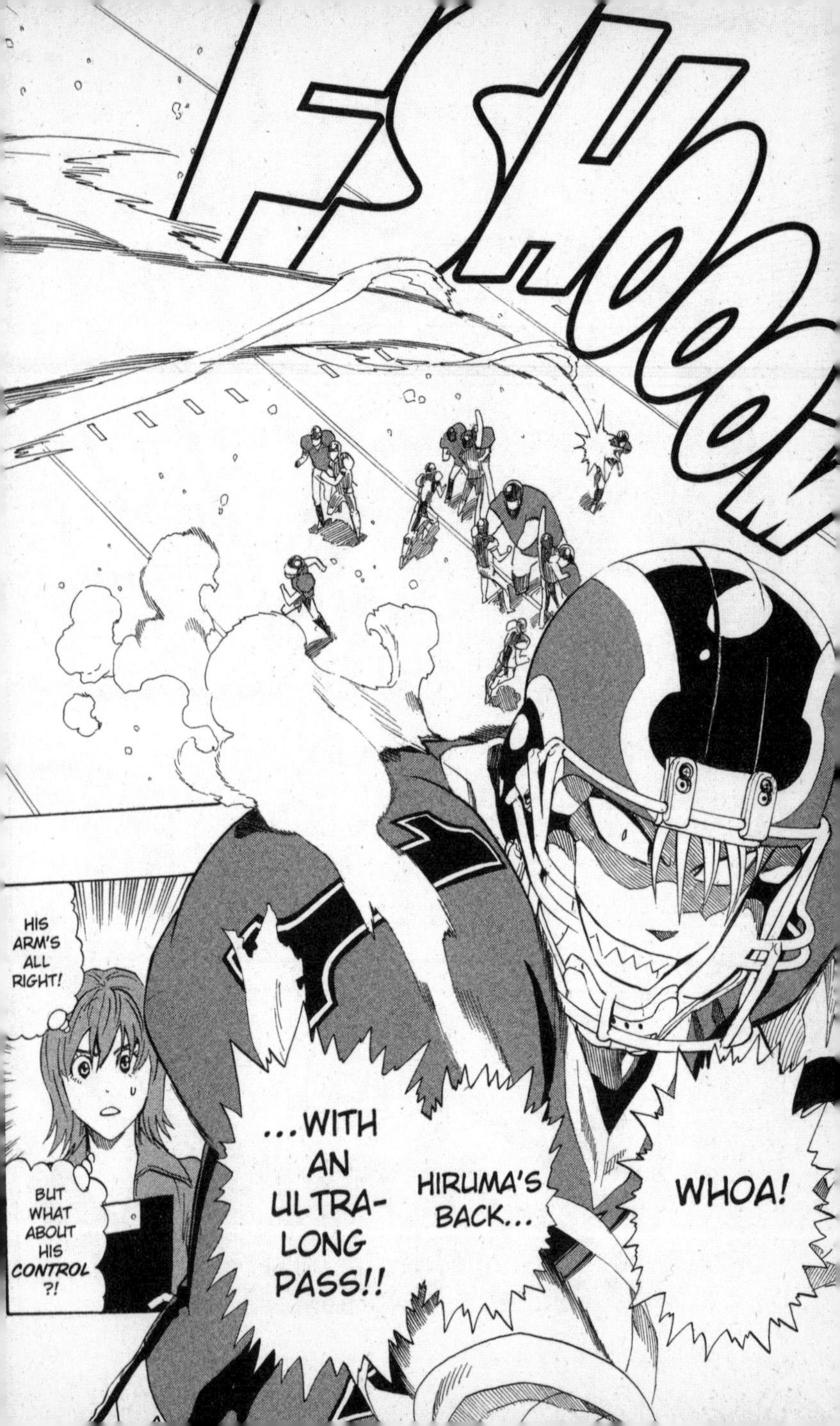
FSHOOOOM
WHOA!
HIRUMA'S BACK...
...WITH AN ULTRA-LONG PASS!!
HIS ARM'S ALL RIGHT!
BUT WHAT ABOUT HIS *CONTROL*?!

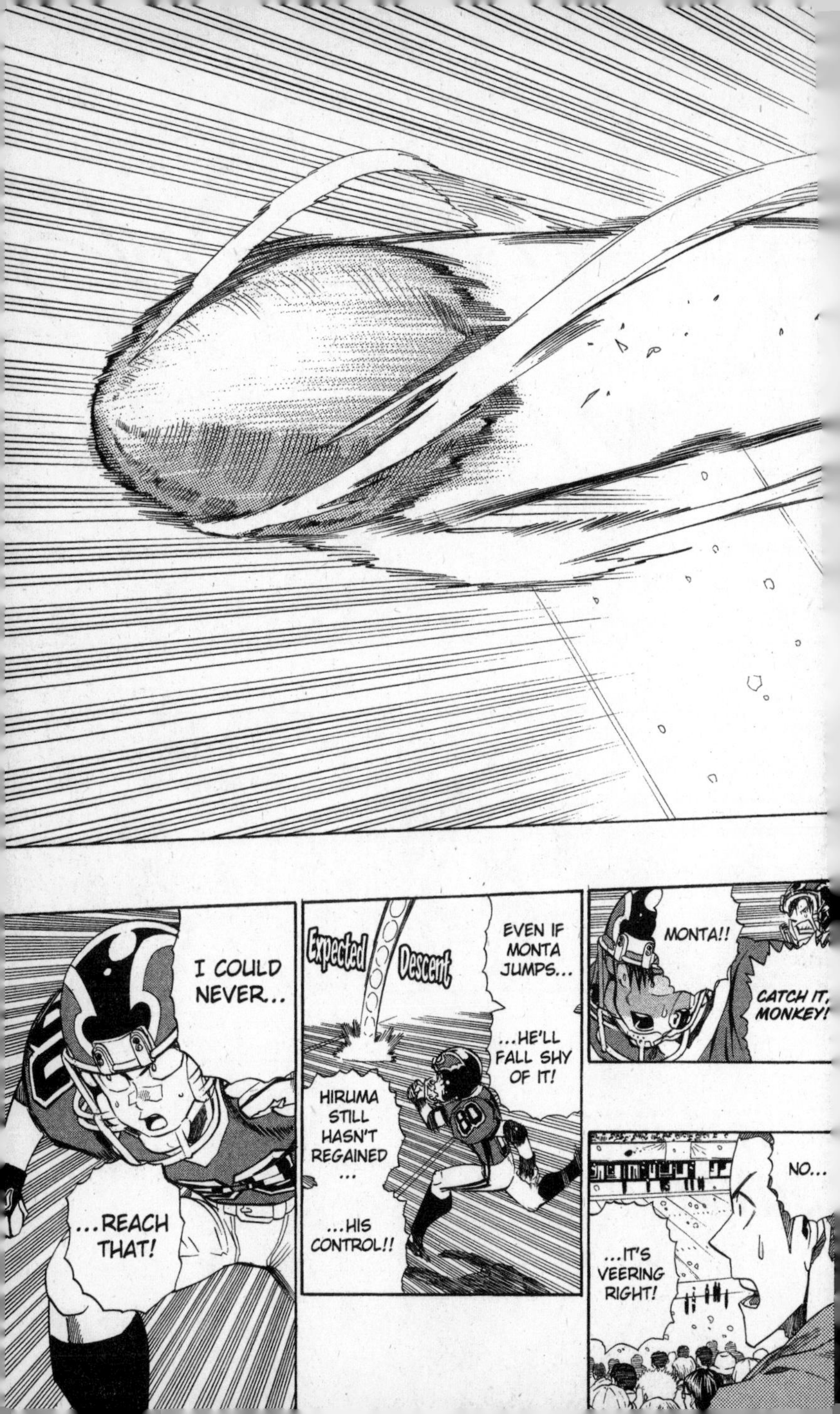
MONTA!!
CATCH IT, MONKEY!
NO...
...IT'S VEERING RIGHT!
EVEN IF MONTA JUMPS...
...HE'LL FALL SHY OF IT!
Expected Descent
HIRUMA STILL HASN'T REGAINED...
...HIS CONTROL!!
I COULD NEVER...
...REACH THAT!

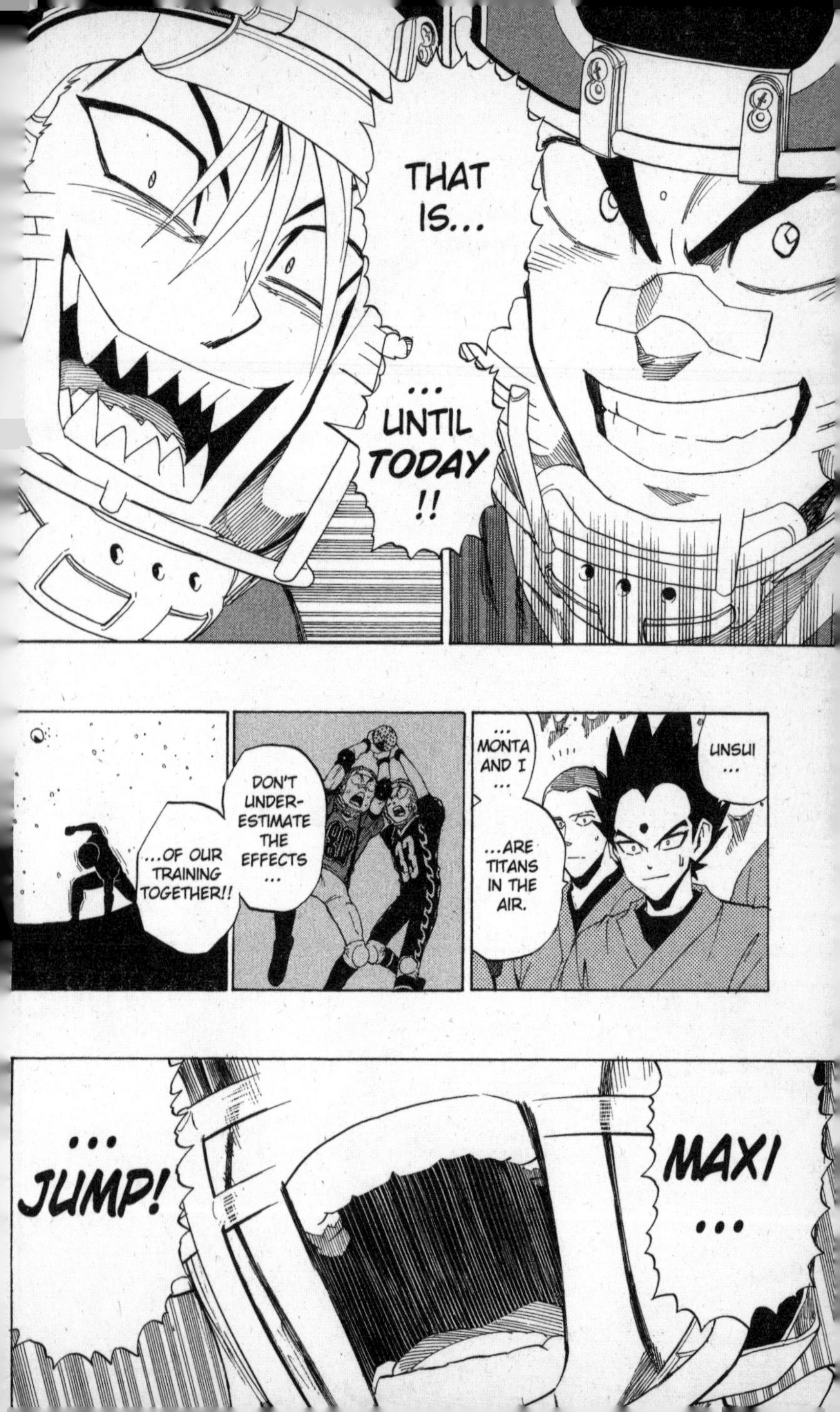
THAT IS...
... UNTIL TODAY !!
UNSUI ...
... MONTA AND I ...
...ARE TITANS IN THE AIR.
DON'T UNDER-ESTIMATE THE EFFECTS ...
...OF OUR TRAINING TOGETHER!!
MAXI ...
... JUMP!

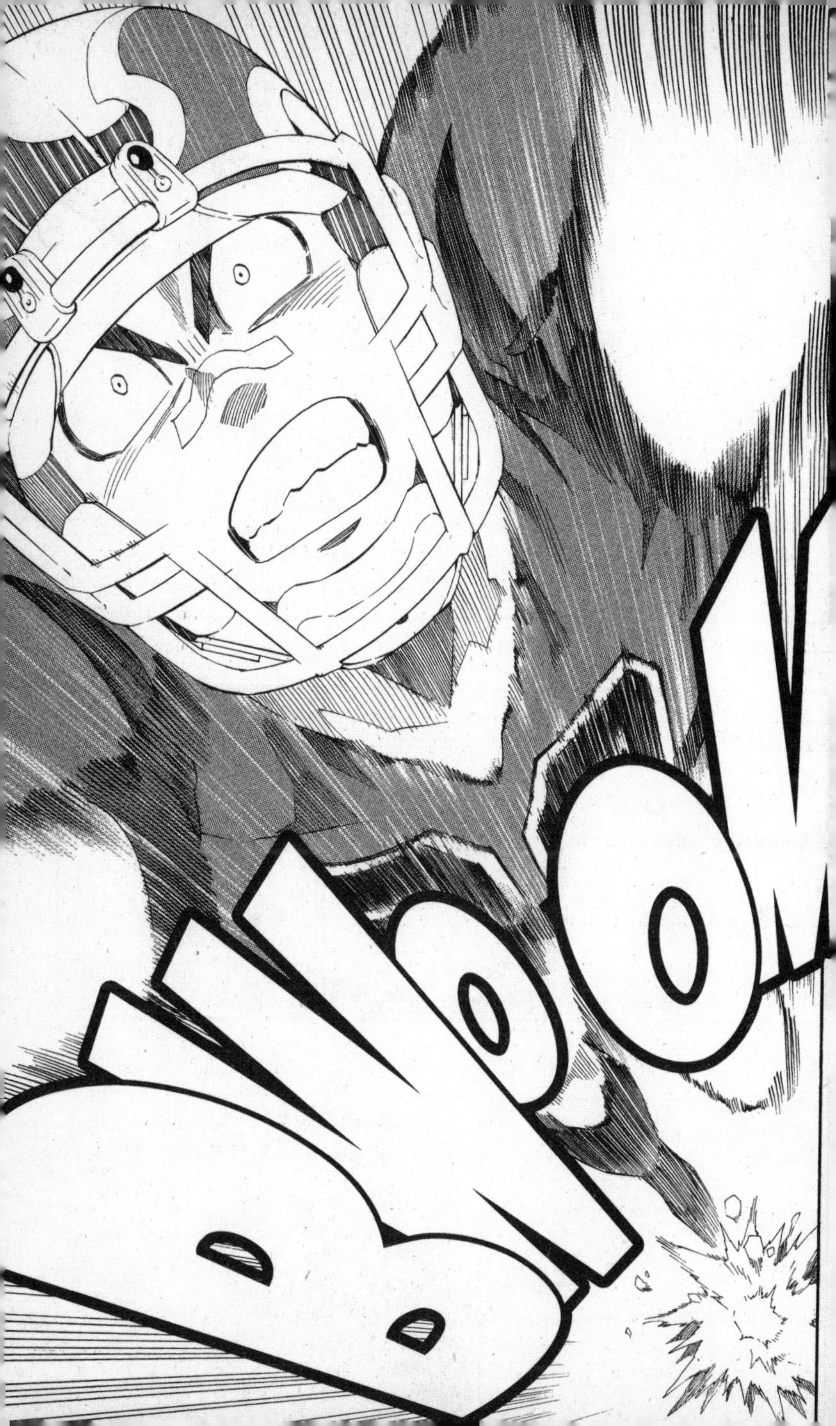
BOOM

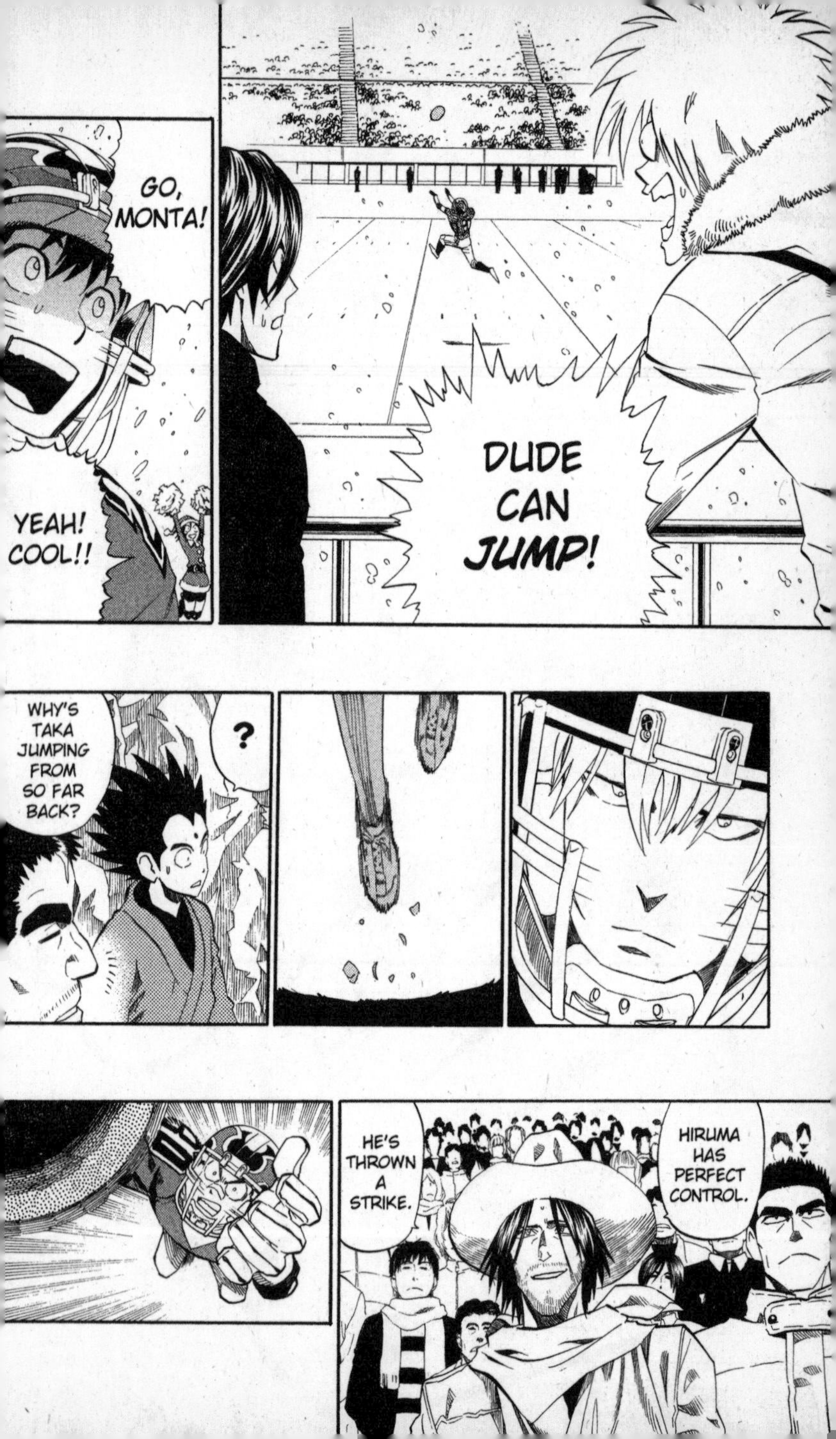
DUDE CAN JUMP!
GO, MONTA!
YEAH! COOL!!
?
WHY'S TAKA JUMPING FROM SO FAR BACK?
HIRUMA HAS PERFECT CONTROL.
HE'S THROWN A STRIKE.

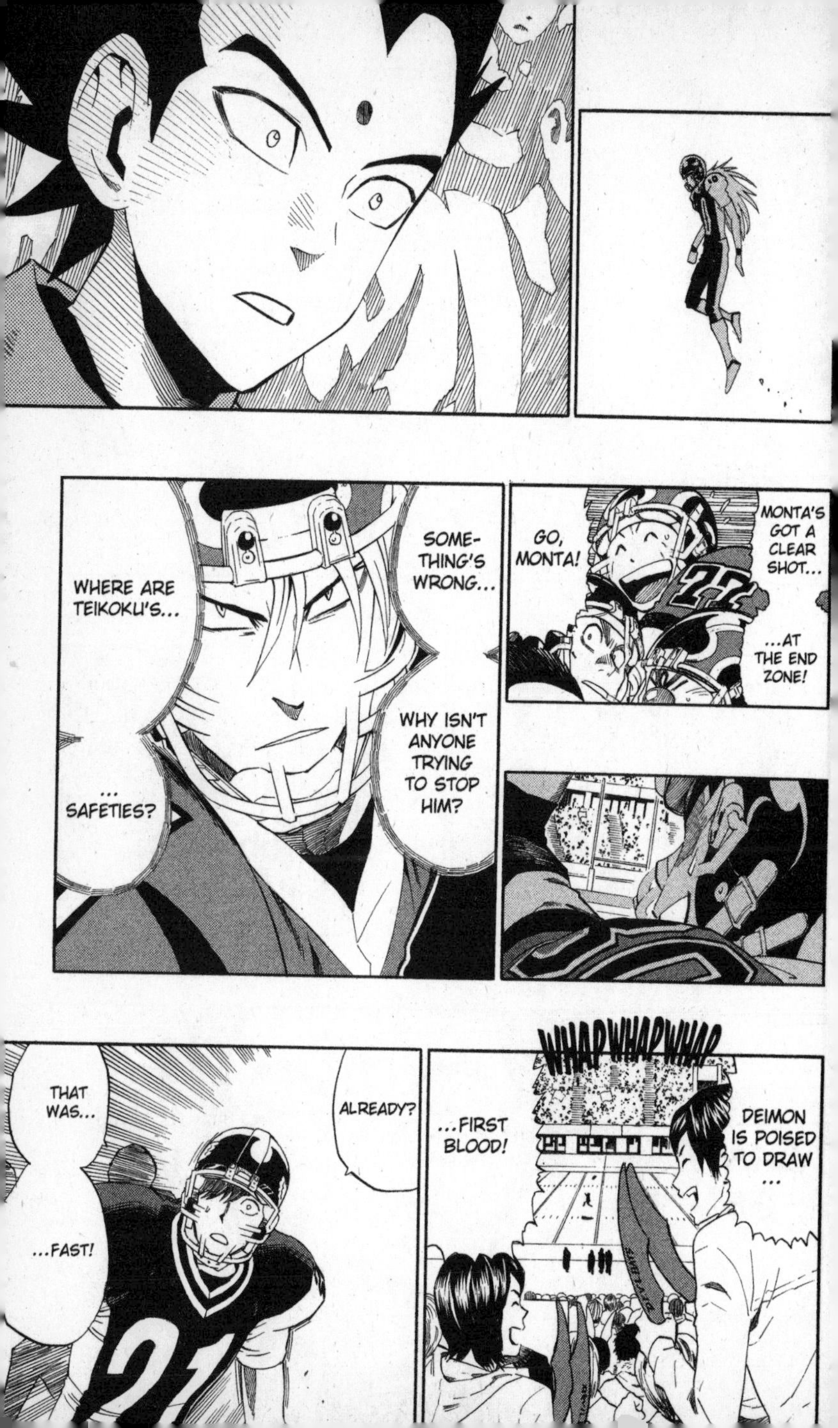
MONTA'S GOT A CLEAR SHOT...
...AT THE END ZONE!
GO, MONTA!
SOME-THING'S WRONG...
WHERE ARE TEIKOKU'S...
WHY ISN'T ANYONE TRYING TO STOP HIM?
...SAFETIES?
WHAP WHAP WHAP
DEIMON IS POISED TO DRAW...
...FIRST BLOOD!
ALREADY?
THAT WAS...
...FAST!

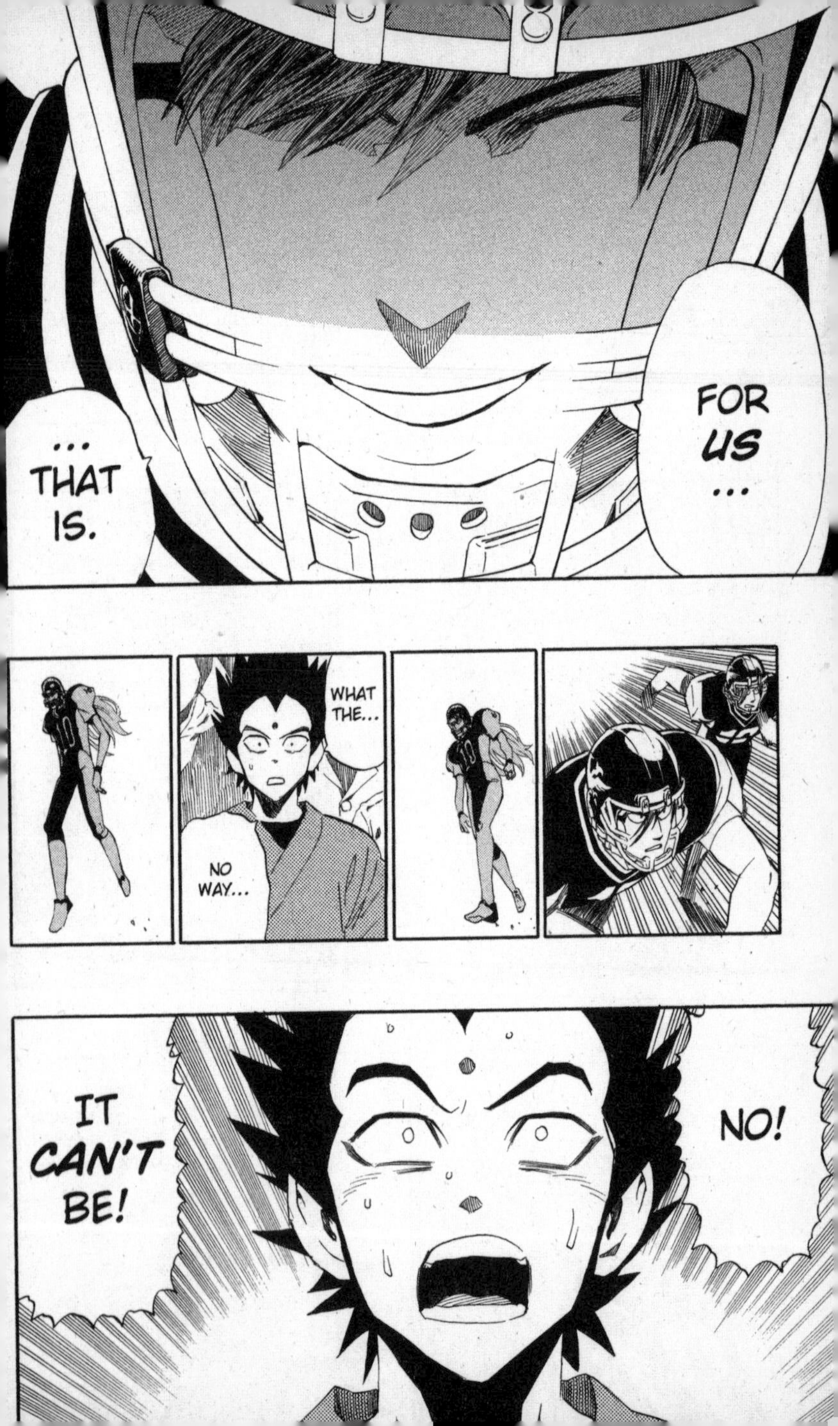
FOR US...
...THAT IS.
WHAT THE...
NO WAY...
NO!
IT CAN'T BE!

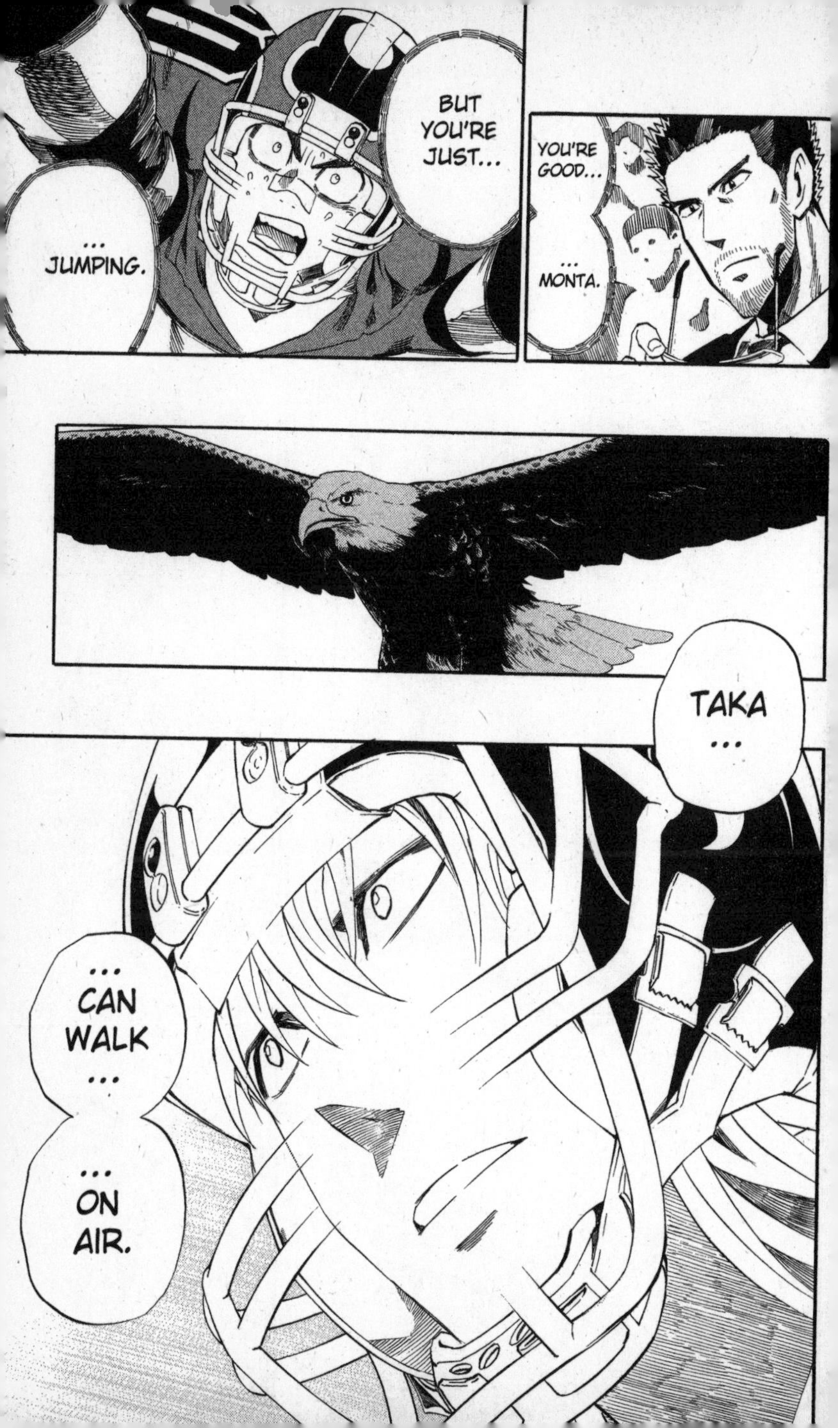
YOU'RE GOOD...
...MONTA.
BUT YOU'RE JUST...
...JUMPING.
TAKA ...
...CAN WALK ...
...ON AIR.

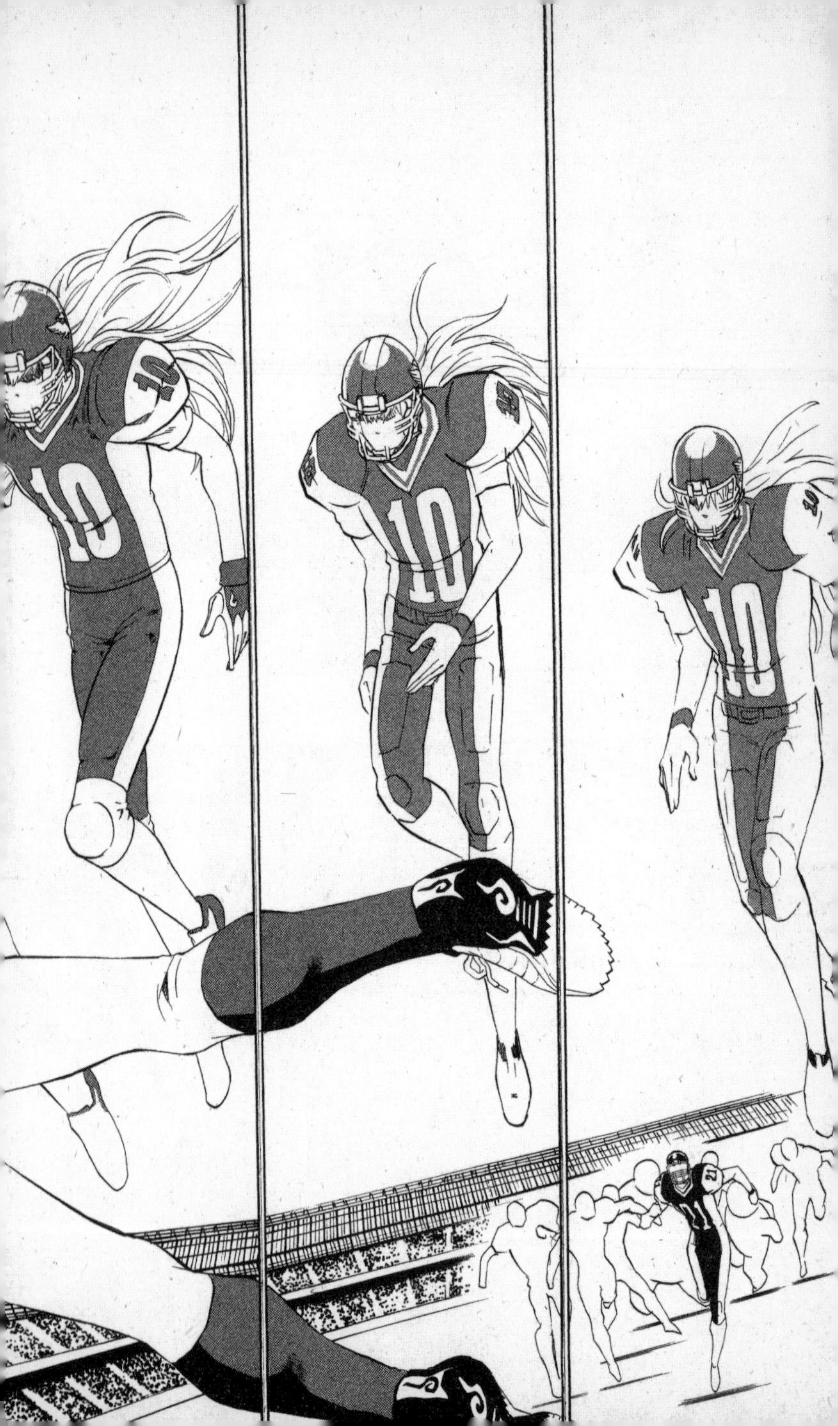

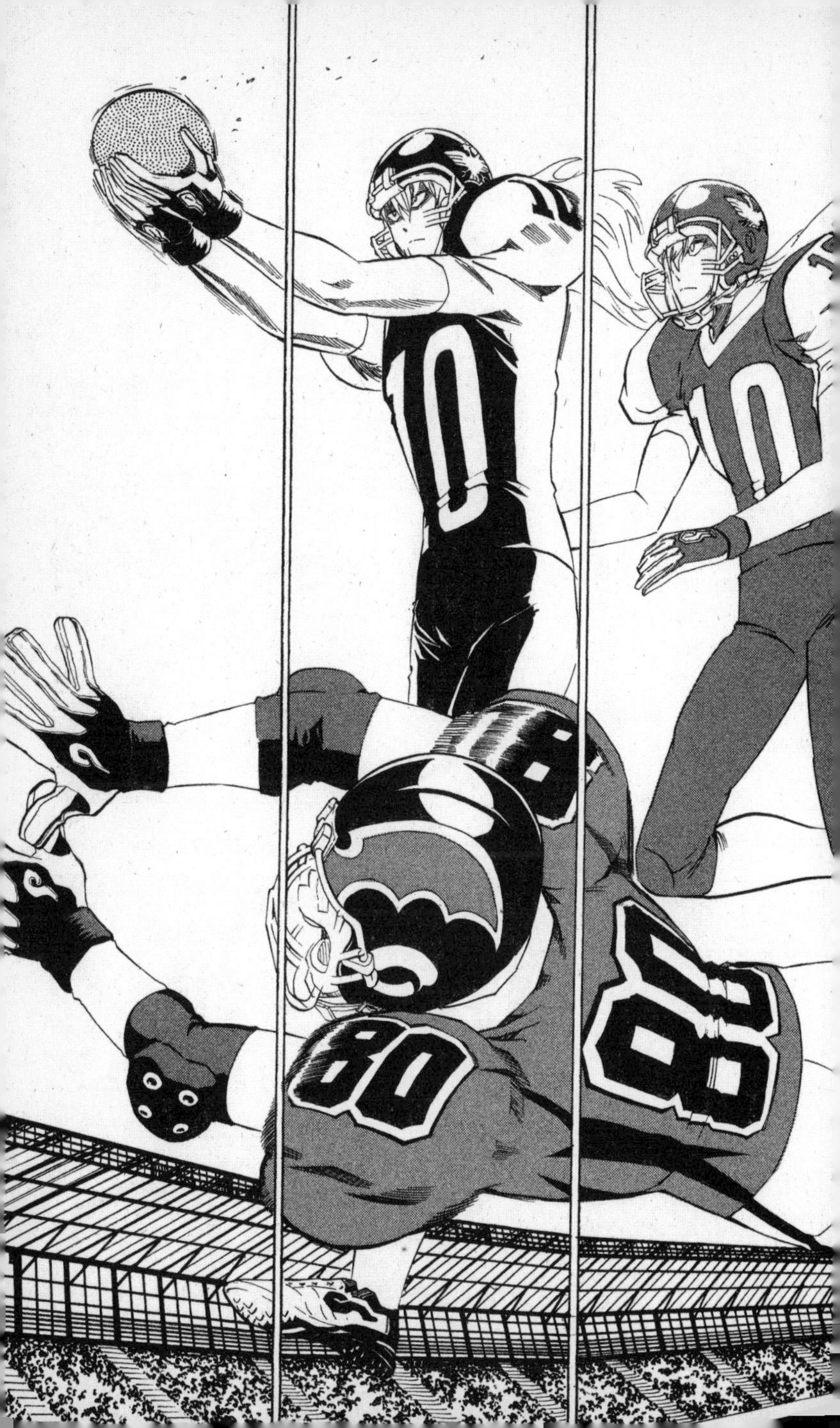

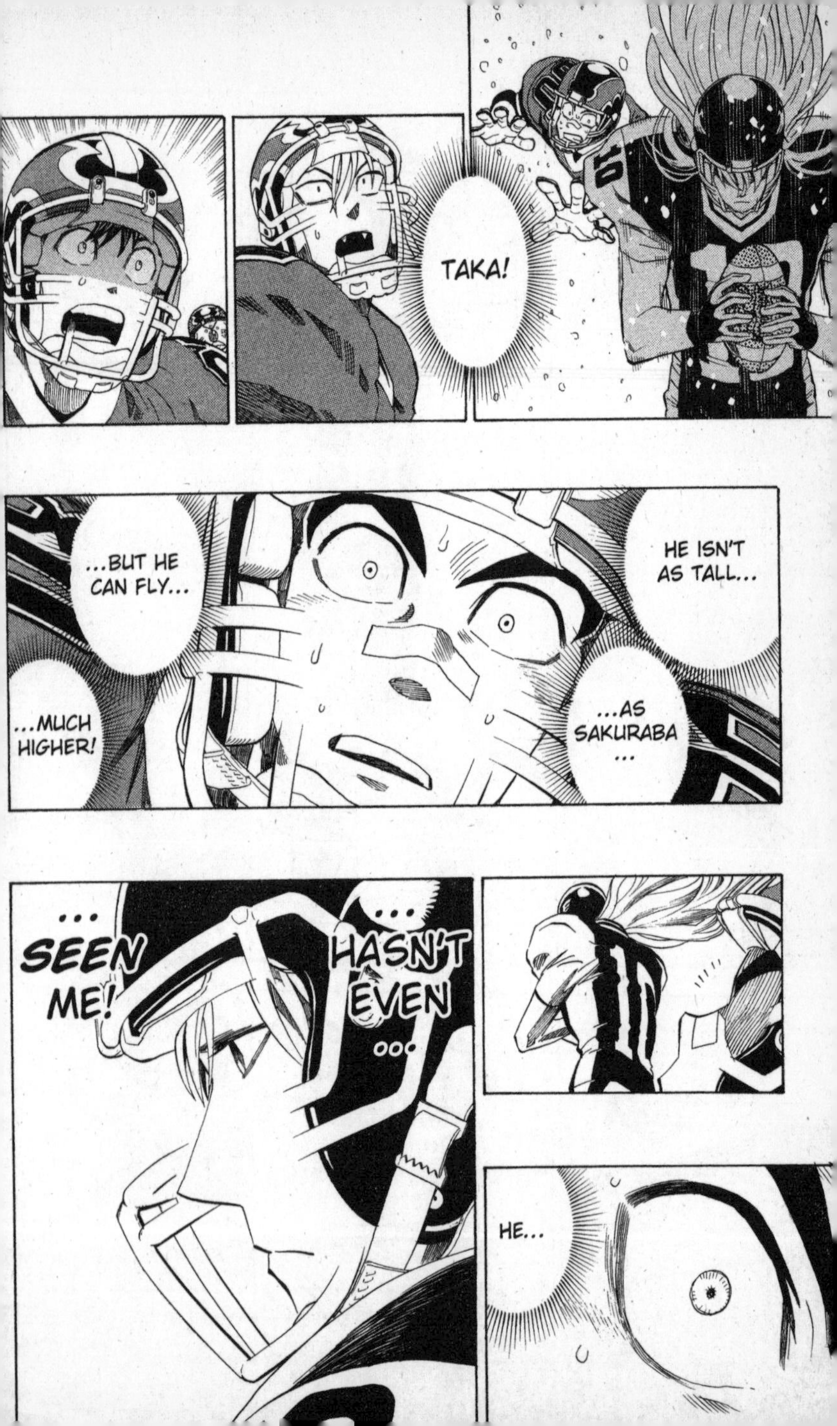
TAKA!
HE ISN'T AS TALL...
...AS SAKURABA ...
...BUT HE CAN FLY...
...MUCH HIGHER!
HE...
... HASN'T EVEN ...
... SEEN ME!

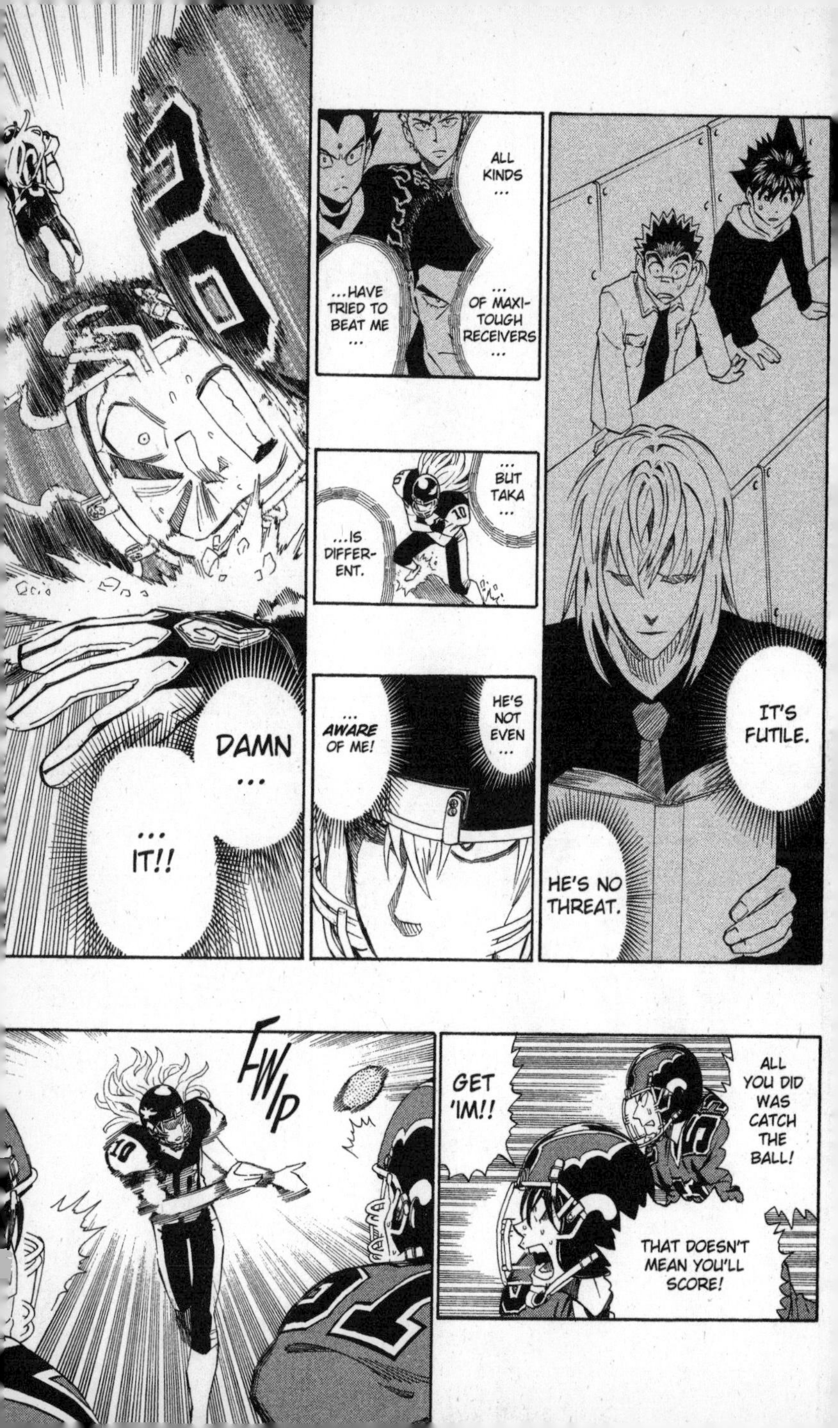
IT'S FUTILE.
HE'S NO THREAT.
ALL KINDS ...
... OF MAXI-TOUGH RECEIVERS ...
...HAVE TRIED TO BEAT ME ...
... BUT TAKA ...
...IS DIFFERENT.
HE'S NOT EVEN ...
... AWARE OF ME!
DAMN ...
... IT!!
ALL YOU DID WAS CATCH THE BALL!
GET 'IM!!
THAT DOESN'T MEAN YOU'LL SCORE!
FWIP

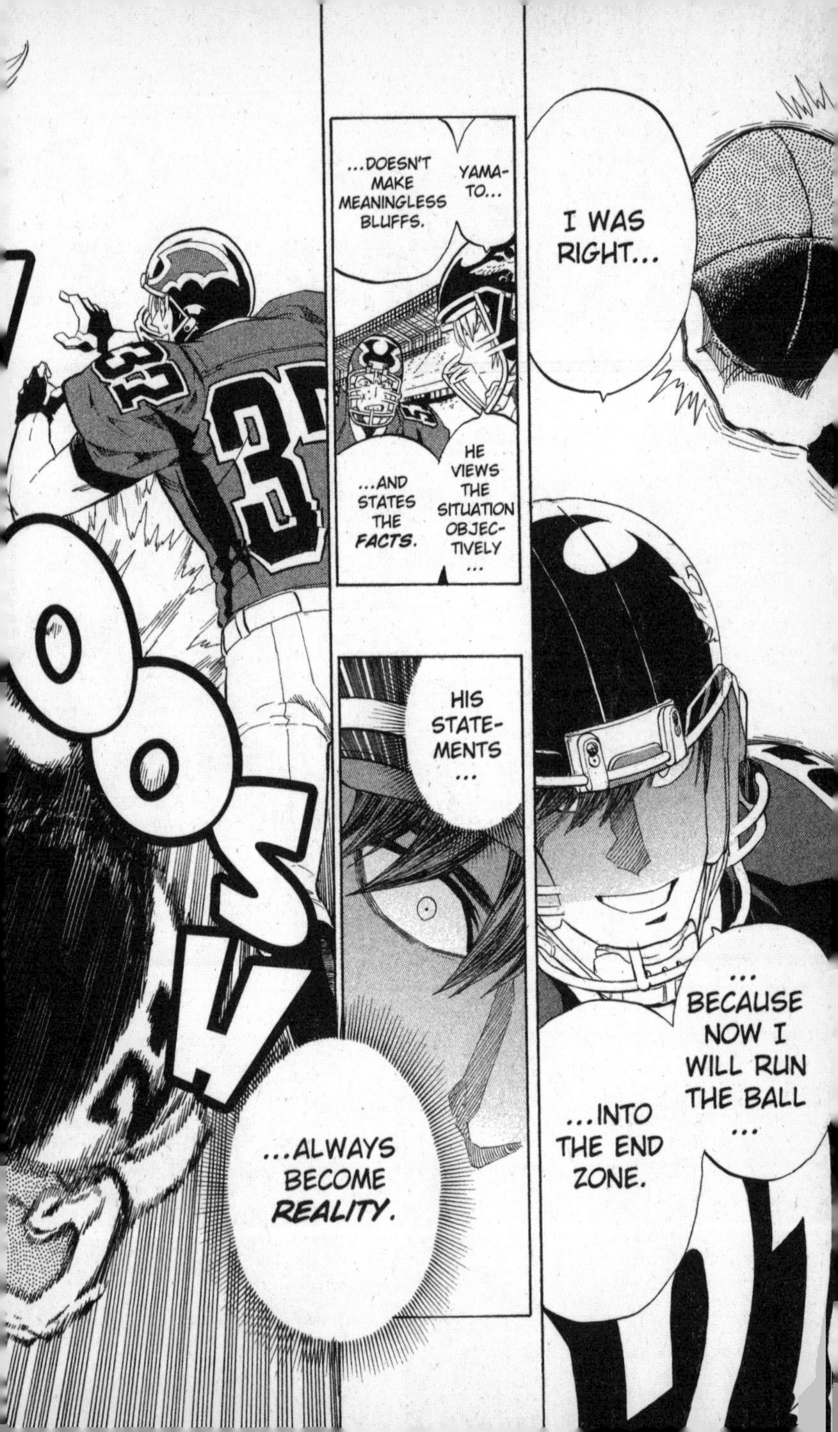
I WAS RIGHT...
...BECAUSE NOW I WILL RUN THE BALL...
...INTO THE END ZONE.
YAMA-TO...
...DOESN'T MAKE MEANINGLESS BLUFFS.
HE VIEWS THE SITUATION OBJECTIVELY...
...AND STATES THE FACTS.
HIS STATEMENTS...
...ALWAYS BECOME REALITY.
OOOSH!

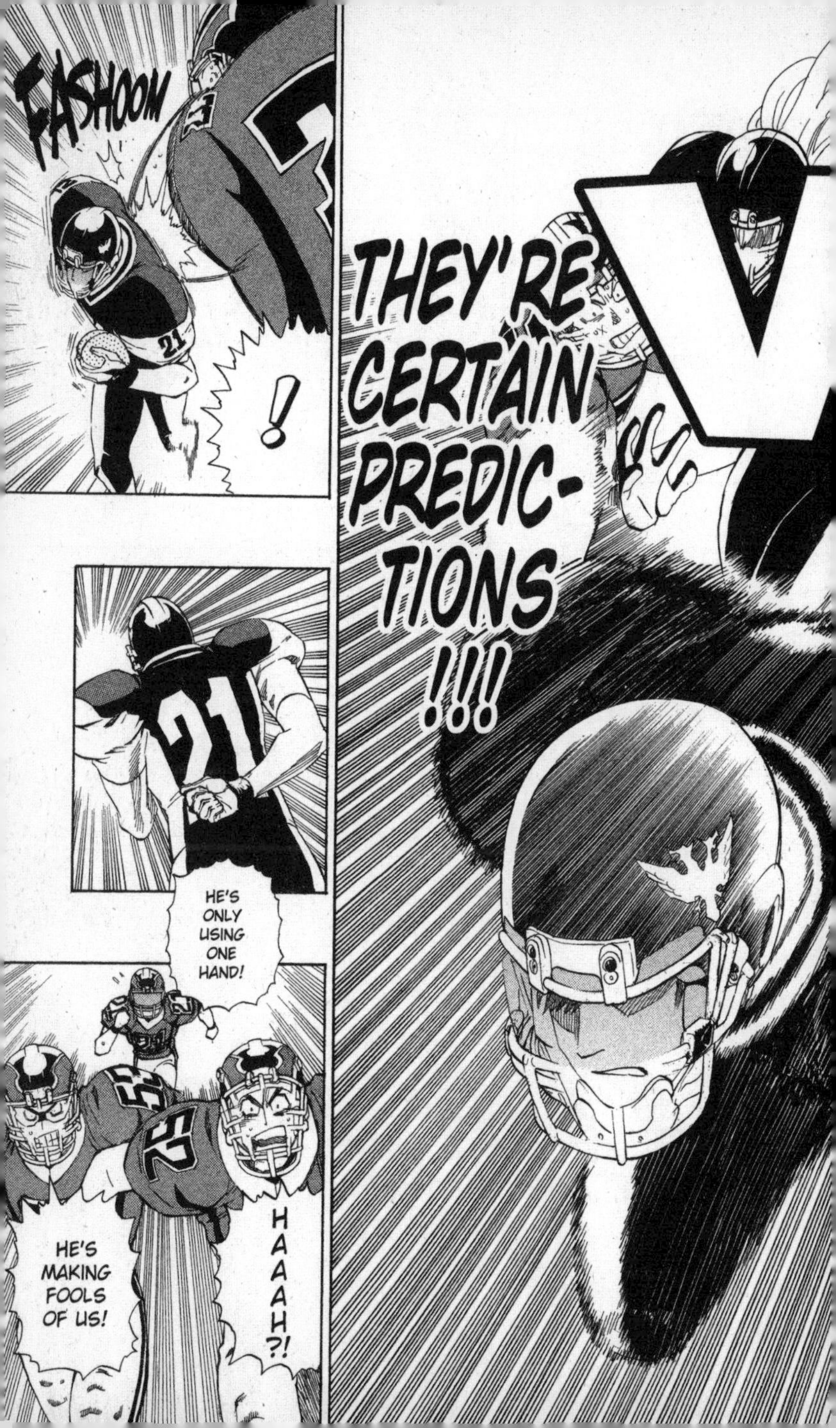
THEY'RE CERTAIN PREDICTIONS!!!
FASHOOM
!
HE'S ONLY USING ONE HAND!
HAAAAH?!
HE'S MAKING FOOLS OF US!

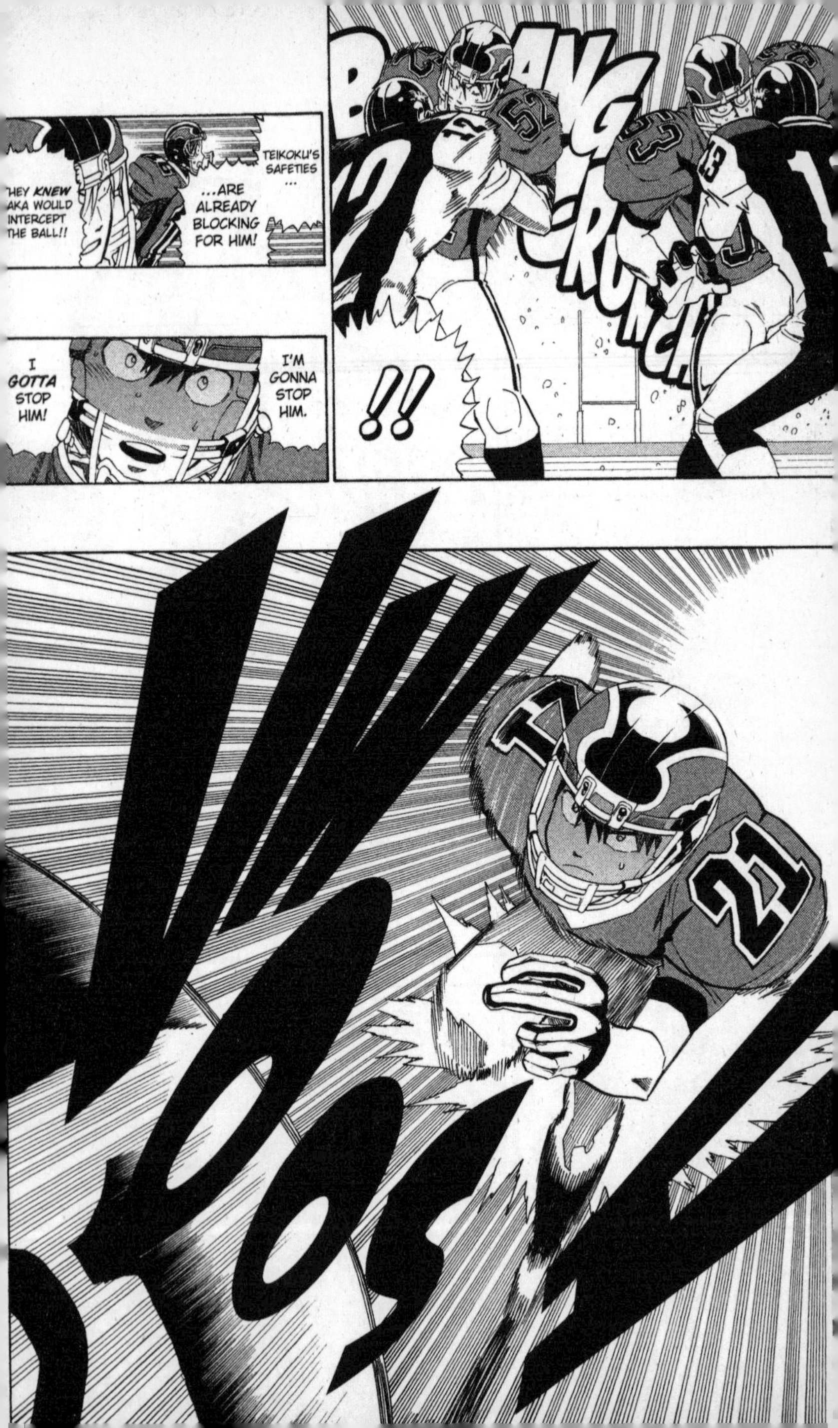
BANG
CRUNCH
!!
TEIKOKU'S SAFETIES ...
...ARE ALREADY BLOCKING FOR HIM!
THEY KNEW AKA WOULD INTERCEPT THE BALL!!
I'M GONNA STOP HIM.
I GOTTA STOP HIM!

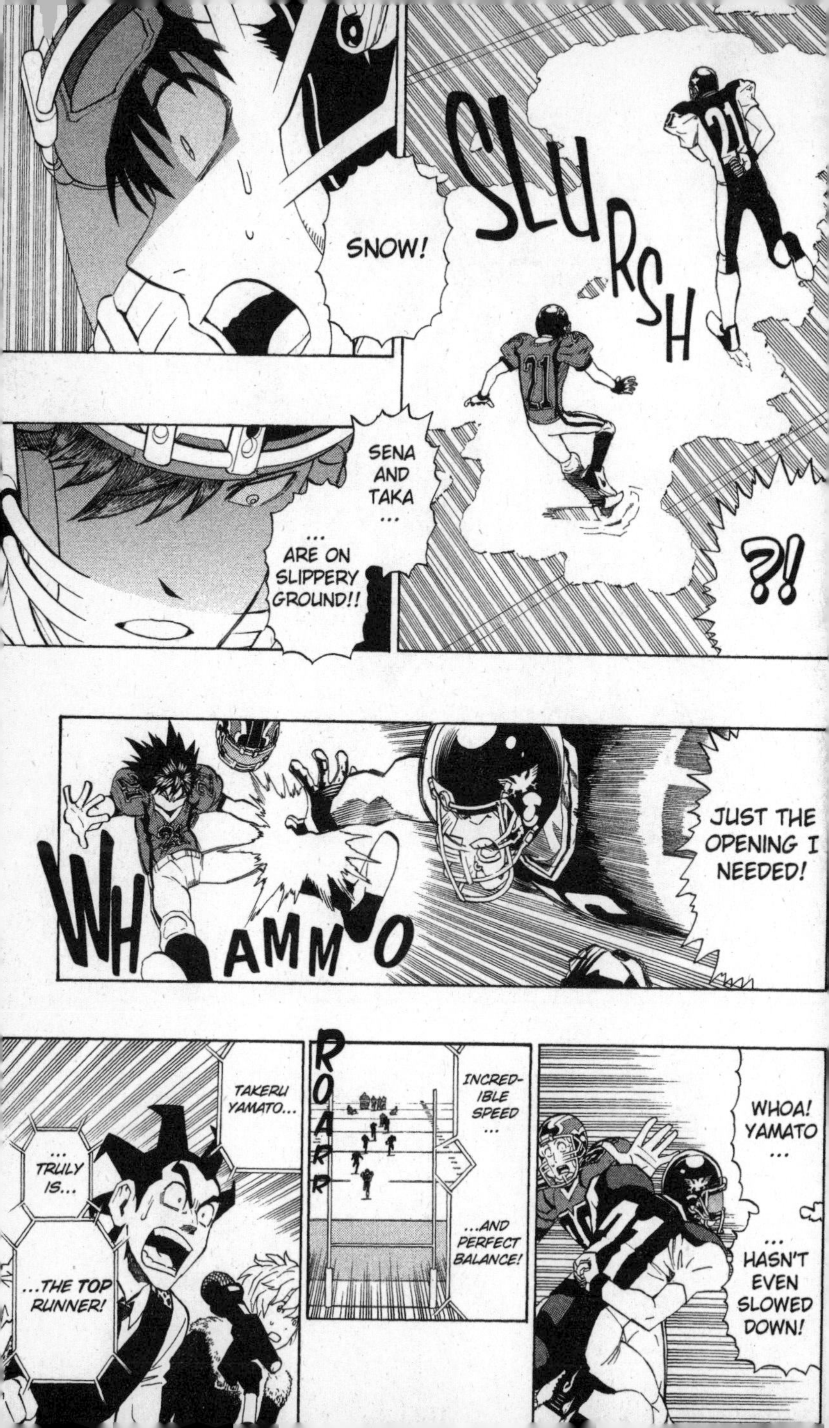
SLURSH
?!
SNOW!
SENA AND TAKA...
...ARE ON SLIPPERY GROUND!!
JUST THE OPENING I NEEDED!
WHAMMO
WHOA! YAMATO...
...HASN'T EVEN SLOWED DOWN!
ROARR
INCRED-IBLE SPEED...
...AND PERFECT BALANCE!
TAKERU YAMATO...
...TRULY IS...
...THE TOP RUNNER!

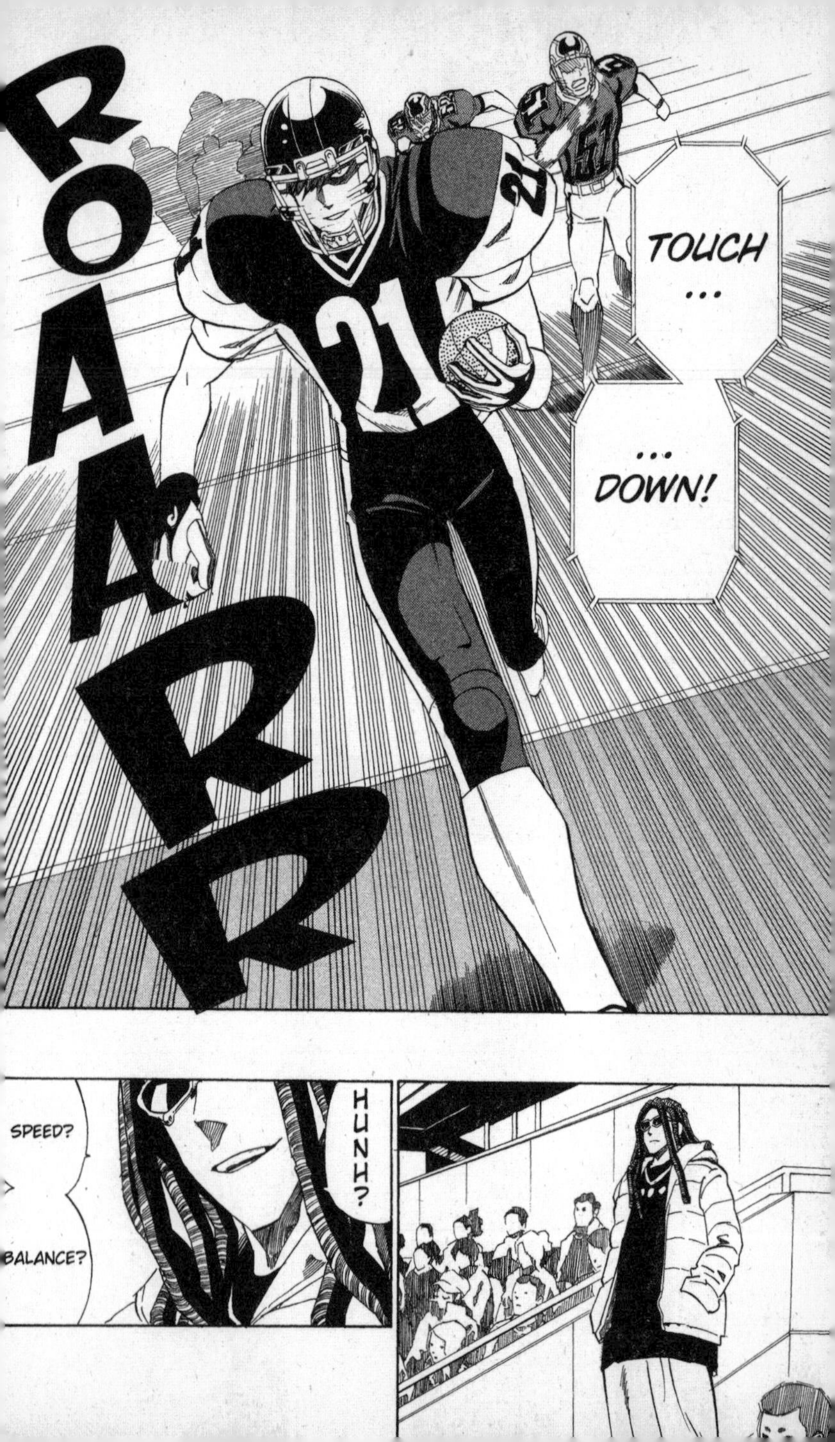
ROARR
TOUCH ...
... DOWN!
HUNH?
SPEED?
BALANCE?

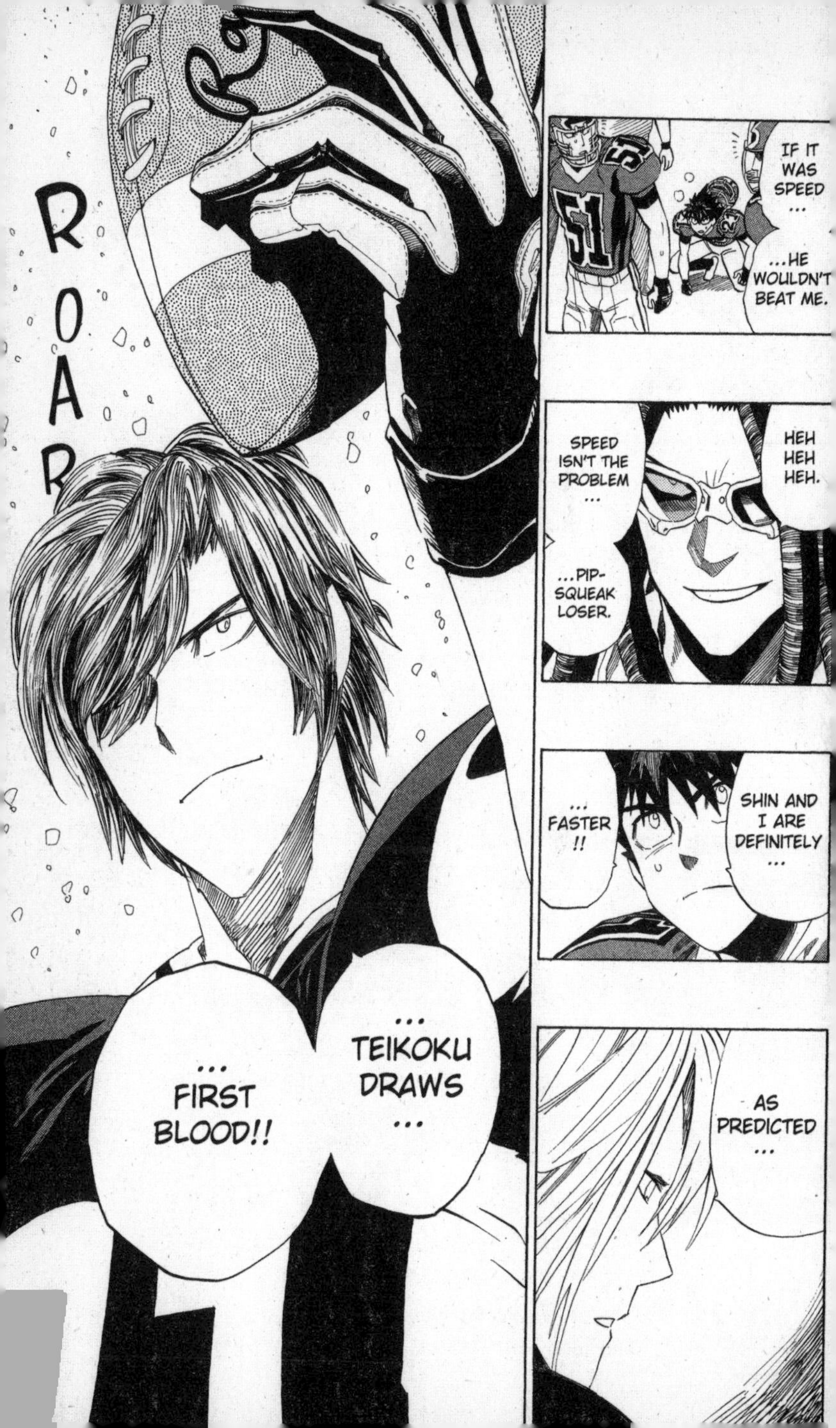
IF IT WAS SPEED ...
...HE WOULDN'T BEAT ME.
HEH HEH HEH.
SPEED ISN'T THE PROBLEM ...
...PIP-SQUEAK LOSER.
SHIN AND I ARE DEFINITELY ...
... FASTER !!
AS PREDICTED ...
ROAR
... TEIKOKU DRAWS ...
... FIRST BLOOD!!

Investigation File #137

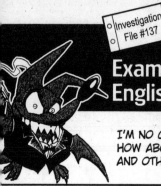

Examine the players' English ability!

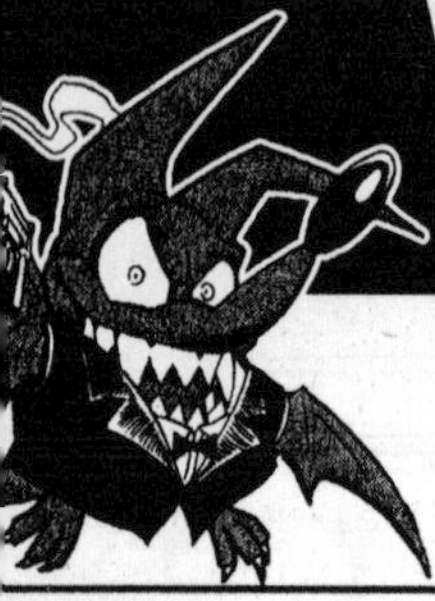

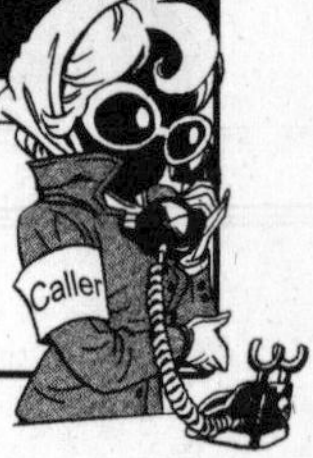
Caller

I'M NO GOOD AT ENGLISH. HOW ABOUT THE DEVIL BATS AND OTHER TEAMS?

Caller name: Bean Rice in Tokyo Prefecture

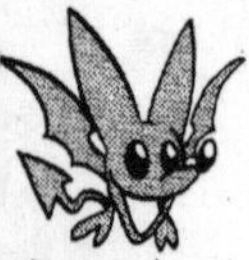

HERE'S WHAT WE DUG UP ON THE GUYS WHO KNOW SOME ENGLISH! YA-HA!

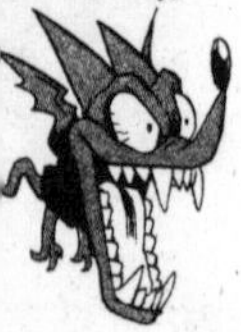

OF COURSE, EVERYONE AT NASA HIGH SCHOOL IS GOOD AT ENGLISH, SO WE LEFT THEM OUT!

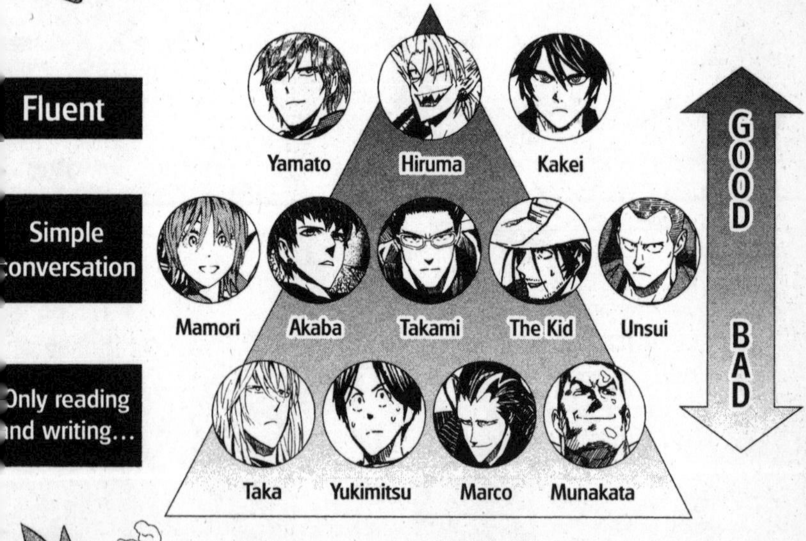
Fluent
Yamato
Hiruma
Kakei
Simple conversation
Mamori
Akaba
Takami
The Kid
Unsui
Only reading and writing...
Taka
Yukimitsu
Marco
Munakata
GOOD
BAD

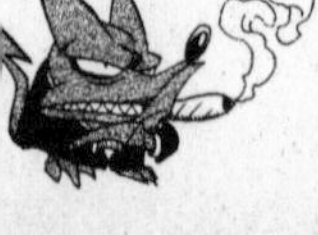

ALL THE OTHER GUYS ARE STUCK AT A "THIS IS A PEN" LEVEL...ESPECIALLY SENA...

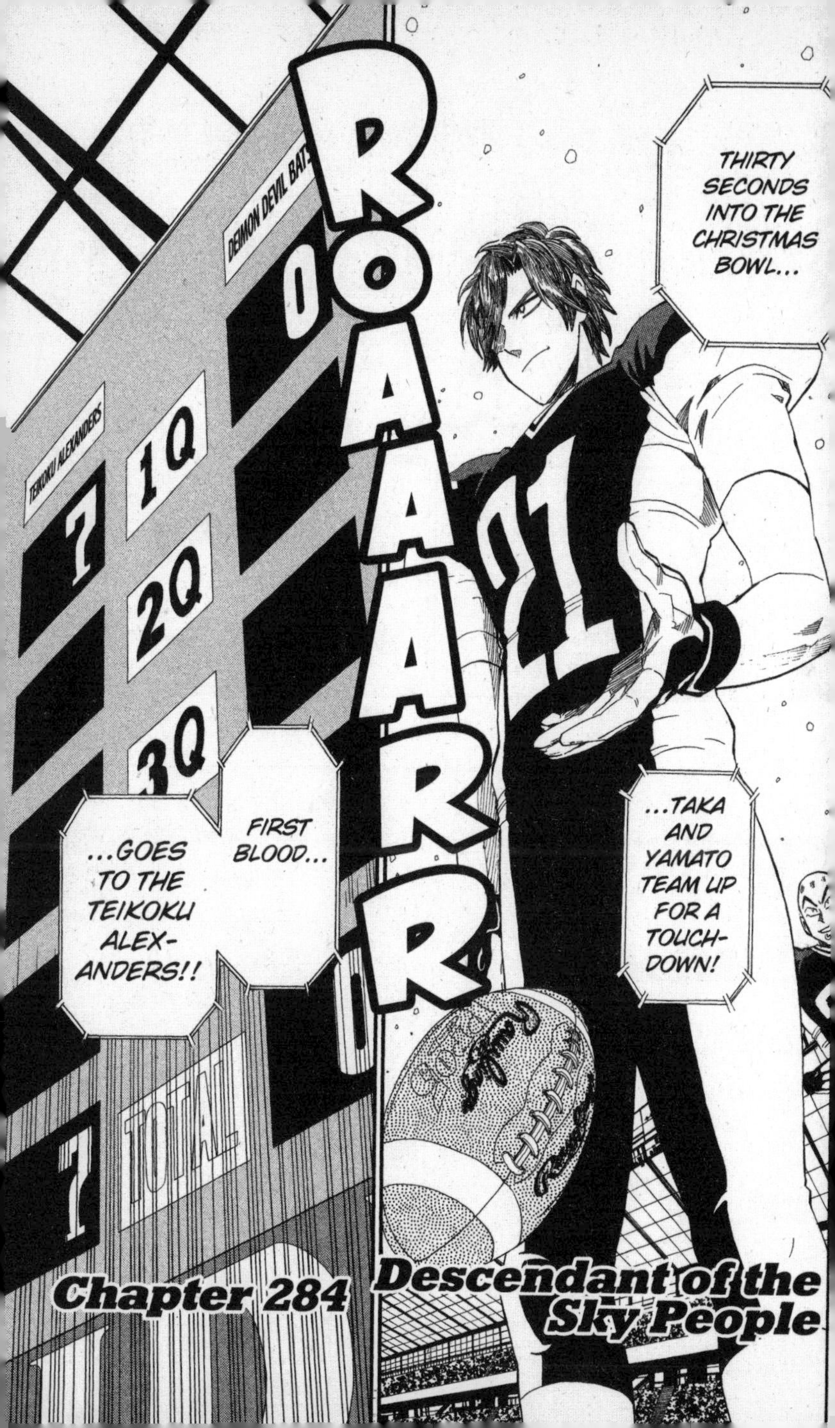
THIRTY SECONDS INTO THE CHRISTMAS BOWL...
...TAKA AND YAMATO TEAM UP FOR A TOUCHDOWN!
ROAAARR
DEIMON DEVIL BATS
TEIKOKU ALEXANDERS
0
1Q
7
2Q
3Q
FIRST BLOOD...
...GOES TO THE TEIKOKU ALEX-ANDERS!!
TOTAL
7

Chapter 284 Descendant of the Sky People

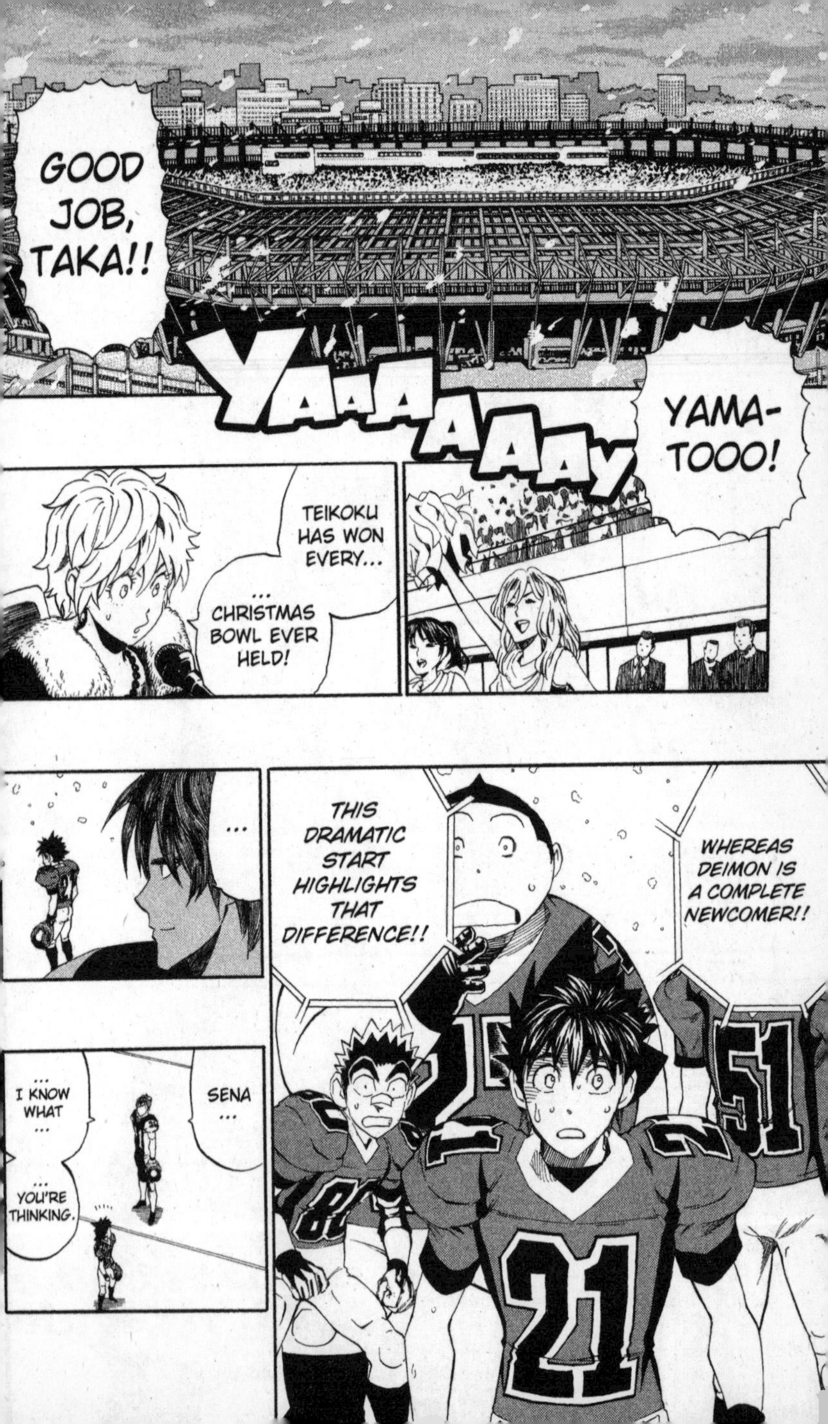
GOOD JOB, TAKA!!
YAAAAAAY
YAMA-TOOO!
TEIKOKU HAS WON EVERY...
...CHRISTMAS BOWL EVER HELD!
WHEREAS DEIMON IS A COMPLETE NEWCOMER!!
THIS DRAMATIC START HIGHLIGHTS THAT DIFFERENCE!!
...
SENA...
...I KNOW WHAT...
...YOU'RE THINKING.

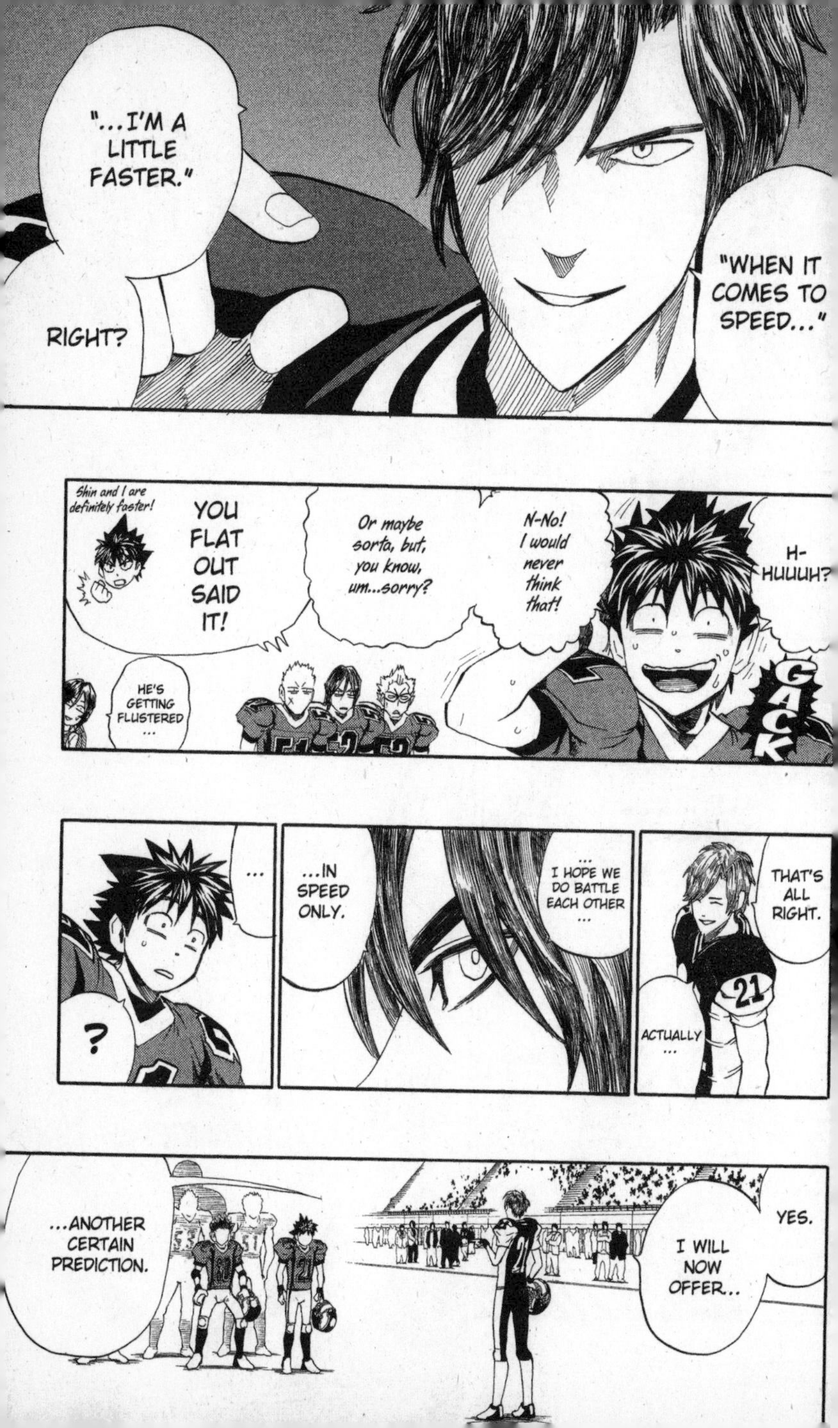
"WHEN IT COMES TO SPEED..."
"...I'M A LITTLE FASTER."
RIGHT?
H-HUUUH?
GACK
N-No! I would never think that!
Or maybe sorta, but, you know, um...sorry?
YOU FLAT OUT SAID IT!
Shin and I are definitely faster!
HE'S GETTING FLUSTERED...
THAT'S ALL RIGHT.
ACTUALLY...
...I HOPE WE DO BATTLE EACH OTHER...
...IN SPEED ONLY.
...
?
YES.
I WILL NOW OFFER..
...ANOTHER CERTAIN PREDICTION.

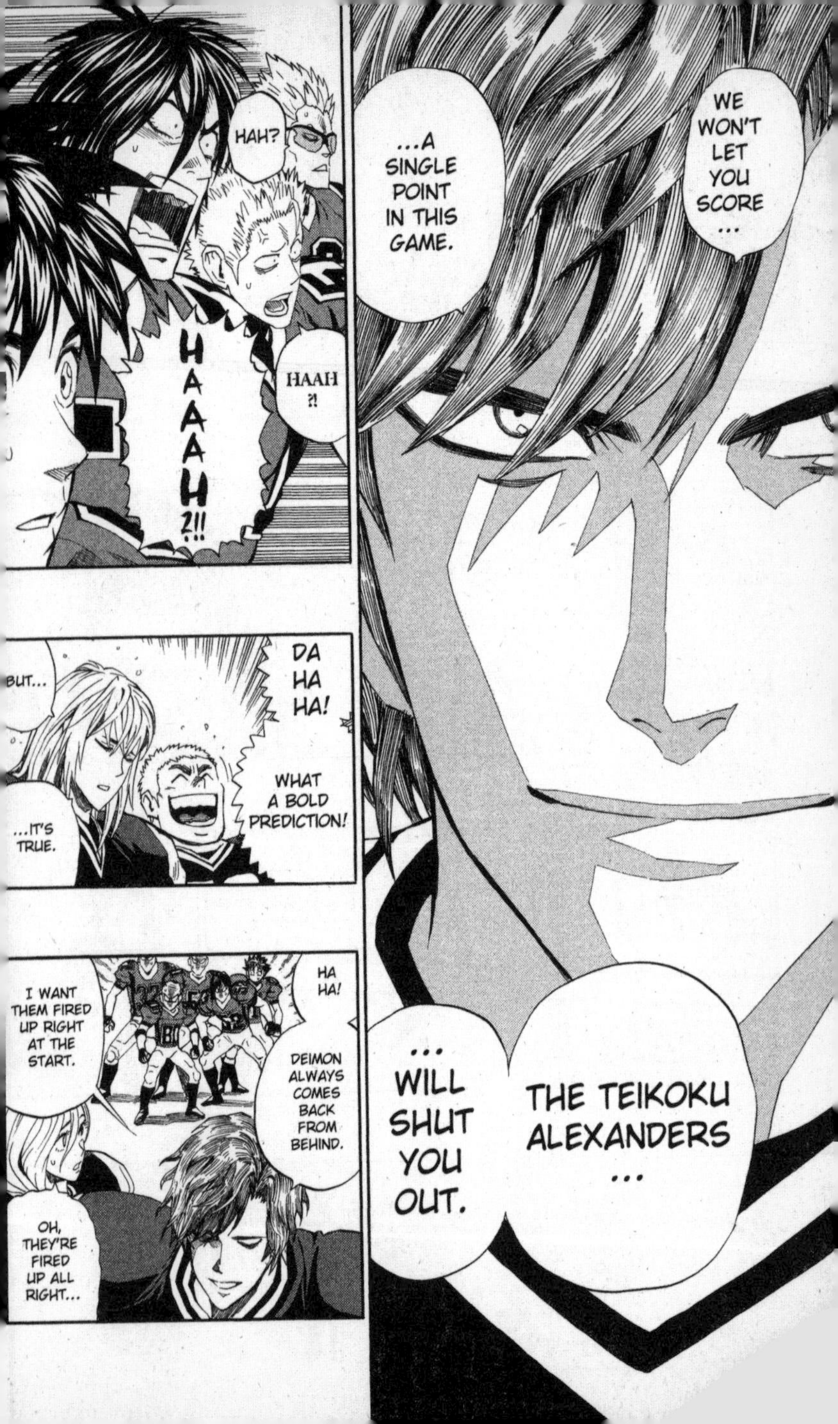
WE WON'T LET YOU SCORE ...
...A SINGLE POINT IN THIS GAME.
THE TEIKOKU ALEXANDERS ...
... WILL SHUT YOU OUT.
HAH?
HAAH ?!
HAAAH ?!!
DA HA HA!
WHAT A BOLD PREDICTION!
BUT...
...IT'S TRUE.
HA HA!
DEIMON ALWAYS COMES BACK FROM BEHIND.
I WANT THEM FIRED UP RIGHT AT THE START.
OH, THEY'RE FIRED UP ALL RIGHT...

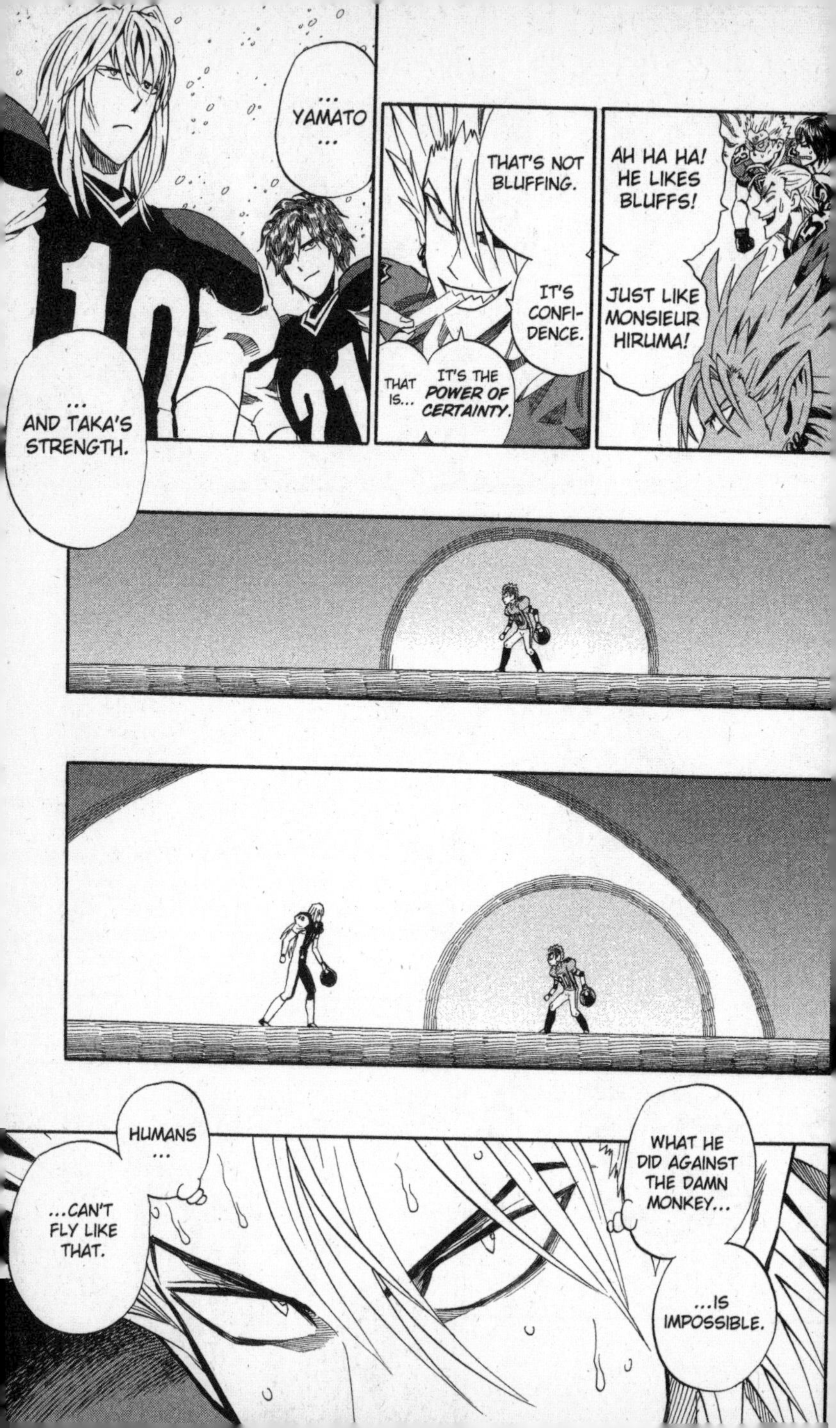
AH HA HA! HE LIKES BLUFFS!
JUST LIKE MONSIEUR HIRUMA!
THAT'S NOT BLUFFING.
IT'S CONFIDENCE.
THAT IS...
IT'S THE *POWER OF CERTAINTY*.
... YAMATO ...
... AND TAKA'S STRENGTH.
WHAT HE DID AGAINST THE DAMN MONKEY...
...IS IMPOSSIBLE.
HUMANS ...
...CAN'T FLY LIKE THAT.

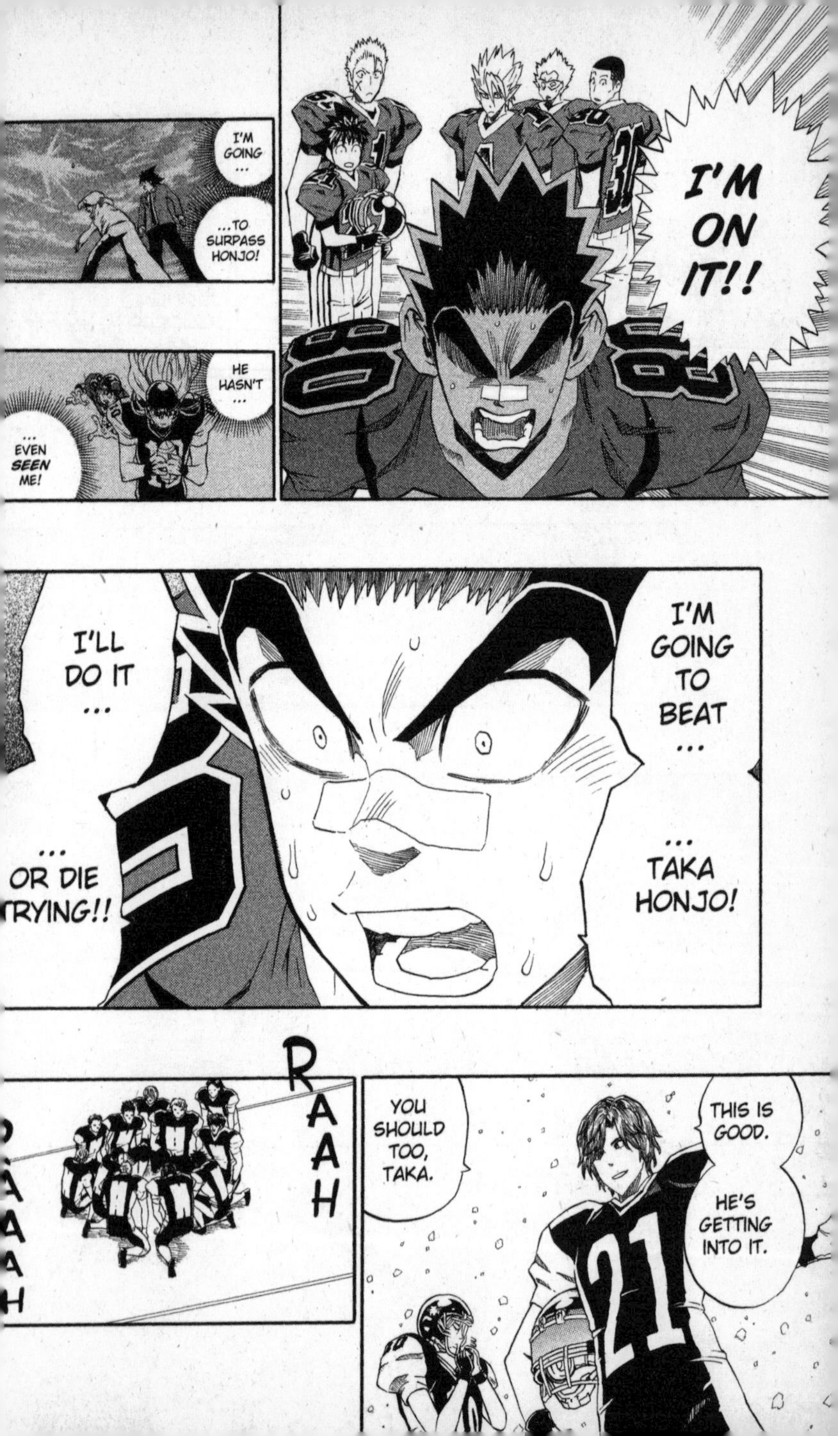
I'M ON IT!!
I'M GOING ... ...TO SURPASS HONJO!
HE HASN'T ... ... EVEN SEEN ME!
I'M GOING TO BEAT ... ... TAKA HONJO!
I'LL DO IT ... ... OR DIE TRYING!!
THIS IS GOOD.
HE'S GETTING INTO IT.
YOU SHOULD TOO, TAKA.
RAAH

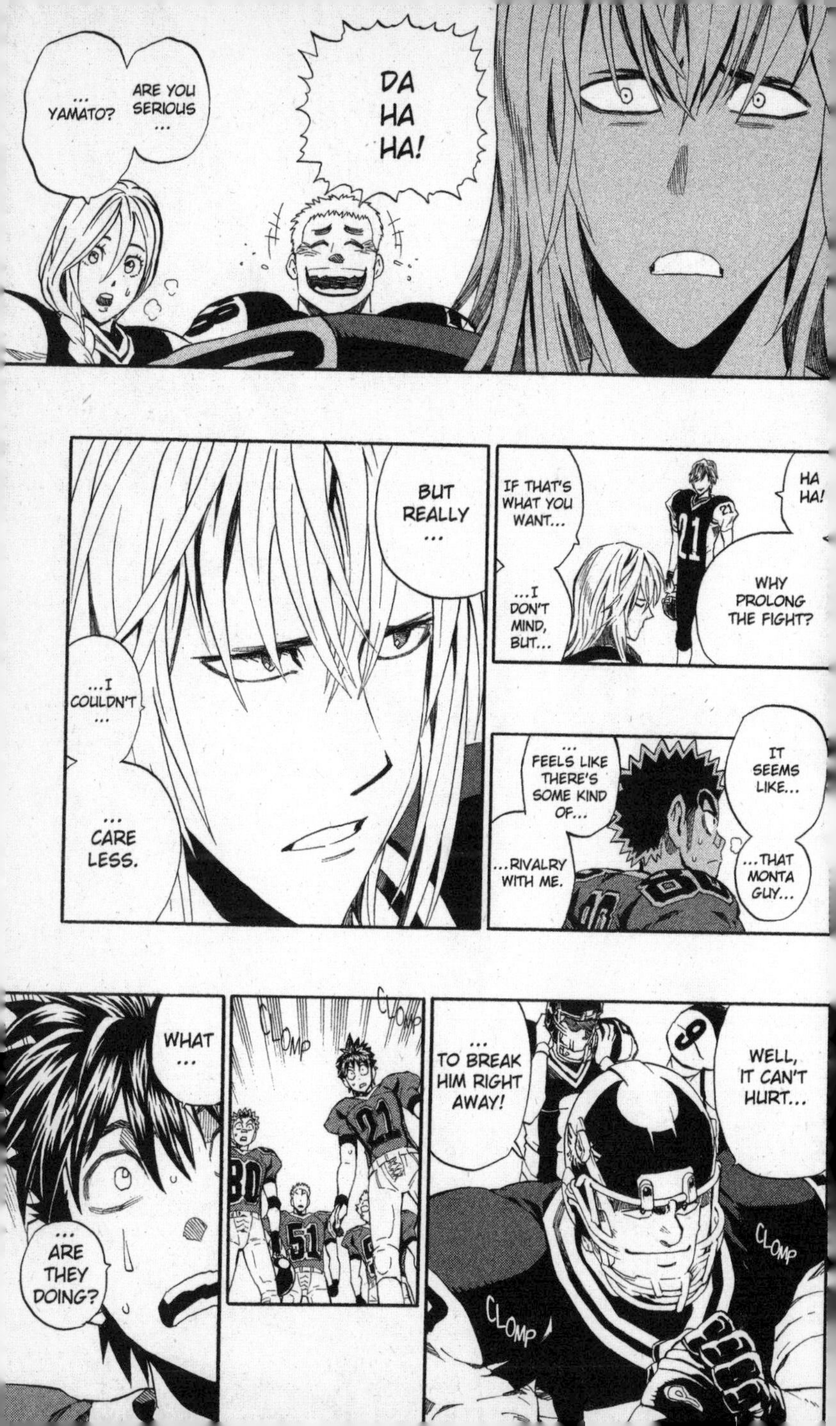

DA HA HA!
ARE YOU SERIOUS ... ... YAMATO?
HA HA!
WHY PROLONG THE FIGHT?
IF THAT'S WHAT YOU WANT...
...I DON'T MIND, BUT...
IT SEEMS LIKE...
...THAT MONTA GUY...
... FEELS LIKE THERE'S SOME KIND OF...
...RIVALRY WITH ME.
BUT REALLY ...
...I COULDN'T ...
... CARE LESS.
WELL, IT CAN'T HURT...
... TO BREAK HIM RIGHT AWAY!
CLOMP
CLOMP
CLOMP
CLOMP
CLOMP
WHAT ...
... ARE THEY DOING?

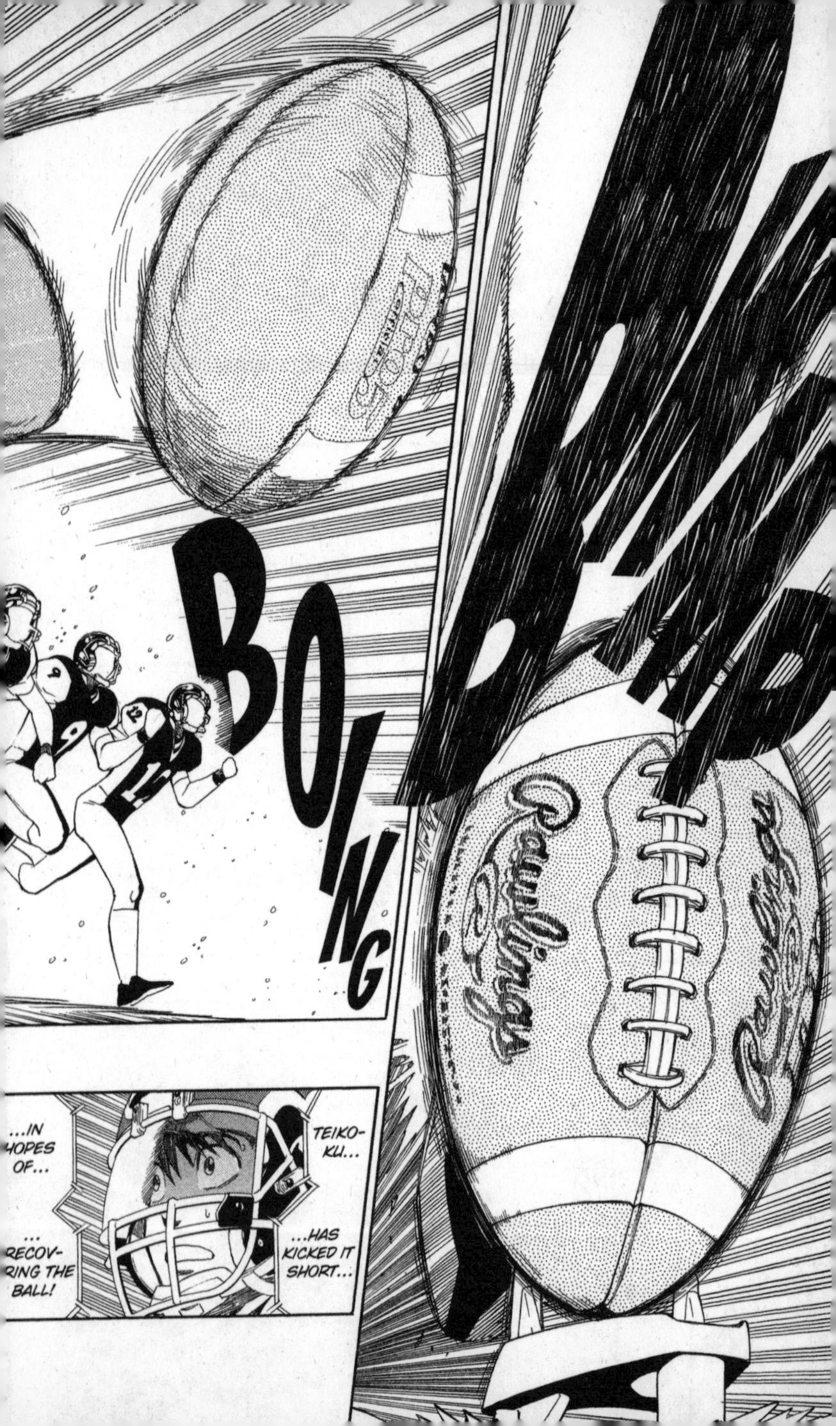
Rawlings
BOING
TEIKO-KU...
...HAS KICKED IT SHORT...
...IN HOPES OF...
...RECOV-RING THE BALL!

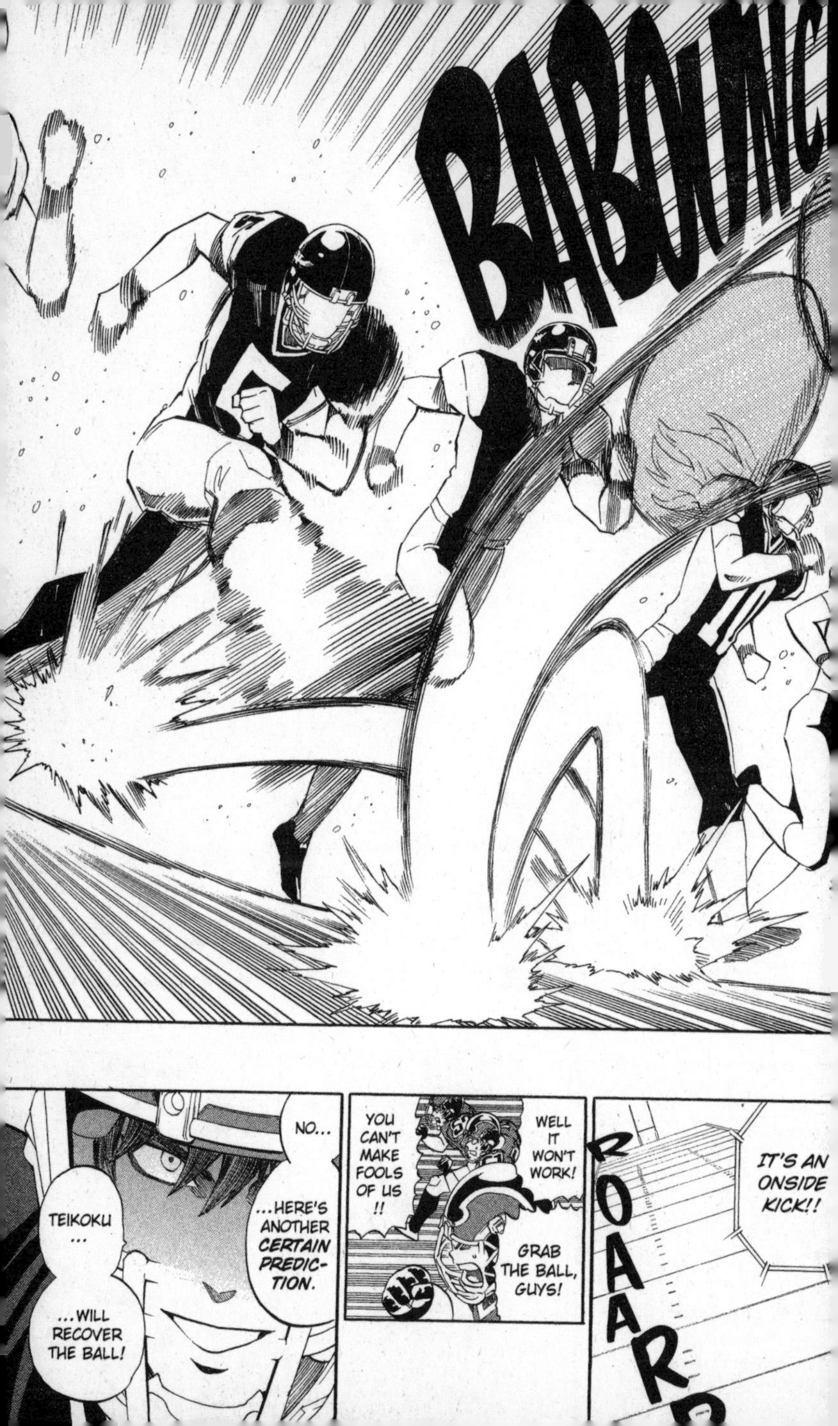
BABOUNC
IT'S AN ONSIDE KICK!!
ROAR
WELL IT WON'T WORK!
YOU CAN'T MAKE FOOLS OF US !!
GRAB THE BALL, GUYS!
NO...
...HERE'S ANOTHER CERTAIN PREDICTION.
TEIKOKU ...
...WILL RECOVER THE BALL!

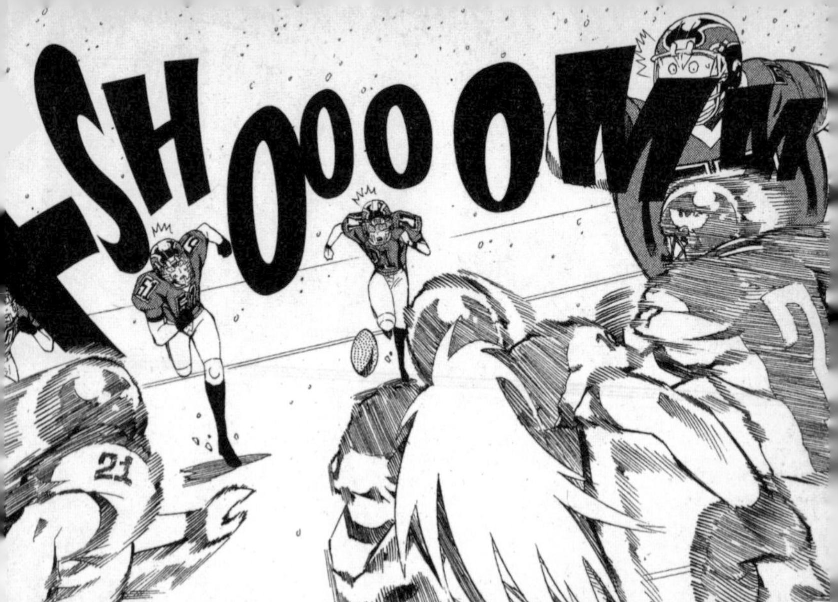
SHOOOOM
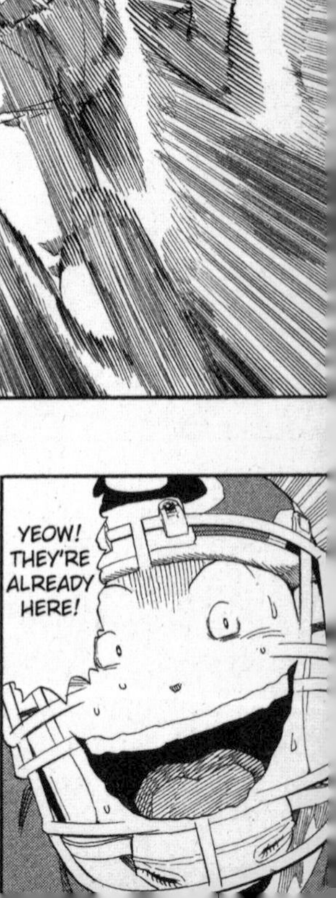
YEOW! THEY'RE ALREADY HERE!
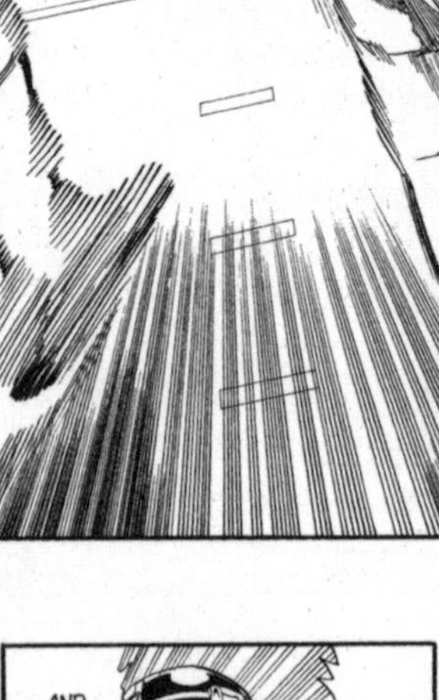
IDIOTS!
AND WE'RE ALL SUPER SPRINTERS!
THIS IS A SPEED CONTEST!
YOU CAN'T BEAT US!
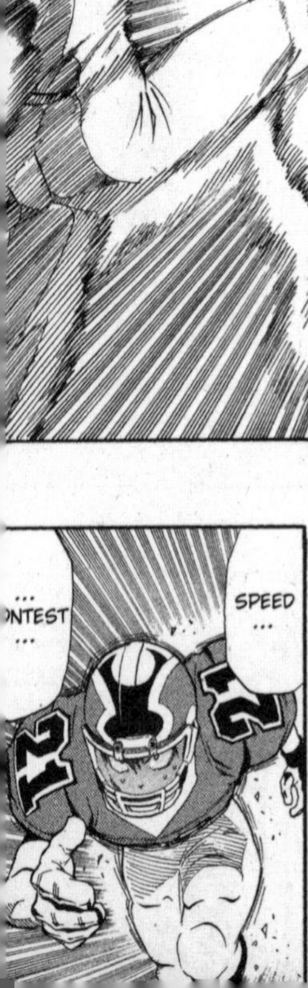
SPEED ...
... ONTEST ...

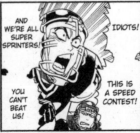

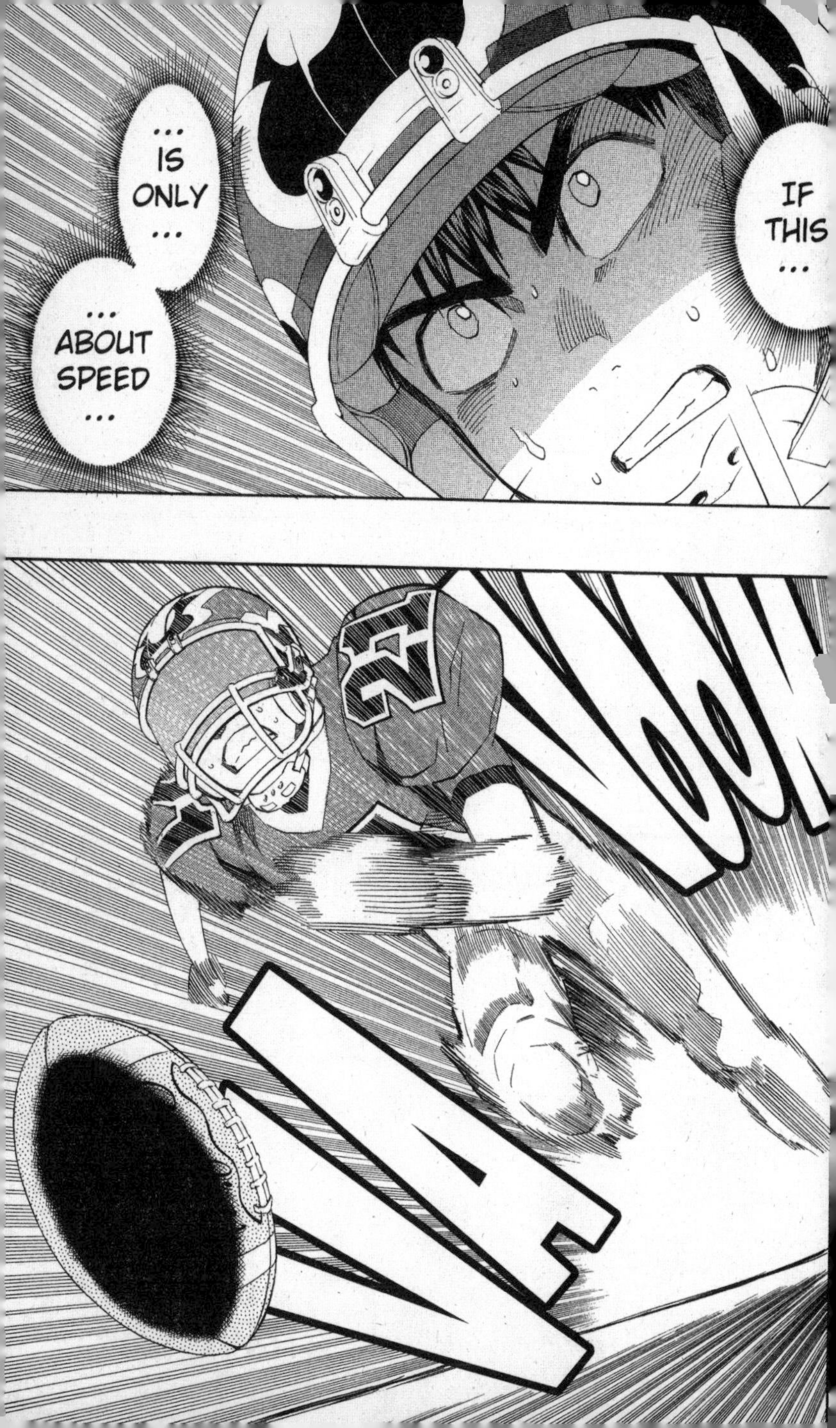
IF THIS ...
... IS ONLY ...
... ABOUT SPEED ...

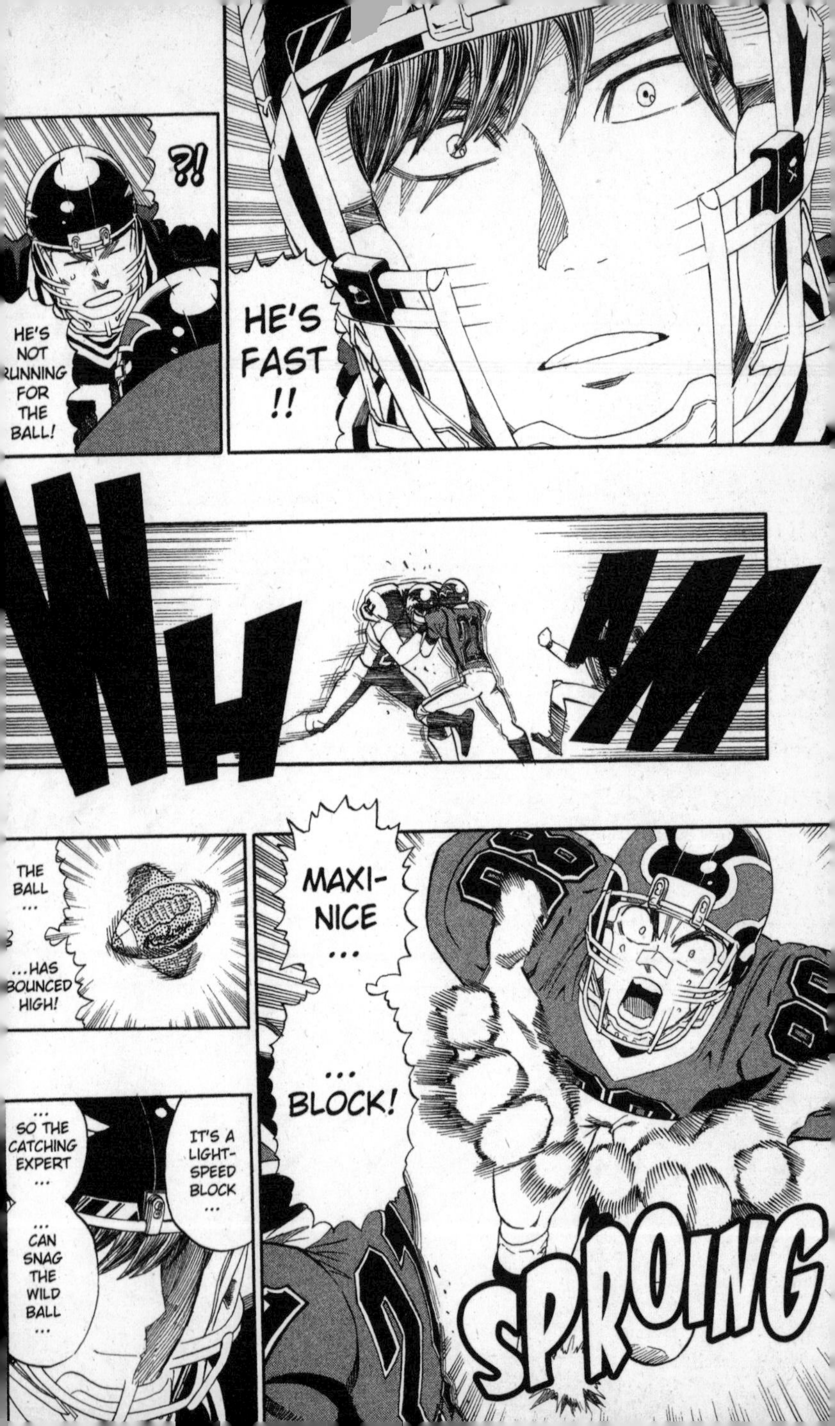
HE'S FAST !!
?!
HE'S NOT RUNNING FOR THE BALL!
WHAM
MAXI-NICE ...
... BLOCK!
SPROING
THE BALL ...
...HAS BOUNCED HIGH!
IT'S A LIGHT-SPEED BLOCK ...
... SO THE CATCHING EXPERT ...
... CAN SNAG THE WILD BALL ...

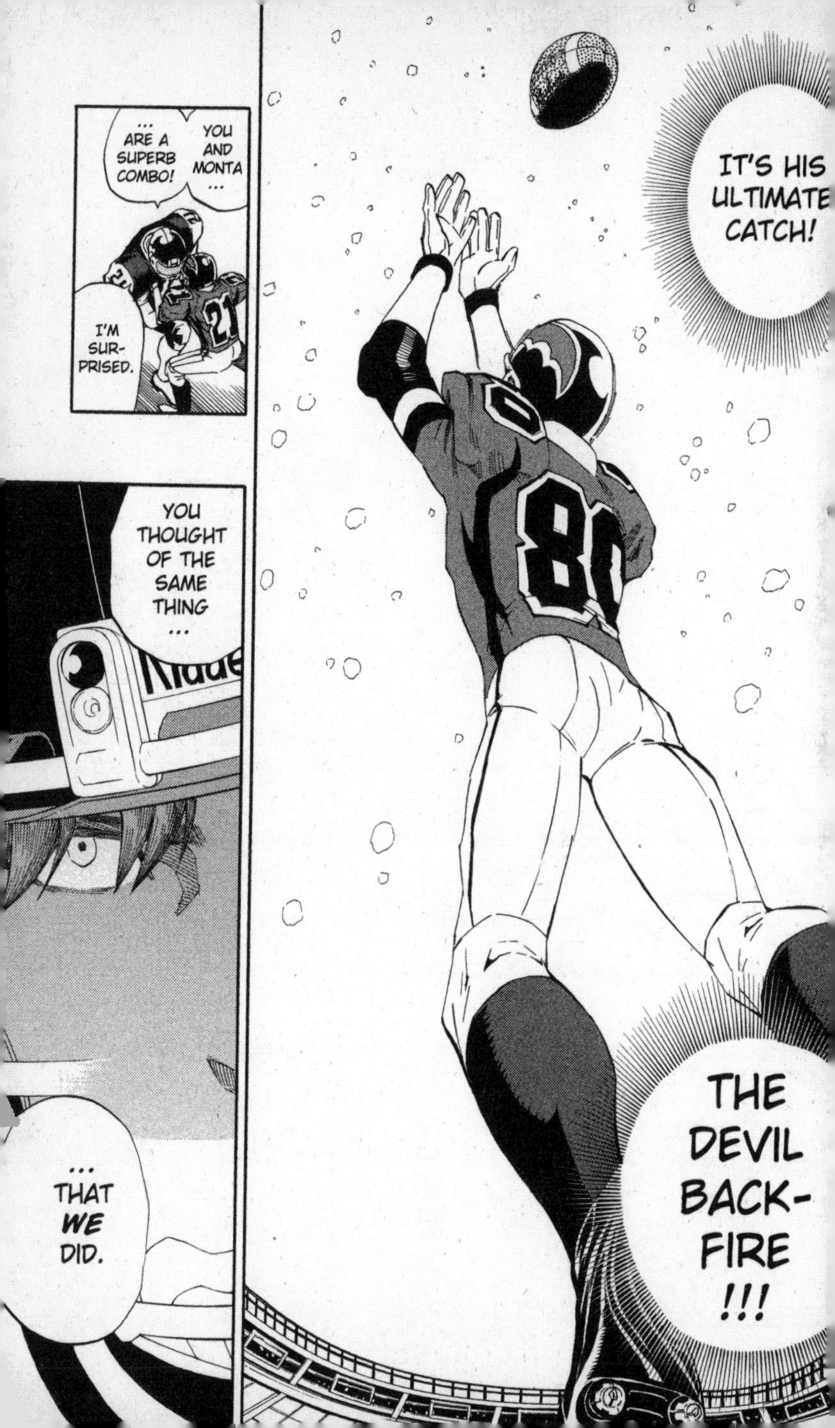
IT'S HIS ULTIMATE CATCH!
THE DEVIL BACK-FIRE!!!
YOU AND MONTA...
...ARE A SUPERB COMBO!
I'M SUR-PRISED.
YOU THOUGHT OF THE SAME THING...
...THAT WE DID.

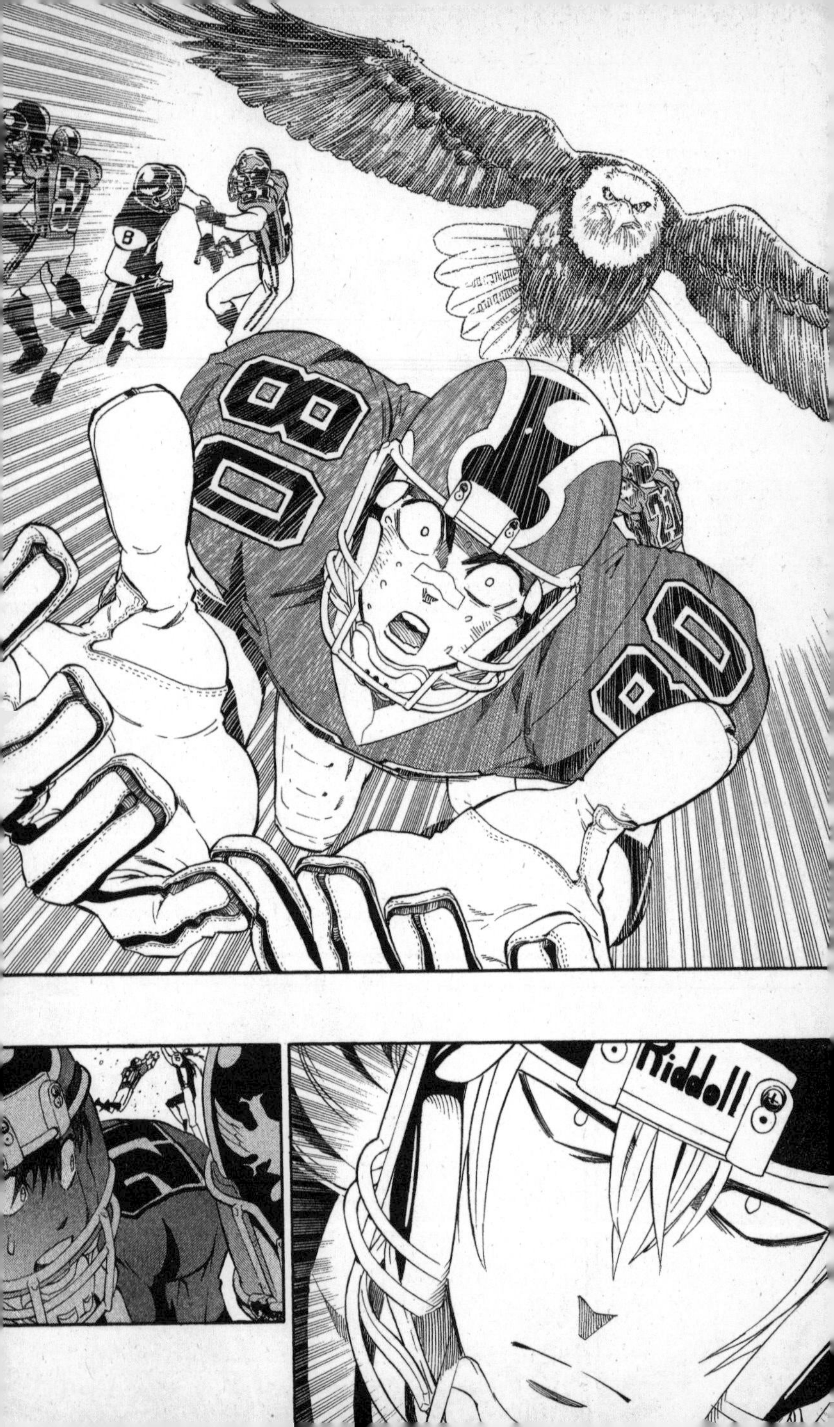
Riddell

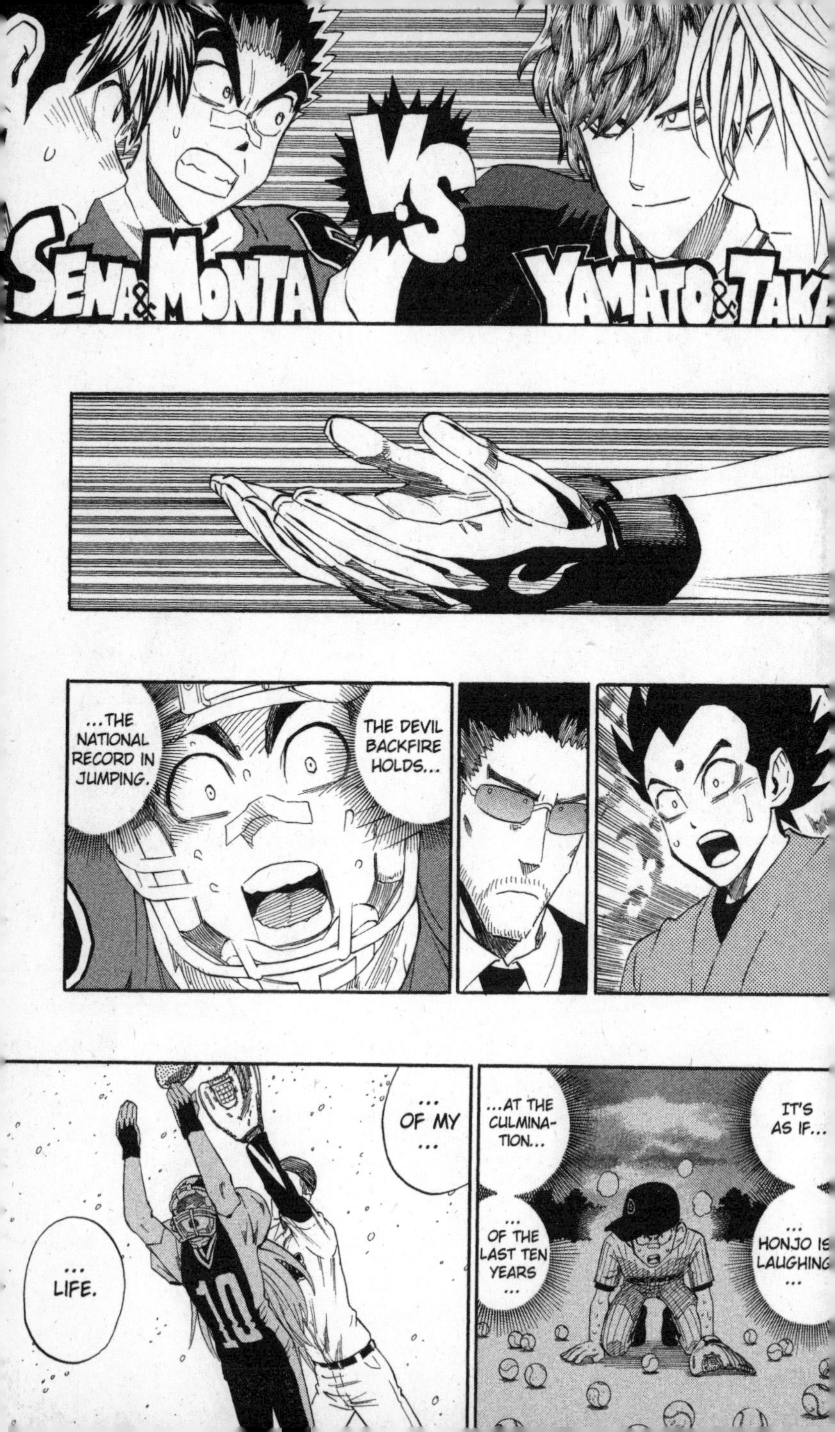
SENA & MONTA
VS.
YAMATO & TAKA
THE DEVIL BACKFIRE HOLDS...
...THE NATIONAL RECORD IN JUMPING.
IT'S AS IF...
...HONJO IS LAUGHING...
...AT THE CULMINATION...
...OF THE LAST TEN YEARS...
...OF MY...
...LIFE.

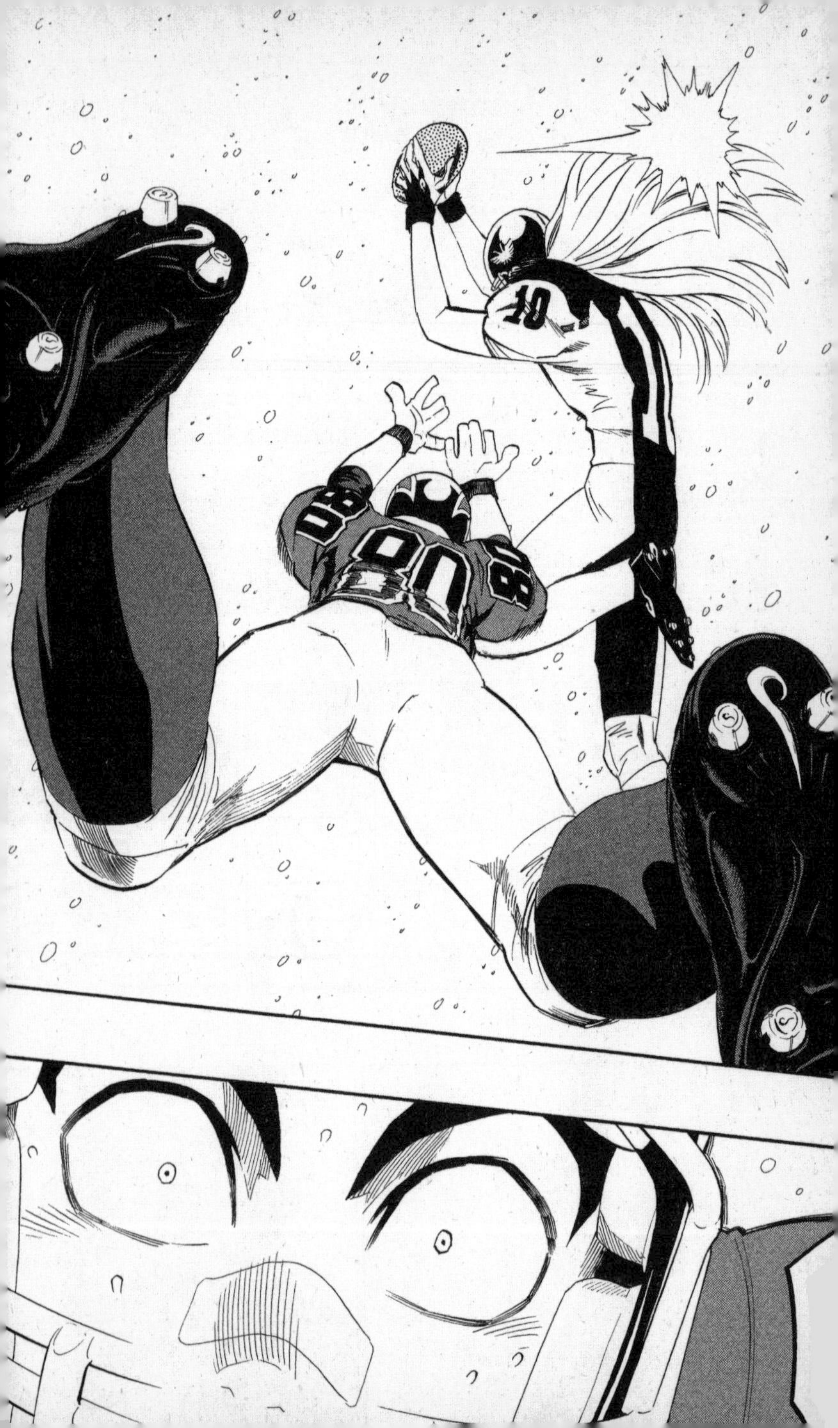

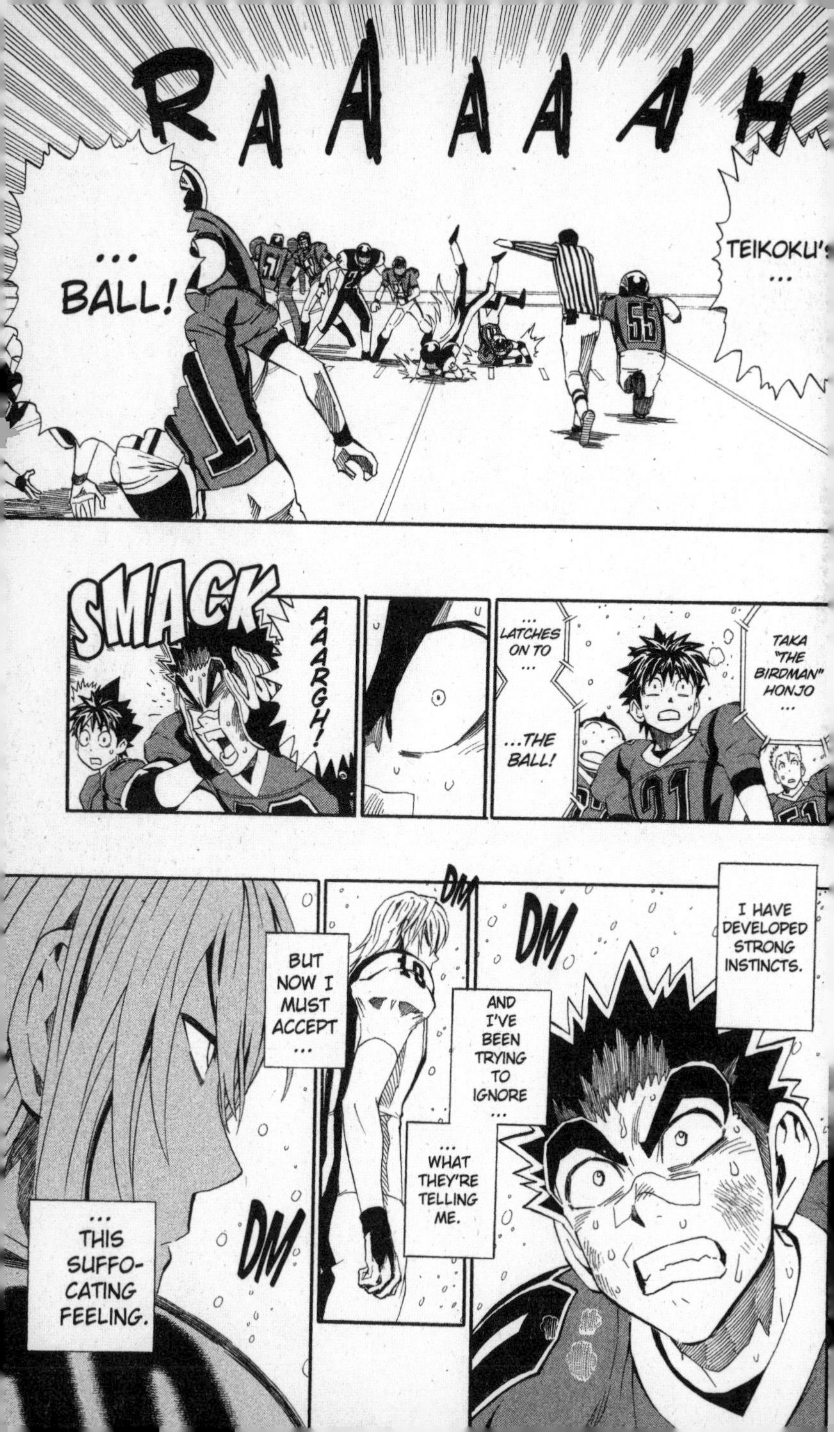
RAAAAAH
TEIKOKU'S ...
... BALL!
TAKA "THE BIRDMAN" HONJO ...
... LATCHES ON TO ...
...THE BALL!
AAAARGH!
SMACK
I HAVE DEVELOPED STRONG INSTINCTS.
DM
DM
AND I'VE BEEN TRYING TO IGNORE ...
... WHAT THEY'RE TELLING ME.
DM
BUT NOW I MUST ACCEPT ...
... THIS SUFFO-CATING FEELING.

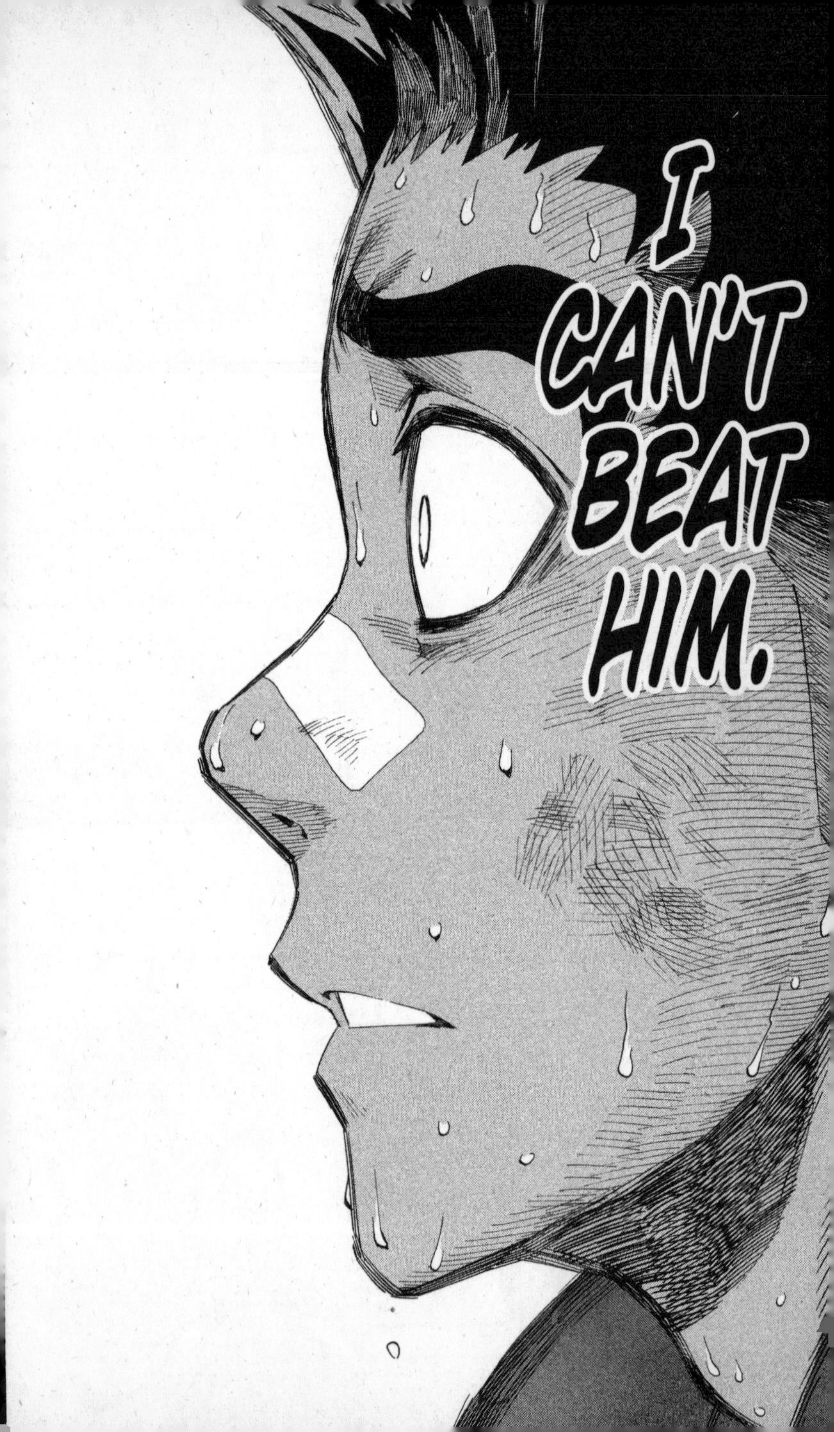
I CAN'T BEAT HIM.

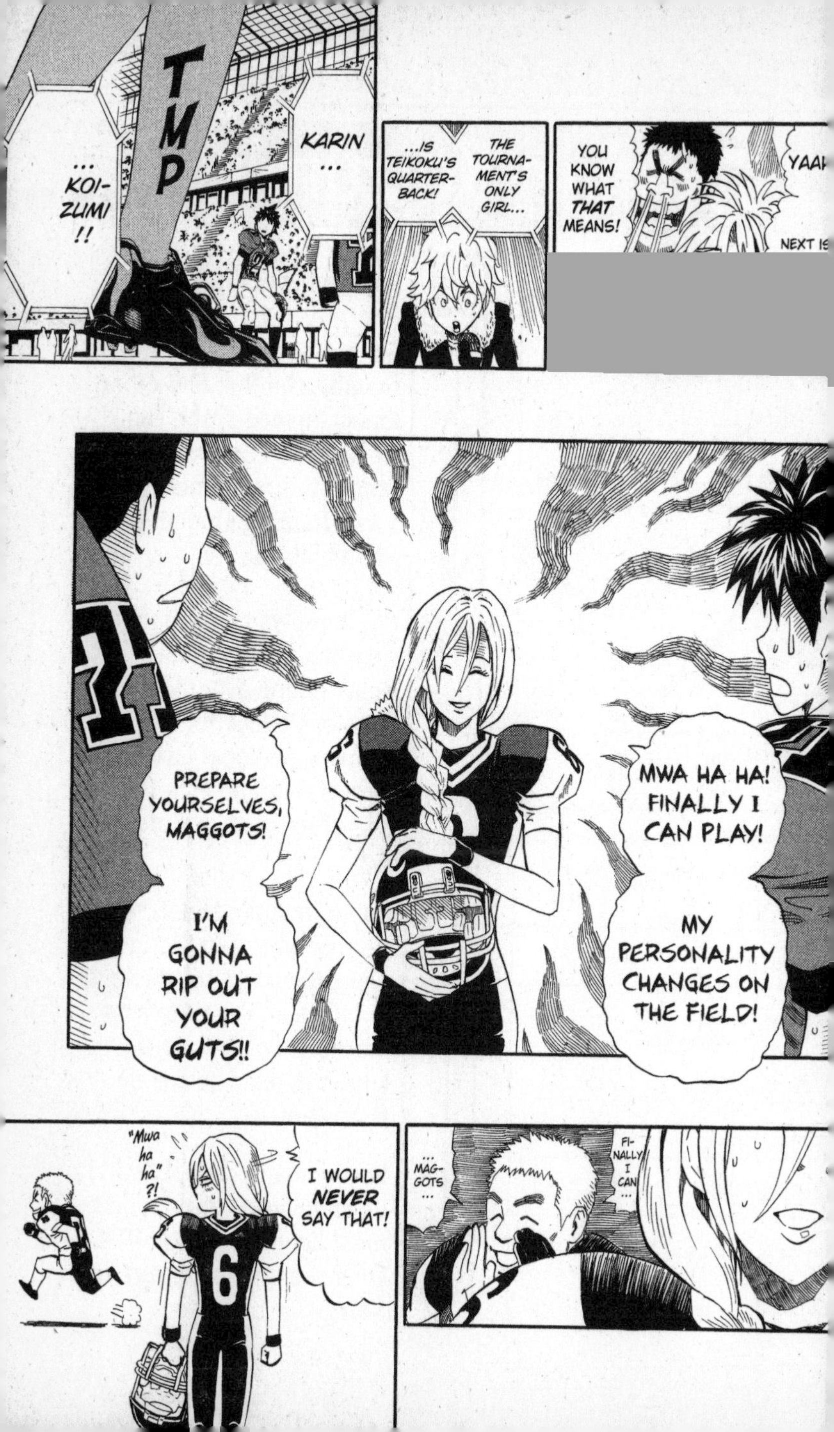
YAAH
NEXT IS
YOU KNOW WHAT THAT MEANS!
THE TOURNA-MENT'S ONLY GIRL...
...IS TEIKOKU'S QUARTER-BACK!
KARIN...
...KOI-ZUMI!!
TMP
MWA HA HA! FINALLY I CAN PLAY!
MY PERSONALITY CHANGES ON THE FIELD!
PREPARE YOURSELVES, MAGGOTS!
I'M GONNA RIP OUT YOUR GUTS!!
FI-NALLY I CAN...
...MAG-GOTS...
I WOULD NEVER SAY THAT!
"Mwa ha ha"?!

●TEIKOKU PERSONAL HISTORIES

◂Karin Koizumi▸

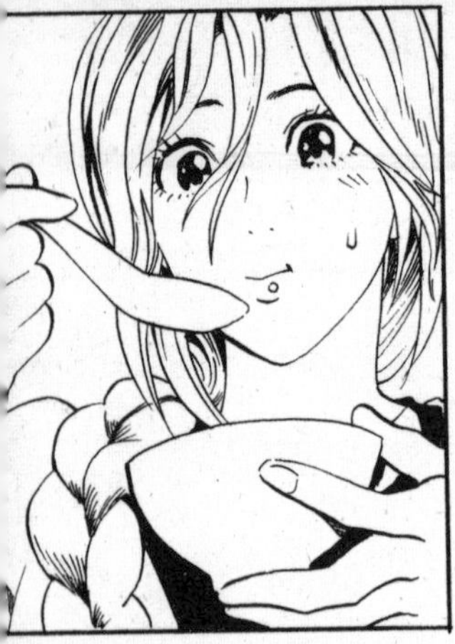

CURRENT AGE: 16

Height	157 cm
Weight	44 kg
Blood type	O
Birthday	July 7
Siblings	One older brother
Talents/Hobbies	Drawing, Piano
Favorite type of boy	
A boy who will listen to her…	

0 YEARS OLD ↓

Born in Kyoto Prefecture.

Surrounded by her loud-mouthed brother and other family members, she can ***never*** speak up around home. This is her own personal ***Dark Age***, full of fear and trembling.

10 YEARS OLD ↓

She borrows shojo manga from her friends, spends hours poring over them and develops a love for drawing. Enjoying personal pastimes for the first time in her life, she experiences a ***Golden Age***.

15 YEARS OLD ↓

Due to her rare talent, she is persuaded to join the football team. She lacks the courage to refuse joining or to skip practices, and before she knows it, finds herself on the first team!

She wants to draw, but ends up standing on this world's most dangerous battlefield. Thus she enters her ***Age of Sorrow***.

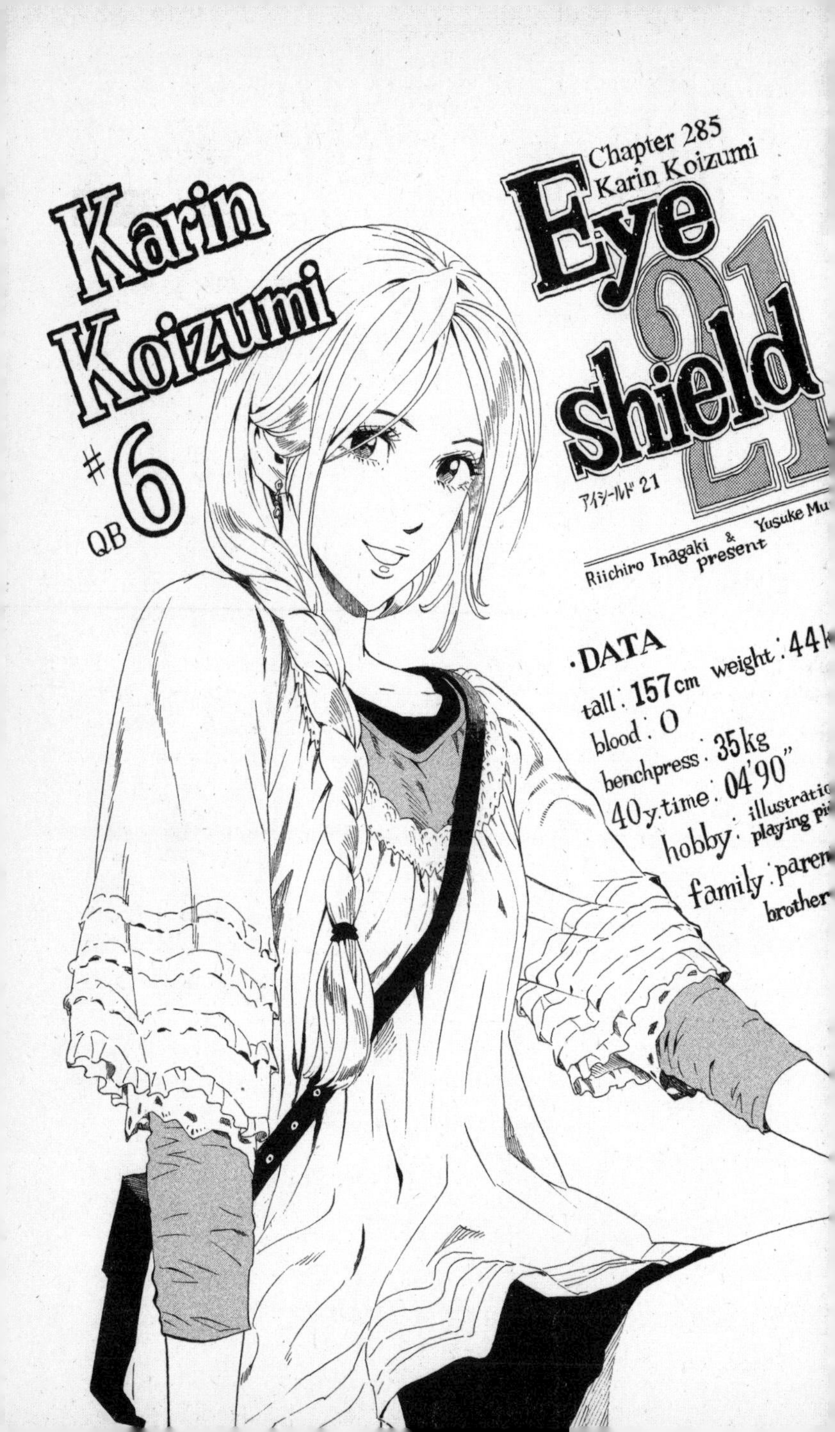
Karin Koizumi
#6
QB
Chapter 285
Karin Koizumi
Eyeshield 21
アイシールド21
Riichiro Inagaki & Yusuke Mu
present
·DATA
tall: 157cm weight: 44k
blood: O
benchpress: 35kg
40y.time: 04'90"
hobby: illustratio
playing pi
family: paren
brother

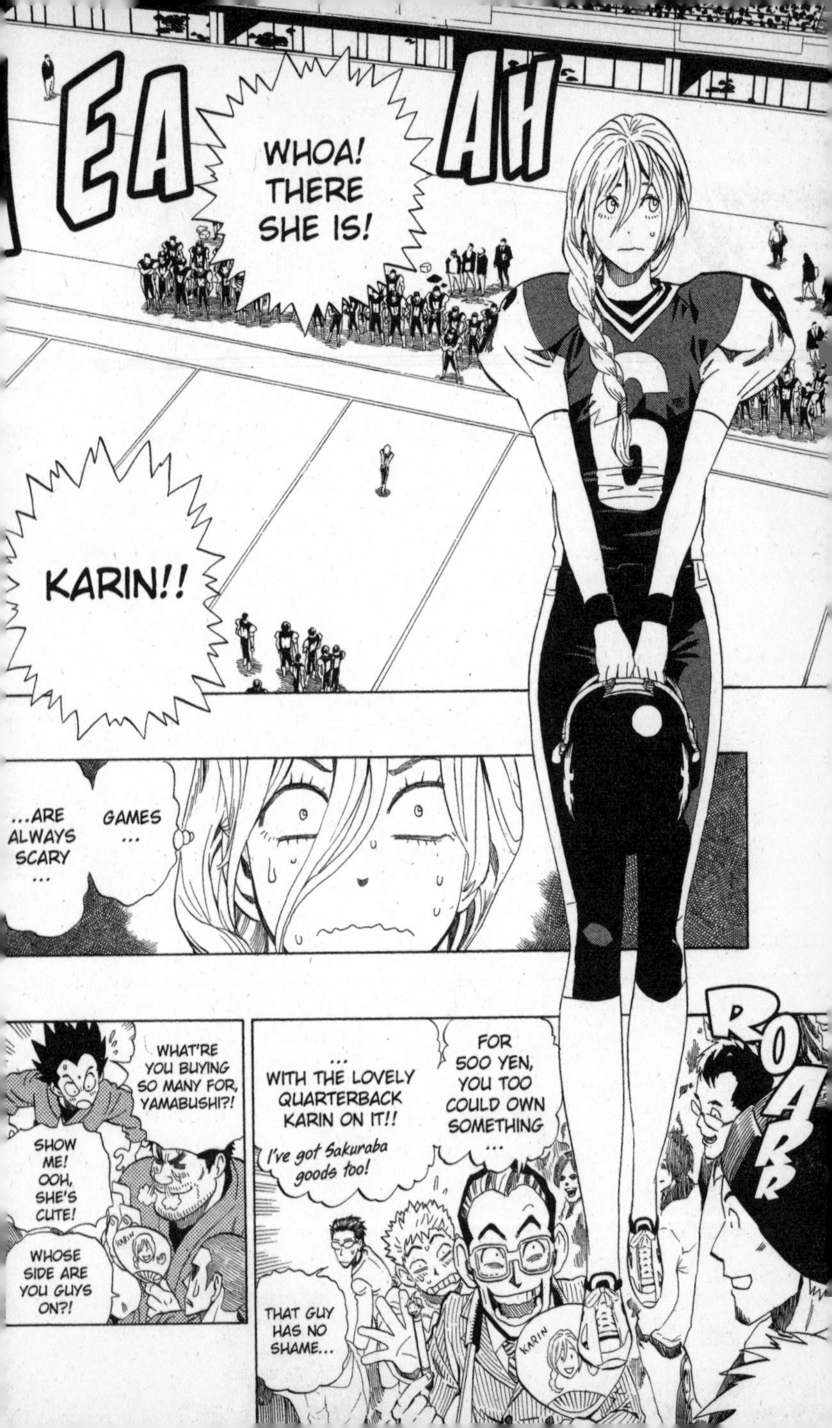
EA AH
WHOA! THERE SHE IS!
KARIN!!
GAMES ...
...ARE ALWAYS SCARY ...
ROAR
FOR 500 YEN, YOU TOO COULD OWN SOMETHING ...
... WITH THE LOVELY QUARTERBACK KARIN ON IT!!
I've got Sakuraba goods too!
KARIN
THAT GUY HAS NO SHAME...
WHAT'RE YOU BUYING SO MANY FOR, YAMABUSHI?!
SHOW ME! OOH, SHE'S CUTE!
KARIN
WHOSE SIDE ARE YOU GUYS ON?!

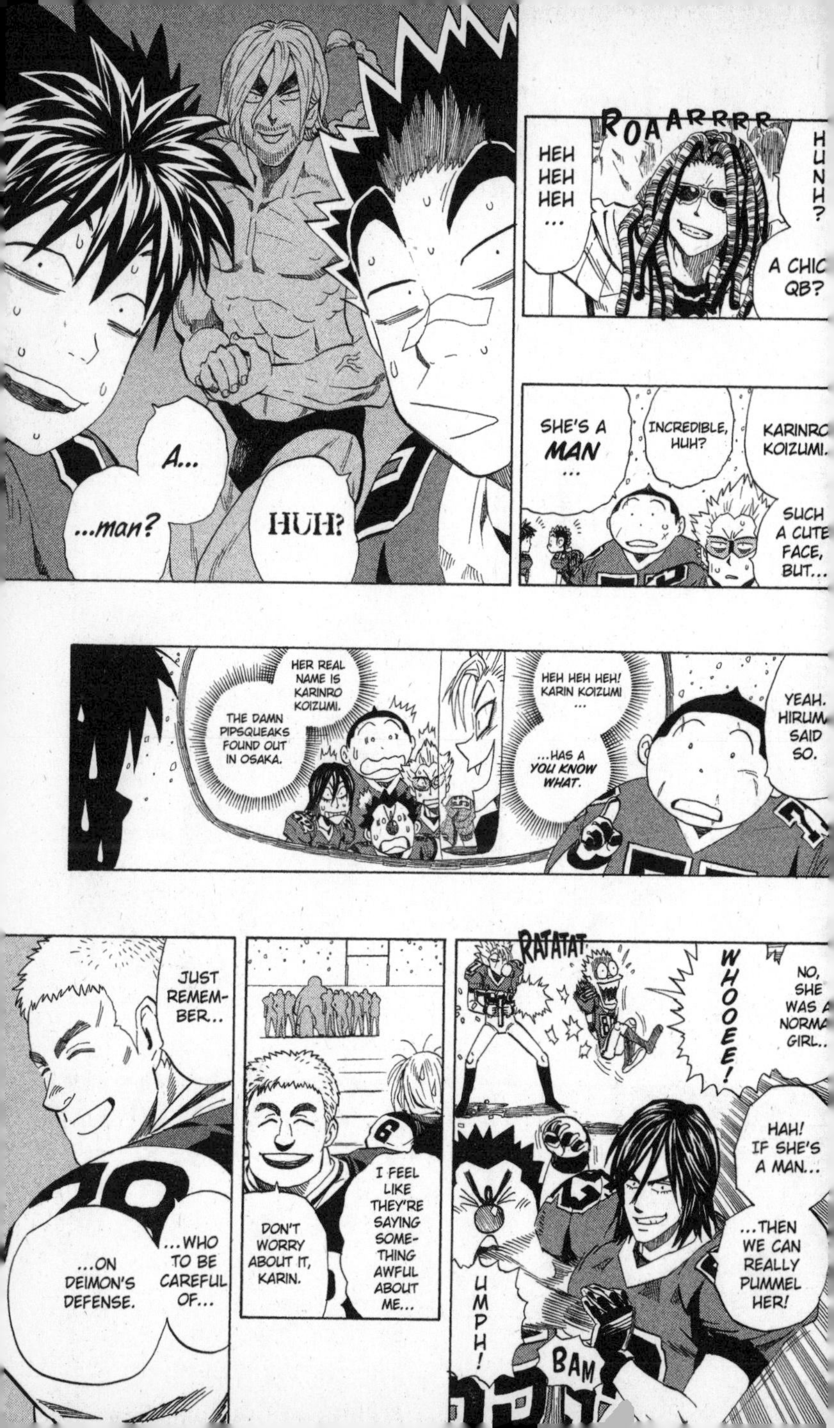
ROAARRRR
HUNH?
HEH HEH HEH ...
A CHIC QB?
KARINRO KOIZUMI.
INCREDIBLE, HUH?
SHE'S A MAN ...
SUCH A CUTE FACE, BUT...
A...
HUH?
...man?
YEAH. HIRUMA SAID SO.
HEH HEH HEH! KARIN KOIZUMI ...
...HAS A YOU KNOW WHAT.
HER REAL NAME IS KARINRO KOIZUMI.
THE DAMN PIPSQUEAKS FOUND OUT IN OSAKA.
NO, SHE WAS A NORMA GIRL..
WHOOEE!
RATATAT
HAH! IF SHE'S A MAN...
...THEN WE CAN REALLY PUMMEL HER!
UMPH!
BAM
I FEEL LIKE THEY'RE SAYING SOMETHING AWFUL ABOUT ME...
DON'T WORRY ABOUT IT, KARIN.
JUST REMEMBER...
...WHO TO BE CAREFUL OF...
...ON DEIMON'S DEFENSE.

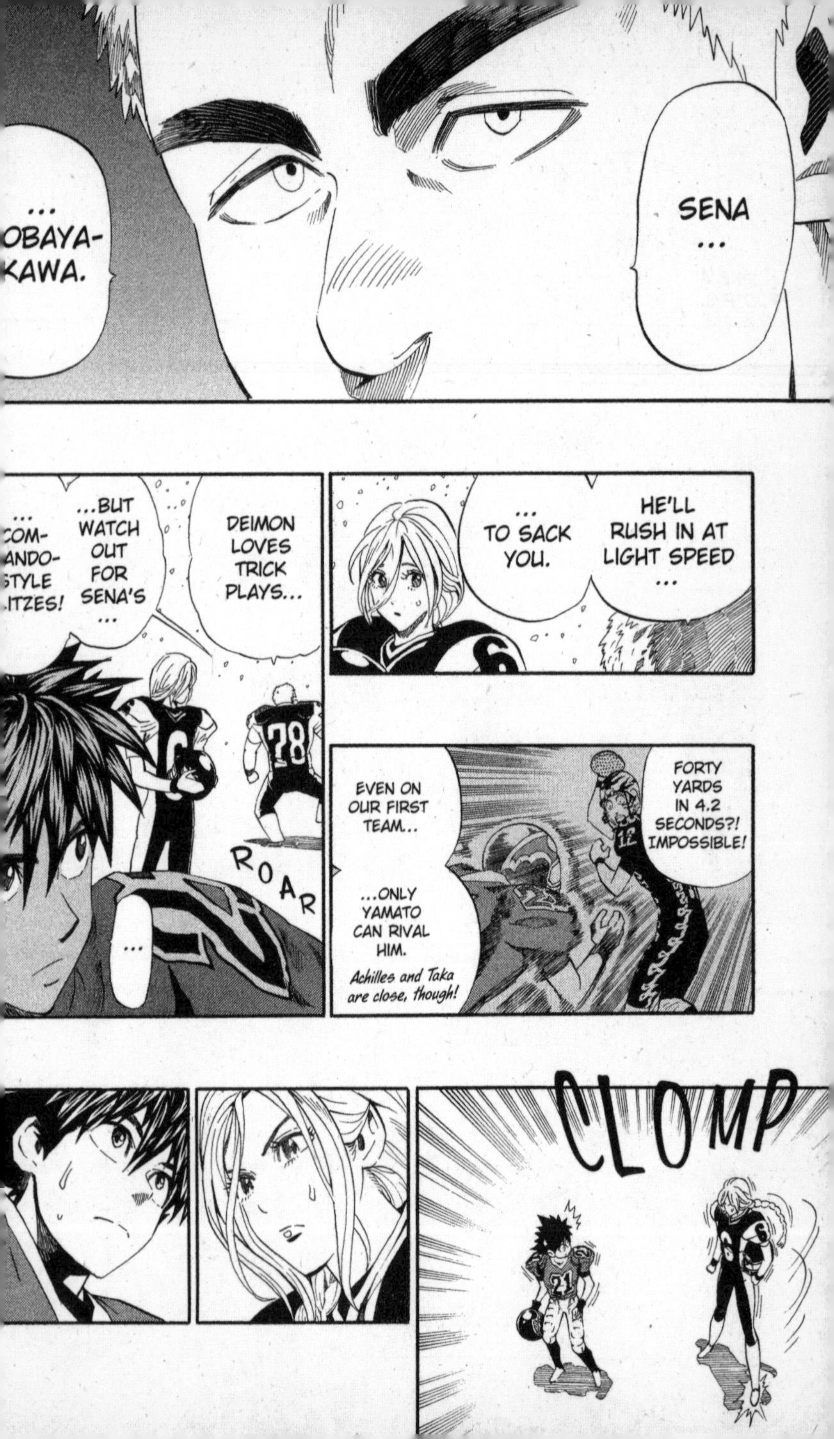
SENA ...
... OBAYA-KAWA.
HE'LL RUSH IN AT LIGHT SPEED ...
... TO SACK YOU.
DEIMON LOVES TRICK PLAYS...
...BUT WATCH OUT FOR SENA'S ...
... COM-ANDO-STYLE ITZES!
ROAR
...
FORTY YARDS IN 4.2 SECONDS?! IMPOSSIBLE!
EVEN ON OUR FIRST TEAM...
...ONLY YAMATO CAN RIVAL HIM.
Achilles and Taka are close, though!
CLOMP

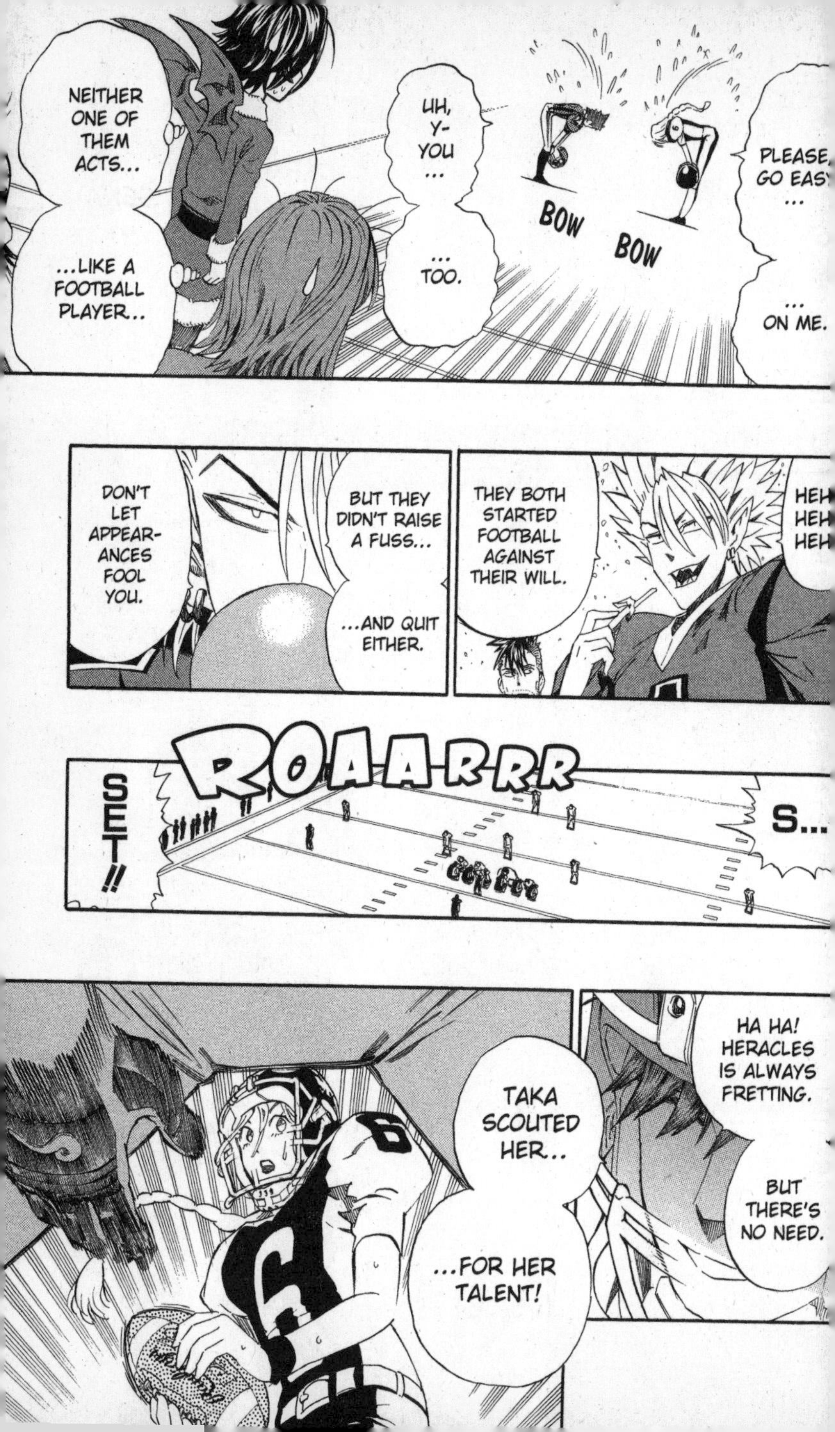
PLEASE GO EAS ...
... ON ME.
BOW
BOW
UH, Y-YOU ...
... TOO.
NEITHER ONE OF THEM ACTS...
...LIKE A FOOTBALL PLAYER...
HEH HEH HEH
THEY BOTH STARTED FOOTBALL AGAINST THEIR WILL.
BUT THEY DIDN'T RAISE A FUSS...
...AND QUIT EITHER.
DON'T LET APPEARANCES FOOL YOU.
S...
ROAARRR
SET!!
HA HA! HERACLES IS ALWAYS FRETTING.
BUT THERE'S NO NEED.
TAKA SCOUTED HER...
...FOR HER TALENT!

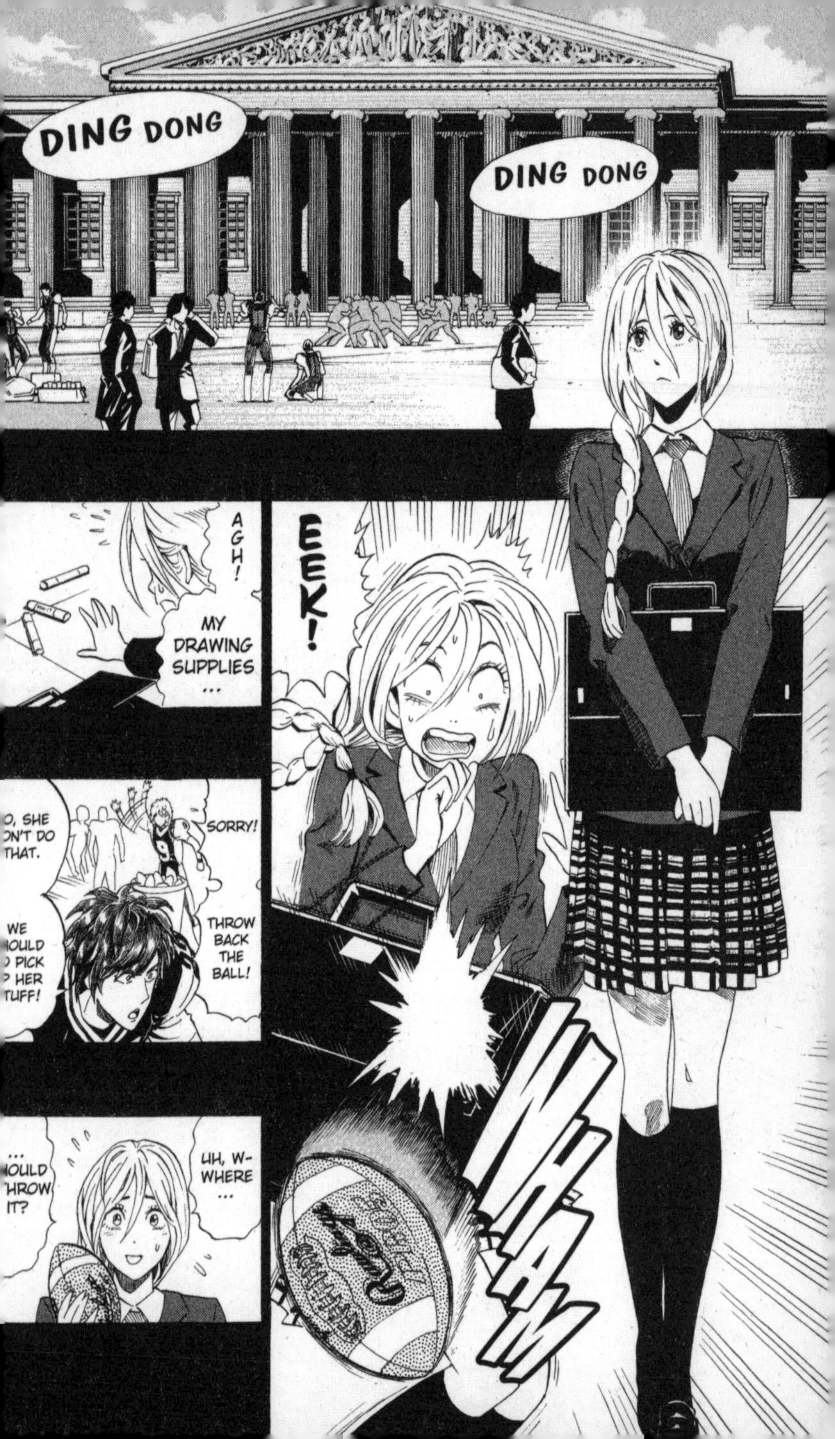
DING DONG
DING DONG
EEK!
WHAM
AGH!
MY DRAWING SUPPLIES ...
SORRY!
THROW BACK THE BALL!
O, SHE ON'T DO THAT.
WE HOULD O PICK P HER TUFF!
UH, W-WHERE ...
... HOULD THROW IT?

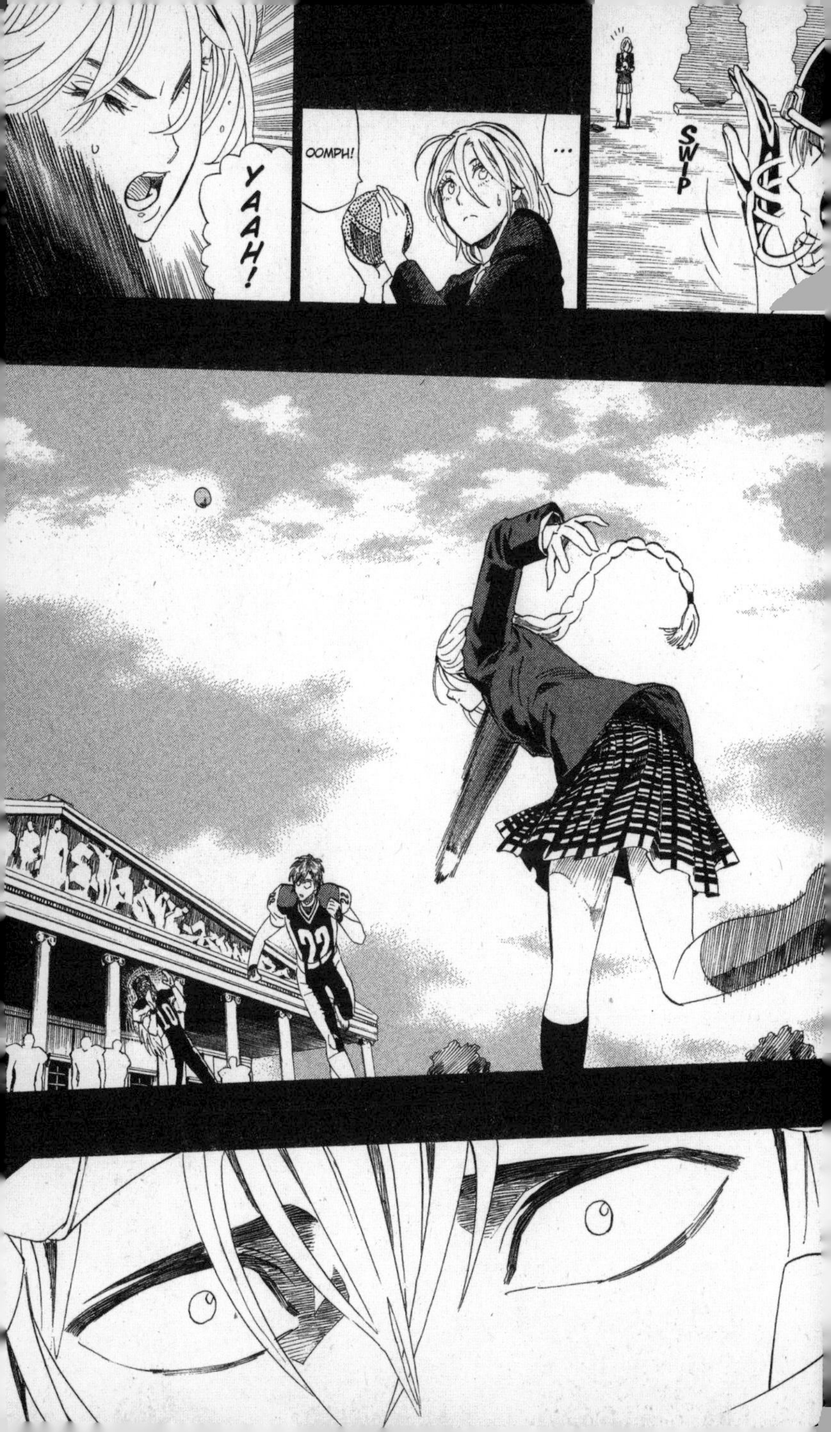
SWIP
...
OOMPH!
YAAH!

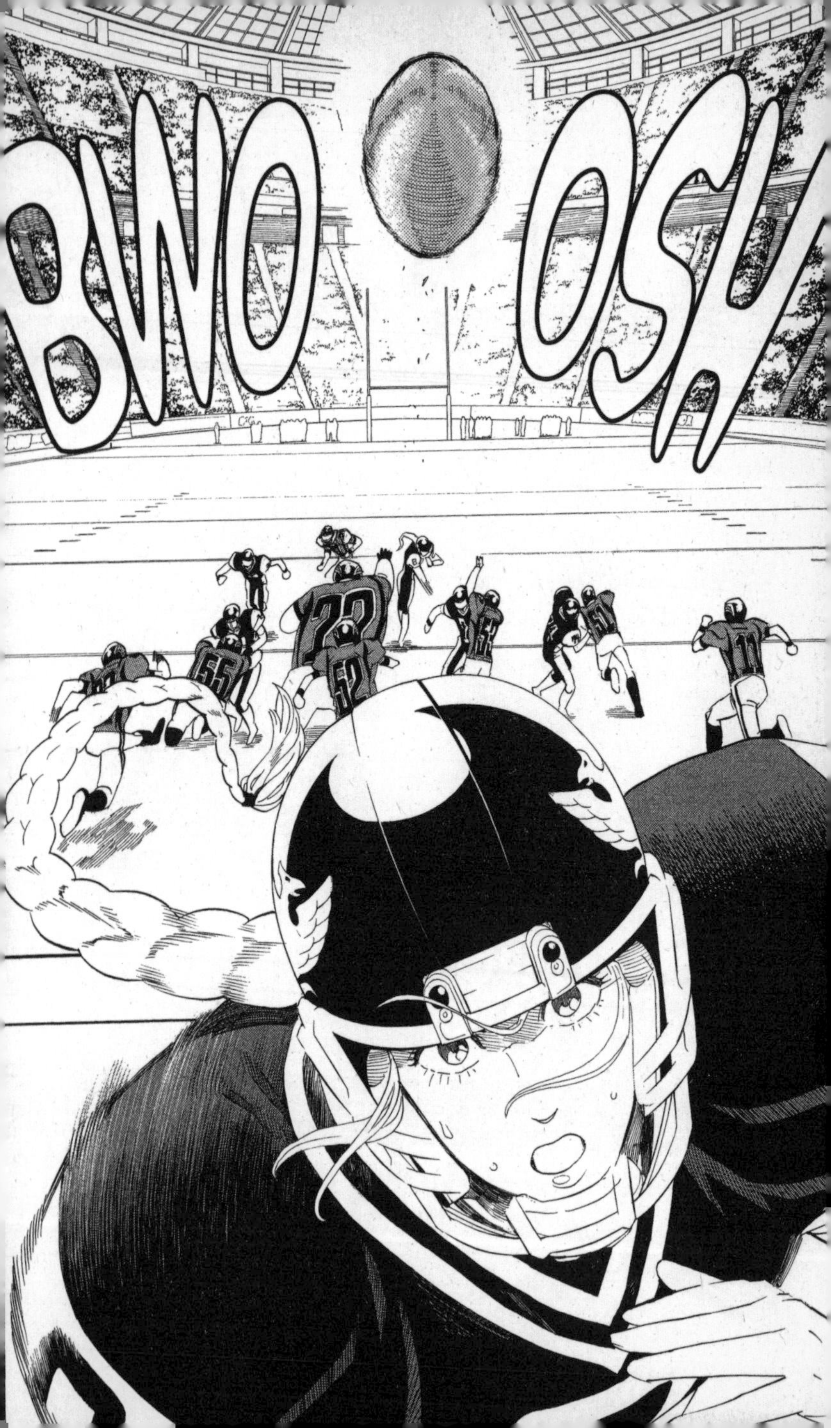
BWOOOSH

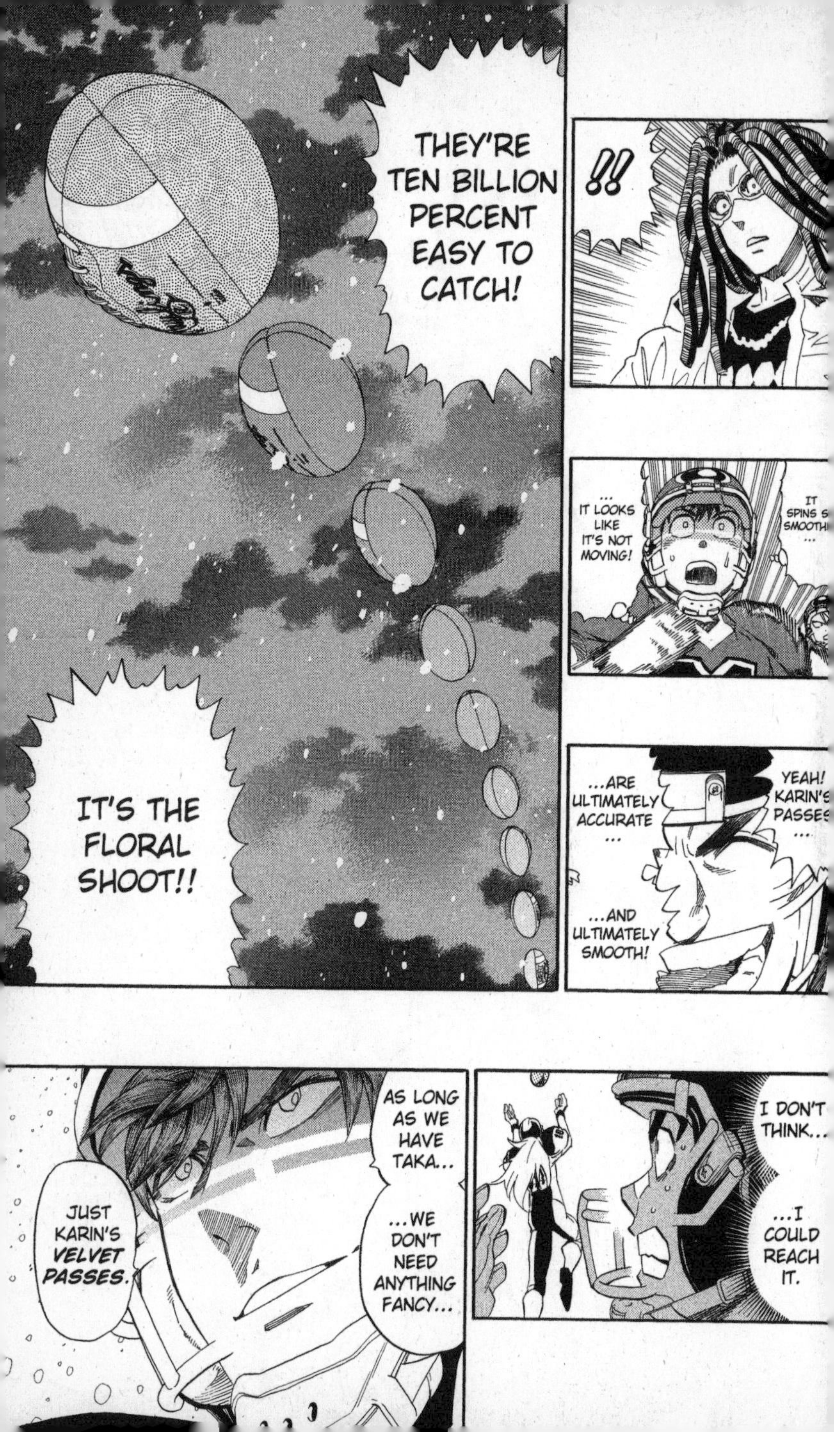
!!
IT SPINS S SMOOTH ...
... IT LOOKS LIKE IT'S NOT MOVING!
YEAH! KARIN'S PASSES ...
...ARE ULTIMATELY ACCURATE ...
...AND ULTIMATELY SMOOTH!
THEY'RE TEN BILLION PERCENT EASY TO CATCH!
IT'S THE FLORAL SHOOT!!
I DON'T THINK...
...I COULD REACH IT.
AS LONG AS WE HAVE TAKA...
...WE DON'T NEED ANYTHING FANCY...
JUST KARIN'S VELVET PASSES.

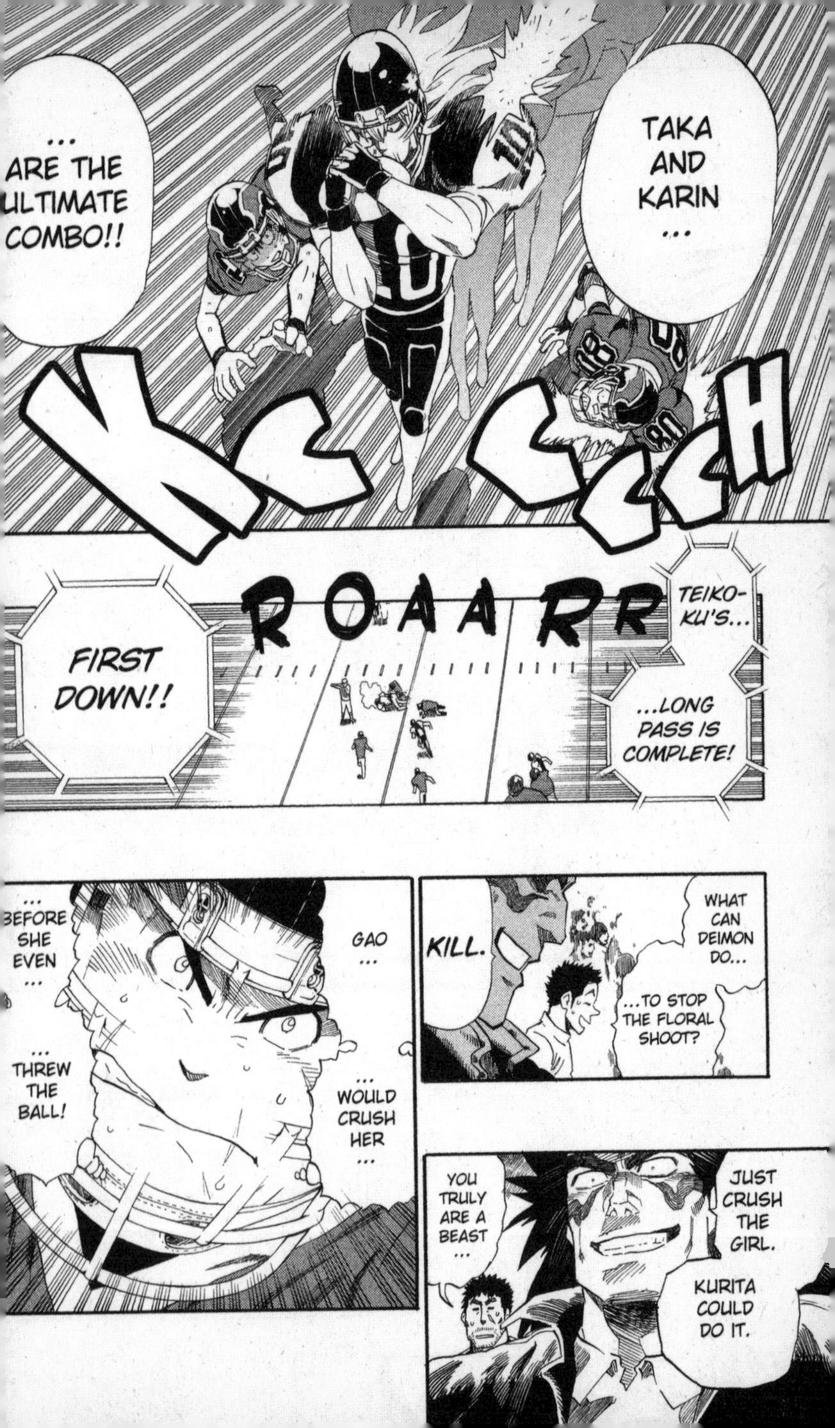
TAKA AND KARIN...
...ARE THE ULTIMATE COMBO!!
KCCCCH
TEIKOKU'S...
...LONG PASS IS COMPLETE!
ROAARR
FIRST DOWN!!
WHAT CAN DEIMON DO...
...TO STOP THE FLORAL SHOOT?
KILL.
GAO...
...WOULD CRUSH HER...
...BEFORE SHE EVEN...
...THREW THE BALL!
JUST CRUSH THE GIRL.
KURITA COULD DO IT.
YOU TRULY ARE A BEAST...

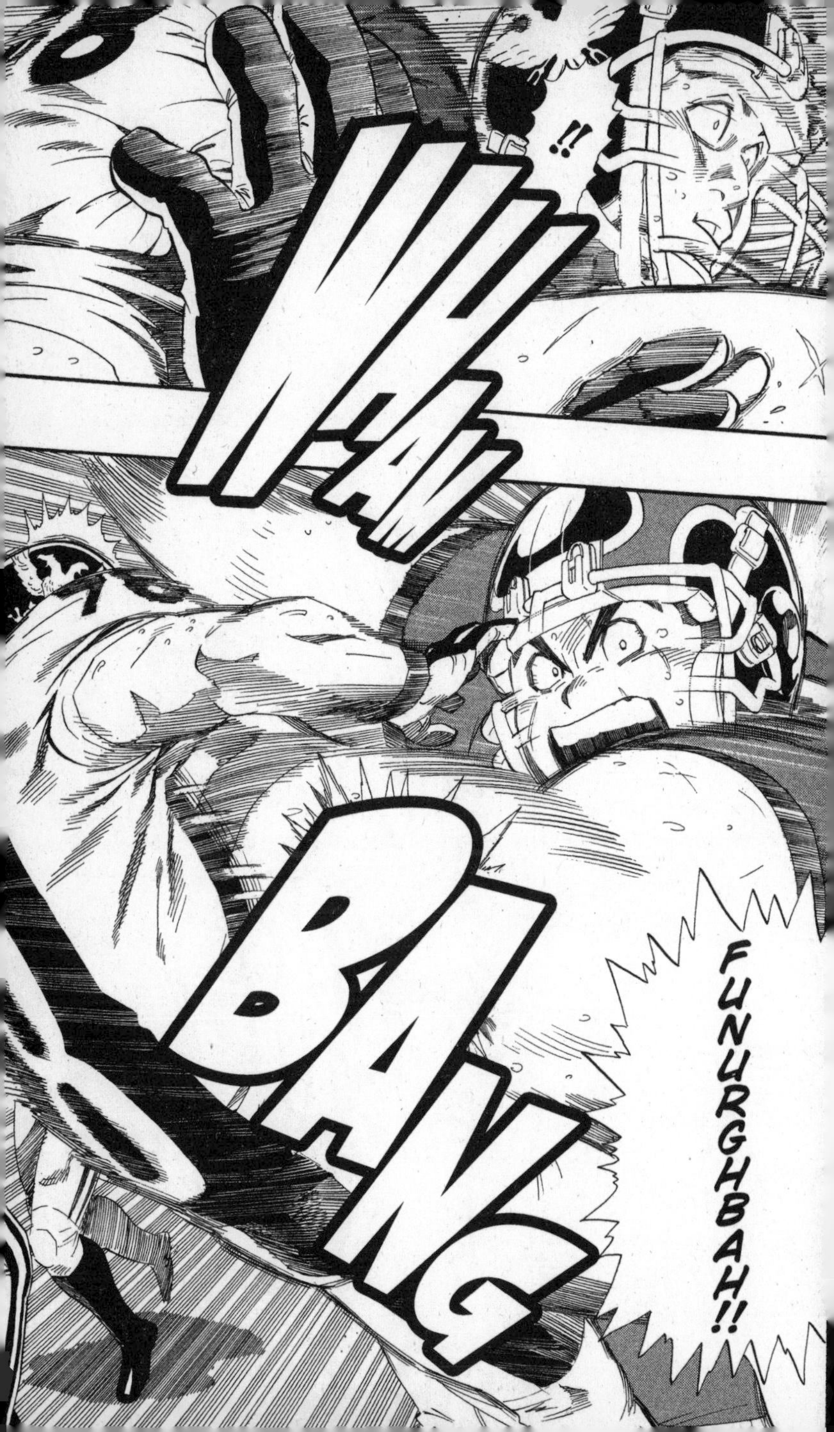
!!
WHAM
FUNURGHBAH!!
BANG

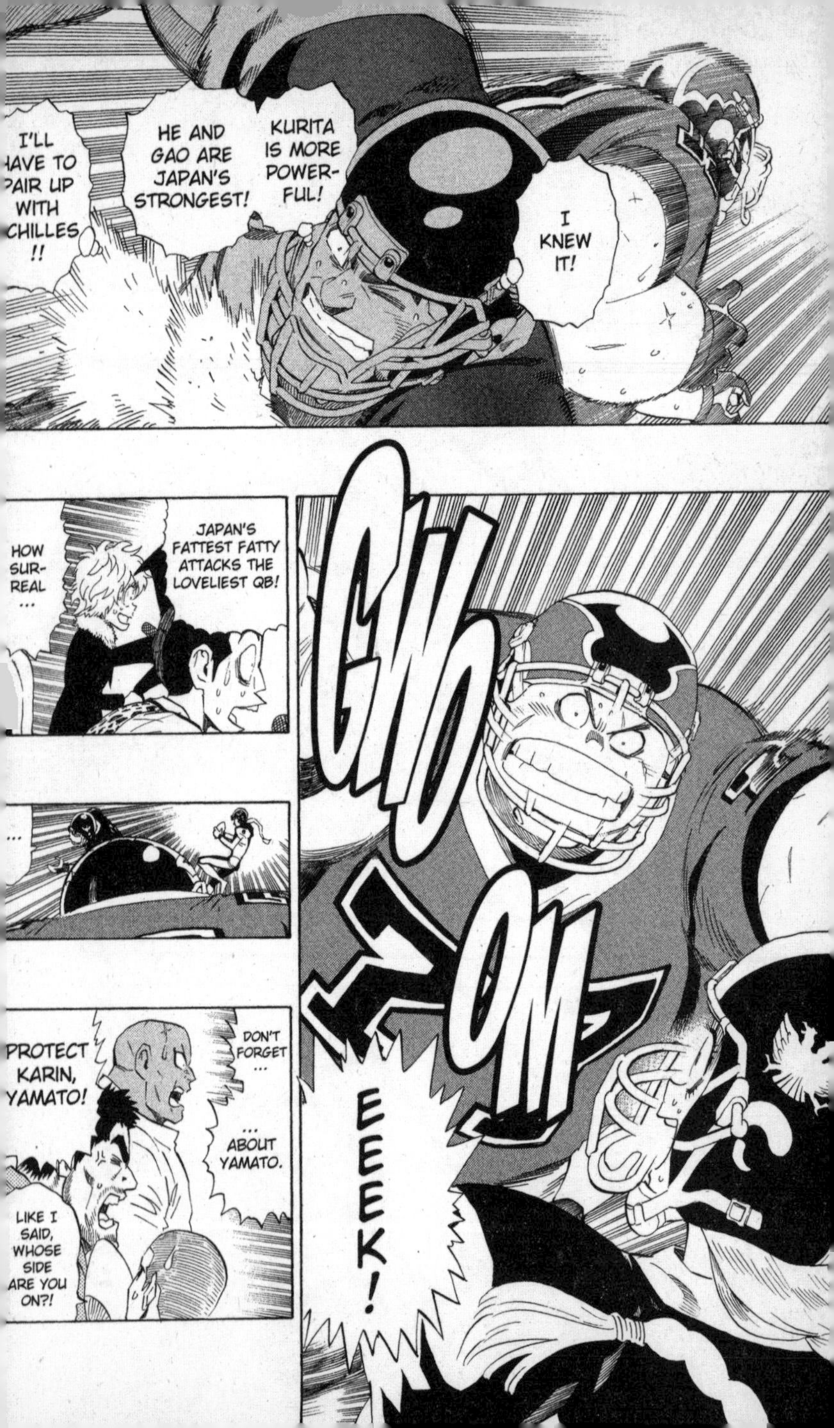
I KNEW IT!
KURITA IS MORE POWERFUL!
HE AND GAO ARE JAPAN'S STRONGEST!
I'LL HAVE TO PAIR UP WITH CHILLES!!
GWOOM
EEEK!
JAPAN'S FATTEST FATTY ATTACKS THE LOVELIEST QB!
HOW SURREAL...
...
DON'T FORGET...
...ABOUT YAMATO.
PROTECT KARIN, YAMATO!
LIKE I SAID, WHOSE SIDE ARE YOU ON?!

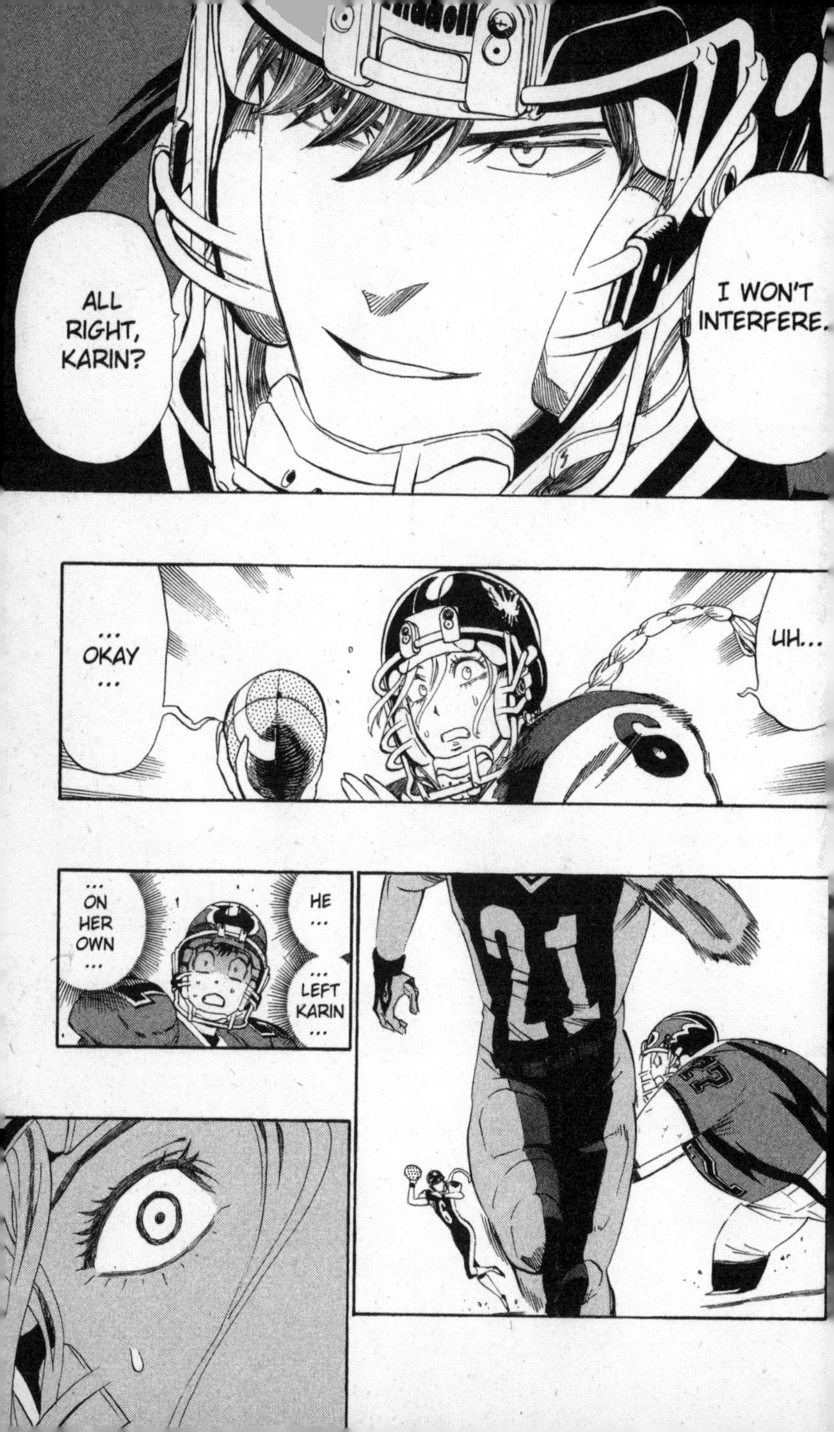
I WON'T INTERFERE.
ALL RIGHT, KARIN?
UH...
...OKAY...
HE... ...LEFT KARIN...
...ON HER OWN...

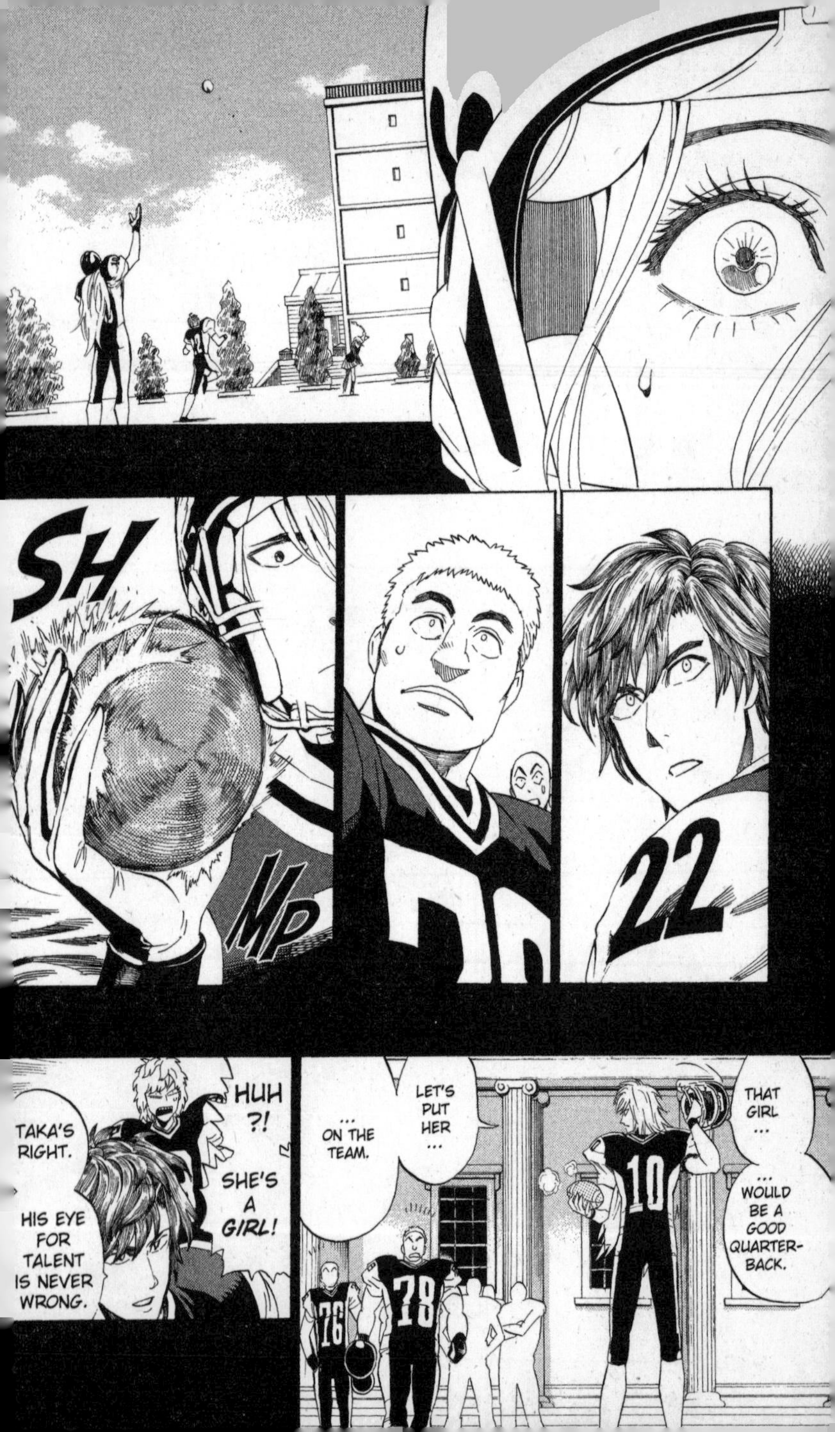
SH
MP
THAT GIRL ...
... WOULD BE A GOOD QUARTER-BACK.
LET'S PUT HER ...
... ON THE TEAM.
HUH ?!
SHE'S A GIRL!
TAKA'S RIGHT.
HIS EYE FOR TALENT IS NEVER WRONG.

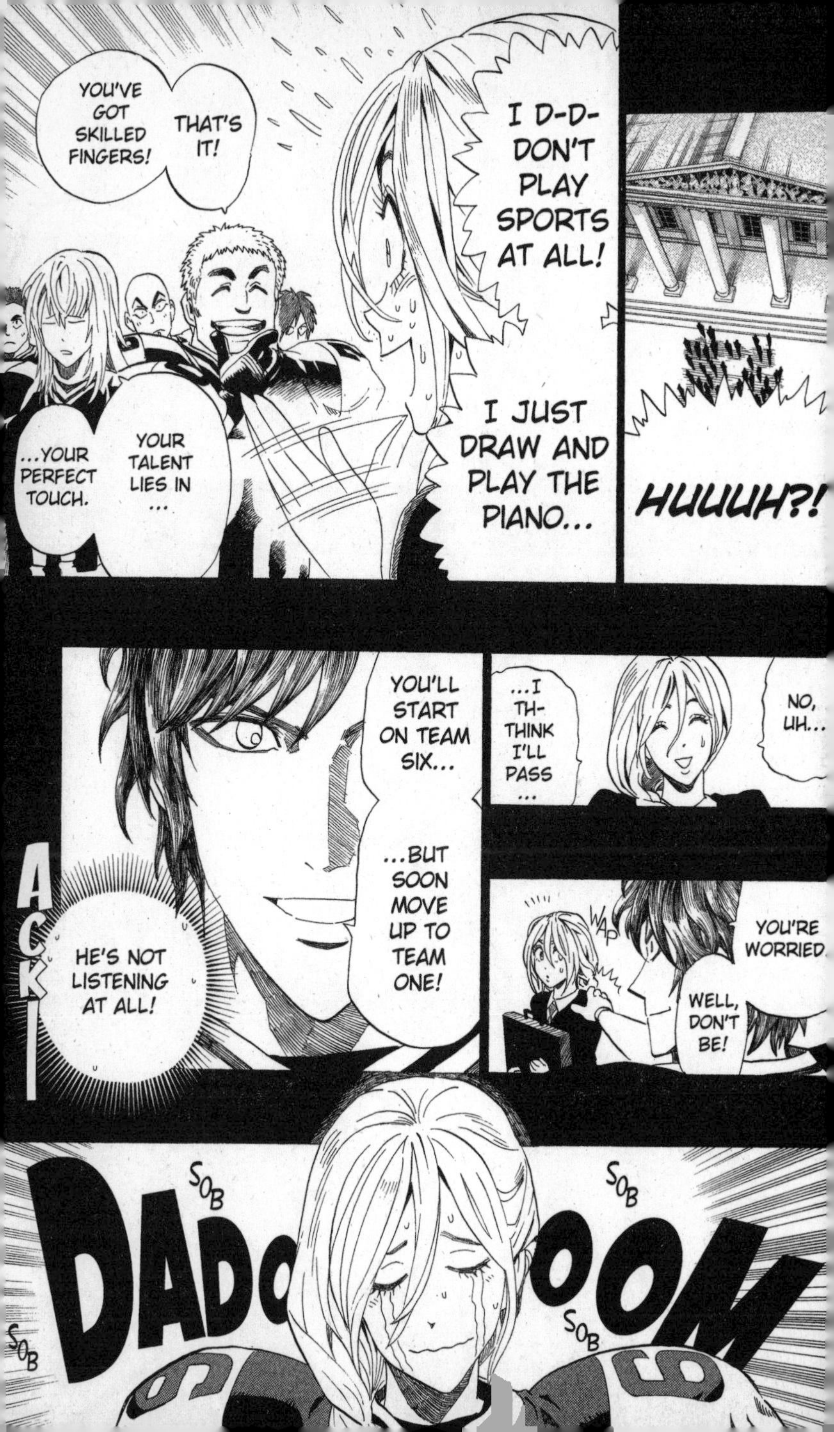
HUUUH?!
I D-D-DON'T PLAY SPORTS AT ALL!
I JUST DRAW AND PLAY THE PIANO...
THAT'S IT!
YOU'VE GOT SKILLED FINGERS!
YOUR TALENT LIES IN ...
...YOUR PERFECT TOUCH.
NO, UH...
...I TH-THINK I'LL PASS ...
YOU'RE WORRIED.
WAP
WELL, DON'T BE!
YOU'LL START ON TEAM SIX...
...BUT SOON MOVE UP TO TEAM ONE!
HE'S NOT LISTENING AT ALL!
ACK
SOB
SOB
SOB
SOB
DADOOOM

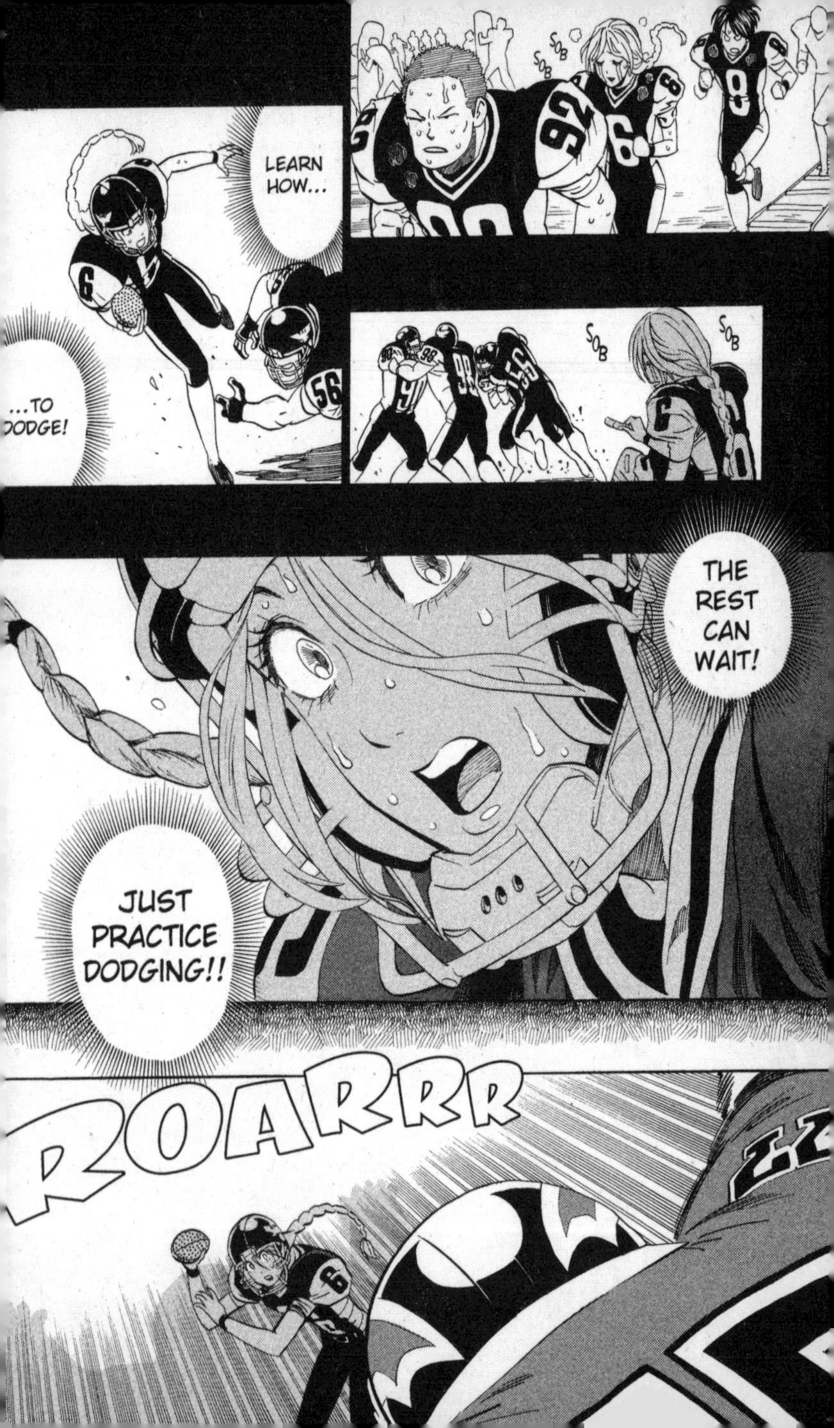
SOB
SOB
SOB
SOB
LEARN HOW...
...TO DODGE!
THE REST CAN WAIT!
JUST PRACTICE DODGING!!
ROARRR

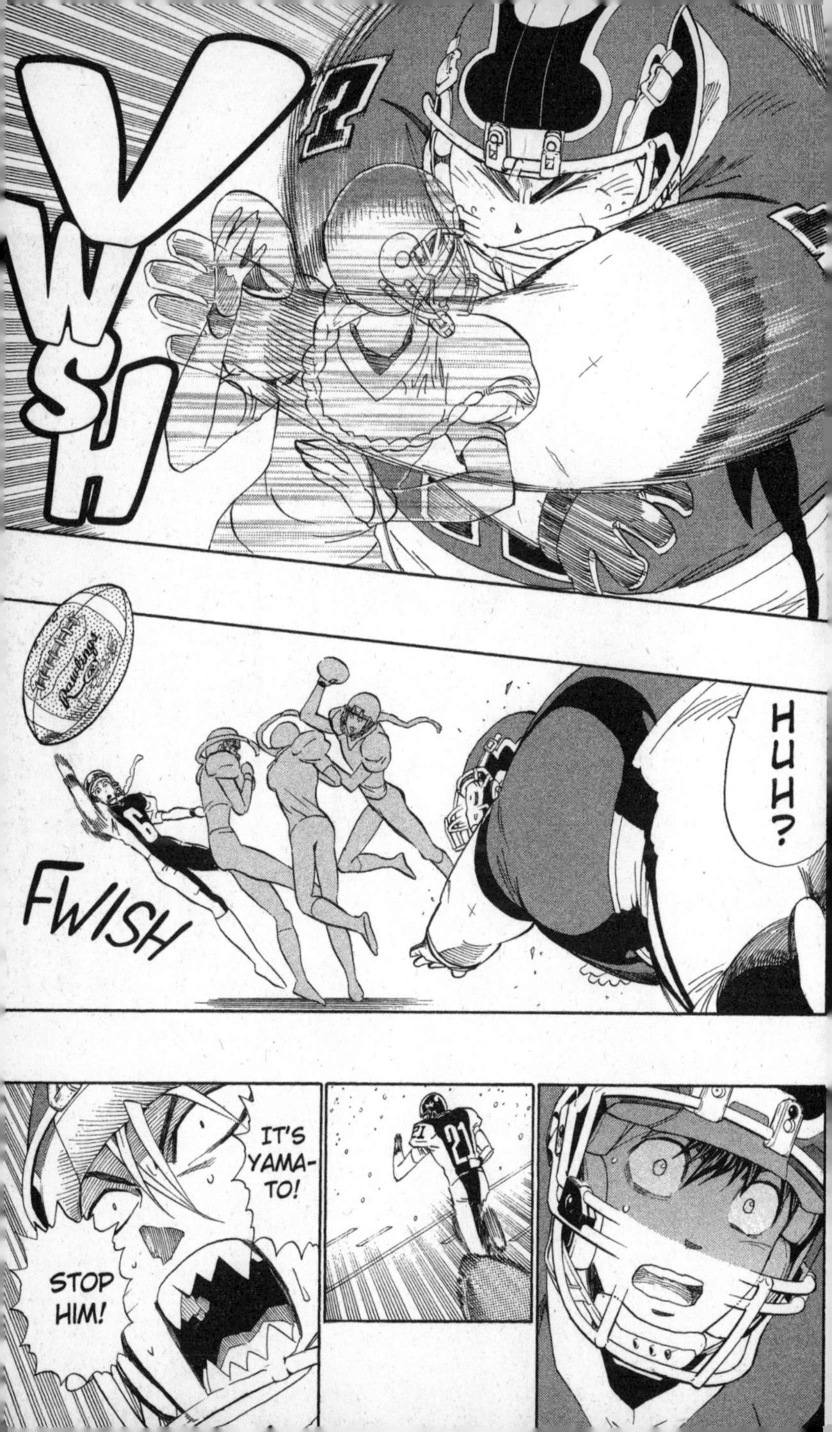
VWSH
HUH?
Rawlings
FWISH
IT'S YAMA-TO!
STOP HIM!

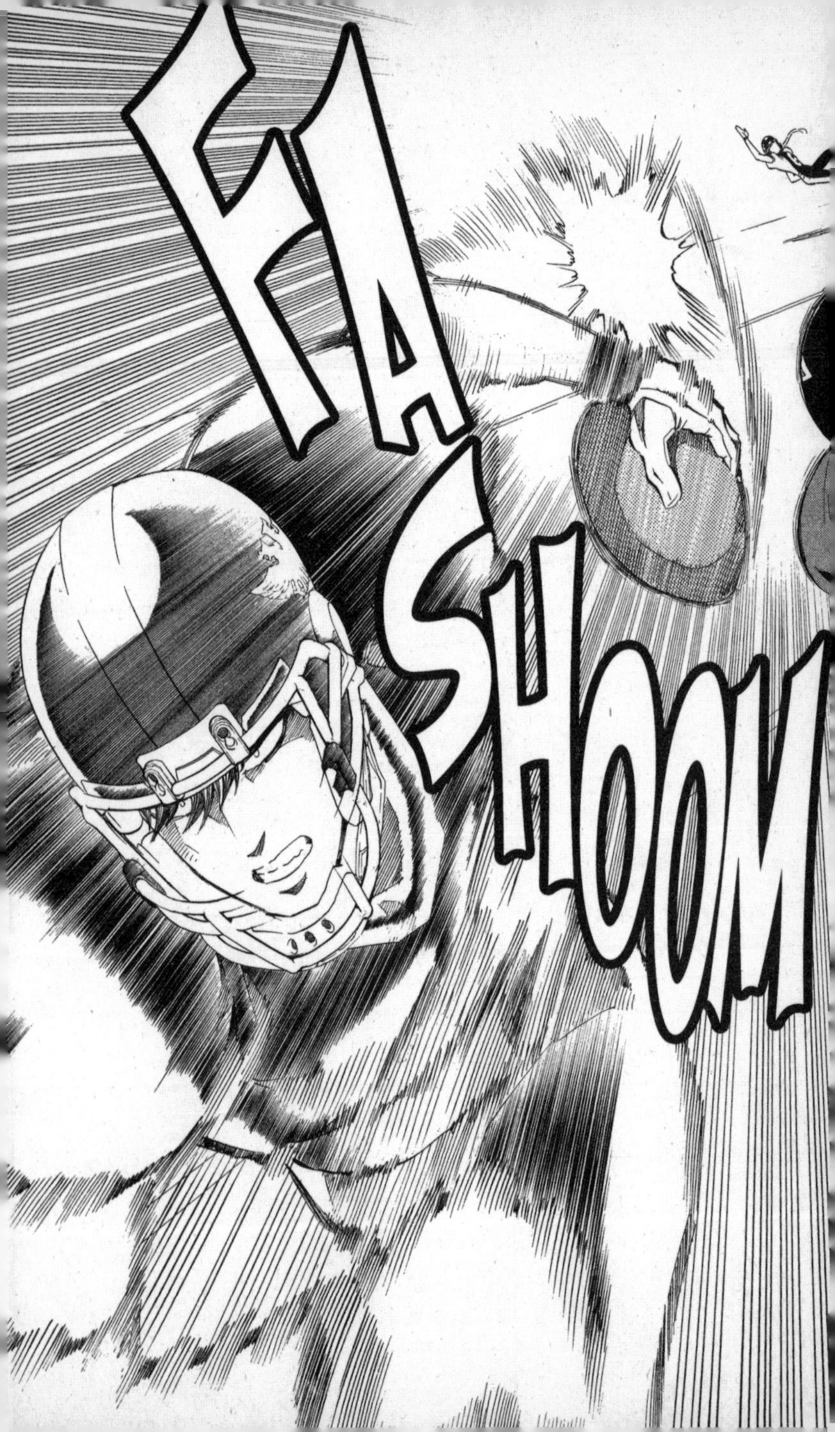
FWA SHOOM

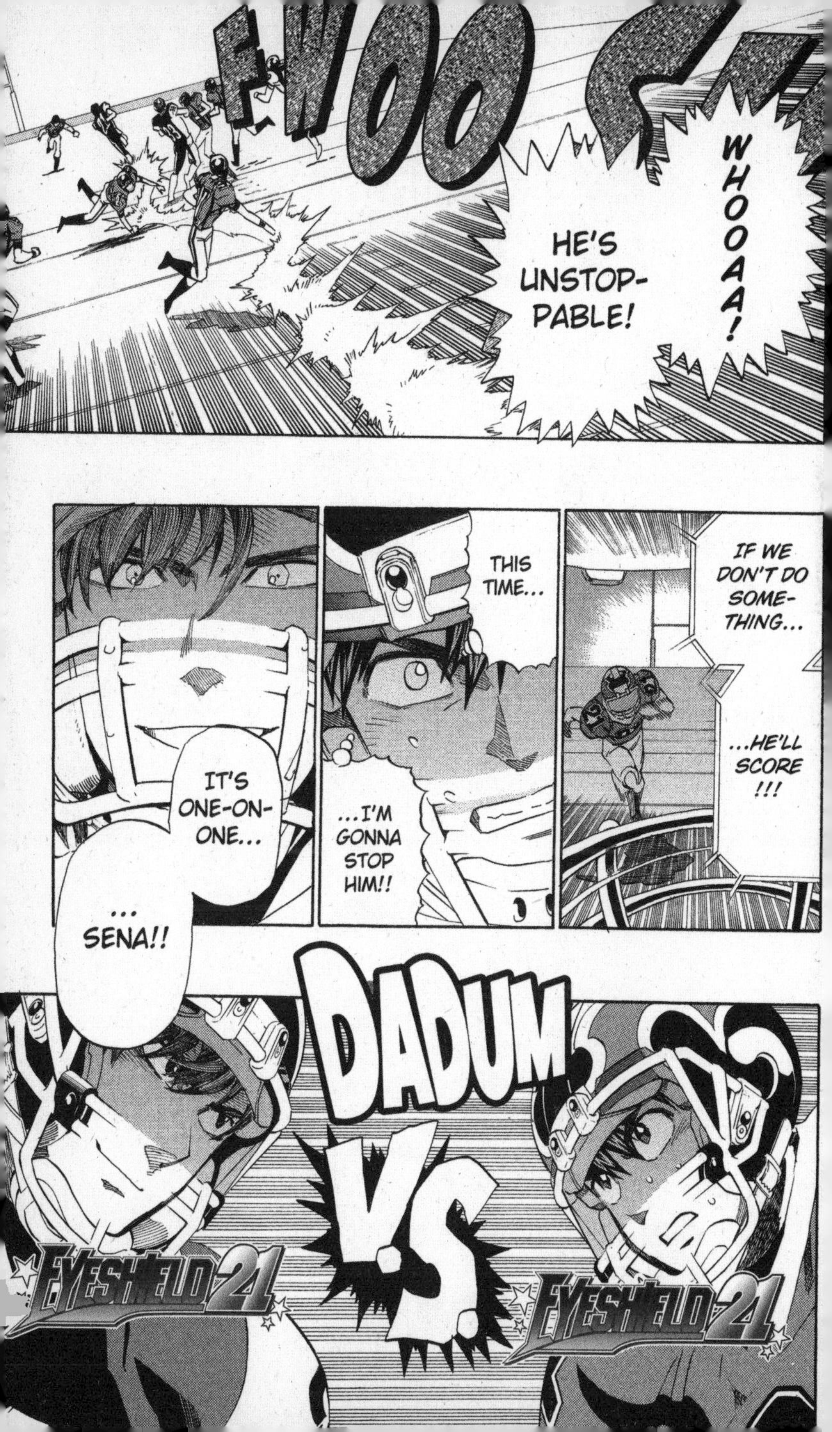
FWOO
WHOOAAA!
HE'S UNSTOP-PABLE!
IF WE DON'T DO SOME-THING...
...HE'LL SCORE!!!
THIS TIME...
...I'M GONNA STOP HIM!!
IT'S ONE-ON-ONE...
...SENA!!
DADUM
EYESHIELD 21
VS
EYESHIELD 21

Devil Bat 021

Investigation File #138

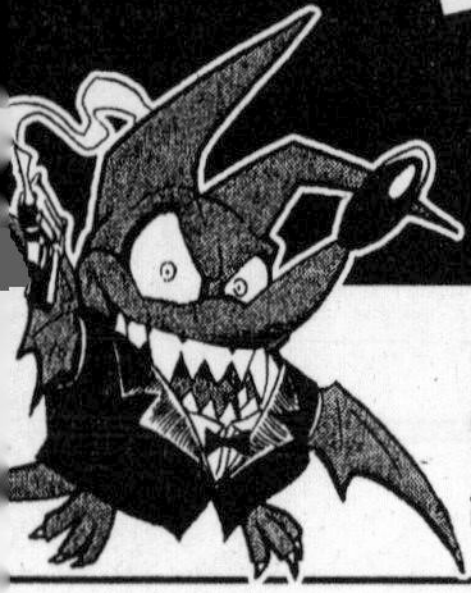

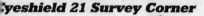

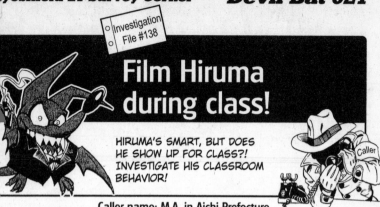

Film Hiruma during class!

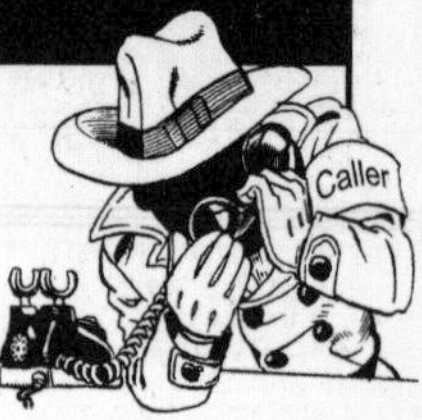
Caller

HIRUMA'S SMART, BUT DOES HE SHOW UP FOR CLASS?! INVESTIGATE HIS CLASSROOM BEHAVIOR!

Caller name: M.A. in Aichi Prefecture

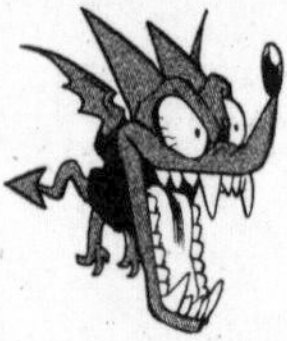

YOU CAN'T PLAY SPORTS UNLESS YOU ATTEND CLASSES, SO HE'S ALWAYS PRESENT!

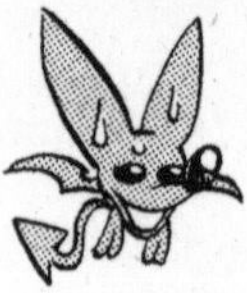

YEAH, BUT HE ONLY LISTENS WITH ONE EAR...

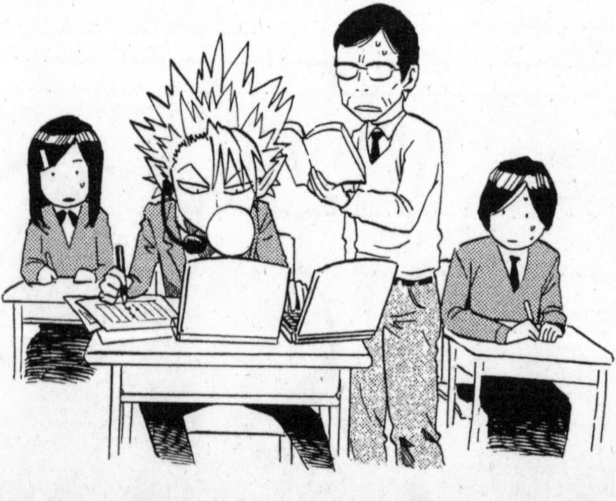

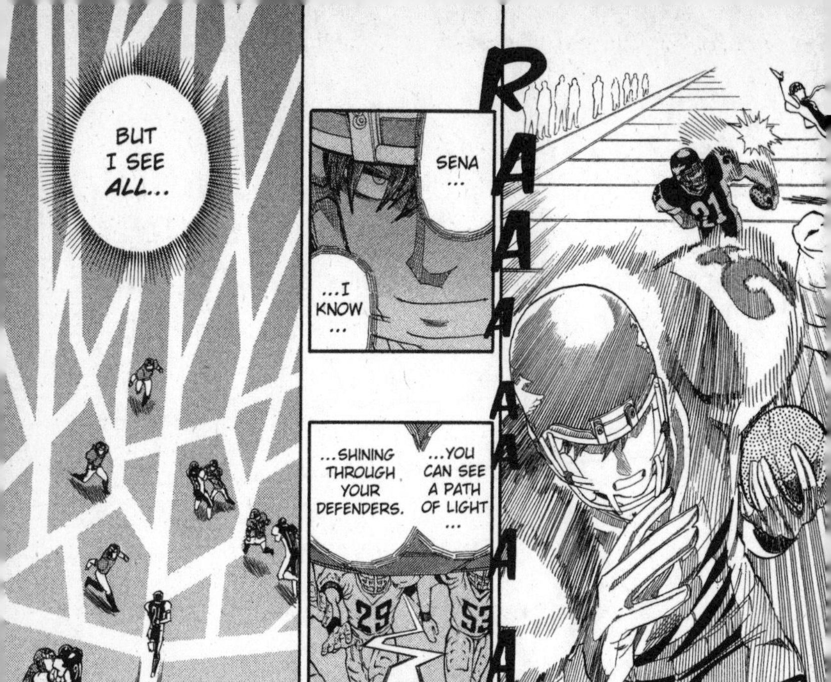
RAAAAAAAAH
FSHOOM
SENA...
...I KNOW...
...YOU CAN SEE A PATH OF LIGHT...
...SHINING THROUGH YOUR DEFENDERS.
BUT I SEE ALL...
...THE POSSIBLE ROUTES.

Chapter 286 Running vs. Running

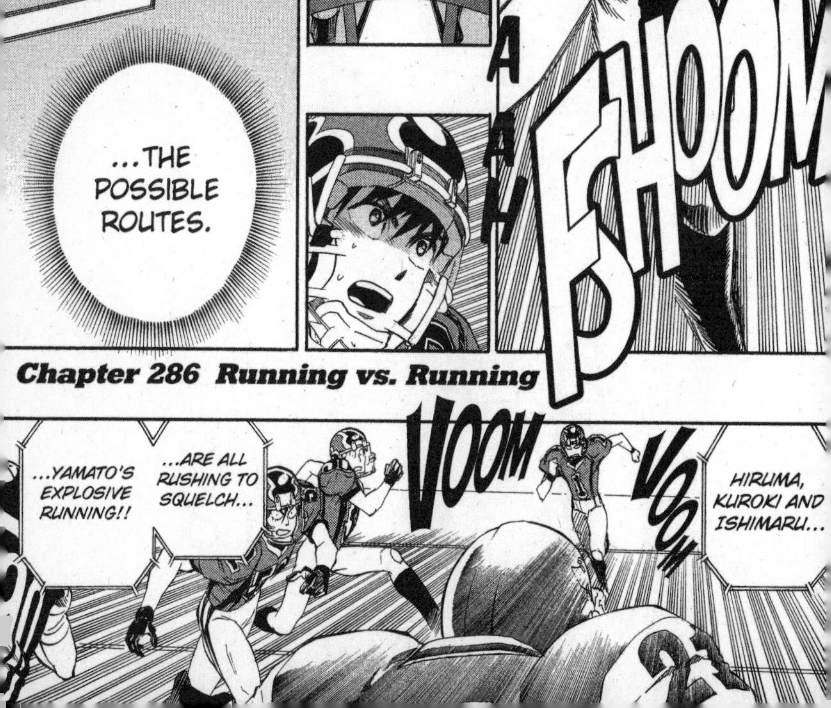
HIRUMA, KUROKI AND ISHIMARU...
VOOM
VOOM
...ARE ALL RUSHING TO SQUELCH...
...YAMATO'S EXPLOSIVE RUNNING!!

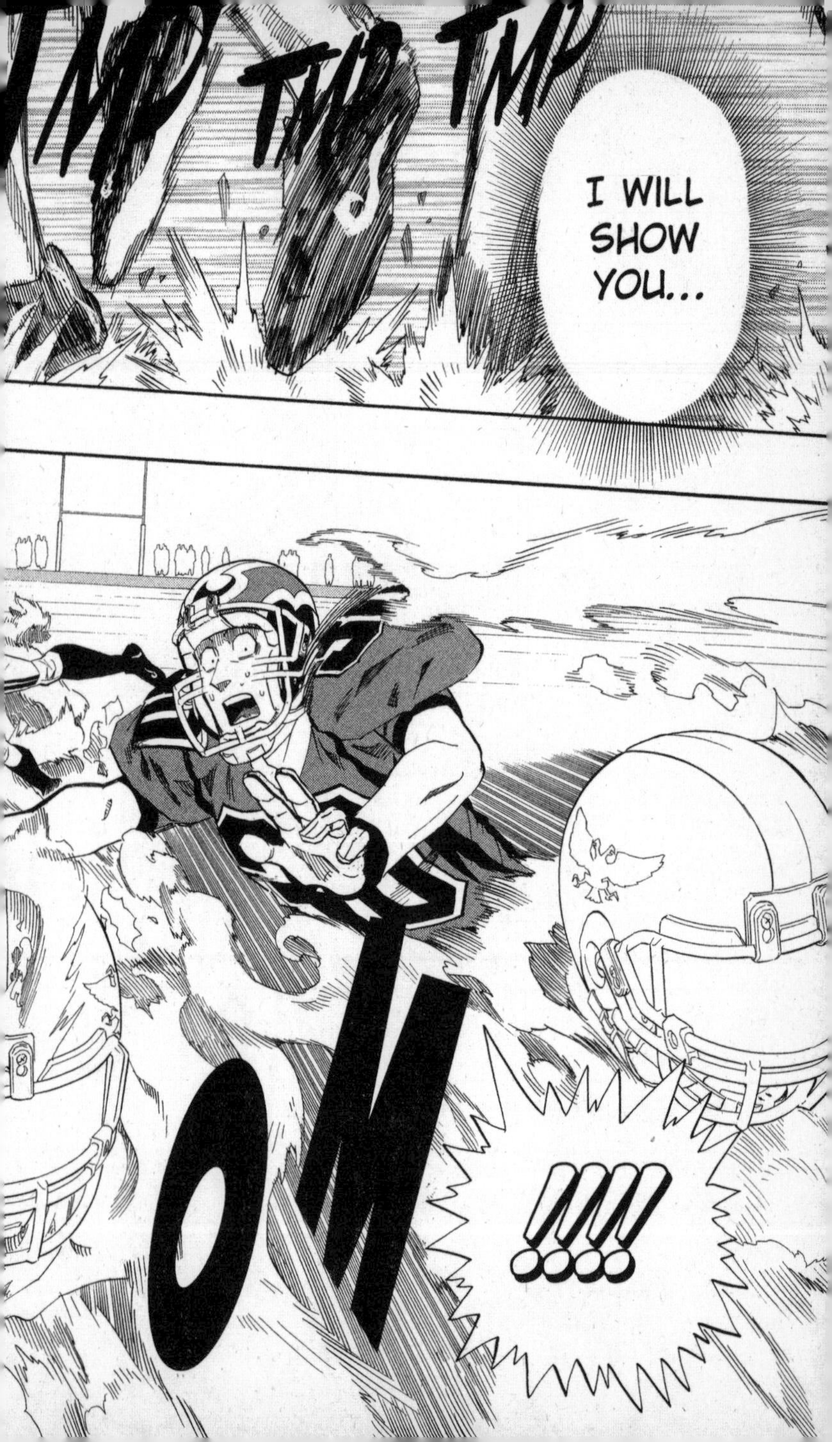
I WILL SHOW YOU...
TMP TMP TMP

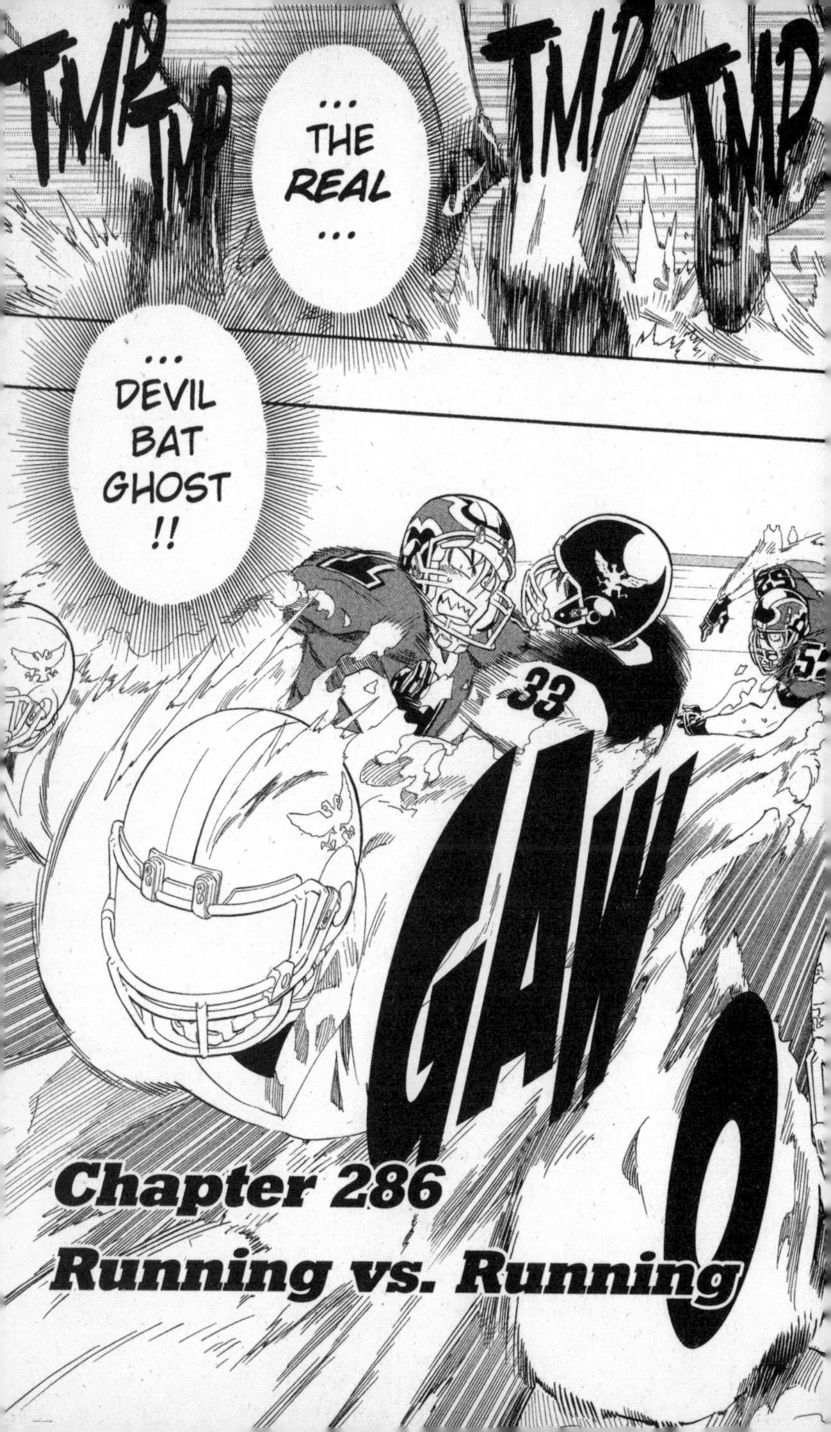

TMP TMP
... THE REAL ...
TMP TMP
... DEVIL BAT GHOST !!
GAWO
Chapter 286
Running vs. Running

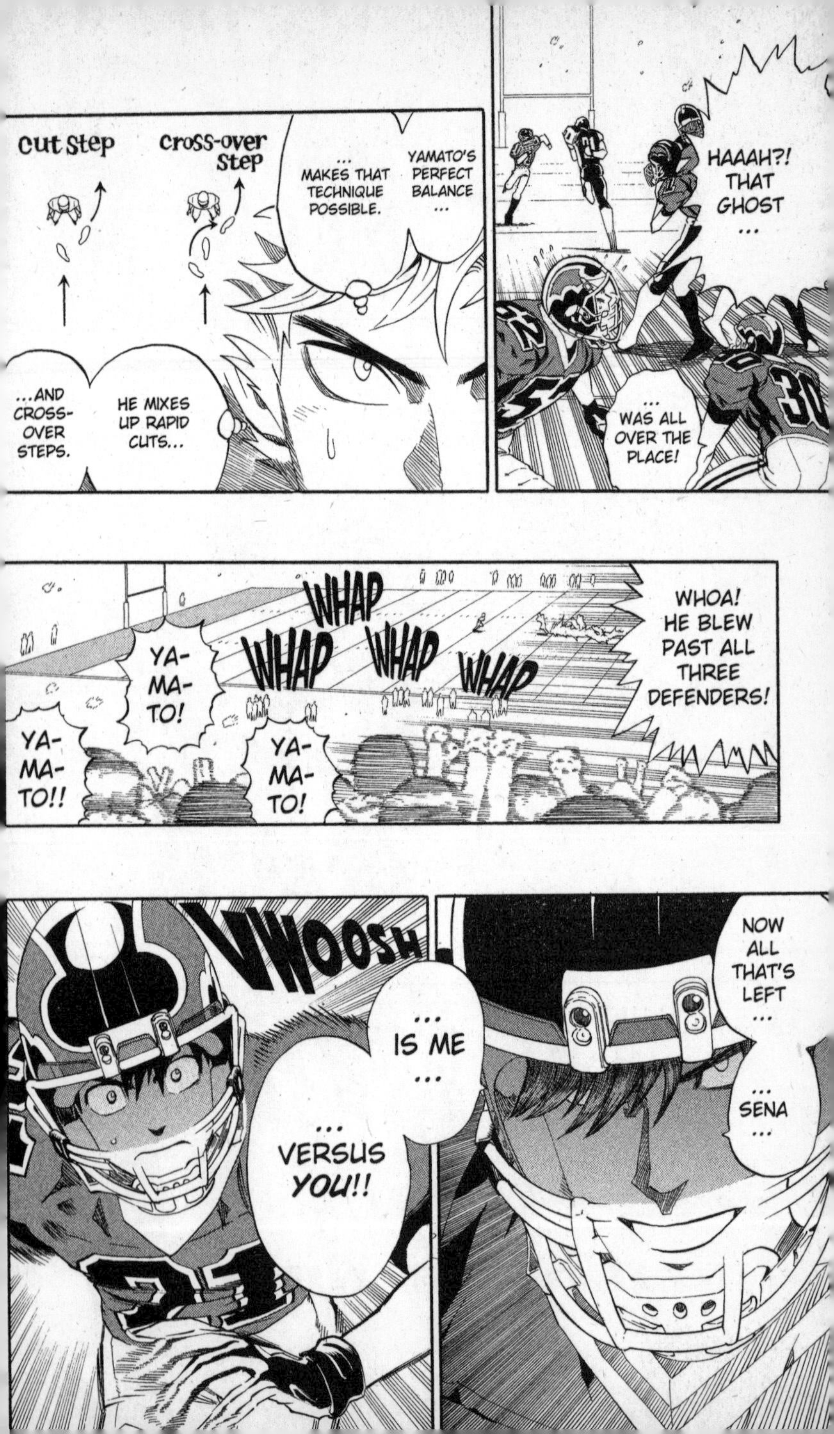
HAAAH?! THAT GHOST ...
... WAS ALL OVER THE PLACE!
YAMATO'S PERFECT BALANCE ...
... MAKES THAT TECHNIQUE POSSIBLE.
Cross-over Step
Cut Step
HE MIXES UP RAPID CUTS...
...AND CROSS-OVER STEPS.
WHOA! HE BLEW PAST ALL THREE DEFENDERS!
WHAP
WHAP
WHAP
WHAP
YA-MA-TO!
YA-MA-TO!
YA-MA-TO!!
NOW ALL THAT'S LEFT ...
... SENA ...
VWOOSH
... IS ME ...
... VERSUS YOU!!

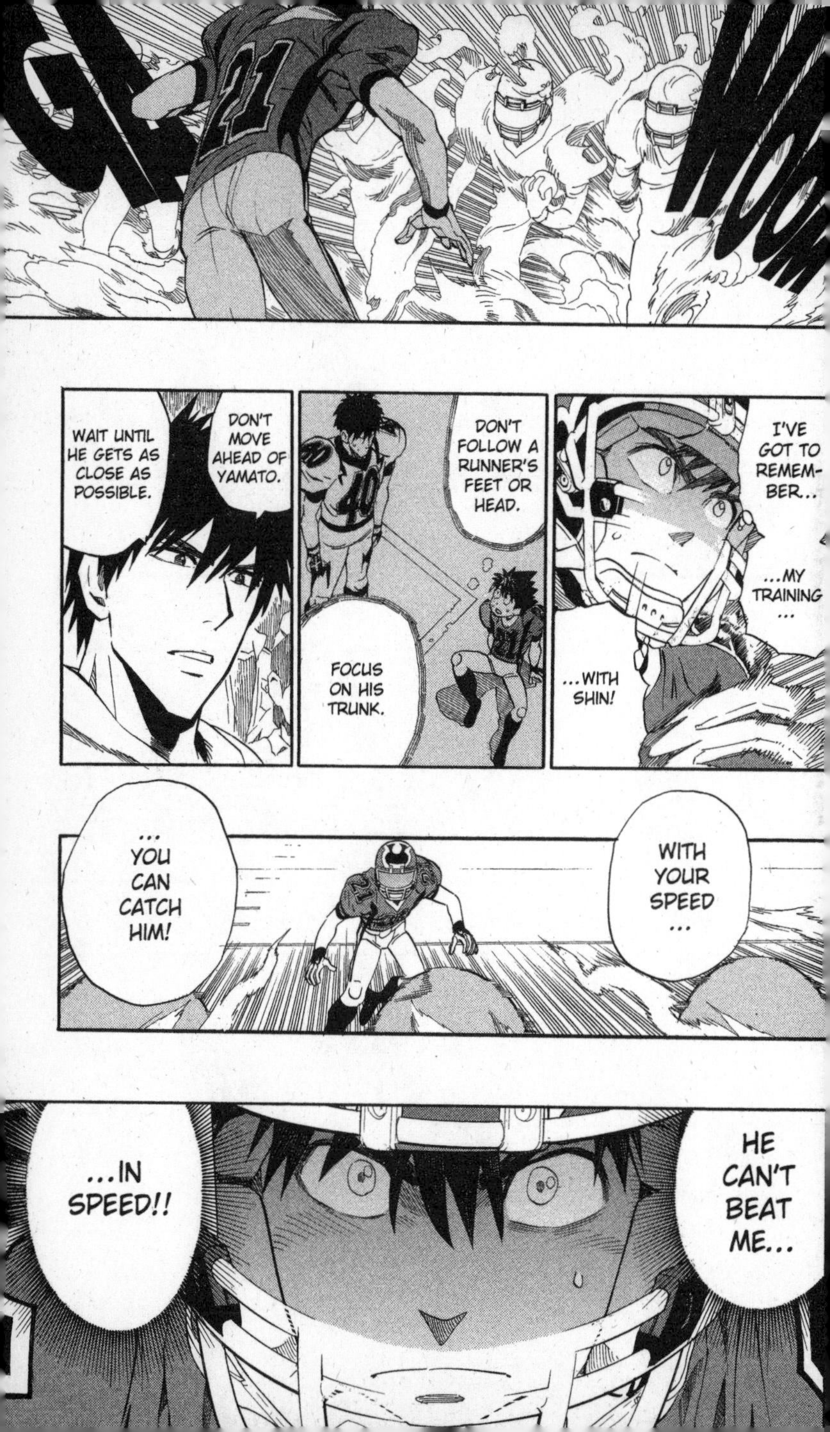
I'VE GOT TO REMEM-BER...
...MY TRAINING...
...WITH SHIN!
DON'T FOLLOW A RUNNER'S FEET OR HEAD.
FOCUS ON HIS TRUNK.
DON'T MOVE AHEAD OF YAMATO.
WAIT UNTIL HE GETS AS CLOSE AS POSSIBLE.
WITH YOUR SPEED...
...YOU CAN CATCH HIM!
HE CAN'T BEAT ME...
...IN SPEED!!

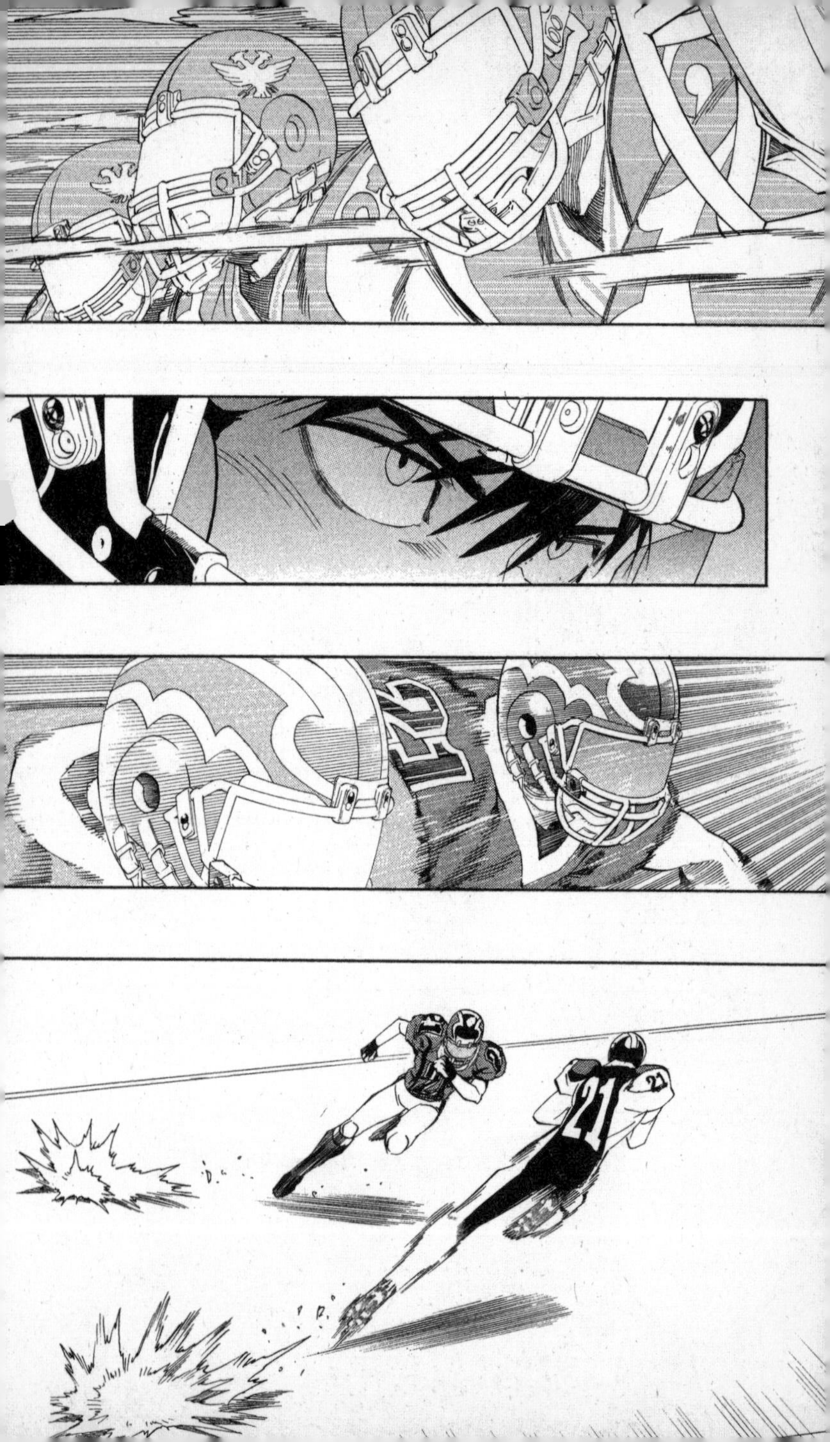

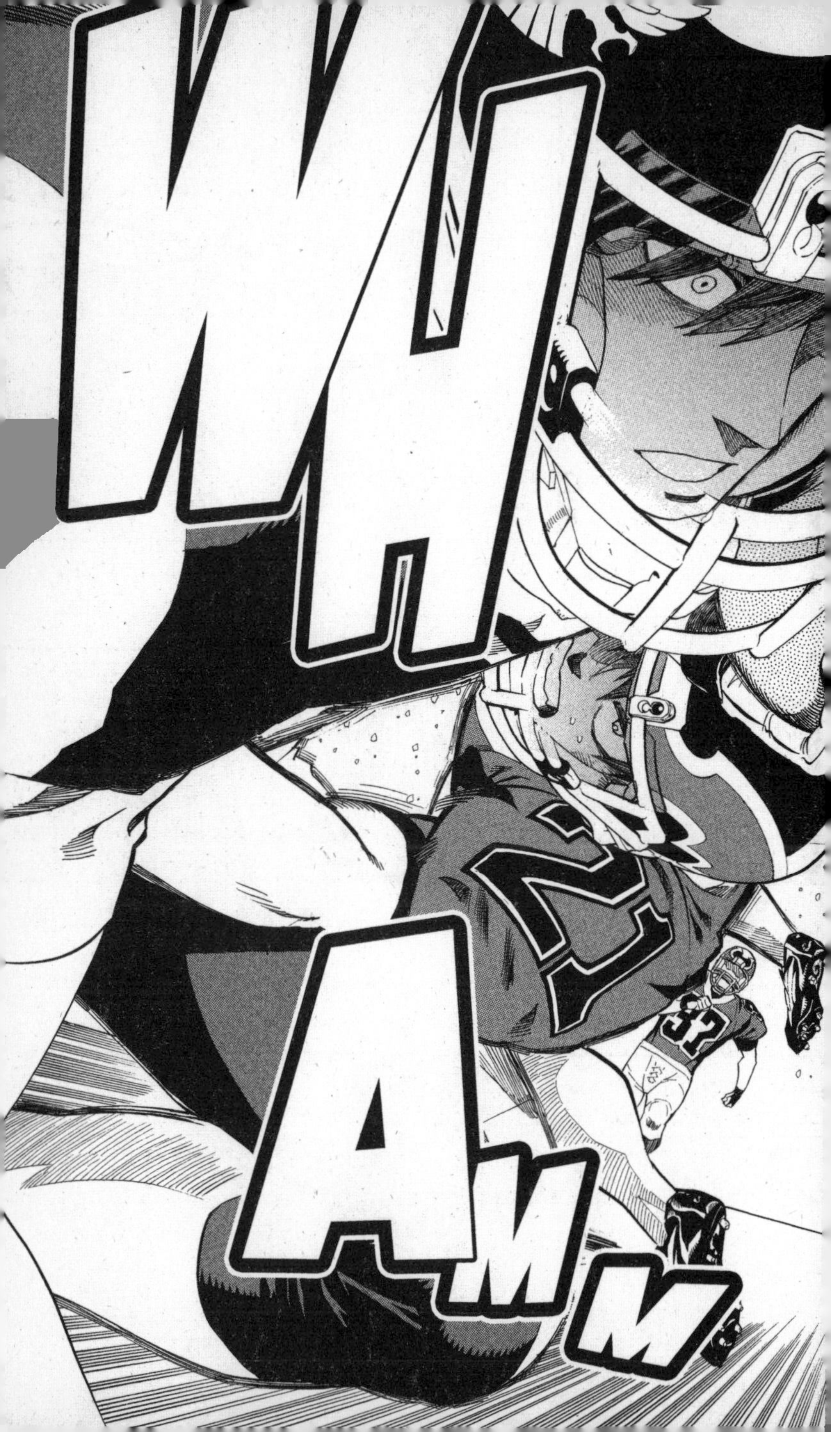
WHAMM

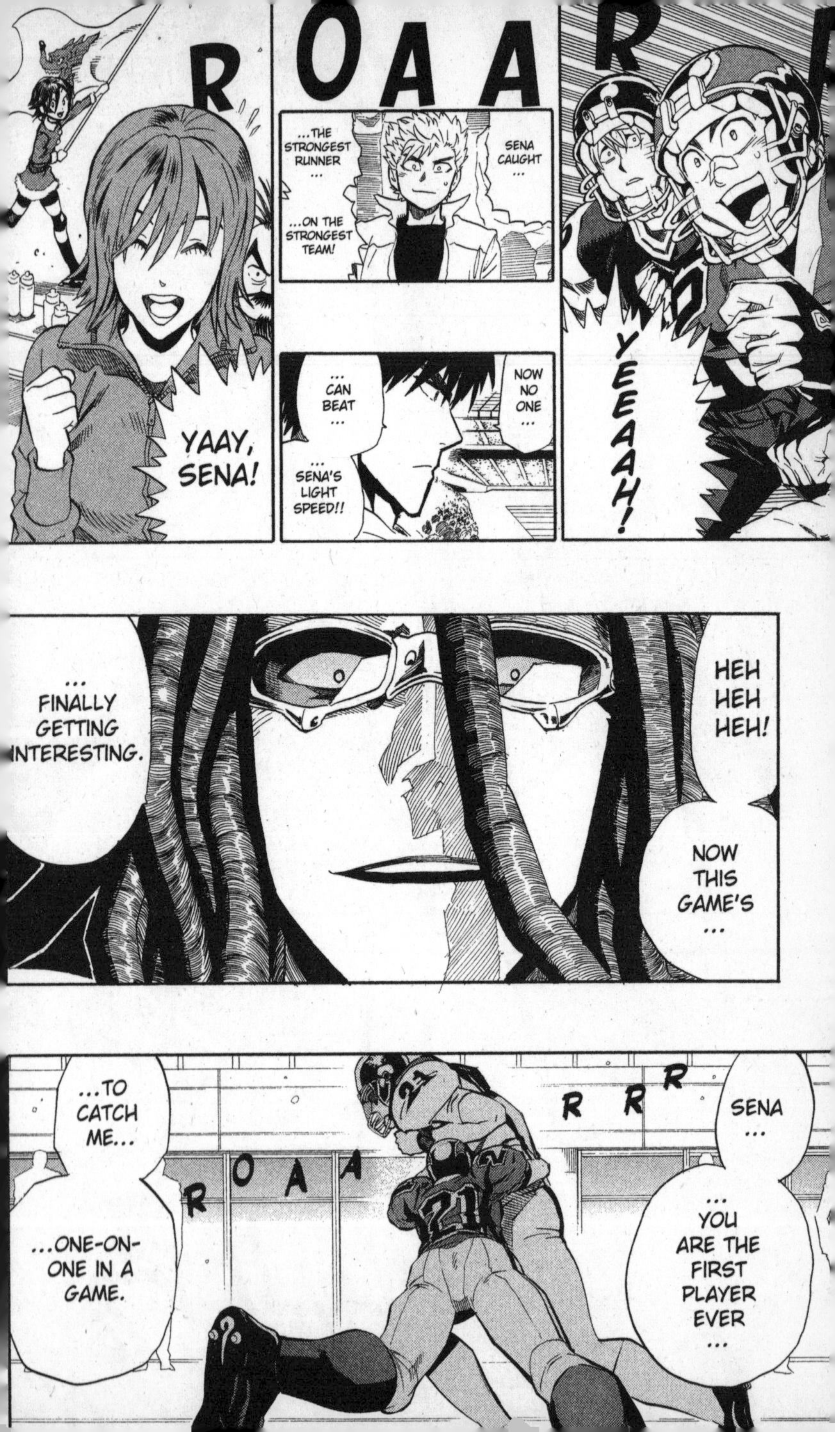

ROAARR
YEEAAAH!
SENA CAUGHT...
...THE STRONGEST RUNNER...
...ON THE STRONGEST TEAM!
NOW NO ONE...
...CAN BEAT...
...SENA'S LIGHT SPEED!!
YAAY, SENA!
HEH HEH HEH!
NOW THIS GAME'S...
...FINALLY GETTING INTERESTING.
SENA...
...YOU ARE THE FIRST PLAYER EVER...
...TO CATCH ME...
...ONE-ON-ONE IN A GAME.
ROAARRR

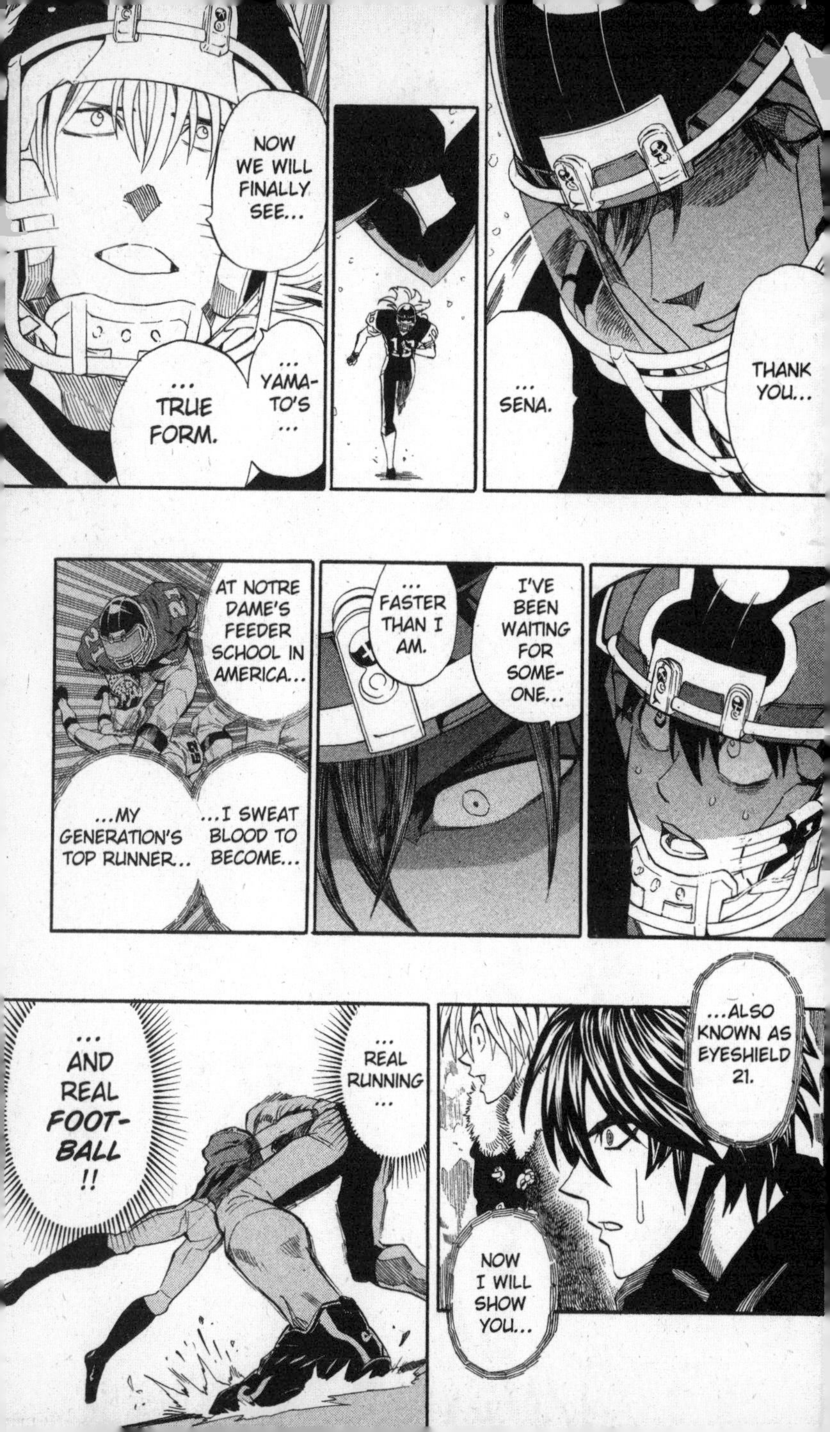
THANK YOU...
...SENA.
NOW WE WILL FINALLY SEE...
...YAMATO'S...
...TRUE FORM.
I'VE BEEN WAITING FOR SOMEONE...
...FASTER THAN I AM.
AT NOTRE DAME'S FEEDER SCHOOL IN AMERICA...
...I SWEAT BLOOD TO BECOME...
...MY GENERATION'S TOP RUNNER...
...ALSO KNOWN AS EYESHIELD 21.
NOW I WILL SHOW YOU...
...REAL RUNNING...
...AND REAL FOOTBALL!!

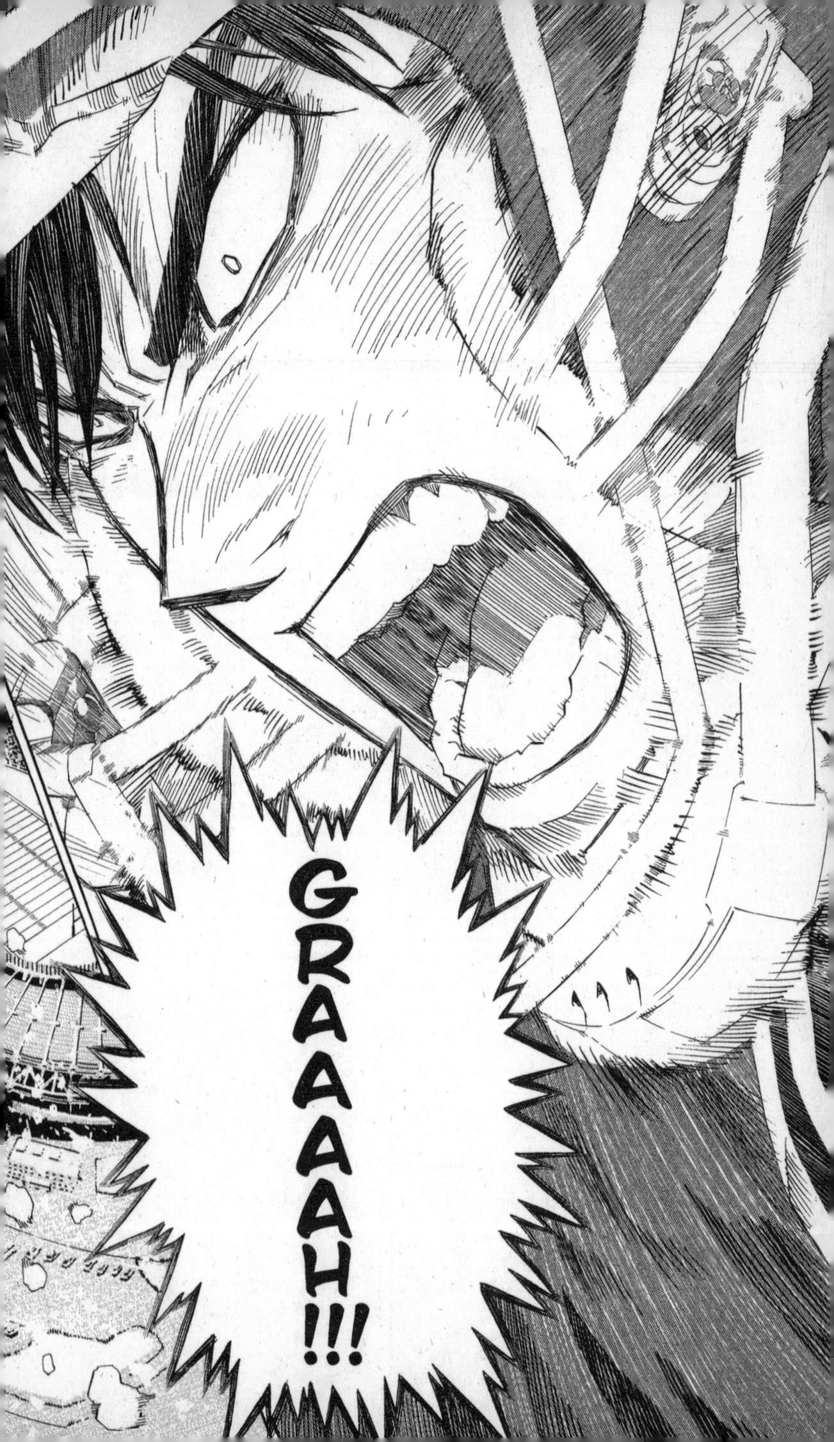
GRAAAAH!!!

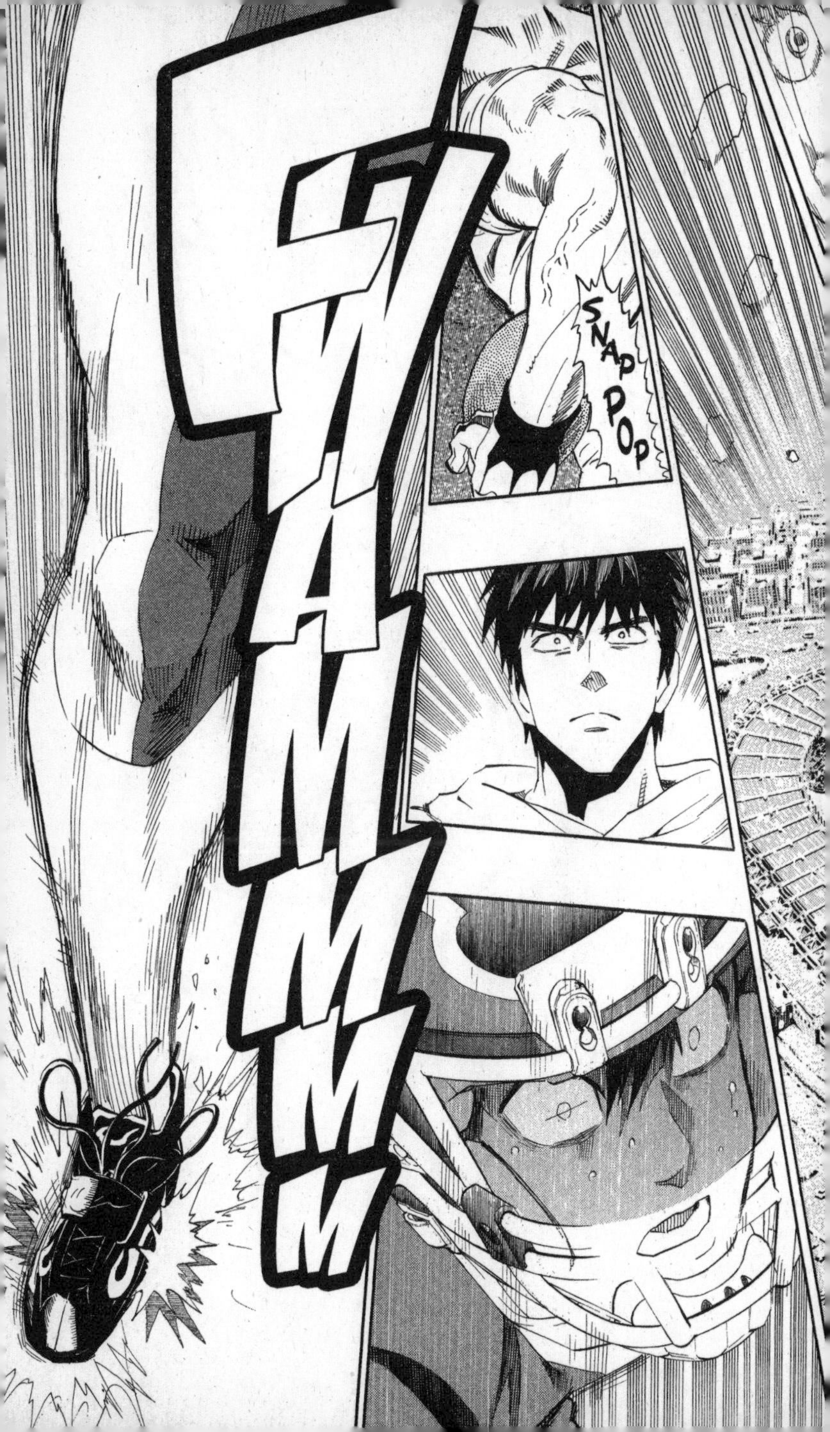
SNAP POP
FWAMMM!

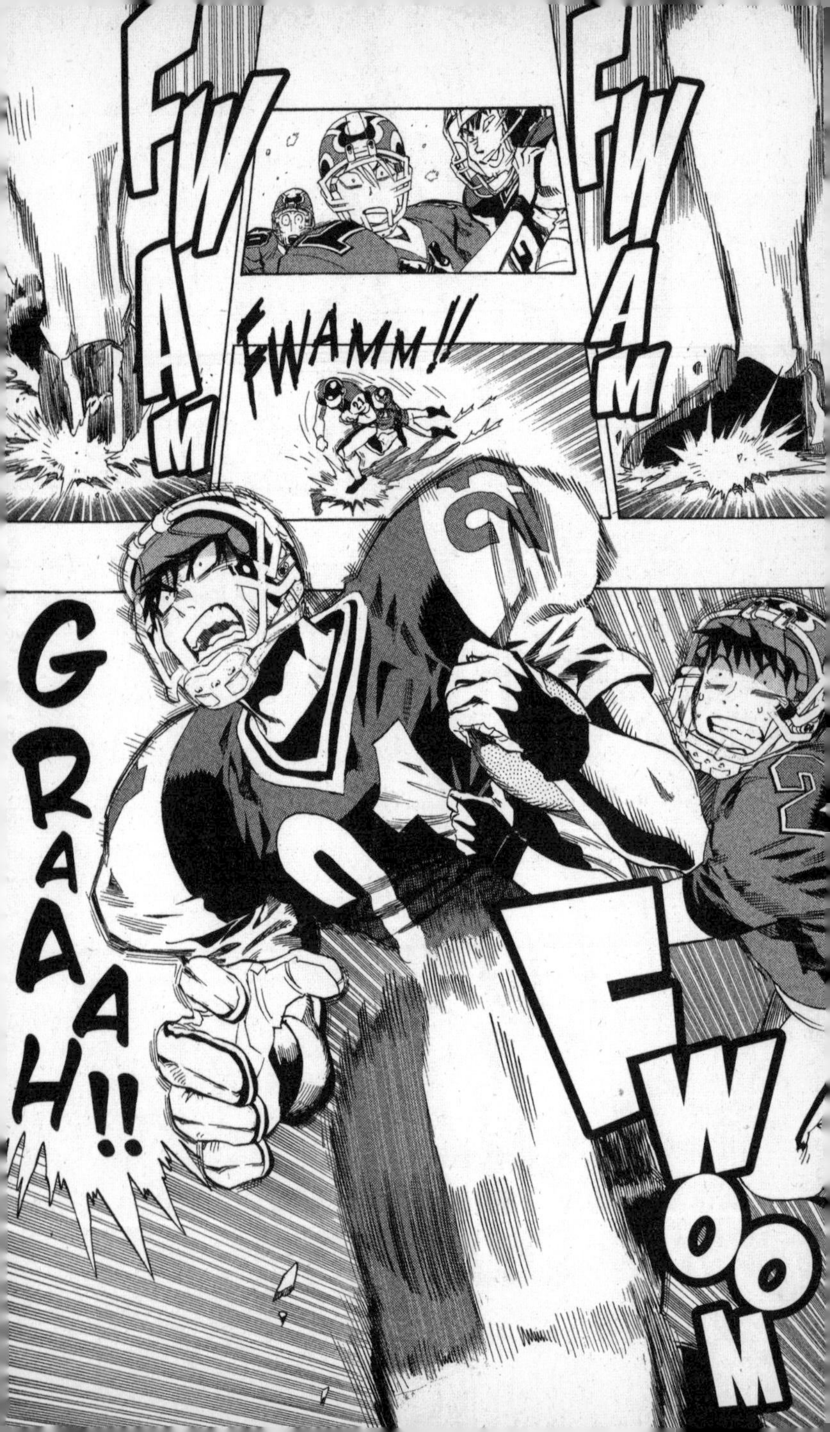
FWAM
FWAMM!!
FWAM
FWOOM
GRAAAH!!

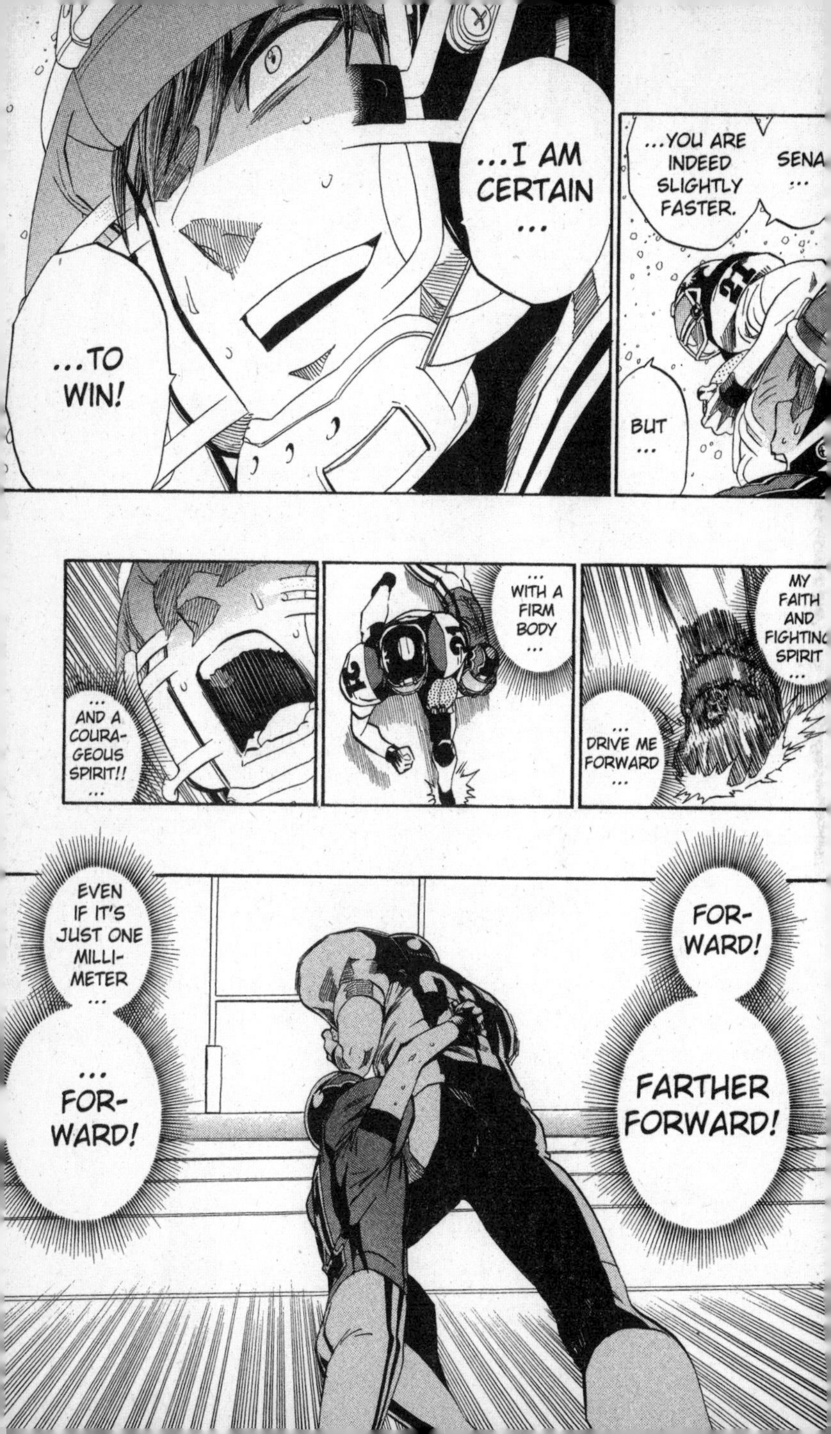
SENA ...
...YOU ARE INDEED SLIGHTLY FASTER.
BUT ...
...I AM CERTAIN ...
...TO WIN!
MY FAITH AND FIGHTING SPIRIT ...
... DRIVE ME FORWARD ...
... WITH A FIRM BODY ...
... AND A COURAGEOUS SPIRIT!! ...
FORWARD!
FARTHER FORWARD!
EVEN IF IT'S JUST ONE MILLIMETER ...
... FORWARD!

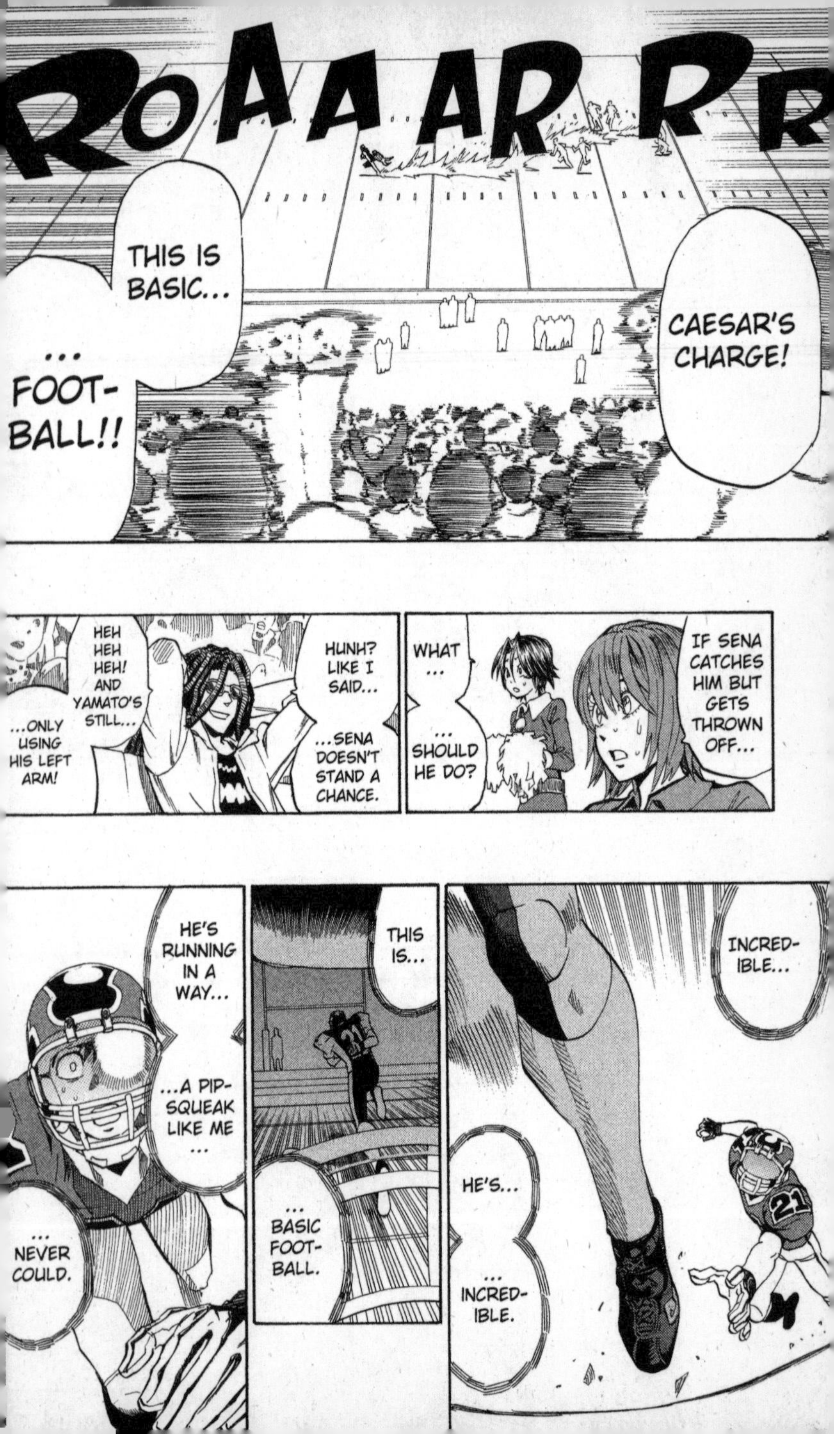
ROAAARRR
CAESAR'S CHARGE!
THIS IS BASIC...
...FOOT-BALL!!
IF SENA CATCHES HIM BUT GETS THROWN OFF...
WHAT...
...SHOULD HE DO?
HUNH? LIKE I SAID...
...SENA DOESN'T STAND A CHANCE.
HEH HEH HEH! AND YAMATO'S STILL...
...ONLY USING HIS LEFT ARM!
INCRED-IBLE...
HE'S...
...INCRED-IBLE.
THIS IS...
...BASIC FOOT-BALL.
HE'S RUNNING IN A WAY...
...A PIP-SQUEAK LIKE ME...
...NEVER COULD.

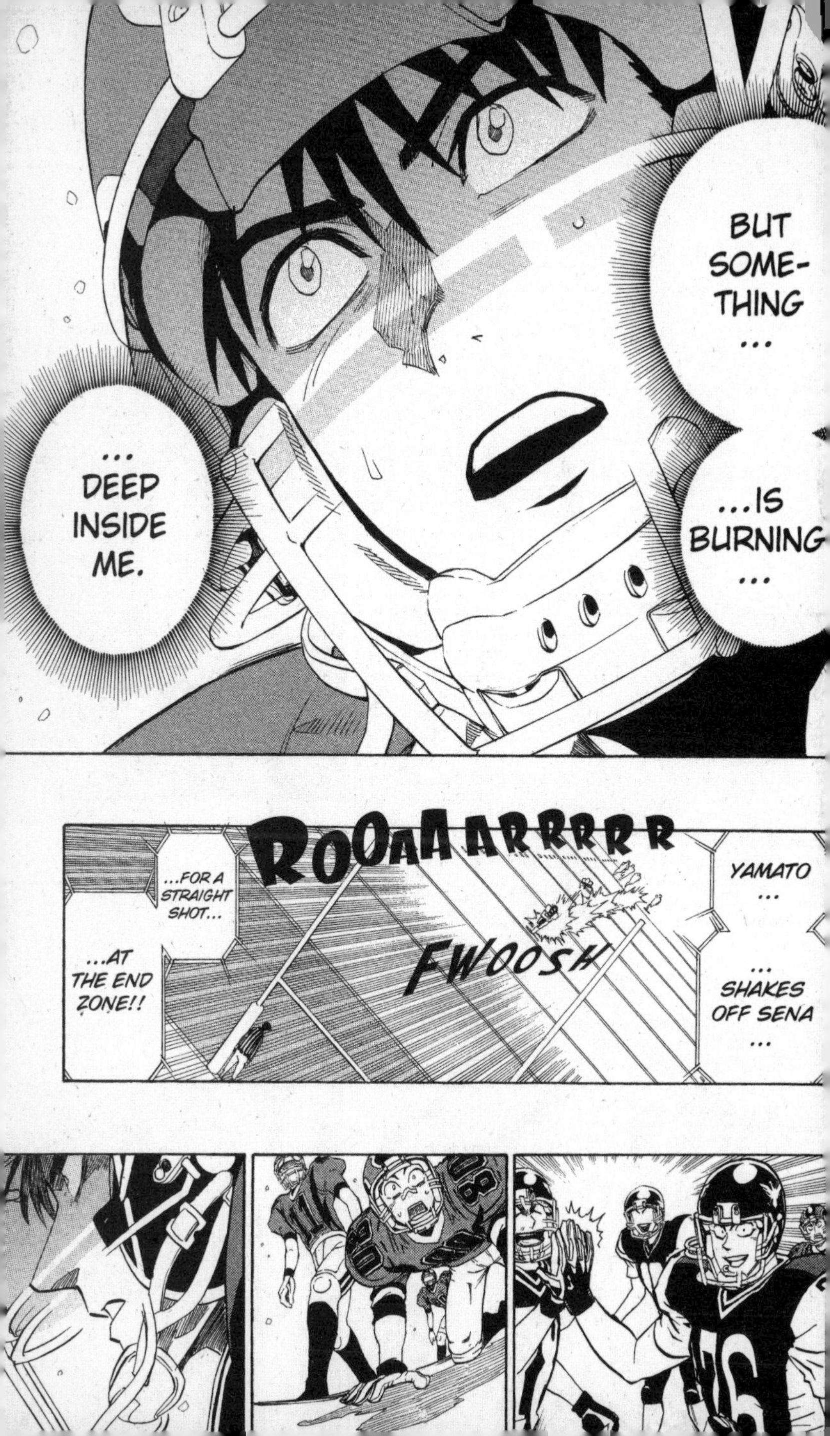
BUT SOME-THING ...
...IS BURNING ...
... DEEP INSIDE ME.
ROOAAARRRRR
YAMATO ...
... SHAKES OFF SENA ...
FWOOSH
...FOR A STRAIGHT SHOT...
...AT THE END ZONE!!

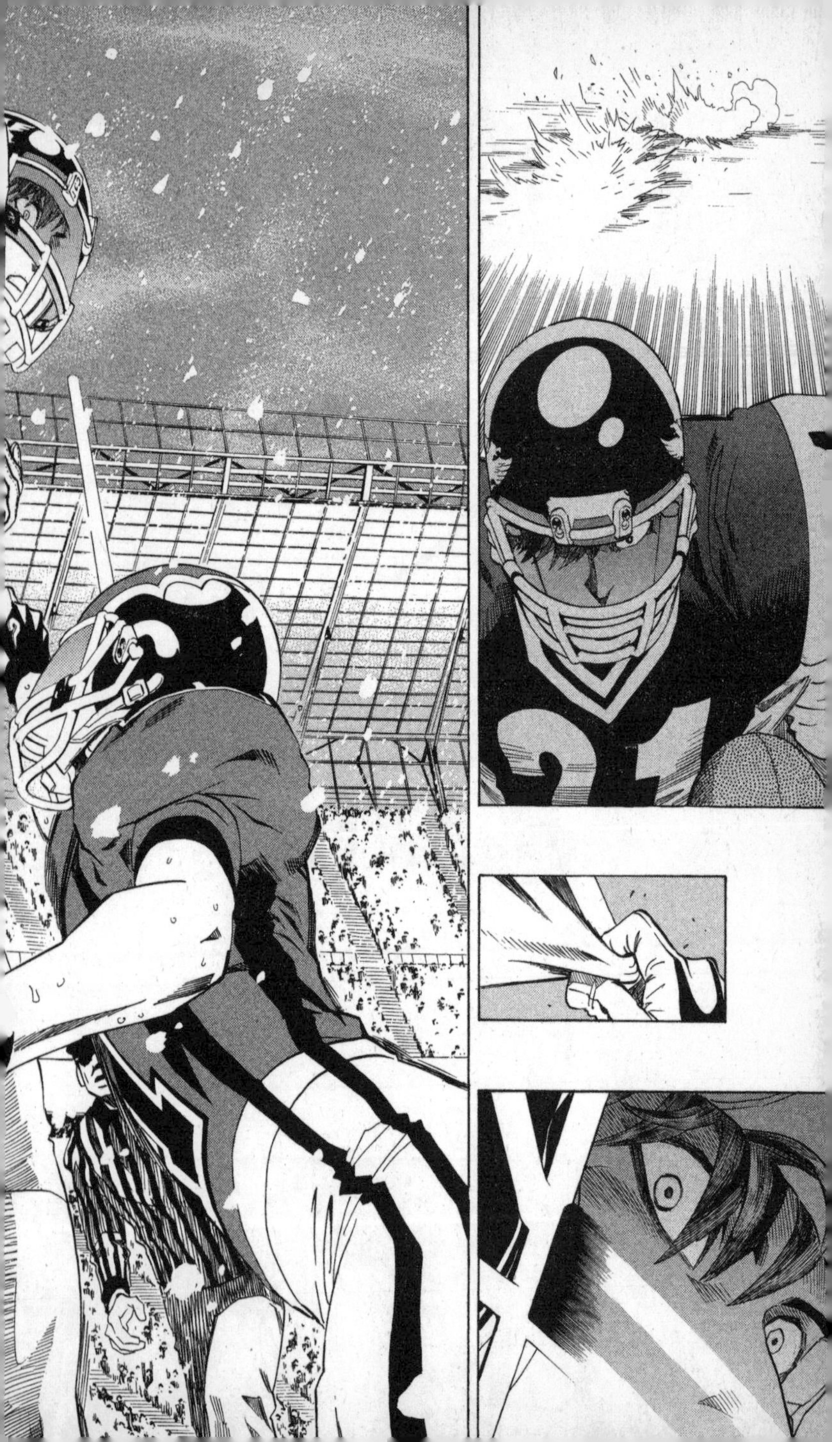

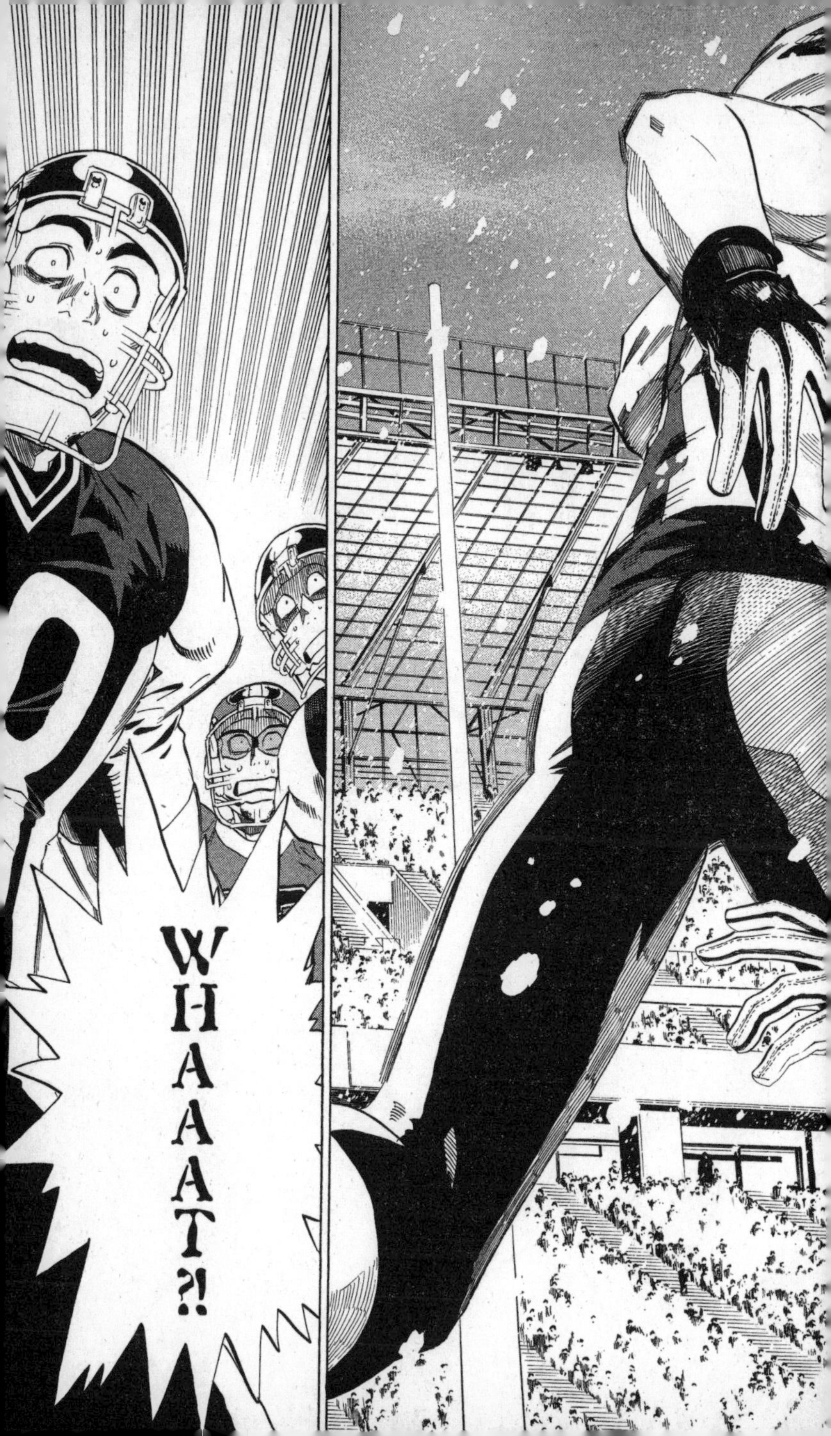
WHAAAT?!

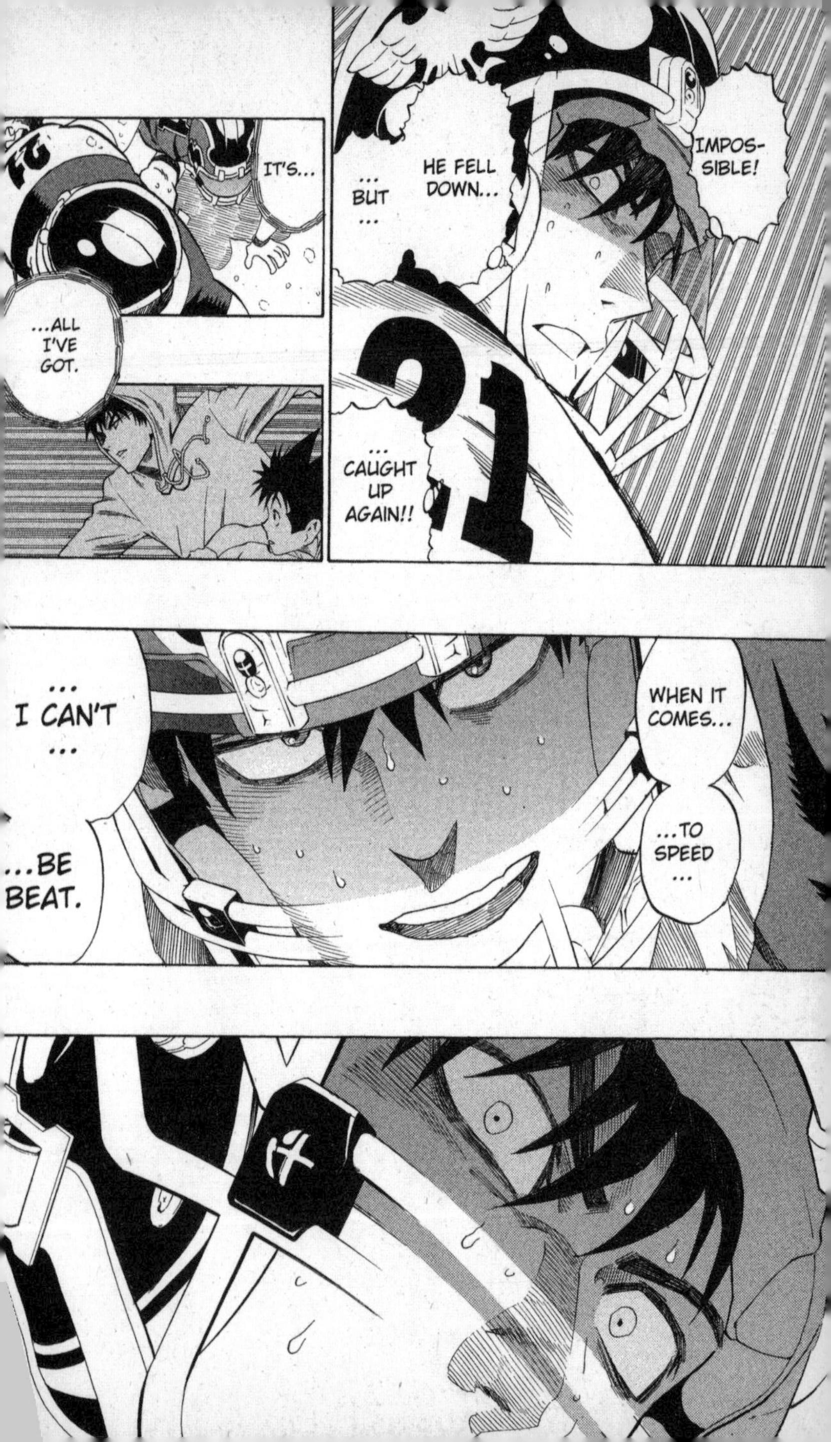
IMPOS-SIBLE!
HE FELL DOWN...
...BUT...
...CAUGHT UP AGAIN!!
IT'S...
...ALL I'VE GOT.
WHEN IT COMES...
...TO SPEED...
...I CAN'T...
...BE BEAT.

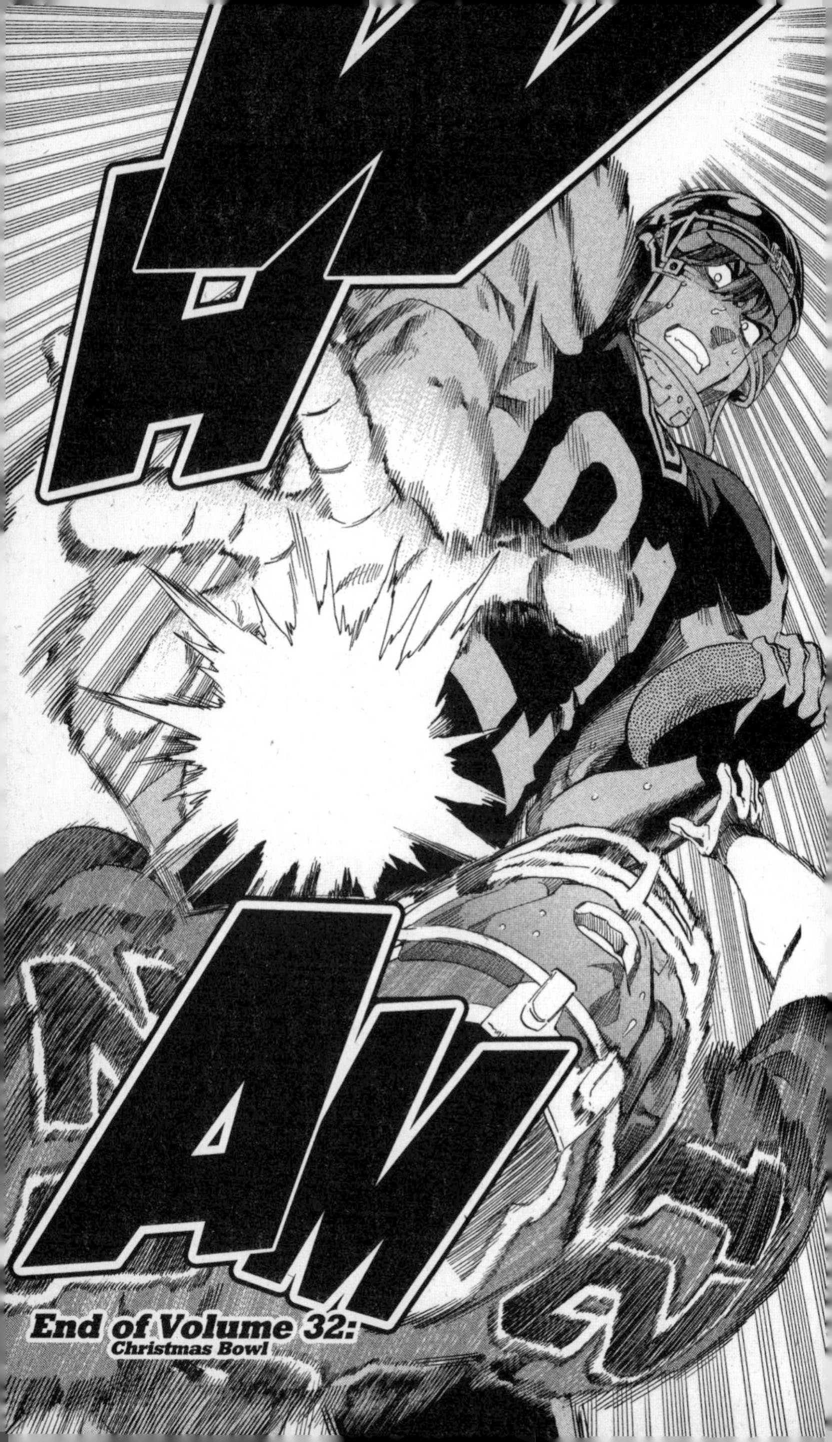
End of Volume 32:
Christmas Bowl

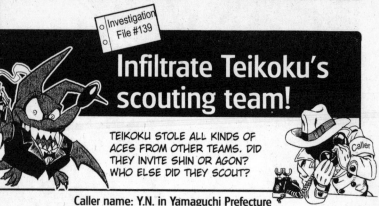

Investigation File #139

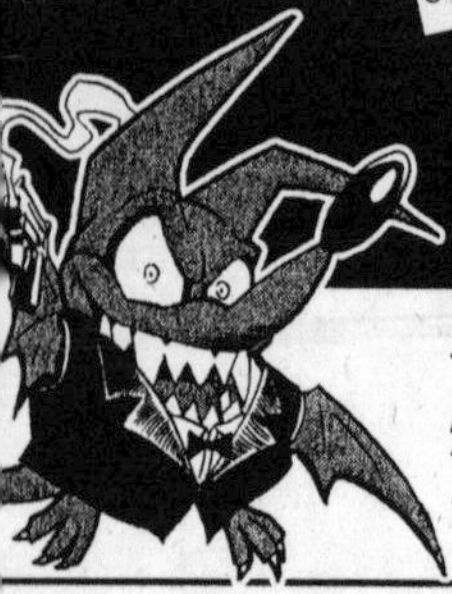

Infiltrate Teikoku's scouting team!

TEIKOKU STOLE ALL KINDS OF ACES FROM OTHER TEAMS. DID THEY INVITE SHIN OR AGON? WHO ELSE DID THEY SCOUT?

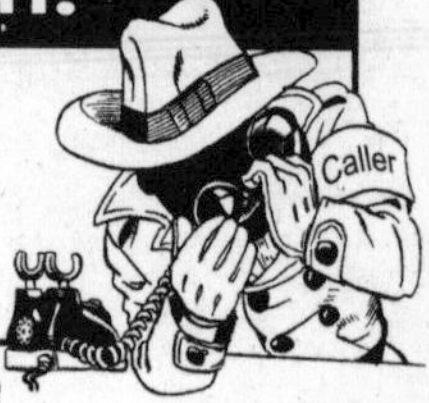
Caller

Caller name: Y.N. in Yamaguchi Prefecture

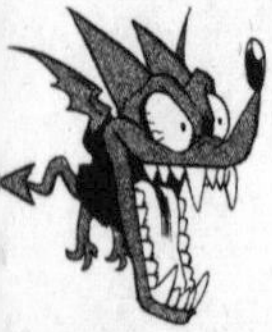

HEH HEH HEH! WE SNUCK A VIRUS INTO TEIKOKU'S COMPUTERS AND RETRIEVED SOME OF LAST YEAR'S SCOUTING FILES!

HINRYUJI NAGAS

gon: Evaluation:

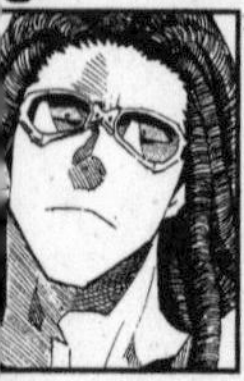

☆☆☆☆☆

"When it comes to the real hard-nosed guys, you have to get right up in their face. Then they'll ten to what you say."

e scout who said that just before proaching Agon is currently missing.

Ikkyu: Evaluation:

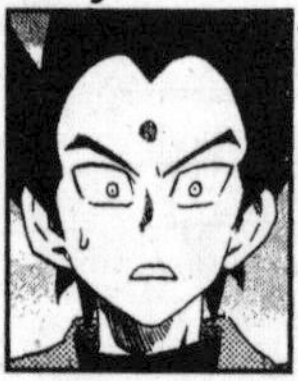

☆☆☆☆☆

On hold due to the aforementioned scout's disappearance.

JO WHITE KNIGHTS

Shin: Evaluation:

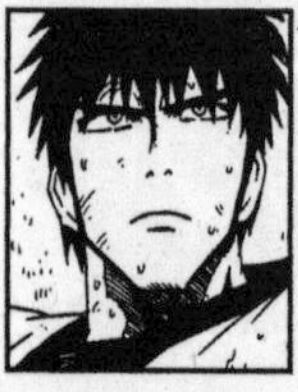

☆☆☆☆☆

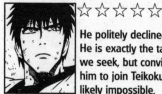

He politely declined. He is exactly the talent we seek, but convincing him to join Teikoku is likely impossible.

Otawara: Evaluation:

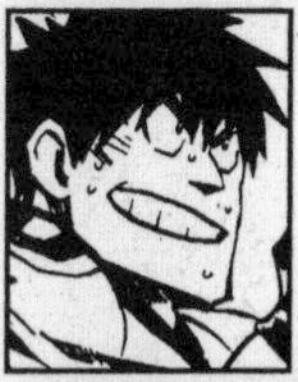

☆☆☆☆

Just prior to negotiations, he farted. The scout is currently in the hospital.

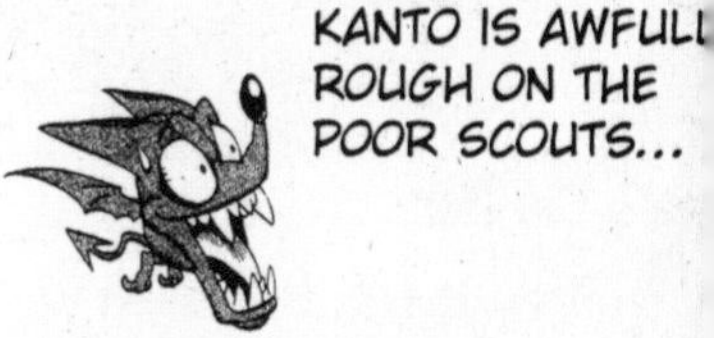
KANTO IS AWFULL ROUGH ON THE POOR SCOUTS...

TAIYO SPHINX

Banba: Evaluation:

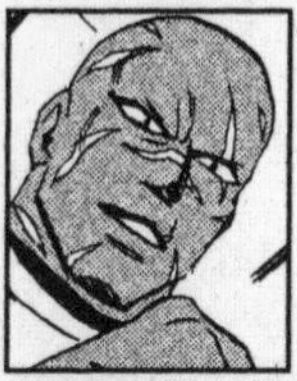

☆☆☆☆

He aggressively opposed the activity of scouting itself. Further scouting at Taiyo is considered dangerous.

DEIMON DEVIL BATS

Kurita: Evaluation:

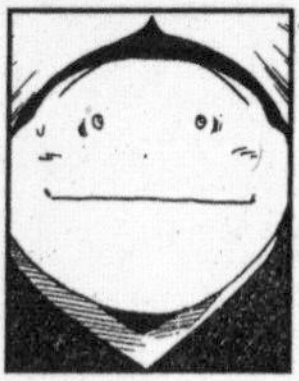

☆☆

Slower than molasses. He's of no use to Teikoku's speed football.

Hiruma: Evaluation:

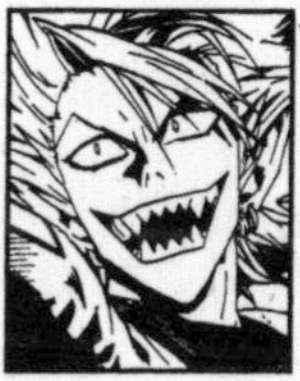

☆

Lacks physical ability. There's no point in scouting him.

Send your queries for Devil Bat 021 here!!

Devil Bat 021
Shonen Jump Advanced/Eyeshield 21
c/o VIZ Media, LLC
P.O. Box 77010
San Francisco, CA 94107

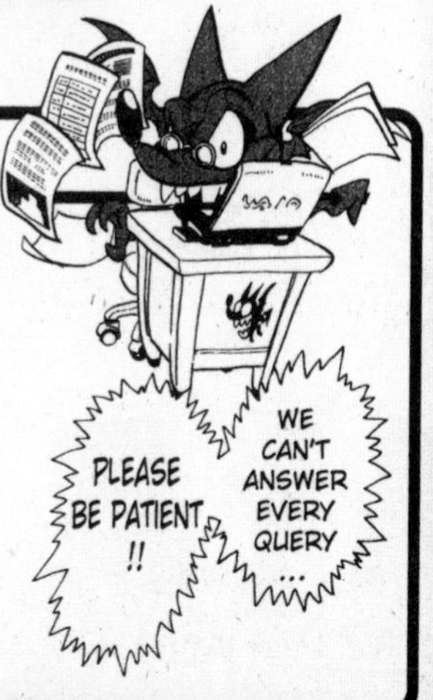
WE CAN'T ANSWER EVERY QUERY...
PLEASE BE PATIENT!!

Deluxe Biographies of the Supporting Cast

na's Cat Pitt

a's cat, which his mother even
ught to the Christmas Bowl.
e pg. 70.)

en Sena tries to cut Pitt's claws,
cat uses the light-speed ***Devil Cat
ost*** to ***run away***, so caring for it is
d.

his way, Sena even gets to
tivate his speed at home!!

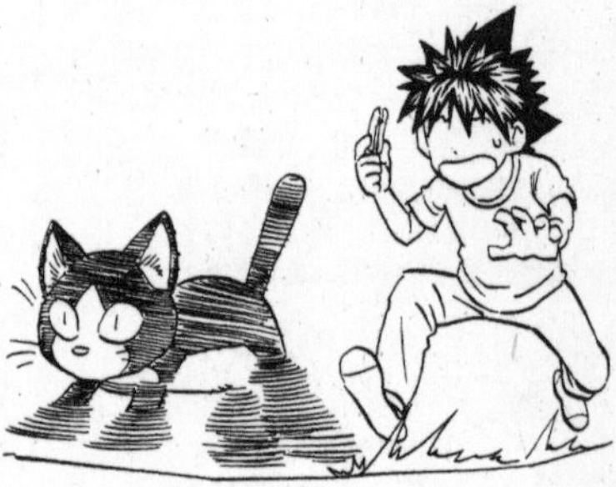

Jumonji's Father

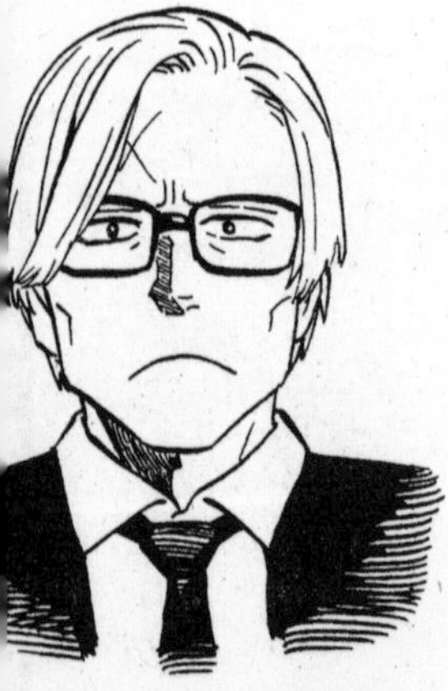

He's super (X10³) uptight and possesses absolutely no interest in sports. When he heard about football, he asked, "Oh, does that taste good?"

[FOOTBALL IN JAPANESE IS "AMEFUTO," WHICH SORT OF SOUNDS LIKE A FOOD, ESPECIALLY SINCE "AME" MEANS "CANDY."]

Relations with his son are incredibly cold, but in order to watch Jumonji play in a game for the very first time, he stayed up all night studying the rules of football. He's serious about everything.

The Teikoku Cheerleaders

They all come to cheer at first-team games, but when Teikoku's other teams play, not a single one shows up. This group of beauties is the epitome of a hierarchical society.

More than once, they have mistakenly included Karin in their practices!

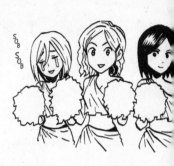

SOB SOB

Karinro Koizumi

Is Karinro based on me?
HOMER

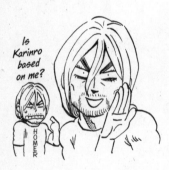

Something Hiruma made up. Supposedly, while Sena was in Osaka, he discovered Karin had a ***you know what*** when he touched it.

But if you think about it, why would he be touching there?! Without even knowing it, poor Sena has become a kind of ***hero***...

The Receiver's Gloves

Monta keeps these in his box of treasured possessions. The sweat on them from games gives off a ***faintly sweet aroma***!

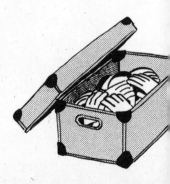

He won't wash them, though.
He would never do that. That's all part of what makes them a treasure for him.

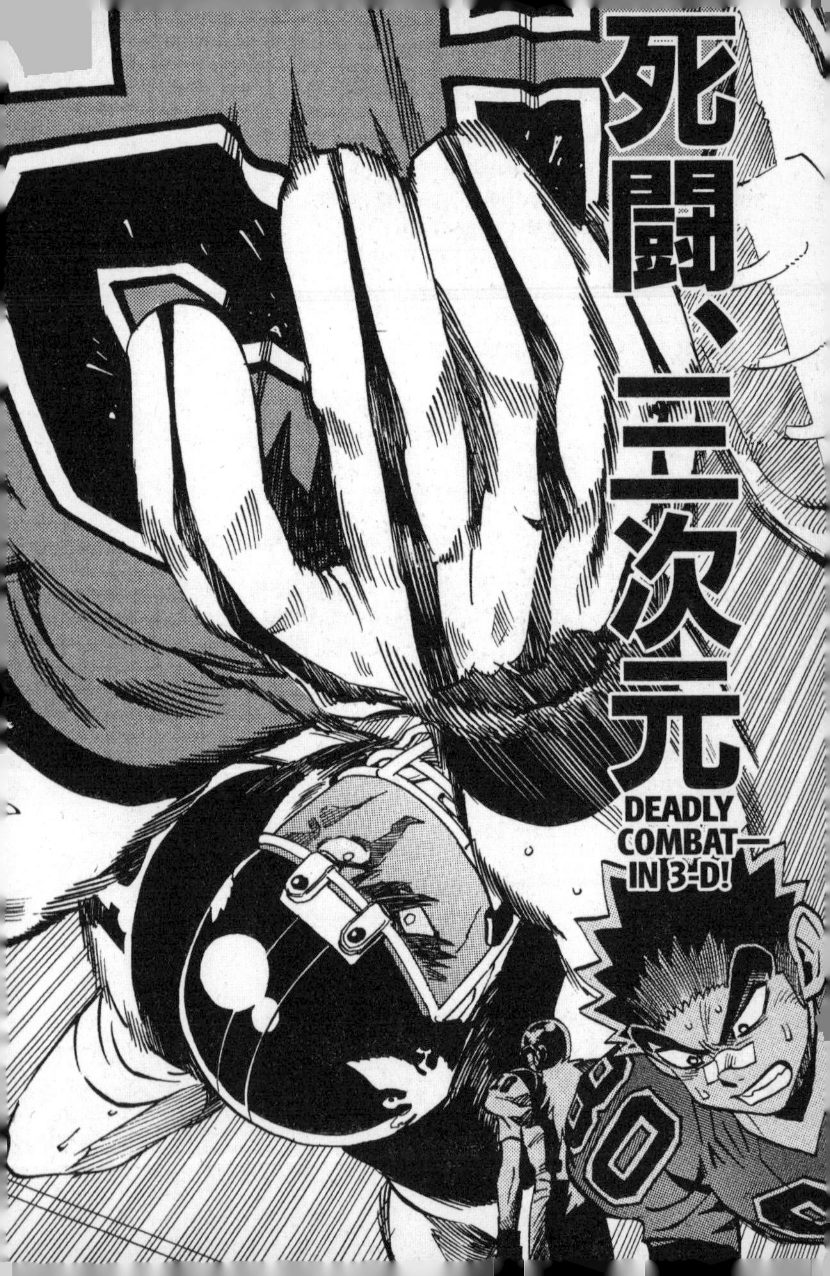
死闘、三次元
DEADLY COMBAT—IN 3-D!

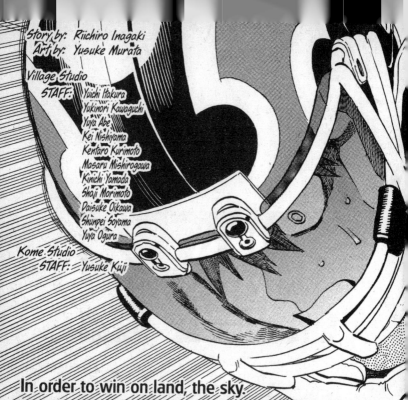

Story by: Riichiro Inagaki
Art by: Yusuke Murata

Village Studio
STAFF: Yuichi Itakura
Yukinori Kawaguchi
Yuya Abe
Kei Nishiyama
Kentaro Kurimoto
Masaru Mishirogawa
Kiichi Yamada
Shoji Morimoto
Daisuke Oikawa
Shunpei Soyama
Yuya Ogura

Kome Studio
STAFF: Yusuke Kuji

In order to win on land, the sky.
In order to win in the sky, the land.
Deimon must master the whole field
to finally achieve a breakthrough against Teikoku!!

EYESHIELD 21 Volume **33**

On sale October 2010!!